Routledge Revivals

Nigerian Land Law and Custom

Originally published in 1951, *Nigerian Land Law and Custom* (now with a new preface by Olusoji Elias), the first of its kind, is an excellent comparative study of the whole system of land tenure in Nigeria. There are, of course, a few anthropological attempts, almost invariably designed as or inspired by Government Reports on some specific areas of the country, and their aim is therefore often administrative or fiscal. This book is accordingly an attempt to create a legal order out of the chaos of lay approaches and to examine and systematize, as far as possible, such principles of indigenous tenure as are discernible in available materials in the light of the growing body of case-law.

This book will be of value to students and researchers of African law and custom, and of comparative jurisprudence.

Nigerian Land Law and Custom

T. Olawale Elias

Routledge
Taylor & Francis Group

First published in 1951
by Routledge & Kegan Paul Ltd

This edition first published in 2024 by Routledge
4 Park Square, Milton Park, Abingdon, Oxon, OX14 4RN

and by Routledge
605 Third Avenue, New York, NY 10017

Routledge is an imprint of the Taylor & Francis Group, an informa business

© 1951 T. Olawale Elias

Publisher's Note
The publisher has gone to great lengths to ensure the quality of this reprint but points out that some imperfections in the original copies may be apparent.

Disclaimer
The publisher has made every effort to trace copyright holders and welcomes correspondence from those they have been unable to contact.

A Library of Congress record exists under LCCN: 52028040

ISBN: 9781032846064 (hbk)
ISBN: 9781003514138 (ebk)
ISBN: 9781032846163 (pbk)

Book DOI 10.4324/9781003514138

NIGERIAN LAND LAW
AND CUSTOM

by

T. OLAWALE ELIAS
LL.M., PH.D.(LOND.)

of the Inner Temple, Barrister-at-Law

*Formerly Yarborough-Anderson Scholar of the Inner
Temple, and Holder of University of London
Postgraduate Studentship in Law*

ROUTLEDGE & KEGAN PAUL LTD
Broadway House, 68–74 Carter Lane
London

*First published in 1951
by Routledge & Kegan Paul Limited
Broadway House, 68–74 Carter Lane
London, E.C.4
Made and printed in Great Britain
by William Clowes and Sons, Limited
London and Beccles*

To my beloved brother
A. W. ATANDA ELIAS, ESQ.
this book is dedicated
in grateful acknowledgment
of his love for me
and his responsibility
for my legal education

New Preface

It gives me immense pleasure firstly to have been asked to provide this brief preface to my father's *Nigerian Land Law and Custom* by Ms. Ria Goyal of the publishers' 'Routledge Revivals Series'. It comes on the back of a certain personal recognition as 'African Lawyer of the Year 2024', and secondly, to have the authority of my siblings to do so as I am doing.

First offered in 1951, this entirely unredacted seminal tome is the archetypal handsome monograph, timeless and elegant, and eternally so in all of its intellectual heavyweight and rigorous simplicity. It happens to be one of the earlier definitive texts from the desk of my all-time personal hero—after my mother of course—who just so happens to be my father. For reasons of subject-matter consonance, I would suggest a reading of it alongside his equally epochal *The Nature of African Customary Law* (1956).

I myself was required to have studied *Nigerian Land Law and Custom* and a few of his other books as part of the requirements for call to the Bar in Nigeria some forty years ago. The book certainly fulfils the curiosity of academic pursuit of its culturally specific subject-matter and the demands of professional engagement therewith.

The book is timeless because of its ground-breaking precedences and for the trail it persists with having blazed. This is evidenced in the enduring quality of the concepts it introduces and unpacks such as customary landholding and rights of occupancy which now exist in substantial statutory form with wide-ranging ramifications in the Nigerian Land Use Act 1978.

As a matter of course I conscientiously recommend this book to everyone with an interest in Nigerian land law.

Olusoji Elias

Preface

THIS book is my thesis for the Degree of Doctor of Philosophy (Laws) in the University of London, and was recommended by the examiners as suitable for publication as presented. It has nevertheless been edited by me just before being finally committed to the publishers' care.

There seems to be no existing comparative study, sociological or legal, of the whole system of land tenure in Nigeria. There are, of course, a few anthropological attempts, almost invariably designed as or inspired by Government Reports on some specific areas of the country, and their aim is therefore often administrative or fiscal. This book is accordingly an attempt to create a legal order out of the chaos of lay approaches and to examine and systematise, as far as possible, such principles of indigenous tenure as are discernible in available materials in the light of the growing body of case-law.

The ground traversed may be briefly stated as follows. The opening chapter contains an Historical Introduction to the Colony and Protectorate of Nigeria and the Trust Territory of Cameroons, which together form the 372,000 square miles of the administrative unit of Nigeria. Next follow in separate chapters a critical analysis of (*a*) The problems of Crown ownership of Nigerian lands (still largely an unsettled question in Colonial jurisprudence) and its impact upon the customary legal concepts of the people, dealing also at some length with the relevant Government legislation since 1861, (*b*) the indigenous ideas about the various land tenure systems of the country, and the changes incident to European contacts since 1852, (*c*) the respective rights and duties of local chiefs, of heads of families and of the ordinary members of the family or extended family within the social context of community usufruct of land, (*d*) factors in the development (within the last 80 years or so) of the conception of individual ownership and of alienation by lease, sale and mortgage—themselves essentially alien to ancient customary ideas—and the economic incidents of these on Nigerian polity, (*e*) the customary rules of inheritance of land as well as the

changes therein due to the introduction of Wills and other factors
and (f) the system of Registration of Titles and of Land necessi-
tated by the partial break-up of traditional land usages in many
urban and semi-urban areas of the country. There is a final chapter
of Summary and Conclusions.

If in the elaboration of many of the foregoing topics the cases
appear to have been given rather extended discussion perhaps one
can plead in extenuation three factors: (a) the fact that the volumes
of the Nigerian Law Reports and of the West African Court of
Appeal Reports are hard to come by, especially for those outside
the British Empire, (b) the paucity of recorded judgments of the
Superior Courts when compared with the vast fields of Nigerian
tenurial problems yet untouched by judicial decisions and (c) the
modest hope that a detailed critique of the various judgments cited
might help in pointing the path along which could tend the future
developments of some of the problems awaiting solution.

It is to be hoped that this book will be found useful by students
of African law and custom, by the British Administrative personnel
in Colonial areas and not least by all students of comparative jurisprudence. Experts in colonial land tenure systems as well as my
colleagues practising at the Nigerian (and West African) Bar may
find it of some value, and I should be particularly grateful for any
suggestions from them for its improvement.

I wish to thank the Nigerian Government for making a grant
to the publishers towards the expenses of publication.

T. OLAWALE ELIAS

London
7 September, 1950

Contents

Table of Cases

Table of Ordinances, Proclamations and Imperial Statutes

(*referred to*)

A. ORDINANCES

B. PROCLAMATIONS

C. ENGLISH STATUTES

Table of Abbreviations of Reports cited

1. (1924), 5 N. L. R. 90=Volume V of Nigeria Law Report, page 90. The year is throughout added to the citations so as to show the date of the judgment, which is otherwise not easy to ascertain merely from a bare statement of the Volume. Each Volume generally covers a period of years.

   A precedent for this can be found in the American method of citing Federal Court cases: e.g. (1930), 209 U. S. 71.
2. (1936), 4 W. A. C. A. 1=Volume 4 of West African Court of Appeal Reports of 1936, page 1.
3. Colonial Nigeria A (wherever used)='Lagos: Reports of Certain Judgments of the Supreme Court. Vice-Admiralty Court and Full Court of Appeal (1884–1892). Law Reports (Colonial), Nigeria A.' This Volume of reports exists only in the Colonial Office Legal Library in London.
4. (1921), 2 A. C. 399=the English Law Report of that name, i.e. Volume 2 of 1921 Appeal Cases Report, usually (for our purpose) Privy Council judgments for the Dominions and the Colonies.
5. (1936), 2 A. E. R. 1632=the English Law Report of that name. i.e. Volume 2 of the 1936 All England Report, at page 1632.

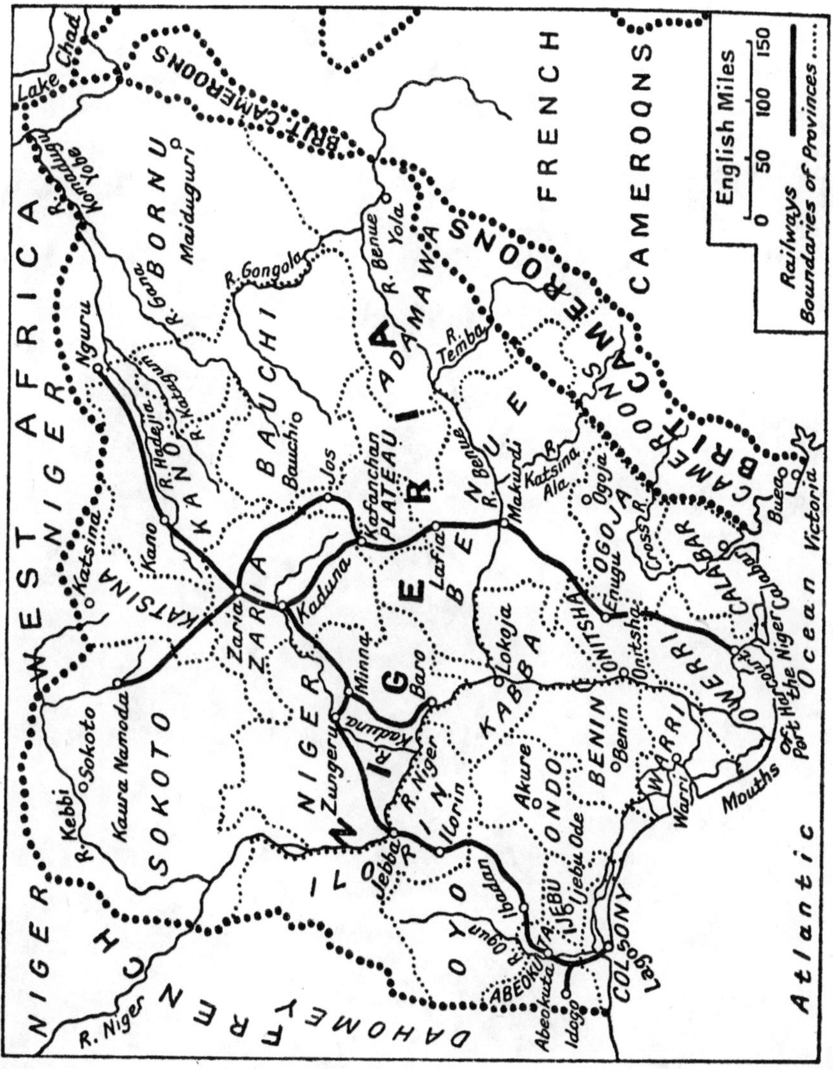
WEST AFRICA
NIGER
FRENCH
DAHOMEY
FRENCH CAMEROONS
BRIT. CAMEROONS
BRIT. CAMEROONS
Lake Chad
R. Yobe
Komadugu
BORNU
Maiduguri
R. Gongola
R. Gana
Nguru
R. Hadejia
R. Katagum
KANO
Kano
KATSINA
Katsina
SOKOTO
Sokoto
R. Sokoto
R. Kebbi
Kaura Namoda
ZARIA
Zaria
BAUCHI
Bauchi
Jos
PLATEAU
Kafanchan
Kaduna
R. Kaduna
Minna
Zungeru
NIGER
Baro
NIGERIA
ADAMAWA
R. Benue
Yola
R. Temba
BENUE
Makurdi
R. Katsina Ala
Lafia
KABBA
Lokoja
R. Niger
Jebba
ILORIN
Ilorin
OYO
Ibadan
R. Ogun
ABEOKUTA
Abeokuta
Idogo
IJEBU
Ijebu Ode
COLONY
Lagos
ONDO
Akure
BENIN
Benin
WARRI
Warri
ONITSHA
Onitsha
Enugu
OGOJA
Ogoja
Cross R.
CALABAR
Calabar
OWERRI
Port Harcourt
Mouths of the Niger
Buea
Victoria
Atlantic Ocean
English Miles
0 50 100 150
Railways
Boundaries of Provinces

Chapter One

HISTORICAL INTRODUCTION

---

1. *General Description of the Country.* 2. *History of the Colony, Protectorate and Mandated Territory.* 3. *Constitution.*

---

1. GENERAL DESCRIPTION OF THE COUNTRY

NIGERIA, as the largest British West African possession, consists of a Colony, a Protectorate and a Mandated Territory—by the way, the three main types of British Dependencies—all of which together embrace also the largest territorial unit in the Colonial Empire. It covers an area roughly equal to 'one third of British India or the size of France, Belgium and the United Kingdom put together',[1] i.e. about 372,700 square miles of territory, inclusive of the 34,081 square miles of the Cameroons under British Mandate. The Colony and what now goes under the generic name of Protectorate have had a slow political evolution, a knowledge of which will be helpful when we come to consider the nature of the differing tenurial systems and the problems which these present.

The Colony is made up of Lagos, the capital of Nigeria and the principal West African port, and its narrow outlying coastal strip of the mainland of Ikeja, Badagry, Ikorodu and Epe. The Protectorate, which represents the rest of Nigeria, divides into the three administrative units of (*a*) the Northern Provinces whose population is mainly Hausa, (*b*) the Western Provinces with a mainly Yoruba population and (*c*) the Eastern Provinces which are mainly Ibo.[2] These administrative divisions, corresponding roughly to the three large groups of tribes with diverse customary land tenures, carry a total population of 19,928,171 (according to

[1] British Govt. White Paper: Cmd. 6599 of 1945, p. 1.
[2] See map of Nigeria on p. xxvii.

1

the 1931 census), though the Government Statistician computed it at 21,902,000.[1] The Northern region alone supports about $11\frac{1}{2}$ millions of the population and is roughly 5/6ths of the entire territory of Nigeria.

2. HISTORY OF THE COLONY, PROTECTORATE AND MANDATED TERRITORY

(i) Colony

With respect to the Colony area of Nigeria the story[2] can be briefly told for our present purpose. Early in the eighteenth century a Chief called Olofin, who had crossed over with a large body of his followers from the mainland, lived on Iddo Island and soon became the overlord of the adjacent island of Lagos which, along with a portion of the adjoining mainland, he parcelled out among some fourteen or sixteen[3] important subordinates later known as the 'White-cap Chiefs'. These Chiefs held full dominion over their respective allotments until about 1790 when the neighbouring Benins over-ran Lagos which was, however, not formally occupied but left in the charge of a representative of theirs as ruler under the title of 'Eleko'. There followed a succession of Elekos who thus became the Kings of Lagos and who paid tribute to the successive Kings of Benin in acknowledgment of the latter's sovereignty over Lagos and its environs. But in the course of the next half-century or so the Kings of Lagos had so consolidated their position that about 1850 the reigning King of Lagos refused to pay further tributes to the King of Benin, and openly declared his independence.

But since about 1840 Lagos had become one of the principal centres of the slave trade, and the Kings of Lagos were rich and powerful chieftains. In 1841, King Akitoye came to the throne on the death in that year of his predecessor, Oluwole; but King Akitoye was deposed by Kosoko, his nephew, whose encouragement of the slave trade led, towards the end of 1851, to the British

[1] It is believed that the actual figure is even very much higher, since during the census many false returns were made by a large majority of natives anxious to escape, or help their relations to avoid, payment of income-tax!

[2] For a fuller political history reference must be made to books like: Rev. J. B. Wood, *Historical Notices of Lagos, West Africa*; A. C. Burns, *Short History of Nigeria* (1936 edition); Lord Lugard, *Dual Mandate in British Tropical Africa* (1929).

[3] The number was sixteen according to C. W. Alexander, *Native Land Tenure in Colony and Protectorate of S. Nigeria* (1910): Colonial Office Legal Library; Legal Pamphlets, Vol. 1, No. 26 (folio).

bombardment of Lagos and the consequent reinstatement of Akitoye after the defeat of Kosoko. A Treaty was signed on 1 January 1852, between Akitoye and the British Consul, whereby the slave trade was finally abolished in Lagos; a new trade in palm-oil and ivory soon sprang up in its place. Later in 1852 King Akitoye died and was succeeded by Docemo whose comparative weakness as a ruler was the occasion of Her Majesty's Government's decision to occupy Lagos Island.

Thus, in 1861, King Docemo of Lagos, who was the thirteenth in succession, and his chiefs, were accordingly induced to make with Her Majesty the Queen of England's representatives a treaty dated 6 August on behalf of himself and chiefs, ceding to the British Crown 'the Port and Island of Lagos with all the rights, profits and territories and appurtenances whatsoever thereunto belonging'.[1]

On 13 March 1862, a new government, officially called the Settlement of Lagos, was by Commission established over these ceded territories, which, on 19 February 1866, became by another Commission merged into what was known as the West African Settlements, having a separate Legislative Council but being subject to the Governor-General-in-Chief whose headquarters were at Sierra Leone. Then, a little more than eight years later, Letters Patent dated 24 July 1874 saw the formal inauguration of the Colony of the Gold Coast in which Lagos was for administrative purposes included for nearly twelve years. On 13 January 1886, however, Lagos was separated from the Gold Coast as an independent Colony.

(ii) Protectorate

In the years immediately following the cession of the coastal areas, certain small British trading companies had penetrated inland and carried on their business with much overlapping of functions as of interests, but the impending Conference of Berlin in 1885 led Sir George Goldie to effect an amalgamation of these rival companies trading on the river Niger so as to strengthen the hands of the British delegates at the Conference in their demand for their Country's overriding claims over the Niger trade. In that year also was established the British Oil Rivers Protectorate and, in 1886, the new company under Sir George Goldie, with the name of the 'Royal Niger Company' was granted a charter having 'power to administer, make treaties, levy customs and trade in all

[1] See text of the Treaty of Cession in Appendix I.

territories in the basin of the Niger and its affluents'. There took place, between 1885 and 1900, further extension of British power inland, largely through these administrations, but native resistance to the virtual trade monopoly of the Royal Niger Company, the need to strengthen the Western border against the French, coupled with the necessity for the suppression of internal slave traffic in the North, soon proved too much for a commercial company. Added to this was the fact that the Fulani, very early in the nineteenth century, had conquered Sokoto, Kano and other ancient Hausa Kingdoms in the North, as well as the still pagan groups of central Nigeria; but the Moslem State of the north-eastern peoples of Bornu and the Lake Chad area alone successfully defied Fulani intrusion. All these have deeply affected land tenure in Northern Nigeria.

The task of taking over the Royal Niger Company's administrative functions was left to Sir Frederick Lugard, the British Commissioner who, after three years of negotiation and of war-like operations which eventually over-powered the Northern emirates, formally proclaimed, in 1900, the Protectorate of Northern Nigeria. By the terms of the resulting Agreement between the Company and the Crown, the Company, while reserving its purely commercial rights and privileges, surrendered its other rights and interests, including all the land hitherto acquired by means of various agreements with native chiefs and princes, to the Crown for the lump sum of £865,000, subject, however, to the payment to the Company of fifty per cent of the mining royalties for a period of ninety-nine years.

In the case of the Company's territory south of the Niger, what used to be the Oil Rivers Protectorate was thrown together with it to form the Protectorate of Southern Nigeria. By Letters Patent dated 28 February 1906, which became operative as from 1 May 1906, this new Protectorate was merged with the Colony of Lagos under a unified administration known as 'Southern Nigeria'.

However, on 1 January 1914, Lord Lugard, who had fourteen years earlier proclaimed the Protectorate of Northern Nigeria, amalgamated the Northern Protectorate and the new Southern Nigeria into the Colony and Protectorate of Nigeria.

(iii) Mandated Territory

As a result of the first world war, Great Britain was, by the League of Nations exercising its powers under Article 22 of the League Covenant, granted the mandate of the adjacent ex-German territory lying east of Nigeria. This, in official language, is known as the Cameroons under British Mandate, and is administered as part and parcel of Nigeria.

3. CONSTITUTION

It remains to add that, until very recently, the Governor of Nigeria, with the assistance of an Executive and a Legislative Council, was responsible for the administration of the whole country, the Legislative Council legislating only for the Colony and the Southern Provinces, that is, what became in 1906, Southern Nigeria. The Governor alone legislated for the Mandated Territory and for the North, so that Ordinances of the Central Legislature (including those relating to land) which affected these areas of Nigeria had to be specially re-enacted by His Excellency the Governor in order to be applicable thereto.

A British Government White Paper,[1] published in March 1945 under the title of 'Proposals for the Revision of the Constitution of Nigeria' (now the operative Constitution of Nigeria with effect from January 1947), provides for three regional Councils based upon the traditional ethnical groupings of the Country (i.e. the North, the South-West, and the South-East respectively), which act as electoral colleges from which representatives are selected by the three groups of native administrations. These sit on the reconstituted Central Legislative Council which, while retaining the Governor's casting vote and other powers, now legislates for the whole country as a political unit.

[1] Cmd. Paper 6599 (cit. *supra*).

Chapter Two

PROBLEMS OF OWNERSHIP
(THE COLONY)

---

1. *The Treaty of Cession of* 1861. 2. *Judicial Opinion thereon.*
3. *Protests by Chiefs.* 4. *Docemo had no Seigneurial Rights over Lagos Land.* 5. *Conclusion.* 6. *The Plea of Act of State.* 7. *Legal Effect of Cession.* 8. *Definition of Crown's Title.* 9. *General Effects of Treaty.* 10. *Crown Grants not Evidence of Crown's Ownership.*
11. *Crown Grants re-determined.* 12. *Crown Title subject to Native Rights.*

IN Nigeria, as in practically all the British West African Colonies, ownership of land in the accepted English sense is unknown. Land is held under community ownership, and not, as a rule, by the individual as such. It is true that the impact of English ideas of property law upon indigenous conceptions, largely due to (*a*) the efforts of practising African lawyers trained in English law, (*b*) the change from the subsistence economy of the autonomous household or village to the market economy of cocoa and palm-oil plantations of 'urban' areas and (*c*) the increased pressure of population upon the land consequent upon this change, has produced tendencies towards a partial break-up in the existing system, and many individuals now own lands in their own right, particularly in the Colony and some other developed areas of Nigeria. But the indigenous customary law of land tenure remains essentially communal.[1]

But before we stop to examine the real nature of this community ownership we may well pose the legal problem: Assuming that land in Nigeria is collectively owned, in whom is the legal title? Now,

---

[1] i.e. 'communal' in the sense explained in Chap. V.

with regard to the Colony, there are at least four possible hypotheses on which jurists could frame an answer:

(i) That the real ownership of land in the Colony is by the Treaty of Cession of 1861 in the British Crown to which belong, in constitutional theory, all the territories of the British Commonwealth and Empire; [1]

(ii) That King Docemo of Lagos owned all Lagos and adjacent lands forming the Colony area, which he ceded to the British Crown in 1861;

(iii) That the land belongs to the White-Cap Chiefs, the land-owning political and administrative rulers of the native communities;

(iv) That land belongs to all the members of native communities on a joint and inalienable basis, the head chiefs being merely in the position of trustees holding the 'legal' title for and on behalf of the individuals forming the various communities in whom rests the 'equitable' estate.[2]

Let us analyse each of these suggestions in turn and see what inferences of fact and law can be made therefrom on the vexed question of title to land in Nigeria. All the four problems will be discussed in their appropriate places since (a) they are really inter-related aspects of the same enquiry and (b) a separate treatment of each would involve much overlapping and needless repetition.

1. THE TREATY OF CESSION OF 1861

Frequently cited in favour of Crown ownership is, of course, the following portion of Article I of the Treaty of Cession of 1861:

'I, Docemo, do, with the consent and advice of my Council, give, transfer, and by these presents grant and confirm unto the Queen of Great Britain, her heirs and successors for ever, the Port and Island of Lagos, with all the rights, profits, territories and appurtenances whatsoever thereunto belonging . . .'.[3]

The wording of this excerpt has been variously interpreted: Some argue that what King Docemo purported to transfer under

[1] This theory of Crown ownership only applies to Colonial, and not to Protectorate or Mandated, territories, as to which more will be said anon.

[2] Whether the exact nature of these 'equitable' interests can be regarded as 'tenancy in common' or as 'joint tenancy' (using these terms to denote their original English idea) will be examined in a later Chapter.

[3] See Appendix 1 for the text of the treaty.

the treaty was 'a mere cession of rights, and not a cession of territory'.[1] What precise meaning is to be given to 'rights' in this context is not often clearly defined, but it seems that the term includes,
if it does not exhaust, the general administrative control and social
precedence enjoyed by Docemo under local law and custom.
Others again aver that the King's political sovereignty alone passed
to the Crown in 1861, since Docemo, not being the owner of the
land, had nothing else to give, on the principle *nemo dat quod non
habet.*

2. JUDICIAL OPINION THEREON

But judicial opinion is that the terms of the Treaty mean what
they say, namely, that the territory of Lagos and its environs as
therein described passed to the Crown; these 'grant and confirm
unto the Queen of Great Britain, her heirs and successors for ever,
the Port and Island of Lagos, with all the rights, profits, territories, . . . freely, fully, entirely and absolutely'.[2] Lord Shaw, in
delivering the judgment of the Privy Council in *Attorney-General
of Southern Nigeria* v. *John Holt*,[3] made short shrift of the point
in these crisp words: 'Their lordships do not refer to the Treaty
further than to say that, in their opinion, property was not excluded from the grant; and they think also that this is subject to
the condition that all rights of property existing in the inhabitants
under grant or otherwise from King Docemo and his predecessors,
were to be respected.'[4]
   But in the leading case of *Amodu Tijani* v. *Secretary, Southern
Provinces*,[5] Viscount Haldane held: 'No doubt there was a cession
to the British Crown, along with the Sovereignty, of the radical
or ultimate title to the land, in the new Colony, but this cession
appears to have been made on the footing that the rights of property of the inhabitants were to be fully respected. . . . The general
words of the cession are construed as having related primarily to
sovereign rights only. . . . Where the cession passed any proprietary rights they were rights which the ceding king possessed
beneficially and free from the usufructuary qualification of his
title in favour of his subjects.' [6]
   It will, therefore, be seen that the effect of the Treaty would at

---

[1] *A.-G. of S. Nigeria* v. *John Holt* (1910), 2 N. L. R. 1, at p. 8.
[2] Ibid., at pp. 58–9.   [3] (1910), 2 N. L. R. 1.
[4] Ibid., at p. 58.   [5] (1921), 3 N. L. R.
[6] Ibid., at p. 55.

first appear to be that both territory [1] and sovereignty passed to the Crown thereunder, but that in practice the general words of the cession are construed as having related primarily to sovereign rights only. If that is so, the crucial question is: What was the nature of King Docemo's rights with respect to Lagos land? Did he possess it beneficially? The answer is partly to be found in these words of Osborne, C.J., in *A.-G. of S. Nigeria* v. *John Holt & Co.*,[2] where, after referring to the abolition of the slave trade in Lagos by a Treaty of 1852 and the influx into the island of liberated slaves from Sierra Leone since that date, his Lordship observed that 'the practice of alienation (of land) sprung into vogue, and another new feature, totally foreign to native law which knew not writing, was introduced, in the shape of written grants by the King of Lagos. The land in Lagos was originally attached to the stools of the White-Cap Chiefs, who were in no way subordinate to the early Kings of Lagos, but, as has been pointed out in a historical treatise to which the Court has been referred, in later times there appears to have been a gradual diminishing of the original owners' interest in the land, and a corresponding increase in it on the part of the King. It was customary when land was sold, as, for example, to European slave exporters, for one half of the proceeds to be taken by the King, and the other half by the White-Cap Chiefs, who were landowners.' The increase of the King's interest continued to grow after the abolition of the slave trade to such an extent, that he came to be looked upon as the proper party to execute grants of Lagos land. In fact, one of the witnesses for the defendants, Chief Eletu, went so far as to say that the King was the superior lord of the chiefs with regard to land.[3]

There are three points which this excerpt seems to imply, namely, (i) that between 1852 and 1862 Lagos land, contrary to the traditional native concept of the absolute inalienability of land, had become alienable; (ii) that King Docemo was already issuing written grants of land to certain donees and that that was evidence of ownership; and (iii) that Docemo was, therefore, competent, even without the concurrence or participation of the White-Cap Chiefs, to cede Lagos territory and its environs to the British Crown.

As to (i), we must accept the new practice of alienation in the

[1] Indeed, Art. 3, para. 2 speaks of 'the Port and Island and Territories of Lagos'!
[2] (1910), 2 N. L. R. 1, at p. 3.
[3] 2 N. L. R. 1, at p. 3.

period following 1852 as a historical fact, while leaving the detailed account of the process to a later Chapter.[1] With respect to (ii), the issue of written grants of land by King Docemo was inspired, if not induced, by contact with Europeans, and the full legal implications of it were hardly understood by the grantor. The grants were more a regulative and protective measure than an investitive one, for in the general uncertainty of titles to land which ensued upon the social and economical upheaval resulting from the abolition of the slave trade, and because of the enhanced position of the King, who had now secured a degree of hegemony over the land-owning chiefs, it was only natural that the right to 'allocate' unused lands to strangers, whether native or non-native, should be conceded to him, just in the same way as chiefs who were also heads of families were endowed with exactly these powers. Nor is the theory of Docemo's derivative authority from the King of Benin through his (Docemo's) predecessors as Eleko [2] of any avail; [3] the Treaty of cession clearly omits any reference to the King of Benin, obviously because whatever right he might have had as a result of his predecessor's conquest of Lagos, had actually been abandoned at the time of the cession.[4] Docemo could not, therefore, have acquired any new rights thereunder.[5]

Winkfield, J., in *A.-G. of Southern Nigeria* v. *John Holt & Co.*[6] thus stated his view of the grants by Docemo: 'Under the native law, strangers could not obtain the ownership of land, but only a right of occupation. Though the grants by Docemo purport to

[1] i.e. the Chapter on Alienation, *infra*.

[2] For the point of this reference, see Historical Introduction, *supra*.

[3] But Speed, C.J., at pp. 24 and 25, in the Divisional Court at Lagos, and Ross, J., at pp. 33 and 34, in the Full Court, both made much of the King of Benin, and thought that the *Onisiwo Case* might have been differently decided if the Court in that case had taken evidence as to the position of the King of Benin.

[4] The argument briefly was: In Benin, the King owned all the land and, in virtue of Benin conquest of Lagos about 1790, Lagos land became Benin land. The Eleko, as representative of King of Benin, therefore, owned all the land in Lagos and its suburbs which he could alienate at will. That the Benin conquest had no such effect was abundantly clear from the judgment of Viscount Haldane in the Privy Council—(1921), 3 N. L. R., at p. 58.

[5] Viscount Haldane, delivering the judgment of the Privy Council in the *A. Tijani* v. *Secry.* 1921, cited the statement of the Under-Secretary for Foreign Affairs in the House of Commons in 1862: 'The slave trade was to be suppressed, but Docemo was not to be maltreated. He was to have a revenue settled on and secured to him. *The real possessors of the land were considered to be, not the native kings, but the White-Cap Chiefs*' (3 N. L. R., at p. 55).

[6] (1910), 2 N. C. R. 1, at p. 43.

grant, assign and to make over land for the use of the grantees and the use of their heirs and assigns for ever, yet, according to native law, the grantees and their heirs and assigns had *a right of occupation only* [1] determinable if they contested the ownership of the grantor in certain other events.' That this is no more than the ordinary administrative right of control exercisable to this day by heads of families all over Nigeria is obvious. Hence it is that Docemo's alleged right of 'ownership' cannot be buttressed by the fact that he was already issuing grants of land at the date of the cession.

In regard to (iii), though Osborne, C.J., was of the opinion[2] that the White-Cap Chief's consent or participation was not necessary to the validity of the alienation by Docemo, it is illuminating to recall Webber, J's., citation in *Amodu Tijani* v. *Secry. Southern Provinces* [3] of a dictum of Chief Justice Smalman Smith who, in defining the position of Idejo Chiefs in the case of *Ajose* v. *Efunde & Ors.*, decided in 1892, observed as follows:

'The absolute ownership of territory has never, so far as my experience teaches me, been acknowledged in this Yorubaland as inherent in the sovereignty of the kings of the Country, but there is undoubtedly *a national proprietary right* which is vested *in the king and his chiefs or Council* as representing the community who elect and appoint them originally and who *conjointly* may exercise the right of alienation.' [4]

[1] The italics are mine.

[2] In *Oduntan Onisiwo* v. *A.-G. of South Prov.* (1912), 2 N. L. R. 77, at pp. 82–3 where the learned C.J. had said that the Treaty was not in the 'nature of a conveyancing transaction, a private grant by an individual who had no title to the land, . . . but was an Act of State by the supreme executive authority in Lagos, viz. the King and the White-Cap Chiefs.' He went on to assert (i) that the signatures of at least two Idejo Chiefs, Aromire and Obanikoro, could be discerned in the copy of the Treaty in Mr. Algernon Montagu's compilation of the Laws of Lagos, published in 1874, and (ii) that 'the signature of the Idejos was not necessary. An Idejo's land belonged to the family of which he was the elected head; the community of Lagos at large had no interest in it or right over it as Lagosians. . . . They were under the sovereignty of Docemo. . . .'

It is clear that this sweeping generalisation has been largely inspired by the learned Chief Justice's ideas of English constitutional monarchy based upon the feudal theory that the King owns all the land. The fact is that there never has been anything in the Nigerian notions of kingship to parallel this peculiarly English theory. Thus, Osborne, C.J's., error is no less grave than Griffith, J's., or Speed C.J's.,., 'seigneurial' idea of the relationship between Docemo and his Chiefs and, therefore, his subjects.

[3] 3 N. L. R. (Full Court Judgment), at p. 39.

[4] All the italics are mine.

3. PROTESTS BY CHIEFS

The White-Cap Chiefs strongly protested at the time of the cession against the giving away of their lands by Docemo, but 'were assured that the Treaty did not deprive them of their private property'.[1] According to native ideas, King Docemo no more owned Lagos land at the time of the cession than did the White-Cap (or Idejo) Chiefs, who however, had a more valid but joint claim to Lagos land by virtue of their headships of their respective families who are the ultimate land-owners of Lagos and its surroundings.

4. DOCEMO HAD NO SEIGNEURIAL RIGHTS OVER LAGOS LAND

'Seigneurial rights are not known to native law and cannot be introduced under s. 19 of the Supreme Court Ordinance.'[2] It follows that, whether we are considering the relation between Docemo and his chiefs or that between the chiefs and their families or communities (or, *a fortiori*, that between Docemo and the community), we would do well to remember that the term 'seigneurial' is a misnomer unless used within the context of Speed,

[1] (a) Winkfield, J., at 2 N. L. R. 41; (b) Osborne, C.J., also recorded the chiefs' protest at p. 9 of 2 N. L. R.; (c) also per Webber, J., in *Amodu Tijani* v. *Secry. Southern Nigeria* (1915), 3 N. L. R. at p. 39; (d) at p. 27 of 2 N. L. R. Griffith, J., remarked: '. . . the root contention in this appeal is that King Docemo was *not* the owner of Lagos land and the implication is that the White-Cap Chiefs were the owners of Lagos land. . . . There can be no doubt that there is some basis for the contention that the White-Cap Chiefs were owners of the land of Lagos Island in 1861; this is shown by the reply in Parliament of the Under-Secretary of State for Foreign Affairs, in June 1862, and by the despatch of Consul Freeman, of March 1862. But the evidence is to my mind overwhelming that Lagos land and therefore Lagos foreshore was the *property* of King Docemo, *at least for the purpose of ceding it to the British Government*' (italics mine).
    If, by this 'property' of King Docemo, Griffith, J., meant what had been described by Chief Justice Smalman Smith in the passage above quoted as 'a national proprietary right which is vested in the King and his Chiefs or Council', all would be well. If, however, it is intended to enhance Docemo's title and erect it into a feudalistic prerogative, on the analogy of European medieval feudalism, it stands contradicted by sounder, if because later, judicial decisions and unsupported by native law and custom (see *dicta* cited later).
[2] *Per* Shyngle, a Nigerian lawyer, acting for the appellant in *Amodu Tijani* v. *Secry., Southern Provinces* (1915), 3 N. L. R. (Full Court Judgment), at p. 28.

C.J.'s, definition in the Divisional Court:[1] 'Such right is merely a seigneurial right, giving the holder the ordinary rights of control and management of the land in accordance with the well-known principles of native law and custom, including the right to receive payment of the nominal rent or tribute payable by the occupiers (and that compensation should be calculated on that basis and not on the basis of absolute ownership of the land).' [2] But their Lordships of the Judicial Committee of the P.C. discounted this idea [3] and awarded compensation to Chief Oluwa on the basis of absolute ownership,[4] even though the latter was no more than a trustee of the land (and, therefore, of the compensation money) on behalf of his family. No doubt, their lordships took this line because they believed themselves to be thereby compensating the ultimate 'owners' of the land, the members of the Oluwa family, through their representative, the Chief Oluwa.

Finally, there is one more point to be considered with reference

[1] 3 N. L. R., at p. 27; cf. Pennington, J., at p. 43 ibid.: '. . . the expression "seigneurial right" may not be strictly accurate if used by itself; it is however amply qualified and explained by the words which follow.'

[2] Of course, the learned C.J. was immediately concerned with describing the nature of a chief's right to family land. It is submitted, however, that Docemo's right, with respect to his own family land, is precisely no more than that of a chief.

[3] 3 N. L. R., at p. 58; (1921), 2 A. C., at p. 409: 'Their lordships think that the learned Chief Justice in the judgment thus summarised, which virtually excludes the legal reality of the community usufruct, has failed to recognise the real character of the title to land occupied by a native community.' Earlier, at p. 40 of 3 N. L. R., Webber, J., in delivering his Full Court Judgment in the *Amodu Tijani's Case*, had dissented from Speed, C.J.'s, *obiter* in the *Onisiwo Case* when he remarked: 'And the position of the King of Lagos over the lands controlled by the Idejos before the cession is clearly stated by the native assessors in this case in answer to a question put by the Court; they stated : 'Before the Cession, if the King of Lagos wanted to give land to any person in that district (i.e. the district of Ottoh), he would send to the chief to say that he wanted land in that part for the person and the chief would give it to him. And the Chief could not say that he had no land to give to the King. The Chief dare not refuse.' The whole evidence, historical, oral and documentary, shows that this right possessed by the Idejos from the earliest times, when all land was communal and there was no fixity of tenure and the idea of private ownership entirely unknown, up to the time of the cession when the influence of civilisation introduced this idea of private ownership, was *a public right*, a right which they acquired by virtue of their chieftaincy.' This 'public right', far from being 'seigneurial', is substantially the 'national proprietary right' of Chief Justice Smalman Smith to which we have referred on p. 12, footnote.

[4] Ibid., at p. 59. But this was done under s. 7 of the Public Lands Acquisition Ordinance, 1917.

to this problem. An attractive ditch of dialectics sometimes employed by protagonists of Docemo's ownership of Lagos land is the argument that the Crown's promise to him of the payment of an annual pension is an acknowledgment of his absolute ownership. Now, when by Article 3 (2) of the Treaty [1] of 1861 a revenue was made payable by the Crown to Docemo, it surely was not an annuity, representing the economic value of the ceded territory, a genuine block estimate rolled into a number of years' purchase in the form of a rentcharge on the basis of a recognised right of Docemo to the absolute ownership of the land, but rather as an earnest of a desire on the part of the Crown to secure Docemo's co-operation in stamping out the (to him) lucrative slave trade in which he had hitherto taken a leading role. Thus, the Privy Council:[2] 'In 1862, a debate took place in the House of Commons which is instructive as showing the interpretation by the British Government of the footing on which it had really entered. The slave trade was to be suppressed, but Docemo was not to be maltreated. He was to have a revenue settled on and secured to him. The real possessors of the land were considered to be, not the native kings, but the White-Cap Chiefs. . . . The object was to suppress the slave trade, and to introduce orderly conditions.' [3] We may, therefore, conclude that the reservation of an annual pension to Docemo in the Treaty does not prove anything with respect to the ownership of the ceded lands; it relates only to the policy which animated the Treaty, a desire to abolish the slave trade in Lagos.

[1] Art. 3, para. 2, reads: 'In consideration of the Cession as before mentioned of the Port and Island and territories of Lagos, the Representatives of the Queen of Great Britain, do promise, subject to the approval of Her Majesty, that Docemo shall receive an annual pension from the Queen of Great Britain, equal to the net revenue hitherto annually received by him; such pension to be paid at such periods and in such mode as may hereafter be determined.'

[2] *Per* Viscount Haldane in *Amodu Tijani* v. *Secry. Southern Provinces* (1921), A. C., at pp. 406–7; (1921), 3 N. L. R., at p. 55.

[3] Cf. Webber, J., in *Chief Young Dede* v. *African Association, Ltd.* (1910), 1 N. L. R. 130, at pp. 136 and 142, where the learned judge dealt with the payment of personal subsidies to the King and Chiefs of Kula, in the Brass district of Eastern Nigeria, under a commercial Agreement of 1856 between certain British merchants and the said chiefs. Since the sole aim of these subsidies (Art. 20 of the Agreement) was 'the abandonment of the slave traffic', it is probable that this Treaty, preceding as it did the Treaty of Cession of 1861 by a period of only five years, might have been the precedent for the latter Treaty's provision to pay Docemo also for the identical purpose of discouraging the slave trade. It might equally be a recognition of Common British practice.

5. CONCLUSION

In the result, our proper inference from the preceding investigations is that (i) Docemo was not the owner of Lagos land and the territory around it [1]; (ii) the four White-Cap Chiefs, as heads of the land-owning families, held and still hold the land on behalf of their respective families or communities who are the ultimate 'owners' of the land.[2]

The immediate conclusion that leaps to the mind is that, since Lagos land was neither Docemo's nor the White-Cap Chiefs' to alienate, the Treaty of Cession is to that extent invalid and the Crown has no title to the land covered by the Treaty. That this is a clear case of *non sequitur* can be demonstrated: Even under strict native law and custom, land may be given to strangers by chiefs or family heads with the consent of the family. Our own earlier account of the influx of liberated slaves from Sierra Leone into Lagos and the consequent practice of alienation of land about the time of the Treaty of Cession, amply bears this out. There can be no doubt that by the time of the Cession the King and his Executive Council were the proper authority to negotiate such treaty.

6. THE PLEA OF ACT OF STATE

(a) On behalf of Docemo

It has therefore been argued with much force that in making the Treaty Docemo, together with his Council of Chiefs, was exercising an Act of State. Osborne, C.J., in *Oduntan Onisiwo* v. *A.-G. of Southern Provinces* [3] had said that the Treaty was not in the 'nature of a conveyancing transaction . . . but was an Act of State by the supreme executive authority in Lagos, viz. the King and the White-Cap Chiefs. . . . The Cession itself was, of course, an Act of State, and it was an act from which, according to the ordinary usages of civilised nations, juristic consequences would follow.' [4] Whatever

---

[1] See Dr. C. K. Meek, 'A Note on Crown Lands in the Colonies' in the *Journal of Comparative Legislation and International Law*, 3rd series, Vol. XXVIII (1946), Parts III and IV, pp. 87–91, at p. 89 where the learned writer briefly referred to the supposed sovereignty of King Docemo.

[2] What the nature of this ownership really is will appear in Chap. V, *infra*.

[3] (1912), 2 N. L. R. 77, at pp. 82–3.

[4] The same view of the 1861 Treaty of Cession was held by E. C. S. Wade in 'Act of State in English Law: Its relations with International Law' in *The British Year-Book of International Law*' (1934), pp. 109–12, where the learned writer would seem to have regarded the Treaty as a kind of international treaty between the Crown and the Lagos King and Chiefs.

moral objection one may have to the attribution to illiterate and
unwary native kings and chiefs of such technical acts in the law,[1]
the elementary legal implications of which were hardly present to
their minds when signing the Treaty, any attempt to impugn the
latter, on that ground would fail since, if we accept the international character of the Treaty, international law does not invalidate a treaty on a ground such as the present one.[2]

(b) On behalf of the Crown

If, however, we deny the international validity of the Treaty,
we have to admit that, from the point of view of British Constitutional Law and practice,[3] the annexation of foreign territory,
howsoever brought about, is an Act of State by the Crown and is
as legally valid as ever. Thus said Viscount Simon, L.C., in delivering the judgment in the recent *New Zealand Maoris' Case* as to the
effect of the Treaty of Waitangi (6 February 1840) in *Hoani te
Heuheu Tukino* v. *Aotea District Maori Land Board:* [4] 'It is well
settled that any rights purporting to be conferred by such a treaty
of cession cannot be enforced in the Courts, except in so far as
they have been incorporated in the municipal law. The principle
laid down in a series of decisions [5] was summarised by Lord
Dunedin, in delivering the judgment of this Board in the Gwalior
Case, *Vajesingji Joravarsingji* v. *Secretary of State for India* (1924),

[1] See Lord Hailey, *An African Survey*, p. 833: 'The agreements under which
such lands were ceded to European governments dealt with conditions which
in almost every case were outside the experience of the Chiefs who made them,
and their implications must usually have been beyond the power of their
makers to envisage.'

[2] See Oppenheim-Lauterpacht, *International Law*, Vol. I, 6th edition,
pp. 802–4; Hall, *P.I.L.* (1924), 8th edition, pp. 380–1 and Lawrence, *International Law* (1927), 7th edition, pp. 302–3.

[3] See Wade and Phillips, *Constitutional Law*, p. 363; M. F. Lindley, *The
Acquisition and Government of Backward Territory in International Law* (1926),
p. 337; 'The Case of the Cayuga Indians', in 20 *A.J.I.L.*, 1926, p. 574; 'The
Fiji Land Claims', in 18 *A.J.I.L.*, 1924, pp. 814–35.

[4] (1941), A. C. 308, at p. 324.

[5] Of which the font and fountain is the famous Apapa Case, *Amodu Tijani
Oluwa* v. *Secretary, Southern Nigeria* (1921), A. C. 399, referred to at p. 315
of this 1941 case: 'The interpretation put on the cession in *Amodu Tijani* v.
Secretary, Southern Nigeria, 399, 400, 404, is really the same as is to be found
in the express terms in the present case.'

Thus Lord Hailey's observation (at p. 714 of his *An African Survey*), which
seems to distinguish the New Zealand land policy from that of the Fiji Islands
and, therefore, of West African Colonies, would appear to need modification
in the light of *Hoani, etc.* v. *Aotea* (1941), A. C. 308.

L. R. 51 I. A. 357 in these words (at p. 360): "When a territory is acquired by a sovereign State for the first time that is an Act of State. It matters not how the acquisition has been brought about. It may be by conquest, it may be by cession following on treaty, it may be by occupation of territory hitherto unoccupied by a recognised ruler. In all cases the result is the same, etc., etc.'"

7. LEGAL EFFECT OF CESSION

The legal effect of the cession of 1861, then, is that the root title to the land comprised in the Treaty thereby passed to the Crown. On the principle that the Crown owns Lagos lands, which has been the consistent judicial view, we naturally want to see stated a clear idea of the nature of this right.[1] In the first case in which the issue as to the nature of Crown rights under the Treaty directly arose, *A.-G. of Southern Nigeria* v. *John Holt & Co.*[2] (where the defendant company had claimed ownership of a certain portion of the Lagos foreshore), it had been held that the Crown was by the Cession the owner of Lagos Island and, therefore, of the whole of Lagos foreshore.[3] Only in a casual manner did the Privy Council observe [4] that the residual rights of the land in Lagos and its surroundings passed to the Crown; no attempt was made to define the nature and scope of these rights.

In the earlier case of *Oduntan Onisiwo* v. *A.-G. of Southern Provinces* [5] in which the extent of the ceded territory fell to be determined, it was held (i) that land at Abekun Lighthouse was *outside* the territory ceded to the Crown in 1861 and (ii) that the land was in fact the property of the Onisiwo Chieftaincy family. On the vexed question as to the real nature of land rights of the

[1] See Dr. C. K. Meek's *Land Law and Custom in the Colonies*, p. 294: 'Lagos was ceded to Queen Victoria by King Docemo in 1861, but the precise nature of the rights and powers which passed to the British Crown were not clearly defined *and are still in some respects a subject of dispute.*'

Cf. Hailey, *An African Survey*, pp. 801–2, where, after raising the issues, the learned writer considered that they were henceforth of merely historical interest. But at p. 833, he opined that the Treaty 'still remains of importance, however, in regard to the disposal of land to natives'.

[2] (1915), A. C. 599; 2 N. L. R. 1.

[3] The other important point decided, viz. that the defendant Company had acquired something in the nature of an easement entitling them to continued enjoyment of the land held by them, will be considered in the Chapter on Servitudes, Easements, Profits, etc.

[4] At pp. 58–9 of 2 N. L. R.

[5] (1912), 2 N. L. R. 77.

Crown, all that was vouchsafed to us by Osborne, C.J., was[1]: 'I am quite clear that *whatever* lands the Idejos owned as heads of their respective families at the time of the Cession passed under the Treaty. . . . I am clearly of opinion that the ownership rights of private land-owners, including the families of the Idejos, were left entirely unimpaired, and as freely exercisable after the Cession as before. . . .'

Instructive as is this general statement about the Crown having acquired whatever it was competent to the Idejos to have alienated under the Cession, it is submitted that we are left none the wiser about the precise nature of the Crown's land rights.[2] Was it a fee simple that passed to the Crown under the treaty, or what was it?

At this stage it is important to bear in mind that the English idea of *a fee simple ownership* is quite foreign to traditional native law and custom. As we have shown above, neither Docemo nor the White-Cap Chiefs, both of whom negotiated the Treaty, were 'owners' of the land *in their own rights*.[3] The ultimate 'owners' were the respective communities represented by them; then, we have to delimit the type of ownership enjoyed by these communities, because on that must finally depend the nature of the Crown's title to the ceded territory.

8. DEFINITION OF CROWN'S TITLE

The first case in which a somewhat salutary, if heroic, effort was made to define the Crown's title is *Amodu Tijani* v. *Secretary, Southern Nigeria*,[4] which has since become the *locus classicus* on the whole subject of the nature of Crown ownership of colonial lands.[5] The facts can be briefly stated: Under the Public Lands Acquisition Ordinance of 1903, the Colonial Government acquired certain pieces of land situate at Apapa within the Colony of Lagos. The plaintiff, the head chief of the Oluwa family and one of the

---

[1] 1912, 2 N. L. R. 77 at pp. 82–3. This passage was cited, with approval, at p. 33 of 3 N. L. R., by Ross, J.

[2] Lack of precision as to the nature of native ownership may have been responsible for this amorphous idea of Crown's rights.

[3] For a detailed analysis of the powers of head chiefs with regard to land see Chap. V.

[4] (1921), 2 A. C. 399.

[5] See Lord Hailey, *African Survey*, pp. 768, 802; C. K. Meek, *Land Law and Custom in the Colonies*, p. 146. Also cited in *Hoani Te, etc.* v. *Aotea District Board* (1941), A. C., at p. 315.

land-owning White-Cap Chiefs of Lagos, claimed compensation for these lands, first as absolute owner thereof but later as representative of his family. Speed, C.J., had held in the Divisional Court that the plaintiff, having exercised a kind of seigneurial right of control and management over the land in accordance with the well-established principle of native law and custom which involved the receipt from the occupiers of some nominal tribute or rent, was entitled to compensation, not on the basis of absolute ownership as provided by para. 6 of the Public Lands Acquisition Ordinance (1903),[1] but on the basis of 'seigneurial' control and management. This decision was on appeal affirmed by the Supreme Court of Nigeria; whereupon the plaintiff appealed to the Judicial Committee of the Privy Council which, consisting of Viscount Haldane, Lord Atkinson and Lord Phillimore, delivered its judgment on 11 July 1921. With respect to the effect of the Treaty of Cession upon land ownership in the Colony, Viscount Haldane, who delivered the judgment of their Lordships, held in very guarded but trenchant language as follows: [2]

'Their Lordships make the preliminary observation that in interpreting the native title to land, not only in Southern Nigeria, but in other parts of the Empire, much caution is essential. There is a tendency, operating at times unconsciously, to render that title conceptually in terms which are appropriate only to systems which have grown up under English law. But this tendency has to be held in check closely. As a rule, in the various systems of native jurisprudence throughout the Empire, there is no such full division between property and possession as English lawyers are familiar with. *A very usual form of native title is that of a usufructuary right, which is a mere qualification of or burden on the radical or final title of the Sovereign where that exists.* In such cases the title of the Sovereign is a pure legal estate, to which beneficial rights may or may not be attached. But this estate is qualified by a right of beneficial user which may not assume definite forms analogous to estates, or where it has assumed these, have derived them from the intrusions of the mere analogy of English jurisprudence. . . . As the result of cession to the British Crown by former potentates, *the radical title is now in the British Sovereign. But that title is throughout qualified by the usufructuary rights of communities,* rights which,

---

[1] Para. 6 reads: 'The head chief of such community may sell and convey the same for an estate in fee simple.' This was intended as a device to secure to the members of the community full and substantial value for their land.

[2] (1921), A. C. 399, at pp. 402–4; also, 3 N. L. R. 21, at pp. 52–3.

as the outcome of deliberate policy, have been respected and recognised.'

After reviewing Speed, C.J.'s,, judgment in the two Courts below in which he had held that all for which Chief Oluwa could claim compensation in respect of the family land at Apapa was 'merely a seigneurial right' of control and management of the land in accordance with the well-known principles of native law and custom, their Lordships questioned whether the Chief Justice considered that by the Treaty of Cession the Crown's title to Lagos land was so absolute that the members of the community could be expropriated without compensation, and proceeded to observe: [1]

'Their Lordships think that the learned Chief Justice in the judgment thus summarised, which virtually excludes the *legal reality of the community usufruct*, has failed to recognise the real character of the title to land occupied by a native community. That title, as they have pointed out, is *prima facie* based, not on such individual ownership as English law has made familiar, but on *a communal usufructuary occupation, which may be so complete as to reduce any radical right in the Sovereign to one which only extends to comparatively limited rights of administrative interference.*'

9. GENERAL EFFECTS OF TREATY

In view of the stricture upon the nature of Crown's right to Lagos land contained in the above definitive pronouncements of their Lordships, we may attempt a summary of the general effects of the Cession in law and in practice as follows:

(i) It is impossible to describe in precise terms of English property law the exact title acquired by the Crown. The attempt [2] to derive a fee simple ownership from the issue of Crown grants, which were often expressed to pass the fee simple to the grantees, must now be abandoned, for Viscount Haldane in the *Amodu Tijani's Case* [3] gave it the *coup de grace* in these words: 'The introduction of the system of Crown grants which was made subsequently must be regarded as having been brought about mainly, if not exclusively, for conveyancing purposes, and not with a view

[1] (1921), 2 A. C., at p. 409.

[2] See, e.g., Osborne, C.J., and all the associate judges in *A.-G. of S. Nigeria* v. *John Holt & Co.* (2 N. L. R. 1) *passim*; *Oduntan Onisiwo* v. *A.-G.* (2 N. L. R. 77) *passim*; *Amodu Tijani* v. *Secry. Southern Provinces* (3 N. L. R. 21) *passim*; in all of which arguments in favour of Crown ownership were based on the circumstance that the Crown was issuing grants as owner of the land.

[3] At pp. 407–8.

to altering substantive titles already existing.' But in spite of this clear statement of principle we still come across some curious attempts to sidetrack this finding on the part of certain judges. Thus, Webber, J., in *Brimah Balogun & Ors.* v. *Saka Chief Oshodi:*[1] 'What was the legal effect of a Crown Grant issued in 1869? Crown grants were given to individuals. These grants conveyed the fee simple in every case.' But Berkeley, J., who came to the same conclusion with the learned judge, had earlier on in the case [2] found that 'Their Lordships also held (in the *Dakolo Case*, a Privy Council decision, 1930 A. C. 667) [3] that the Crown grants to compound heads were only grants in trust, and left the property exactly where it was. Their Lordships also said that Government Grants are in their form inconsistent with the whole idea of native rights. They point to a transition state, but it is for legislation and not for the Board to bring to an end such a peculiar state of affairs as regards title.' No doubt Crown Grants came to be issued for exactly the same purpose as that of Docemo's grants, namely, to settle and regulate questions of native titles to land which had in the period following 1852 become almost chaotic. They were, in fact, no more than certificates of title and were never intended to pass, nor could they have passed, any property in the land which did not exist before.[4] Before 1895, when Sule Raphael died, he had bought the land from Agebodeh, who had a Crown grant of it dated 1866, that is, he had a Crown Certificate; he had no conveyance. It does not appear to have been usual in those days for the Crown to make grants; they granted a certificate of title.[5]

10. CROWN GRANTS NOT EVIDENCE OF CROWN'S OWNERSHIP

It seems quite safe to assume that Crown grants [6] were no more than administrative machinery employed by the local Government

---

[1] 10 N. L. R. 36, at p. 50. [2] At p. 46, ibid. [3] The interpolation is mine.

[4] This was, of course, subject to any special regulative measure which the Government of the day might have taken to confer upon individuals or groups of individuals; e.g. the Governor Glover's 'endowments' at Ebute Metta, but even these were done with the consent of the representatives of the families concerned.

[5] *Sunmonu* v. *Disu Raphael* (1927), A. C., at p. 884.

[6] Dr. C. K. Meek in *Land Law and Custom in the Colonies*, at p. 295: 'Between 1868 and 1912 the British authorities in Lagos issued some 4,000 "Crown Grants". The issue of these grants was in many ways unfortunate.' He then cited a statement of Hon. Kitoyi Ajasa—a Nigerian lawyer—before the West African Lands Commission (1912): 'in their inception they were no more than confirmatory of the rights, titles and interests of persons in possession and occupation of the land to which they related at the time of cession.'

during a troubled period of transition and that, whatever later doubts had been raised as to their legal effect, they did not constitute an exercise of Crown ownership. No fee simple passed under them.[1]

(ii) A corollary of this attractive idea of the Crown's fee simple under the Treaty is the *theory of 'dormant' fee simple* as the title of the Crown, first put forward by Berkeley, J., delivering his judgment in the Supreme Court of Nigeria in *Brimah Balogun & Ors.* v. *Saka Chief Oshodi:*[2] 'What happened after the cession of the territory of Lagos seems to have been that the Crown acquired the *dominium directum* but let the customary tenure undisturbed as between the natives of the territory. This acquiescence in a local form of land tenure among the natives of the land in their dealings with each other would not operate to extinguish the *dominium directum; and a fee simple tenure was lying dormant in this dominium directum.* I think the fee lay dormant, and remained dormant so long as native of the territory was dealing with native of the territory under the communal system, which is the basis of this customary tenure.' The learned Judge went on to assert that as soon as natives treat family land as private property or employ modern modes of alienation like conveyance and mortages, then such procedure 'awakens the dormant fee simple in favour of the purchaser'. In that case, the plaintiff had acquired one of the parcels of land granted by a predecessor of the defendant to certain settlers who had received a Crown grant thereto. He acquired it by purchase from a third party who had himself purchased it from a member of the defendant's family, with the acquiescence of that family. The plaintiff then argued that he had acquired the fee simple by the purchase. *Held*: by a majority of the Supreme Court, Kingdon, C.J., alone dissenting, that the plaintiff had acquired an estate in fee simple. In an unreported decision of the Privy Council on appeal [3] the judgment was reversed and the theory of a dor-

[1] *Per* Lord Blanesburgh in *Idewu Inasa* v. *Oshodi* (1934), A. C., at p. 101: 'It cannot be doubted that this act of Government was a source of misunderstanding, as each grant, on its face, purported to be a disposition in absolute terms in favour of the grantee. But it was at an early stage settled, although apparently not always accepted, that these grants were only grants in trust, and that they left the interests in the properties, whether those of the occupiers or those of the Chief exactly where they had been.'

See also Lord Hailey, *African Survey*, p. 768.

[2] (1931), 10 N. L. R. 36, at p. 48.

[3] See Colonial Office Legal Library: Record of Judgments of the Privy Council for 1936–1945, Judgment No. 51, delivered on 16 July 1936 (Privy Council Appeal No. 46 of 1934).

At p. 7 of the judgment, Lord Maugham significantly observed: 'Their

mant fee simple was exploded. Because of the practical importance of the theory it may be profitable briefly to state the arguments. Counsel for plaintiff claimed for his client a fee simple with the reservation that in case of failure of heirs the property would revert to the family instead of being subject to escheat to the Crown. Counsel for defendant, on the other hand, claimed an estate of absolute ownership under native law which, according to him, implied the right of reversion to the original family on failure of heirs instead of escheat to the Crown. Berkeley, J., while holding that a fee simple passed to the plaintiff in any case, then pointed out that there was no difference between the two standpoints, although Counsel for plaintiff had based his contention on 'the inherent sovereignty of the Crown made applicable to the territory of Lagos by the Treaty of Cession of 1861', [1] while defendant's Counsel had appealed to 'native law' which, however, knew no conception of a fee simple. The dissenting judgment of Chief Justice Kingdon, with which their Lordships of the Privy Council agreed on appeal, is particularly illuminating: [2] 'There is no suggestion of a dormant fee simple. In my view the whole idea of fee simple is so contrary to native law and custom that, whether dormant or otherwise, it cannot exist side by side with native customary tenure in respect of the same piece of land.' The learned Chief Justice had adapted a dictum of the Privy Council in the intervening *Dakolo Case* (1930), A. C. 667, which was decided between the judgment of the Divisional Court (in which Tew, J., had found against the plaintiff and held that he did not acquire the fee simple) and the judgment of the Supreme Court: 'The paramount chief is owner of the lands, but he is not owner in the sense in which owner is understood in this country. *He has no fee simple*, but only a usufructuary title.'

11. CROWN GRANTS RE-DETERMINED

According to a correspondent in 'The Nigerian Daily Times' of Monday, 2 August 1948, the two Privy Council decisions of *Sakariyawo Oshodi* v. *Moriyamo Dakolo & Ors.* and *Brimah Balogun &*

Lordships think it right to express the opinion that the wide differences of opinion of learned Judges as to the titles to lands in Lagos disclosed in the present case and in a number of cases to which reference has been made, and the frequent actions in the Courts to which these doubts give rise, make it very desirable to deal with these questions by legislation.'

[1] For the obvious contradiction in this argument of the plaintiff's Counsel, see Berkeley, J.'s, observation on pp. 46–7 of 10 N. L. R.
[2] 10 N. L. R. 36, at p. 57.

Ors. v. *Saka Chief Oshodi* led to the appointment of Sir Mervyn L. Tew on 29 November 1938, to carry out an enquiry into the title to land in Lagos and Ebute Metta. He arrived in Lagos on 23 February 1939, and, with the assistance of Captain G. Derby, M.C., of the Land Department, received the evidence, oral as well as documentary, of the Lagos Chiefs, The Epetedo Union and other private individuals, including the late Mr. Herbert Macauley, a professional civil engineer, politician, historian and journalist, who had carried out extensive surveys of vast areas of Nigeria. Sir Mervyn submitted his Report to the Nigerian Government in August 1939, whereupon a Committee was set up on 21 February 1940 to advise on the recommendations in the Tew Report. This Committee finally submitted, on 4 September 1942, its own findings which substantially adopted Sir Mervyn's Report.

The following four Ordinances, all of which came into operation on 22 May 1947, were the outcome:

(*a*) *The Crown Grants (Township of Lagos) Ordinance No*. 18 *of* 1947, which strips previous claim to Crown's absolute ownership of all its pretensions and puts all land subject to Crown grants back into their pristine state under native law and custom. Only in certain cases of grants made for terms of years before the Crown Lands Ordinance 1918 will there be a reversion to the Crown on the expiry of their respective terms.

(*b*) *The Arotas (Crown Grants) Ordinance No*. 19 *of* 1947, which declares that all documents of title previously issued by or on behalf of the Crown to persons under the protection of Chiefs and occupying lands under the control of such chiefs, were 'inconsistent with native law and custom and neither enlarged the rights of the grantees nor diminished those of the Chiefs under whose protection they were living, but left unimpaired all rights under native law and custom in the land to which the said grants related.' There is a right of reversion in the Chief representing the family under indigenous law and custom.

(*c*) *The Epetedo Lands Ordinance No*. 20 *of* 1947, which seeks (i) to put back under native law and custom two of the Crown grants in respect of lands now occupied by the descendants of Chief Oshodi Tappa and (ii) to enfranchise lands the subject of all other Crown grants by the extinguishment of certain incidents of tenure operating in favour of the successor in title to Chief Oshodi Tappa. But those already paying rents in respect of their tenements to Chief Oshodi at the date of the Ordinance are not entitled to have their tenements enfranchised. Compensation is payable to

Chief Oshodi by those entitled to enfranchisement of their lands.

(*d*) *The Glover Settlement Ordinance No.* 21 *of* 1947, which is designed to regularise grants of land in the Settlement by the issue, subject to native law and custom, of new certificates of titles in place of those lost or destroyed but so that, in case the family of a person or the family of the successor in title to such person becomes extinct, the Oloto Chieftaincy family has reversionary rights in the lands. The erstwhile claim by the House of Docemo to rights in the land comprised in the Settlement (with the exception of only one parcel of land which is reserved to the Head of the House of Docemo) is expressly denied, as is any collective claim to the aggregate of the plots by refugees from Egba territory and their descendants.

The Crown categorically renounces all claim to ownership of the lands comprising the Settlement, with the exception of such of the lands as the Crown has taken possession of before the coming into operation of this Ordinance.

(iii) If, then, we hold that in the strict sense of the term the Crown has no fee simple, whether dormant or live, under the Treaty of Cession, we may rationalise the situation by saying that the Crown's ownership of Lagos land is on the same footing as its ownership of lands in the United Kingdom, with this difference that whereas the latter derives from the feudal theory of land tenure, the former is a corollary of British constitutional legal theory in cases of annexation of a foreign territory.

12. CROWN TITLE SUBJECT TO NATIVE RIGHTS

This theory, as has just been stated above, gives to the Crown the radical or final title, whatever that may mean, so long as it is not taken as a fee simple, while leaving the 'usufructuary' rights in the native owners. 'It is not admissible to conclude that the Crown is generally speaking entitled to the beneficial ownership of the land as having so passed to the Crown as to displace any presumptive title of the natives. . . . A mere change of sovereignty is not to be presumed as meant to disturb rights of private owners and the general terms of a cession are *prima facie* to be construed accordingly.' [1] This statement of principle goes very far towards

[1] (1921), 2 A. C. 399, at p. 407: Viscount Haldane cited, with approval, the dictum of Osborne, C.J., in the Supreme Court of the Colony in *Oduntan Onisiwo* v. *A.-G. of Southern Nigeria* (1912), 2 Nig. L. R. 77, at p. 83: 'I am

whittling down in practice what in theory at first seems, at least to colonial eyes, an extreme position taken up by the Crown with regard to Colonial lands. But as has been shown earlier [1] the practice seems fairly consistent under British constitution and law, and it is reasonably elastic enough to allow of no absolute *proprietary* right in the Crown while fully ensuring such native rights and usages as existed and still exist.[2]

clearly of opinion that "the ownership rights of private land-owners, including the families of the Idejos, were left entirely unimpaired, and as freely exercisable after the Cession as before." As to the effect of the Cession as an Act of State, Osborne, C.J., further held: 'The doctrine laid down in *Cook* v. *Sprigg* (L.R. Appeal Cases 1899) is, that "a change of sovereignty ought not to affect private property, but no municipal tribunal has authority to enforce such an obligation". If the Crown had chosen to repudiate this obligation, this Court would have had no jurisdiction. But this case is distinguishable from *Cook* v. *Sprigg* in one essential particular; there the obligation repudiated was never expressly recognised by the Crown, whereas here the obligation now sought to be repudiated, i.e. the obligation to recognise rights of private ownership in the ceded territories, has been actually adopted, and such recognition has been made part of the municipal law.' He, therefore, held that, to the extent to which the A.-G. of Nigeria had contended in the Court below that *Cook* v. *Sprigg* deprived the Nigerian Court of all jurisdiction to enquire into the extent of the ceded territory, it must be regarded as wrongly decided since *Walker* v. *Baird* ((1892), A. C. 491) is authority for the proposition that the jurisdiction of a municipal Court is not ousted merely because a question arose as to the construction of a treaty. (See also *West Rand Gold Mining Co. Ltd.* v. *Rex* (L. R. 1905, 2 K. B. D. 391 at 409) where the proposition seems applicable to both *personal* and *real* property.)

[1] See p. 16, *supra*.

[2] A detailed analysis of the exact nature of the various land rights enjoyed by Nigerians, from the head chiefs downwards, will be found in Chap. V.

Chapter Three

PROBLEMS OF OWNERSHIP
(THE PROTECTORATE)

A. The Northern Provinces of the Protectorate. B. The Southern Provinces of the Protectorate. C. The Cameroons under British Mandate (now Trust).

COMING now to the Protectorate of Nigeria we may start off with the constitutional theory that, so far as the British Crown is concerned, land in Colonial Protectorates is *foreign* territory,[1] just in the same way as Colonial territories are considered to be Crown lands. But any discussion about land in the Protectorate must take account of the distinction between Crown territory and Crown-owned land, since the two are not necessarily co-terminous. In the case of British Dominions,[2] there is a unity of both *dominium* and *imperium* and the feudal theory of Crown ownership of such lands avails. With regard to a Colonial Protectorate, however, there is *imperium* without *dominium*, and

[1] See, e.g., Sir J. Salmond, *Jurisprudence*, 10th edition, pp. 514–22; Jennings and Young, *Constitutional Laws of the British Empire*, 1938 edition, p. 7; Wade and Phillips, *Constitutional Law*, 3rd edition, pp. 368–9; M. F. Lindley, *Acquisition and Government of Backward Territory in International Law*, at p. 187; F. Lugard, *Dual Mandate* (1922), p. 36 and footnote 3 thereof; also, A. E. Sockett, *East Africa as a Protectorate* (1917), at p. 4: 'A Protectorate implies more than a Sphere of Influence but it is not an integral part of the British Empire, it is not part of the "Possessions" or "Dominions" of the Crown and has not reached the status of being considered British territory; it is less, therefore, than a Crown Colony.'

[2] i.e. using the word 'Dominion' in the sense of s. 18 of the Interpretation Act, 1889.

But the Nigerian Interpretation Ordinance No. 27 of 1939 provides in s. 3 that the term 'British possession' includes protectorates and mandated territories.

27

the Crown holds its territory but not its land.[1] The immediate practical importance of this theoretical distinction lies in the fact that whatever *dominium* is acquired in part or whole over protectorate land can only be the result of agreement, conquest or annexation by the Crown. Thus, in *Oshuntuyi Ogini* v. *T. S. Thomas (Governor's Deputy) and Owa of Ilesha & Ors.*[2] Webber, acting C.J., remarked:[3] 'Ilesha and Oyo are districts in the Oyo Province which is part of the Protectorate of Nigeria. Protectorates, which are dependencies of the Crown, though governed by Great Britain, are strictly speaking foreign territories.'[4]

We may here briefly review the legal effects of the various treaties entered into by the Royal Niger Company with native rulers and chiefs, and the succession by the Crown to such rights as the Company had, ending in the Proclamation of the Protectorates of Northern and Southern Nigeria which, as we have seen earlier,[5] took place in 1906. We have to treat the Northern and Southern Provinces separately.

A. THE NORTHERN PROVINCES OF THE PROTECTORATE

With regard to the Northern Provinces, two related questions have to be considered:

(1) Could the local Emirs, Chiefs and other rulers in the Protectorate effectively pass, or did they ever intend to pass any title to land by the various treaties they signed with the Royal Niger Company (or, under its earlier name, the National African Company)?

(2) What title really passed to the Crown as a result of the revocation of the Charter, the Government Proclamations as well as the Agreement with Her Majesty's Government in 1900?

Our analysis of each question will be as follows:

(1) As in the case of the cession of the Colony, so here we have to consider the validity of the treaties signed by native rulers with

---

[1] From the principle that Colonial Protectorates are 'foreign' countries has arisen the theory that their inhabitants are not British subjects; they are only British protected persons who may, however, owe extensive duties of allegiance to the Crown. Legislation with respect to Colonial Protectorates is enacted by means of Orders in Council as provided by the Foreign Jurisdiction Acts, 1890 and 1913.

[2] (1928), 8 N. L. R. 41.

[3] Ibid., at p. 42.

[4] To the same effect is *R.* v. *Crewe* (1910), 2 K. B. 576, at p. 603.

[5] Historical Introduction, *supra*.

the National African Company and its successor, the Royal Niger Company, between 1885 and 1890. Even in the Moslem emirates of Northern Nigeria with their central and often autocratic rule, no less than in the pagan areas, the Emirs and other native rulers 'were never lords and masters of the land; they were only political, religious and military rulers of their respective States. . . . In this way the Emirs were looked upon like all other African chieftains merely as trustees of the land on behalf of the people, to whom the land belonged.' [1] They could not, therefore, give away by treaties any rights in land of a proprietary character.[2]

Against Lady Lugard's positive assertion that 'By their treaties with the Royal Niger Company some of them had nominally surrendered their territory with all sovereign rights',[3] one may set Lord Lugard's own official report to the Secretary of State for the Colonies of 2 September 1903, in which he observed: 'The treaty contained certain stipulations which amounted to transfer by the Sultan of a part, at any rate, of his sovereign rights to the Company. That they had ever understood or agreed to this the Sokoto chiefs entirely denied. For the rest it amounted to a compact of friendship, and was understood as such by the Sultan. This maintenance of friendship was in fact the only *quid pro quo* he recognised in return for his subsidy, and this he now no longer maintained.' [4]

The reason assigned for this attitude of the Sultan was, according to Lord Lugard, that the Sultan of Sokoto considered the British attack on Nupe and Gando (confederate and vassal respectively of Sokoto) as having virtually put an end to the treaties which the Sultan and the Sokoto chiefs had always looked upon as treaties of commerce and friendship merely. When a claim to a transfer of sovereignty was first made by the British, the Northern

---

[1] C. K. Meek, *Land Law & Custom in the Colonies* (1946), pp. 12–13; George Padmore, *How Britain Rules Africa*, p. 210.

[2] Lord Hailey, *An African Survey*, p. 771: 'The treaties made by the Royal Niger Company with the Emirs between 1885 and 1890 gave it no general rights over land.' Also, pp. 798–802, ibid.

[3] At p. 417 of her *A Tropical Dependency*.

[4] Annual Report of Northern Nigeria for 1902, at pp. 157–160.

We may here recall also the Sultan's letter of May 1902, to Lord Lugard: 'From us to you. I do not consent that any one should ever dwell with us. I will never agree with you. I will have nothing ever to do with you. Between us and you there are no dealings except as between Mussulmans and Unbelievers ("Kafiri")—War as God Almighty has enjoined on us. There is no power or strength save in God on high. This with salutations.'

chiefs promptly denied that they ever contemplated parting with their lands under the treaties and felt righteously indignant at such an interpretation of their act.[1]

In his *Nigeria under British Rule*, Sir William Geary, Bart., has this to say on the present point: 'Treaties were entered into by the Royal Niger Company with Gando and Sokoto whereby the Company paid an annual subsidy to the Sultan of Sokoto. . . . However these treaties may be interpreted, there would not seem to be any Protectorate, express or implied. The Sokoto chiefs denied that these treaties had ever been understood as a transfer of sovereign rights, but amounted to a compact of friendship and was understood as such. The two letters of the Sultan of Sokoto received May–June 1902 protested against the British intervention. . . . England was clearly an uninvited ruler in Northern Nigeria.' [2]

Lady Lugard pointed out [3] that the arrangements between the Company and the African rulers were really private agreements and not treaties in the international sense; it was the grant of the Royal Charter [4] which lifted them out of their obscurity to the status of international treaties. Even so, it does not seem that such a view satisfactorily disposes of the argument that, in the words of C. L. Temple at p. 140 of his *Native Races and their Rulers*, 'All those acts of Native Chiefs, which, by means of treaties made with strangers, alienated the tribal lands, are . . . according to Native law and custom, *ultra vires*.' [5]

[1] See P. T. Moon's *Imperialism and World Politics*, at p. 102 where, amidst a somewhat melodramatic account of the general mode of treaty making with native chiefs by Sir George Goldie of the Royal Niger Company, he ended: 'Such, in a general way, was the process of treaty-making by which the Negro tribes accepted Great Britain's protectorate. A courageous but nervous explorer bravely concealing his fears; a half explained treaty of "friendship"; presents of beads and cloth (and of liquor in the case of less high-minded explorers)—these were the typical elements in the situation.'

[2] At pp. 354–5.

[3] Op. cit.

[4] i.e. the Royal Charter granted to the National African Company on 10 July 1887, the relevant portion of which reads: 'In the administration of justice by the Company to the peoples of its territories, or to any of the inhabitants thereof, careful regard shall always be had to the customs and laws of the class, or tribe, or nation to which the parties respectively belong, especially with respect to the holding, possession, transfer and disposition of lands and goods and testate and intestate succession thereto, and marriage, divorce, and legitimacy, and other rights of property and personal rights.'

[5] And this, in spite of Lord Lugard's statement: 'The system of Fulani rule was a feudal one, in which the right of all land was vested in the Emir, and fief-holders paid a rent or tribute to the overlord.' That this view is incorrect

The highest claim, then, which the Royal Niger Company could have staked was the right to the use only of the land comprised in any particular agreement relating thereto, since, in the view of Sir Charles Orr in his *The Making of Northern Nigeria*, at p. 248, 'the use of land by the inhabitants throughout the Protectorate could be, and was by custom, transferred and inherited, but that it was the use of the land and not the land itself, which was thus dealt with'.

In the result, such a clause as the following, which occurred in a treaty between the Emir of Katsina and the National African Company, can only be regarded as *ultra vires*. It could pass no more rights to the Company than the African ruling signatories had the right to convey under native law and custom. The clause in question reads:

'We, the Undersigned King and Chiefs of .... with a view to the bettering of the condition of our country and people, do this day cede, *with all sovereign rights*, to the National African Company (Ltd.) *for ever*, the whole of our territory extending from .... to ....' [1]

It is, therefore, clear that the absolute terms in which the purported conveyance was couched could not have meant the transfer by the African ruler of the fee simple in native communal and family lands, and no claim founded on such treaties could be valid *per se*.

On the same principle, any title to land purporting to have been granted to the Royal Niger Company by alien bodies like the Roman Catholic Missionary Society [2] is *a fortiori* weaker still.

(2) (a) On the revocation of the Charter of the Royal Niger Company and the Proclamation of the Protectorate of Northern Nigeria, agreements were concluded between Sir Frederick Lugard

---

appears, e.g., from para. 8 of Cmd. 5102 of 1910 (the Report of the Northern Nigeria Lands Committee of 1908). But cf. para. 17 of same. Many other later writers have expressed similar views against this feudal theory with respect to land.

[1] Cited in R. L. Buell's *The Native Problem in Africa*, Vol. 1, p. 682, from Sir Edward Hertslet's *Map of Africa by Treaty*, Vol. 1, 1909, p. 472. It should be noted that the clause above quoted is very typical of the many agreements and treaties between the African rulers in the Protectorate and the Company. See also C. N. Cook's *British Enterprise in Nigeria* (1943), pp. 91–2, where the method of treaty-making is described as 'quite ridiculous'. A typical treaty form is also analysed there.

[2] See the Third Schedule to the Niger Lands Transfer (Protectorate) Ordinance—Cap. 86 of The Laws of Nigeria (1923), Vol. I.

as High Commissioner and certain representatives of the Company whereby all lands, rights and easements (with one or two minor exceptions then held by the Company), were vested in the High Commissioner for the time being in trust for His Majesty, his heirs and successors.

S. 2 of 'The Crown Lands Proclamation, 1902' enacts that, subject to certain collateral agreements between the High Commissioner and the Company's representative, 'the lands, rights, and easements mentioned or referred to in the Agreements and Instruments set out in the Schedule are to the extent and in the degree to which such lands, rights, and easements were vested in the Royal Niger Company, Chartered & Ltd. hereby vested in the High Commissioner for the time being, in trust for His Majesty his heirs and successors.' And, although s. 7 of the same Proclamation speaks of such lands and rights as '*the property* of His Majesty etc.' we must remember that such expressions claiming beneficial ownership for the Crown are not terms of art but merely describe the administrative attitude towards, rather than a claim to proprietary ownership in, Northern Nigeria lands. This is probably why, after s. 4 has laid down certain wide powers of the High Commissioner in the matter of the disposal of the lands, s. 5 goes on to provide that 'all moneys derived from such sales, leasing, or otherwise dealing with the said lands, rights and easements aforesaid shall form part of the general revenue of the Protectorate'.

Moreover, the presence of a number of African towns and villages on certain of these pieces of land for which the Crown paid such a large sum of money, in virtue of which the lands have been claimed as 'Crown lands', makes it at least doubtful whether a private right of an absolutely proprietary character could be claimed by the Crown in these village lands inhabited by the local 'owners'. Many of the inhabitants, pagan as well as Moslem, holding lands in communal tenure, had no knowledge that their lands had ever been thus given away, and might well have been alarmed at such an idea.[1]

In the light of these further encumbrances on the lands thus

---

[1] Lord Lugard, in para. 1 of his Memo. No. 16: 'These lands are, by presumption, the absolute property of the Government, though, as a matter of fact, native towns are situated upon them, the inhabitants of which, so far as I am aware, have no knowledge that their rights in the land they occupy have ever been alienated. Since, moreover, the greater part are situated in pagan districts, where rights in land are communal, it is doubtful whether it was in point of fact alienable by any chief under treaty.'

taken over by the Imperial Government, one hesitates to say that they are properly described as the absolute property of the Crown —i.e. as Crown lands. We have already seen how the relevant legislation has so far shrunk from asserting a fee simple ownership on the Crown's behalf: All proceeds of sale, lease, etc., of these so-called 'Crown lands' form part of the general revenue of the Protectorate. It seems, therefore, an inevitable conclusion that all the Crown really meant to do is to assume rights of absolute administrative control over the lands while leaving the indigenous inhabitants to enjoy their customary rights, even such as they are.

(b) By s. 3 of the Niger Lands Transfer Ordinance (No. 2 of 1916) [1] all lands and rights belonging to the Royal Niger Company in the Northern Provinces of the Protectorate on 1 January 1900, 'shall be and are hereby vested as from 1st January, 1900, in the Governor in trust for Her Majesty, her heirs and successors', subject to certain rights reserved to the Company under the agreements therein referred to.[2]

Then, s. 5 expressly reserves to the Company under the said agreements certain pieces of land and other rights in the Northern Provinces. The lands were mostly the Company's trading stations and commercial sites.

Of the other rights reserved to the Company by the relevant agreement, its mineral concessions were, as we have seen,[3] bought off for a lump sum of £865,000 and an additional fifty per cent. royalty payable to the Company and its successors for a period of ninety-nine years reckoning from 1 January 1900.

(c) In addition to these so-called *private* lands of the Company thus transferred to the Government as 'Crown lands', all other lands in the Protectorate were regarded as 'Public lands' the ultimate title to which the Government claimed by right of conquest.[4] To give it legal effect, Proclamation No. 13 of 1902 (which must be read as one with Proclamation No. 8 of 1900) provides in s. 2 as follows:

'The High Commissioner may by writing under his hand and the Seal of the Protectorate declare to be public lands:

[1] Now Cap. 86 of *The Laws of Nigeria* (1923), Vol. I.

[2] A. F. Calvert, *Nigeria and Its Tin Fields*, London, 1912, 'Because of the transfer of the mining rights under the Royal Niger Company's concessions to the Government, the natives were debarred from further mining of tin which, according to the Northern Nigeria Lands Committee, they were in the habit of mining from time immemorial.'

[3] See Historical Introduction, *supra*.

[4] For an able criticism of this claim to ultimate title by the Crown, see L. P. Mair, *An African People in the Twentieth Century* (1936), p. 133.

(1) All lands not in the actual occupation of persons or of the tenants agents or servants of persons having an original or derivative title to such lands under any Proclamation enacted for the Protectorate or under any law or custom prevailing in that part of the Protectorate where such lands are situated.

(2) Lands being the property of any conquered or deposed ruler'.

These 'Public lands', comprising 'unoccupied' lands as well as those formerly subject to the control of the Fulani rulers to whose title the Crown hereby claims succession by right of conquest, are set in direct contrast to those described as 'Crown lands' by Proclamation No. 16 of 1902 (The Crown Lands Proclamation, 1902), already referred to.

But a comparison of the identical provisions of ss. 3–6 of the two Proclamations shows that there is really no justification for the distinction of Northern Nigeria Protectorate lands into 'Crown' and 'Public', and one may give the following reasons therefor:

(a) Both types of land were places under the administrative control of the High Commissioner with identical powers of disposal—sale, lease, etc.

(b) The money accruing from dealings in both types forms part of the public revenue of the Protectorate.

(c) The Government assumes the same rights with regard to the lands of conquered pagan tribes as it does in a Fulani emirate or over unconquered and 'waste' lands.

(d) Conquest, like cession, does not *ipso facto* confer upon the conqueror the right to confiscate private property.

(e) The very proclamation of a Protectorate, all-embracing as it is in its constitutional effect, makes nonsense of this pedantic dichotomy into Crown and Public lands within the territory covered by the Proclamation. This is the more so when one recalls the trend of subsequent legislation as briefly reviewed above.

Some such ideas as these must have inspired the recommendation of the Northern Nigeria Lands Committee of 1908 to the effect that, because of the fundamental principle that the whole of the land in the Protectorate is under the control of the Crown, 'such distinctions become unnecessary and may be misleading'.[1]

As a correlative of this ultimate right of the Crown over the

---

[1] Cmd. 5102, paras. 14, 23 and 37. Thus, Sir P. Girouard, in his *Memoranda on Land Tenure in Northern Nigeria*, para. 4. 'Both in definition as to class and in definition of rights, the foregoing would appear to me to be, from a legal point of view, cumbersome, and, in practice, indefinite.'

Also Cmd. 5103: Minutes of Evidence of the Committee.

land, the Committee further declared the right of the Government to some form of land revenue imposed upon the occupiers 'rather in the nature of rent than a tax upon agricultural profits,' especially in view of the expanding values of land due to construction of roads and railways, the introduction of new industries and the general progress of the Protectorate.[1]

These, their conclusions, were based upon the two principles :[2]

(1) 'That all the land of the Protectorate is under the control and subject to the disposition of the Government.

(2) That the controlling power of the Government should be exercised in accordance with the customs prevailing throughout the country subject to local variations on the principle laid down in the Supreme Court and Native Court Proclamations above referred to.'

The outcome of these and other submissions of the Committee was Proclamation No. 9 of 1910—'The Land and Native Rights Proclamation', according to s. 2 of which 'the whole of the lands of the Protectorate of Northern Nigeria, whether occupied or un-occupied on the date of the commencement of this Proclamation, are hereby declared to be native lands'. This provision is substantially reproduced in s. 3 of the Land and Native Rights Ordinance No. 1 of 1916, which, as modified by Ordinance No. 18 of 1918, is now the law on the subject.[3] Ss. 3 and 4 provide as follows:

(3) 'All native lands, and all rights over the same, are hereby declared to be under the control and subject to the disposition of the Governor, and shall be held and administered for the use and common benefit of the natives of Northern Nigeria; and no title to the occupation and use of any such lands shall be valid without the consent of the Governor.

(4) The Governor, in exercise of the powers conferred upon him by this Proclamation with respect to any land, shall have regard to the native laws and customs existing in the district in which such land is situated.'

[1] See paras. 43–54, particularly paras. 45 and 46 of Cmd. 5102.

[2] Paras. 20 and 32 of Cmd. 5102.

[3] The term 'native land' had been adopted from para. 6 of the Conclusions to Sir P. Girouard's Memoranda (on p. 27), which para. reads as follows: 'If land were nationalised, and alienation in fee simple made impossible, they would, for the time being, be best described, in my opinion, as "Native Lands", the description "National Lands", which might suggest itself, being, today, for obvious reasons, a misnomer. As the native or national lands would include the land requirements of their government, there would appear to be no necessity for the term "Crown Lands".'

Later sections further provide, inter alia, for the Governor's power:

(a) to grant rights of occupancy to natives as well as to aliens;

(b) to demand and revise rents for such grants;

(c) to render null and void any attempted alienation by an occupier of his right of occupancy without the Governor's consent;

(d) to revoke the grants to occupiers for 'good cause' shown.

The principles of this legislation were trenchantly criticised by Lord Lugard in his *Dual Mandate* on the following main grounds:

(1) That land in the Northern Nigeria Protectorate cannot properly be described, as did the Ordinance, as 'Native lands' where:

(a) the Governor's consent was necessary to the validity of the native occupier's title;

(b) the Governor had the right to demand rents, to nullify all attempted alienations by occupiers, and above all to revoke the grant at will.

(2) That these absolute powers given to the Governor by this legislation were in the nature of '*expropriation*',[1] since they were inconsistent with the fundamental principle that conquest or cession should not affect private property.

But Lord Lugard had earlier in his Memorandum No. 16 on Titles to Land, already cited, maintained the distinction between Crown and Public lands,[2] and while criticising as just stated the policy of the present legislation in his *Dual Mandate*, he also claimed for the Government a right of ownership in 'unoccupied' lands.

While his criticism of the general theory of Crown ownership in the land of Northern Nigeria is sound in principle, and his conclusion that all that the Crown is entitled to is 'trusteeship' and not 'ownership' of the land is correct, Lord Lugard's assertion with respect to Crown ownership of unoccupied [3] lands is doubtful for at least two reasons:

(a) Because it is inconsistent with s. 3 of the Lands and Native Rights Ordinance of 1916 which, by re-enacting s. 2 of the equivalent Proclamation of 1910, provides that 'the whole lands of the

---

[1] F. D. Lugard, *Political Memoranda* (1918), pp. 347–8; Sir W. Geary, *Nigeria under British Rule*, p. 266; One writer has even remarked thus: 'When Lord Lugard annexed Northern provinces, he disregarded the principles of Native law and custom and issued "The Land Proclamation" of 1900 enacting that "title to land can only be acquired through the High Commissioner".'

[2] A criticism of which already appears on p. 34, *supra*.

[3] Lugard's favourite term is 'derelict'.

Northern Provinces, whether occupied or unoccupied on the date of the commencement of this Ordinance, are hereby declared to be native lands'. All lands covered by this Ordinance are expressly excluded from those described in the Crown Lands Ordinance No. 7 of 1918 as Crown lands.[1]

(b) Because under native customary law there has never been any land which can be regarded as 'unoccupied'. The indigenous system does not admit that land can ever be without an 'owner'.[2]

Moreover, certain attempts [3] have been made to show that the Northern Nigeria legislation cannot properly be characterised as expropriation simply for the reason that the requirement of Governor's consent to transfers of titles to land makes native customary titles otherwise invalid. For example, it is contended that, whatever the Ordinance may say in theory, the Governor's consent is in practice given as a matter of course; the Ordinance expressly requires him to have regard to native law and custom,[4] and his consent is, therefore, automatic whenever the transaction is governed entirely by customary law.[5] Another line of argument is that (a) the Crown has used its 'ultimate title' to make only a few grants in favour of tin mine development; (b) land disputes as well as other dealings in land as between the natives are left to the native courts and the respective native authorities; certificates of occupancy, with very few exceptions in urban areas, are not as a rule issued to natives; [6] (c) in spite of the reservation of rents to the Crown from native and non-native occupiers alike, it is only the latter who, in fact, pay rents; even in the case of agricultural and grazing leases granted by the Crown to non-natives, native occupiers of the land covered by such leases are exempt from any form

[1] See s. 2 of the Ordinance, which is considered, *infra*, p. 45.

[2] C. K. Meek, *Land Law and Custom in the Colonies*, pp. 12 and 178; Lord Hailey, *An African Survey*, p. 745.

[3] See Lord Hailey, *An African Survey*, pp. 773–4: 'It is clear that the intention underlying the assertion of "ultimate ownership" by the State was mainly to secure full control over alienations, and the manner in which the provision has been applied in practice is of greater importance than the legal form in which it is expressed' (also, pp. 832–3); C. K. Meek, *Land Law and Custom in the Colonies* (1946), pp. 147 to 148 and footnotes thereof; also L. P. Mair, *Native Policies in Africa* (1936), p. 134.

[4] S. 5 of Cap. 85 of the Laws of Nigeria (1923), Vol. I.

[5] But, because of the dynamic nature of native law and custom, problems are nevertheless bound to arise under such a very elastic arrangement.

[6] Lord Lugard had suggested at p. 293 of his *Dual Mandate* that the one reason why the Government refused to issue certificates of occupancy to natives was because the legislation was never intended to apply to natives.

of rent since they are not regarded as lessees either of the original grantees of the leases or of the Crown.[1]

The language of the land legislation in Northern Nigeria is clearly unfortunate, and the reluctance on the part of the Government to make theory accord with practice has been largely responsible for the controversy which has raged round the question of Crown title to land in the Northern Provinces.[2] In theory, Crown ownership has been couched, particularly in all early legislation,[3] in the most absolute terms; in practice, however, it does not seem that the Crown asserts more than a mere right of administrative control over the land in the Protectorate. The present legal position, then, would appear to be that the Crown claims not as absolute owner, but as trustee of land in the North.[4]

B. THE SOUTHERN PROVINCES OF THE PROTECTORATE

Here we have to consider:

(a) land taken over from the Royal Niger Company;

(b) the remainder of the territory in the Southern Provinces of Nigeria.

As regards (a), it is not necessary to traverse the ground already covered with respect to the legal validity or otherwise of the treaties entered into between the Royal Niger Company on the one hand

---

[1] Another qualification of the Governor's powers of alienation is contained in s. 21 of Chap. LXXXV of *The Laws* requiring that disputes about the Governor's exercise of his authority to grant rights of occupancy should be cognisable in the Supreme Court.

[2] Dr. C. K. Meek in 'A Note on Crown Lands in the Colonies' in the *Journal of Comparative Legislation and International Law*, 3rd series, Vol. XXVIII (1946), Parts III and IV, on pp. 90–91: 'The exact legal position of the Crown, therefore, in the Northern Provinces of Nigeria (the former Protectorate of Northern Nigeria) is not very clear, and it is hardly satisfactory to say that the legal position does not matter so long as the law works satisfactorily, as it admittedly does, for with the changes in economic conditions there will be changes in the native customary law under which land is held, and the Government may have to face native customs to ownership of a kind not contemplated by the earlier legislators.'

[3] e.g. the Lands Ordinance No. 9 of 1907 spoke of 'land the property of the Crown' in dealing with registration of Crown lands.

[4] (a) *Nigeria Handbook*, p. 217: 'In the Northern Provinces today all land is by Ordinance held in trust for the people by the Governor.'

(b) C. K. Meek, op. cit., at p. 91: 'Even where the State has sometimes seemed to have made an unwarranted claim to legal ownership this claim has been made with the express purpose of protecting the actual ownership of the native communities.'

and the local Chiefs and rulers on the other. What has been stated applies with equal force to all similar treaties signed with the Company by ruling chiefs south of the Niger.

We therefore proceed to observe that, just as ss. 3 and 5 of 'The Niger Lands Transfer Ordinance' (Ordinance No. 2 of 1916) provide in the case of lands in the Northern Protectorate, so do ss. 2 and 4 regarding the area under the Company's control in the Southern Provinces. These sections enact that 'all the lands and rights within the Southern Provinces of the Protectorate belonging to the Niger Company, Limited . . . on the 1st January, 1900, . . . shall be and are hereby vested as from the 1st January, 1900, in the Governor in trust for Her Majesty' (s. 3), but that certain pieces of land and certain rights appurtenant thereto which are mentioned in certain collateral agreements 'shall remain vested in the Company' as from 1 January, 1900. These include the Company's trading posts as well as minerals.

Although the Crown thereby obtained control of these areas under this Ordinance in circumstances which would lead one to suppose that a fee simple title was contemplated thereunder, the Crown has nevertheless left the native occupiers in undisturbed possession and enjoyment of their rights under native law and custom.

With respect to (b), we have seen how British rule was gradually extended from the Coast Colony inland until the establishment in 1906 of the protectorate over what are now called the Southern Provinces.[1] We must note the special case of Benin with respect to the lands in which the Crown claimed right of ownership conferred

---

[1] Historical Introduction, *supra*.

Also C. W. Alexander, *Memo. on the Subject of Native Land Tenure in the Colony and Protectorate of Southern Nigeria* (dated 4 November 1910), para. 25 (in part): 'Now all land in the old Lagos Colony was undoubtedly surrendered to the Government. The Benin Empire was crushed by force of arms, and the British sovereignty has been extended step by step over the whole of the Eastern and the remainder of the Central Provinces. It may be said in fact that the greater part of the territory contained in the old Lagos Colony and the Eastern and Central Provinces is in the position of territory acquired by conquest'; para. 26 (in part): 'It is thus clearly recognised that the ultimate control over land acquired by conquest is vested in the Head of the victorious Kingdom, to whom tribute is paid. It follows as a necessary consequence that the ultimate control over the greater portion of the territory of the Colony and Protectorate is vested in this Government, *but I think in trust to use its powers for the benefit of the native races according to the principles of native land tenure*. The fact of this control is recognised under the provisions of the Native Lands Acquisition Ordinance.'

upon itself by the conquest of Benin in 1896. For nearly twenty years afterwards the Crown granted, as absolute owner of the lands, a number of leases in exercise of its sovereignty. But, when the Oba of Benin was re-instated in 1916, his customary rights of control over Benin lands were restored to him.

Apart from this Benin interlude, we need only mention the somewhat dubious legal position of formerly native protected States like Ijebu Ode, Abeokuta, Ibadan, Oyo, Jekriland and Onitsha. The problem is complicated by the various treaties with these States which virtually acknowledged their independence, while recognising the right of the Crown to institute British Commissioners in their territories.[1] One would be inclined to dismiss this as a transient phase of the evolution of the Protectorate were it not the case that claims are still sometimes based by some native chiefs upon aspects of these agreements.[2] On the whole, however, it is clear that the subsequent proclamation of the Protectorate, in itself an Act of State, legally supersedes claims that may now be based upon such agreements with these States.

We may now trace quite briefly the history of Government land policy and legislation in the Southern Provinces generally.

[1] See C. W. Alexander, op. cit., para. 26.

[2] One such very recent claim was the Petition of Right filed in the Supreme Court at Ibadan (Nigeria) by the Akarigbo or Oba of Ijebu Remo against the Attorney-General of Nigeria, claiming the sum of £3,200 as arrears of the annual subsidy of £100 from 1916 to 1947 under an Agreement dated 4 August 1894 made between 'The King, Chiefs, Elders and people of Ijebo Remo Country and His Excellency Sir Gilbert Thomas Cater, Commander-in-Chief of the Colony of Lagos on behalf of Her Majesty the Queen of Great Britain and Ireland, Empress of India'. The prayer of the Petition was that 'the claimant's predecessor, as Akarigbo, undertook on behalf of himself and his successors, to carry out the several terms set out in paras. 1 to 8 of the said Agreement, and the said Agreement is now and has ever since remained in force.

By clause 9 of the said Agreement, the Crown undertook as follows: 'In consideration of the foregoing, the Governor of Lagos on behalf of Her Majesty, the Queen aforesaid, agrees to take the Kingdom of Ijebu-Remo into the British Protectorate and to pay to the King of Ijebu-Remo the sum of £100 annually.'

In November 1894, a British Protectorate was duly proclaimed over the Kingdom of Ijebu Remo. 'In pursuance of the said Agreement, the said subsidy of £100 per annum was duly paid up to the year 1915 by the Government of Nigeria. In breach of the said Agreement, the Government of Nigeria ceased to pay the said subsidy from 1916 onwards, have neglected and refused to pay the claimant the said sum of £100 annually ever since.' ('The Daily Service', Friday, 2 April 1948, front page.)

Under the 'Native Lands Acquisition Proclamation, 1900' (Proclamation No. 1 of 1900) it is provided in s. 1 as follows:

'From and after 1st January 1900, no person other than a Native shall either directly or indirectly acquire any interest in or right over land within Southern Nigeria from the Natives without the written consent of the High Commissioner first had and obtained. . . . Any such interest in or right over land acquired without such consent shall be void.'

Proclamation No. 1 of 1903 repeals in its s. 8 this one of 1900 which it substantially re-enacts, and adds a penalty to the effect that any alien found in wrongful possession of any such lands shall be liable to a fine of £100 or imprisonment not exceeding twelve months, in addition to being ejected from the land and due process issued to enforce any relevant Court Order.

The Crown Lands Management Proclamation, 1906 (Proclamation No. 6 of 1906), which was designed to provide for the management and disposition of Crown lands in the Protectorate of Southern Nigeria, defines 'Crown lands' as 'all lands and all rights in and over lands which at any time or after the commencement of this Proclamation are vested in, held in trust for or otherwise belong to His Majesty, his heirs and successors'. Also this official definition of 'land' was made: ' "Lands" includes messuages, tenements, and hereditaments, minerals, houses and buildings of any tenure.'[1]

Like the analogous provisions of Proclamations No. 13 of 1902 and No. 16 of 1902 relating to the Northern Provinces, s. 3 of this Ordinance provides that 'The High Commissioner shall have the management of all Crown lands in the Protectorate, and may at any time and from time to time sell, lease, exchange or otherwise dispose of such lands as he may think fit'. S. 5 repeats the usual provision as to the application of the revenue accruing from Crown lands: 'All moneys derived from the sale, lease, exchange or other

---

[1] But in the definition clause 2 (10) of 'The Interpretation and General Clauses Ordinance' No. 3 of 1908, Chap. II of Schedule, as reproduced in 'The Interpretation Ordinance, 1914', which applied alike to the Colony and Protectorate of Nigeria, occurs the following: ' "Immovable Property " or " Lands " shall include land and everything attached to the earth or permanently fastened to anything which is attached to the earth and all chattels real, *but shall not include minerals*.' The same exception of minerals from the legal meaning of land in Nigeria was made in s. 19 of Proclamation No. 1 of 1900; and No. 9 of 1910, Chap. I of Schedule, s. 25 (9) Ordinance No. 3 of 1908, was repealed by No. 58 of 1917. Cf. definition of 'Land' in L.P.A. 1925, s. 205.

disposition of Crown lands shall form part of the general revenue of the Protectorate.'

S. 6 (*a*) and (*b*) is a substantial reproduction of s. 5 (*a*) and (*b*) of Proclamation No. 1 of 1903, thus showing a clear assimilation of the principles conceived as underlying Crown and non-Crown lands. Indeed, both with respect to the powers of disposal of the land by the High Commissioner and the ultimate destination of all proceeds from the land, there is a noticeable uniformity of phrasing which reveals a unity of aim and purpose on the part of the Government alike towards 'Crown' as to non-Crown lands.

The next important piece of legislation was the Native Lands Acquisition Ordinance (No. 3 of 1908, Chapter III of Schedule) which re-enacted the main provisions of Proclamation No. 1 of 1903, except that it substituted 'Governor' for 'High Commissioner' in the relevant parts. In the Schedule attached thereto is a provision requiring any alien intending to acquire any interest or right in any lands from a native to furnish to the District Commissioner of the area particulars of the names and addresses of both grantor and grantee, the exact location of the land, and the purpose for which as well as the conditions on which such lands or interests are required.

The District Commissioner was to make enquiries as to the title of the native grantor and the good character of the alien, together with his desirability as a resident or trader in the district. The necessary instruments and plans might, in proper cases, be prepared for a fee by a Government official duly nominated by the District Commissioner. The Governor would then sign certificates of approval to such instruments.

Rule No. 4 of 23 June 1908 amplifies s. 4 of No. 3 of 1908 under consideration by providing that, unless the instrument specifies the purpose for which it is intended that the land be used and used for such purpose within a reasonable time, the Governor may by written notice require the grantee to make good his default within a stipulated time or the instrument shall become null and void, as if the Governor's approval had never been obtained.

The Crown Lands Management Ordinance (No. 3 of 1908, Chapter CVIII of Schedule) substantially reproduces the Crown Lands Management Proclamation of 1906 (already considered) which covered 'the Protectorate of Southern Nigeria'. But the present Ordinance of 1908 applied 'only to the Central and Eastern Provinces of the Protectorate', and the only alteration it made to the earlier legislation was the substitution of 'Governor' for 'High Commissioner' in the relevant parts.[1]

Ordinance No. 3 of 1908, Chapter III of Schedule, was repealed and re-enacted by The Native Lands Acquisition Ordinance (No. 32 of 1917) which, now appearing as Cap. 89 of the *Laws of Nigeria*,[2] regulates the acquisition of land by aliens from the natives of the Southern Provinces. It provides in s. 3 as follows:

(a) No alien shall acquire any interest or right in or over any lands within the Protectorate from a native except under an instrument which has received the approval in writing of the Governor,

(b) Any instrument which has not received the approval of the Governor as required by this section shall be null and void.

It is thus apparent that, running through the entire web of legislation regarding land in the Protectorate of Southern Nigeria from the proclamation of the protectorate onwards, has been the one consistent principle that the right of the Crown has, at least in practice, been confined to an administrative control over the alienation of land by natives to non-natives,[3] the customary use and enjoyment of the land being preserved to the native occupiers. All that any alien [4] can now acquire is a lease, duly approved by the Governor, for a maximum period of ninety-nine years.[5] A limited

[1] Under and by virtue of s. 2 of The Crown Lands Ordinance, 1908, the expression 'Agricultural lease' means a lease granted by the Governor to some person not a native of Nigeria for the purpose of cultivating, planting or farming (s. 1). No agricultural lease will be granted in respect of an area of more than 1,500 acres (s. 2). No agricultural lease will be granted for a longer term than ninety-nine years. Such lease may be renewed for a further term of years if the Governor thinks fit (s. 4). Every agricultural lease shall expressly reserve all existing rights of way and rights to hold markets, sacred trees and groves in respect of which the lessee shall acquire no rights (s. 7). (Irving, *Titles to Land in Nigeria*, 1916), Rule No. 9, of 12 July 1912.

[2] *Laws of Nigeria* (1923), Vol. I, pp. 907–8.
See also the Volume of Nigeria Ordinance for 1917 and 1918.

[3] The Leverhulme project, aimed at obtaining freeholds for the plantation of palm-oil in Nigeria, was for this reason frustrated by the Nigerian Government, partly because it preferred a subsistence economy for Nigeria and partly because it was anxious to preserve, consistently with its avowed policy, the land rights of the native occupiers. See Lord Hailey, op. cit., p. 770; C. K. Meek, op. cit., p. 147; Ward Prince, *With the Prince to West Africa*, p. 154 (1925); T. O. Elias, 'The New Development Corporations', a paper read before the West African Students' Union Conference, in London (1948) at the Caxton Hall.

[4] An alien, in this connexion, is defined in s. 2 of the Ordinance as 'any person who is not a native of Nigeria'.

[5] Note also that s. 4 of Rule 9 of 1912, cited above, footnote (1), limits the period of an agricultural lease to ninety-nine years in the first instance.

number of grants for purposes of trade have been made in certain urban areas,[1] but rights of freehold in land, of which a few had formerly been granted, were henceforth forbidden to aliens.

In the result, therefore, the Government has pursued a policy of restricting alienation of land in the Southern Provinces only to dealings among the natives themselves, while frowning upon any out-and-out transfer to aliens. No claim to absolute ownership has been made, nor has any rigid distinction between drawn between Crown and other lands except, perhaps, that whereas in the case of certain lands taken over from the Royal Niger Company no compensation to any occupier will be paid for their appropriation to public purposes, compensation is as a rule paid in the case of all other lands within the Southern Protectorate.[2] This contrasts markedly with the Northern policy of paying only for unexhausted improvements by native occupiers and not for the acquisition of the land itself.[3] A corollary of this has been that while in the North the Government has formally laid down the policy that no freehold title can exist in land but only a right of occupancy, there has been a benevolent neutrality on the part of the Government with respect to the form which titles to land in the Southern Provinces should take.[4]

This difference of attitude reflects the tyranny of the persistent *communis error* which consists in the idea that whereas Southern Nigeria lands were in effective native occupation at the time of the British advent and were for the most part acquired by voluntary cessions, lands in the North belonged to the Emirs into whose shoes

[1] Thus, the United Africa Company Ltd. have by agreement with Native authorities secured the leaseholds of over 12,4000 acres for the development of rubber, timber and palm-oil industries in certain regions of Benin and Sapele.

[2] *The Nigeria Handbook* (1936), 11th edition (the Chapter on 'Land Tenure'), at p. 218: 'In the Southern Provinces lands are not at the disposal and under the control of the Governor in the same way as are native lands in the Northern Provinces, . . . The greater part of the land in the Southern Provinces is held under rights which, by long occupation, have matured into family rights.'

[3] S. 23 of Chap. LXXXV of *The Laws of Nigeria* (1923), Vol. I.

[4] Ibid., 'The only freehold properties in the strict sense are those which have matured out of family properties in that part of Nigeria which is known as the Colony of Lagos, the freeholds vested in the Niger Company when their charter was revoked, and certain Crown Lands retained for public purposes.' The actual legal position as to all but the first of these three categories of freehold title is, as has been abundantly shown already, as anomalous as it is doubtful.

the Crown considered itself to have stepped by mere right of conquest.[1]

We are, however, up against trouble when we come to consider the Crown Lands Ordinance [2] (No. 7 of 1918) in s. 2 of which 'Crown land' is defined as follows:

' "Crown Land" means all public lands in Nigeria which are for the time being subject to the control of His Majesty by virtue of any treaty, cession, convention or agreement, or by virtue of His Majesty's protectorate, and all lands which have been or may hereafter be acquired by or on behalf of His Majesty for any public purpose or otherwise howsoever, but does not include lands subject to the Land and Native Rights Ordinance.'

Now, the language of this definition is at once too wide and too vague. If taken literally it would, for example, turn all lands in the Protectorate (with the exception of what has been described as 'native lands' under the Land and Native Rights Ordinance) into Crown lands; it might even be stretched to cover lands in the *mandated* (now *trust*) territory of the Cameroons,[3] which is certainly 'subject to the control of His Majesty by virtue of any . . . convention', albeit an international one. Moreover, the express exclusion of lands subject to the Land and Native Rights Ordinance would seem anomalous; for, to leave Northern Nigeria lands, over which the Crown, in theory, claims such absolute powers, out of the category of 'Crown lands' while at the same time including in the term lands in the Southern areas, with respect to which the Crown claims only a right of administrative interference *vis-a-vis* aliens, is curious.

Even if we grant that only areas of the Southern Provinces which are 'public lands' are contemplated by our definition, we are none the wiser for it since there has been no authoritative definition of what constitutes '*public*' lands in the Southern Protectorate as has been the case with the Northern Protectorate, which we have already considered. On the contrary, the official

---

[1] That this arrogation of monarchical absolutism to the Northern Emirs in the matter of land was the result of error as to the actual position on the part of the early British administrators has been borne out by the minutes of evidence and the findings of the Northern Nigeria Lands Committee: Cmds. 5102 and 5103 of 1910. Also, Lord Hailey, *An African Survey* (1945), pp. 832–3.

[2] It is now Chap. LXXXIV of *The Laws of Nigeria* (1923), Vol. I. It repeals in s. 37 (i) The Lands Ordinance, (ii) The Crown Lands Management Ordinance and (iii) The Crown Lands Ordinance, 1908.

[3] The Cameroons is, of course, an integral part of geographical Nigeria, at least for administrative purposes.

attitude has been that lands in the South were in effective native occupation. An attempt has, of course, been made, in s. 2 of the Minerals Ordinance, 1916, to define 'Private Land' as 'any land which is neither Crown land within the meaning of the Crown Lands Ordinance nor native land within the meaning of the Land and Native Rights Ordinance, and includes land held under a grant from the Crown'.[1] Were this definition of private land not limited to the particular field of mineral rights, one might infer that 'public' lands should comprise of all lands in Nigeria outside the category of (a) Crown lands, (b) lands subject to the Land and Native Rights Ordinance, (c) lands held under a Grant from the Crown.

Also, according to this inclusion in the definition of private land of all lands held under a grant from the Crown, the area of Crown land would dwindle with each Crown grant, particularly in the North, while the area of private land would continually increase until a position would be reached where Crown lands would consist of no more than lands held by the Government for purely public purposes. Would it not be simpler and more logical to divide Nigerian lands into the two categories of State [2] and Private lands?

Another aspect of our definition of Crown land is the inclusion of 'all lands which have been or may hereafter be acquired by or on behalf of His Majesty for any public purpose or otherwise howsoever'. Since the necessary funds for the acquisition of such lands would invariably be provided from the general revenue of the country, though nominally 'on behalf of His Majesty', it seems that the term 'Crown lands' as applied to the lands is no more than a convenient administrative device or a generic name for all those lands which are in reality the property of the Nigerian public, held on their behalf by the Government.

Additional support can be had for our view from the provision in s. 3 of the Crown Lands Ordinance (1918) that, although the Governor may grant a *lease* of Crown land (s. 4), he cannot *sell* any Crown lands 'except with the consent of the Secretary of State first obtained'. Happily, there has never been a single case of a sale of so-called Crown lands in Nigeria or elsewhere [3] within the British Empire.

[1] Reproduced in s. 2 of the Minerals Ordinance, 1945.

[2] Dr. C. K. Meek's suggested classification in 'A note on Crown Lands in the Colonies' at p. 91 of the *Journal of Comparative Legislation and International Law* (already referred to) was into Crown or State lands and other lands or Non-State lands.

[3] Although the lease-lend arrangement between the United Kingdom and the United States of America in connexion with the Carribean Islands went perilously near to a sale.

Some judicial opinions on Crown ownership of land in the Southern Provinces have thrown a flood of light on the real legal position regarding both (a) Agreements entered into between Nigerian Chiefs and the Royal Niger Co., and (b) the Niger Lands Transfer Ordinance (1916), regularising the taking-over arrangements between the Royal Niger Co. and the Crown. A case in which both points recently fell to be considered is *Okafo Egbuche & Anor*. v. *Chief Idigo & Anor*.[1] in which in the Provincial Court of Onitsha the plaintiffs, on behalf of the people of Umuleri, claimed as against the defendants, representing the people of Eziagutu (a quarter of Aguleri), a declaration of title to land in Onitsha. An agreement of 1898 whereby the plaintiffs' ancestors had conveyed to The Royal Niger Company the land in question was tendered, inter alia, as evidence of their title. Now, by the Niger Lands Transfer Ordinance (1916), the rights of the Royal Niger Company in this land under the Agreement of 1898 became vested in the Crown. Neither the Royal Niger Company nor the Crown had taken possession of the land in question. *Held*: by the Provincial Court at Onitsha (1) that judicial notice of the 1898 Agreement must be taken as evidence of an overt act of ownership by the plaintiffs' ancestors—namely, a sale of the land to the Niger Company; (2) that the plaintiffs must, therefore, be given judgment for the declaration of title to the land, subject to the limitation, however, that the defendants should not be disturbed in the peaceful possession of the land; (3) that leases to European firms must be set aside in so far as they were contracted by the defendants; and (4) that money due from the lessees by virtue of these leases must be placed upon deposit in the Government Treasury until such time as plaintiffs should have been substituted for defendants as lessors.

The defendants appealed on the main ground that the Court, having found as a fact that the plaintiffs had sold the land in dispute to the Royal Niger Company in 1898, should not have given judgment for them. The appellants' supporting reasons were: (a) that neither in the Court below nor in this Court did the appellants admit that in June 1898, or at any other time the title to the land in question was in the plaintiffs: (b) that the appellants say that the agreement giving effect to the sale to the Royal Niger Company was executed without their knowledge; and (c) that the Royal Niger Company never entered into possession under the agreement or did any overt act of ownership in respect of the land.

[1] (1934), 11 N. L. R. 140.

The Divisional Court at Lagos, which was presided over by Graham Paul, J., held on appeal (1) that the plaintiffs' ancestors having by the Agreement of 1898 divested themselves of all right or title competent to them had no longer any right or title to the land, and that their claim for a declaration of title should have been refused on that score; and (2) that the mere fact that neither the Royal Niger Company, nor the Crown had taken possession of the land did not amount to an abandonment of their rights under the Agreement or under the Niger Lands Transfer Ordinance.[1] Graham Paul, J., said: 'Indeed by this Agreement being included in the Schedule of statutory transfers by the Company to the Crown in 1916 it is apparent that at that date both the Company and the Crown regarded it as a live and effective agreement.' Even if we should interpret the Crown's lack of exercise of ownership since 1916 as evidence of abandonment, the revival of title to the land should be, not in the original plaintiffs, but in the immediate author of the Crown's title, i.e. the Royal Niger Company, argued the learned Judge. He also denied that native law and custom had anything to do with this aspect of the case.

Then came the significant passage:[2] '*I am unable to hold that the defendants-appellants have in the Court below established their title to the land. I am unable to hold that in 1898 the plaintiffs-respondents were in a position to give a good title to the Royal Niger Company to this land. I cannot, therefore, hold that the land in question is Crown land, as the Court below held.*'[3]

Here, Graham Paul, J., would seem to be arguing thus:

(i) The plaintiffs-respondents could not in any case have given a good title in 1898 to the Royal Niger Company:

(ii) The plaintiffs-respondents had proved that they had no right or title left in them after the 1898 Agreement;

(iii) The defendants-appellants had not established their title to the land in the lower Court;

---

[1] 'In my opinion the Court below, in giving the plaintiffs-respondents a declaration of title, failed to appreciate the real effect of the agreement of June 1898. Whatever right or title the plaintiffs-respondents had in that land was by the Agreement sold to the Royal Niger Company; and, being by that Agreement completely divested of their right or title to the land, the plaintiffs-respondents had nothing left to justify the Court in giving them a declaration of title'—*Per* Graham Paul, J., at p. 142.   [2] At p. 143.

[3] And this, in spite of His Honour's earlier finding on p. 141 that 'It must be noted here that under the Niger Lands Transfer Ordinance (1916), (Cap. 86) the rights of the Royal Niger Company in the land in question under the Agreement became vested in the Crown'!

(iv) Therefore, although the plaintiffs-respondents had no right to sell the land to the Company and although whatever title the plaintiffs-respondents had had passed to the Royal Niger Company and hence to the Crown, yet the Crown was not entitled to the land;

(v) Therefore, the defendants-appellants' appeal must be allowed and judgment given in their favour, with twenty guineas as costs of the appeal. This, to say the least, has most of the virtues of a jig-saw puzzle and the decision looks somewhat casuistic. But the seemingly paradoxical result may be rationalised in this way:

(a) To the extent to which legislation has given the land to the Crown, all question as to the legal validity of the 1898 Agreement must be put aside;

(b) To the extent to which plaintiffs, on whom is always the onus of proof of title to land, had failed to establish their claim, the defendants were entitled to judgment.

But since the Niger Lands Transfer Ordinance, which embodies and adopts the 1898 Agreement, has purported to make all the lands covered by the Ordinance 'Crown lands' and since so much was conceded by the learned judge, it is difficult to see how he could nevertheless hold that the land is not Crown land, that the Agreement in fact has the effect of divesting the plaintiffs of all title to the land without at the same time vesting it in the Crown as the ultimate purchaser. It is submitted that the better view seems to be to hold that the land is Crown land under the Ordinance but that the defendants-appellants were entitled to continue in permissive possession of it.[1]

Where, however, land is regarded as Crown land under the Crown Lands Ordinance (1916) a sub-lease made to a third party by an 'occupier' from the Crown in contravention of the Ordinance is clearly an illegal contract. Thus, in *Sam Warri Esi* v. *J. A. Moruku* [2] the plaintiff, who held a lease of Crown land at Warri under the Crown Lands Ordinance, sub-let part of the premises to the defendant at a monthly rent in contravention of both s. 6 (ii) (c) of the Ordinance (and of a corresponding clause in the lease granted to the plaintiff thereunder) which prohibits sub-letting the premises or any part thereof without the Governor's previous

---

[1] For an instance of the Crown's permission given to ancient occupiers of what later became Crown land to continue in such permissive occupation, see the case of *Lieutenant-Governor of Southern Nigeria* v. *Ajakaiye and Laditan* (1927) 7 N. L. R. 21.   [2] (1940), 15 N. L. R. 116.

written consent. The plaintiff later sued the defendant for arrears of rent in the Magistrate Court the judgment of which, to the effect that the plaintiff's sub-lease to the defendant was an illegal contract, was upheld by Jackson, Asst. J., in the High Court at Warri. The learned Judge made the graphic observation that the covenant not to assign without the Governor's consent was 'a covenant designed by the legislature for the management and disposal of *Crown lands in which the whole public have an interest*'.[1] This *judicial* definition of Crown land, more than the facts of the case itself, is a welcome statement of principle as elucidating as it is sanguine.

As regards the facts and the actual decision in the case the analogous conception of the Crown's statutory power over land in Northern Nigeria has provoked a similar finding. In *Domingo Martins* v. *S. A. Molade and two others*[2] A held a plot of land in Zaria under a certificate of occupancy in accordance with the Land and Native Rights Ordinance (1916). A sold the buildings subsequently erected by him thereon to B. Later still, C obtained a judgment against A for debt and wanted to levy execution on the buildings on the ground that under the Ordinance 'all buildings on the plot shall be the property of the occupier'. B resisted this contention of C. *Held*: by the Full Court at Lagos, on appeal from the Divisional Court at Zaria, that A's sale to B was only effective as between the two and could not affect C's right to levy execution on the buildings on the plot in virtue of his claim against A as the reputed occupier. Of course, if A had purported to sell to B, not the buildings but the land itself, such a sale would have been contrary to s.12 of the Ordinance and, therefore, void without the Governor's consent.

The Crown cannot, however, claim any title to land not covered by any agreement with local Chiefs and therefore outside the Niger Lands Transfer Ordinance, even though the land is erroneously thought to be Crown land on account of the absence of proper demarcating boundary.[3]

It is pertinent here to record the recent amendment to the definition of Crown lands in s. 2 of Cap. 84 of the Laws by the Crown Lands Amendment Ordinance No. 5 of 1945, s. 2 of which is in the following terms:

'Section 2 of the Crown Lands Ordinance is hereby amended

---

[1] (1940), 15 N. L. R. 116 at p. 118.   [2] (1930), 9 N. L. R. 53.
[3] *Chief Commissioner, Eastern Provinces* v. *S. N. Ononye & Ors.* (1944), 17 N. L. R. 142.

by deleting the comma after the word "howsoever" where it occurs therein and inserting between that word and the word "but" the following expression: and land acquired under the provisions of the Public Lands Acquisition Ordinance.'

As thus amended, the definition of Crown Lands now runs:

' "Crown Land" means all public lands in Nigeria which are for the time being subject to the Control of His Majesty by virtue of any treaty, cession, convention or agreement, or by virtue of His Majesty's protectorate, and all lands which have been or may hereafter be acquired by or on behalf of His Majesty for any public purpose or otherwise howsoever and land acquired under the provisions of the Public Lands Acquisition Ordinance, but does not include lands subject to the Land and Native Rights Ordinance.'

It is submitted that this does not affect our analysis and criticism of the language of the definition; rather, it strengthens the argument in favour of the Crown's right in Nigerian land, in the North as well as in the South, being merely one of administrative control and not of a strictly proprietary character.

A very interesting instance of the kind of self-denying Ordinance which has lately characterised Government attitude in these matters is the Niger Lands Transfer (Amendment) Ordinance No. 22 of 1945, as amended by the Niger Lands Transfer (Amendment No. 2) Ordinance of the same year. These Ordinances together amend the Niger Lands Transfer Ordinance (1916) by the re-arrangement of its first three sections and the addition of eight new sections with the significant heading: 'Divesting of Land and Procedure relating thereto.' The first provision, which is now s. 9 of the Amended Principal Ordinance of 1916, creates a novel category of 'vested trust lands' in what was hitherto described as Crown lands:

For the purpose of this Ordinance, 'vested trust lands' means any of the lands and interests vested in the Governor in trust for His Majesty, his heirs and successors under the provisions of this Ordinance.

Then follows the most revolutionary s. 10 according to which the Governor may by Order published in the Gazette abandon all right, title or interest vested in him on behalf of His Majesty so long as same is not the subject of a Court suit. This 'debunking' of the Crown's proprietary ownership is neatly rounded off by the later provision of s. 15 which states that the legal effect of the Crown's abandoning any right, title or interest in vested trust lands or part thereof is that the lands so abandoned shall be treated as if not originally transferred to the Niger Company, that is, as if still in effective native occupation.[1]

Finally, it is relevant to refer to s. 16 of the Glover Settlement Ordinance, 1947, whereby the Crown was expressly divested of all title to certain lands situate at Ebute Metta on the mainland which the Crown had claimed by means of a Certificate of Title under the Public Lands Ordinance, 1876. In the light of fuller knowledge of native customary tenure of land, the Crown has, under this and three other Ordinances,[2] renounced its former claim to ownership based upon an imperfect understanding of native rights in land.

Therefore, as regards both the Northern and the Southern Provinces of the Protectorate, the decision[3] in the already considered Colony case of *Amodu Tijani* v. *Secretary, S. Nigeria* (1921), 2 A. C. 399 is universally valid in so far as the actual legal position of the Crown with respect to land in Nigeria is concerned. In theory, the Crown owns under the British Constitution the lands in the Colony but not those in the Protectorate, except those acquired either from the Royal Niger Company or for public purposes; in practice, it limits itself to a mere right of control of native interests in the land *vis-à-vis* alien acquisitiveness.[4] In view of the doubts necessarily raised by the language of certain types of land legislation, which appears inconsistent with the growing recognition by the Government of native rights, and because of the confusion often created by the assertion of the Crown's proprietary title to the land, it would seem that a simple definitive piece of legislation by the Crown would alone clarify the position.

[1] Under s. 14 of Ordinance No. 22 of 1945, there were reserved to the Crown and the Niger Company certain ultimate rights in such abandoned lands. The Amendment No. 2 Ordinance of 1945 did away with even these titles altogether.

[2] The other three Ordinances are: (*a*) Crown Grants (Lagos Township) Ordinance No. 18 of 1947; (*b*) Arotas (Crown Grants) Ordinance No. 19 of 1947; (*c*) Epetedo Lands Ordinance No. 20 of 1947. All four Ordinances had been inspired by the Report of Sir M. L. Tew who arrived in Lagos on 23 February 1939 to carry out an enquiry into the title to land in Lagos.

[3] See the passage previously cited from the Privy Counsel judgment of Viscount Haldane at pp. 19–20.

[4] Lord Hailey, in *An African Survey*, p. 770, commenting on definition of 'Crown lands' wrote: 'It appears, however, that this is in practice interpreted as applying only to land acquired by escheat, purchase, and the like, and not to native lands generally.'

The four Ordinances (Nos. 18–21 of 1947) above referred to should be useful precedents on which to base a general declaratory legislation.

C. THE CAMEROONS UNDER BRITISH MANDATE (NOW TRUST)

On the question of the Crown's relation to land in the Cameroons, it is sufficient to state that neither Article 22 of the League Covenant nor the Mandate Agreement [1] later negotiated in pursuance thereto between Great Britain on the one hand and the League of Nations on the other, contained any provision for the Crown acquisition of property in the mandated territory. Indeed, Great Britain, like all other Mandatory Powers under the League system, was expressly forbidden [2] to annex any mandated territory whether in whole or in part.[3]

The fact that, for reasons purely of administrative convenience, the Cameroon area is run along with Nigeria as one integral political unit does not alter the position. The territory remains under the mandate or, since the establishment of the Trusteeship Council of the United Nations as the successor to the Permanent Mandate Commission, under the trust of Great Britain. Its inhabitants are not British subjects,[4] and the territory is not British.

But the Nigerian Government may, on behalf of His Majesty under current practice, acquire certain land rights therein. Thus, under s. 2 (1) of the British Cameroons Administration Ordinance

---

[1] See Cameroons Ordinance No. 3 of 1924 (An Ordinance to provide for the Administration of the British Cameroons) and the text of the British Mandate: Cmd. 1794.

[2] In Art. 22 of the League Covenant.

[3] Even at International Law, the location of sovereignty of a mandated territory has proved highly controversial. In whom is the sovereignty? As applied to our case, is it: (a) in the League of Nations as the constitutive authority? But this anomalous international institution had no direct control over the mandated territory; (b) in Great Britain as the Power directly responsible for its administration? But this Power itself derives its authority from the League; (c) in the Permanent Mandate Commission as the supervising authority charged with the periodic inspection of mandated territories? But how can one impute sovereignty to a body to which so strictly limited powers were delegated by the League? (d) in the peoples of the territory themselves as being in actual occupation of it? But what about the double restriction on their 'volunte generale' arising from the League's incipient authority on the one hand and Great Britain's derivative competence on the other?

[4] See, e.g., R. v. Ketter (1939), 1 A. E. R. 729, where an inhabitant of Palestine under British Mandate was held not to be a British subject, and the mandated territory not to be British.

(No. 3) of 1924, certain Nigerian Ordinances stated in the First Schedule thereto, including the Crown Lands Ordinance, are made expressly applicable to the Cameroons 'so far as they are applicable and local circumstances permit'.[1]

Under the earlier administration of the Germans a decree of 15 June 1896, provided that Crown land should comprise of (i) all lands to which no claims could be established by a private person, or by a chief on behalf of a native community, and (ii) all lands not the subject of agreements between the imperial government and third parties. But there was never any specifically demarcated areas set apart as belonging to the Crown; in fact, the German Government's practice was to buy out native claimants of the lands and to grant leases of these to intending European speculators. In this way extensive concessions,[2] such as the vast North-West Cameroons Concession, were granted and, when it became quite clear that this seriously diminished native customary land rights, the system of *Reservats* was introduced. These were areas declared to be subject to native law and custom regarding land tenure or to the terms of each particular grant by the Government to native occupiers.[3]

After the first world war of 1914–18, all the plantation estates previously held by the Germans were first auctioned in London, but without any offers by the British public. This led to the passing of the British Cameroons Ex-Enemy Immovable Property Disposal Ordinance No. 22 of 1924, in order to legalise the acquisition by ex-enemy nationals or corporations under ex-enemy control of right, title or interest in ex-enemy immovable property in the British sphere of the Cameroons.[4] As a result, most of the lands found their way back into the hands of their former holders at the subsequent auction of 1925.

[1] By s. 3 of the Interpretation Ordinance No. 27 of 1939 it is provided that the term 'Protectorate' of Nigeria includes the Cameroons under British Mandate.

[2] Fifty estates, about 258,000 acres in all, were alienated to German private individuals. (Hailey, *An African Survey* (1945), p. 775.) The total number of the estates was fifty-six, according to the Cameroons under British Mandate Administration (Amendment) Ordinance No. 9 of 1938 (Third Schedule).

[3] By the amending provision of the Cameroons under British Mandate Administration (Amendment) Ordinance No. 9 of 1938, Third Schedule, all these *reservats* were enlarged for the benefit of the inhabitants and designated 'native lands'.

[4] Such acquisitions by ex-enemy nationals and/or corporations had previously been forbidden under the Cameroons Proclamation No. 38 of 10 October 1922.

By the British Cameroons Administration Ordinance No. 1 of 1925 (which repealed the British Cameroons Administration Ordinance No. 3 of 1926 just discussed) the policy of the Crown towards Cameroonian lands became assimilated to that of the Northern Provinces of Nigeria which we have previously described. This means that the Crown claims a complete power of control over all lands in the Cameroons; the native can enjoy only rights of occupancy and not of freehold; the most that aliens can acquire are mere grants of leases, and then only with the Governor's approval.[1]

Under the Cameroons Development Corporation Ordinance No. 39 of 1946, which came into force on 23 January 1947, a public body was instituted and, 'in pursuance of the Government's declared policy that the natural resources of Nigeria should be developed to the fullest extent in the interests of the Country's inhabitants, a public body has been set up by the Ordinance to hold the captured properties in trust and to develop them until such time as the Government of Nigeria, is in a position to undertake national ownership in a fully representative form'.[2]

There are two immediate inferences one may draw from this statement of policy. One is that this Ordinance envisages an ultimate goal of 'national' ownership of land by the Government of Nigeria in a truly representative capacity; but, for the present, the public corporation holds these properties in trust for the community. The other is that it assumes that the Cameroons will eventually be formally annexed, with the due sanction of the appropriate international authority, to the Nigerian territory, without which assumption this and other legislation would seem to go beyond the original terms of the mandate or the new trusteeship agreement under the United Nations framework.[3]

One other matter closely related to the problem here is the acquisition, under the Ex-Enemy Lands (Likomba Estate) Ordinance No. 22 of 1947, of the land known as the Likomba Estate

[1] All these follow from the fact that the Lands and Native Rights Ordinance (1916) as amended by Ordinance No. 1 of 1927 and No. 47 of 1935, was also made applicable to the Cameroons; see the First Schedule to Ordinance No. 1 of 1925. Also s. 4 of Ordinance No. 38 of 1946.

[2] *Nigeria: Annual Report for* 1946, published by the Colonial Office (H.M.S.O., London, 1947).

[3] Lord Hailey has estimated that the Nigerian Government spent from the inception of the Mandate up to about 1945, the sum of £58,000 on the Cameroons. A further sum of £1,750,000 has just been raised under the Cameroons Development Corporation Ordinance of 1946.

by the Nigerian Government from the British Company which owned ninety-eight per cent. of the whole. The legislative purpose was the planned development of the area by the new Cameroons Corporation for the use and common benefit of the inhabitants of the Cameroons. The enabling Ordinance describes it as 'native lands' subject to the Land and Native Rights Ordinance 1916 (as amended).

Chapter Four

COROLLARIES OF CROWN 'OWNERSHIP'

---

1. Minerals and Mineral Oils. 2. Foreshores and Beaches. 3. Inland Waterways and Rights of Fishing, etc., therein. 4. Un-occupied Lands. 5. Swamp and Grass Lands—Principles of assessing Compensation when acquired. 6. Unsettled Districts. 7. Forest Reserves.

---

1. MINERALS AND MINERAL OILS

IN s. 3 of the Interpretation Ordinance No. 27 of 1939, we find that 'lands' does not include minerals, though, under the native law and custom relating to land, no such distinction appears to have been made. The exclusive use and enjoyment of the land usually carried with it the full right to its minerals, subject of course to the requirements of the prevailing custom and the relation of the particular occupier to the land. If occupation was merely temporary or permissive, conditions might be imposed by the immemorial 'owners'. Otherwise, land usually included minerals.[1] The position is, however, now entirely governed by legislation.

The Minerals Ordinance, 1945, with minor amendments by the Minerals (Amendment) Ordinance No. 8 of 1948, repeals and re-enacts the Minerals Ordinance of 1916 and all subsequent amending Ordinances and came into operation on 22 February 1946. Its relevant provisions are:

S. 3 (1). The entire property in and control of all minerals, and mineral oils, in, under or upon any lands in Nigeria, and of all rivers, streams and water courses throughout Nigeria, is and shall be vested in, the Crown, save in so far as such rights may in any case have been limited by any express grant made before the commencement of this Ordinance.

[1] This indigenous idea closely approximates to the definition of 'land' in s. 205 (1) (ix) of L.P.A. 1925: ' "Land" includes land of any tenure, and mines and minerals, . . .'

S. 3 (2). Except as in this Ordinance provided no person shall prospect or mine on any lands in Nigeria or divert or impound water for the purpose of mining operations.

Also, any native of Nigeria can still take, according to the custom of the community to which such a native belongs, iron ore, salt, soda, potash or galena from lands not subject to a lease or licence. But no mineral oil as defined below may be prospected for or won from any lands, whether by a native or by a non-native except under a licence or lease granted by the Governor under s. 3 of the Mineral Oil Ordinance No. 17 of 1914. Sacred areas and trees or 'other thing which is the object of veneration' are exempt from the operation of the Ordinance,[1] that is, no mineral right will be granted in respect of such areas.

The legal definition of 'mineral' in s. 2 of the 1945 Mineral Ordinance is that 'mineral' does not include mineral oils but that it includes the four large species of (i) *metalliferous minerals* like antimony, arsenic, bismuth, copper, iron, lead, tin, zinc, etc.; (ii) *combustible carbonaceous minerals* like coal, lignite, etc.; (iii) *non-metallic minerals* like asbestos, bauxite, china clay, marble, salt, potash, etc.; (iv) *precious minerals*, including (*a*) precious stones like diamond, emerald, ruby, sapphire, etc., (*b*) precious metals like gold, silver, etc., (*c*) radio-active minerals like pitch-blende and other uranium ores.

And s. 2 of the Amended Mineral Oils Ordinance of 1914 thus defines mineral oils: 'Mineral oils' includes bitumen, asphalt and all other bituminous substances with the exception of coal.

It is to be noted also that, under s. 21 of the Crown Lands Ordinance No. 7 of 1918, any conveyance or lease under that Ordinance does not confer any right to any mineral or mineral oil, using these terms in the sense just stated. The Crown further reserves to itself the right to enter upon any land sold or leased under that Ordinance and (i) to search for, mine and remove any mineral as aforesaid or any mineral oil, and (ii) except in the case of lands for building purposes only, to remove any stone, gravel, soil or other substance required for the construction or repair of any road, Government building or other public work. Any person, duly authorised by the Governor or by or under any Ordinance relating to minerals or mineral oil, may exercise the right thus reserved to the Crown.[2]

[1] Ss. 5 and 6 of the Minerals Ordinance, 1945.

[2] S. 21, subs. (1)–(3) of The Crown Lands Ordinance, 1918. Also G. Stone, *The Mining Laws of the British Empire*, Vol. I (Nigeria), pp. 63–4 (London, 1920).

The result of these statutory provisions would, therefore, appear to be that the ownership as well as control of all minerals and mineral oils in, under and upon any lands in Nigeria is vested in the Crown, but that any native of Nigeria can still take, without prior authorisation, iron ore, salt, soda, potash and galena from lands not under a Crown lease or licence. The express exclusion of coal from the category of 'mineral oils', which nobody could prospect for or win without the Governor's authority, would seem to permit by implication the taking by natives of coal as well. But coal-mining in Nigeria is the monopoly of the Nigerian Government, and its inclusion in the definition of minerals under the Mineral Ordinance of 1945 shows that this mineral cannot be won or prospected for, by natives and non-natives alike, without the Governor's sanction.[1]

Again, since practically all the minerals which natives can still 'take' are included in the list of those defined under the Minerals Ordinances, 1945, it seems a matter of some difficulty whether the reservation of this right to the natives in s. 5 of the Ordinance really entitles them to exploit these minerals without permission. It is possible and indeed logical to take the view that it is a matter of the *purpose* and *quantity* of the particular minerals exploited by the natives in any given case. The Ordinance uses the word 'take' (not deliberately, perhaps) rather than 'win' or 'prospect for' and also gives the right to the natives only where a tradition or custom exists in the community for so doing.[2]

It is, however, clear that these minerals could not have been mined by natives in quantities comparable to those won under

[1] In English Land Law, the Crown owns all gold, silver and 'treasure trove', and to the fee simple owner belongs all other minerals in, under or upon his land. (G. C. Cheshire, *The Modern Law of Real Property*, 5th edition, London, 1944, pp. 116–17.)

On the other hand, in the neighbouring Colony of the Gold Coast, that is to say in the Colony proper and in Ashanti, mineral rights remain in the native 'owners' of the land, though subject to the protection of a Divisional Court in cases of alienation to alien concessionaires—The Concession Ordinance No. 19 of 1939. Also, Ward Price states, with respect to the Yoruba: 'Minerals were owned by the owners of the land; but nothing except iron-ore was dug up for economic use' (para. 29 of his *Land Tenure in the Yoruba Provinces of Nigeria*).

[2] There is abundant evidence of the mining, howbeit on a minor scale, of minerals like tin, iron-ore, salt, etc., by natives in various districts of Nigeria before the advent of the British. See *Nigeria Handbook*, 1936, 10th edition, pp. 91–5; Forde and Scott, *The Native Economics of Nigeria* (1946), p. 79 *et passim*.

more modern conditions. The legislative intention, therefore, is presumably to maintain the *status quo ante*, and not to invest natives with any wide powers of extensive mining or prospecting for minerals, especially now that these minerals have acquired an enhanced commercial value. But there does not seem to be a provision for any clearly defined quantity of minerals, or the nature and purpose of their exploitation, in any particular case. Problems are bound to arise on this score in the future.

2. FORESHORES AND BEACHES

(i) Foreshores

The general principle is that the ownership of the foreshore is in the Crown, since the Nigerian territorial waters, i.e. a strip of three miles of the water skirting the coast of Nigeria, belong, at international law, to the British Crown.[1] This follows from the theory that under British Constitution the Treaty of Cession in the case of the Colony and the fact of the existence of British Protectorate over the rest of the country give the Crown the right to the foreshore. In the first and only case in Lagos that the point has so far arisen for a judicial pronouncement, *Attorney-General of Southern Nigeria* v. *John Holt and others*,[2] the facts were briefly as follows: The foreshore of the lagoon around the coast of the island of Lagos and of the arms and creeks thereof between high-water and low-water mark as also the bed of the said lagoon and arms and creeks thereof, as far as the tide ebbs and flows, and all land accruing to the foreshore by reclamation or silting belong to the Crown. Certain rights of user of the foreshore, and such land accruing thereto, had become vested in the grantees of adjoining land by presumed licence from the Crown based upon the latter's acquiescence and other facts. The defendants disputed the Crown's title and themselves claimed ownership of the foreshore adjoining their lands through their predecessors in title. *Held*: (i) the Crown is entitled to the foreshore including the area since reclaimed by the defendants; (ii) but this radical title of the Crown is subject to a perpetual right in the two defendant companies to place and store things thereon, to erect buildings thereon and generally to use such foreshore as they might deem expedient for the purposes of their business.

[1] In the Divisional Court at Lagos. Lord Shaw at p. 61 of 2 N. L. R. 1 speaks of the limits of 'territorial waters'.

[2] (1910), 2 N. L. R. 1, at p. 11 *per* Osborne, C.J.

'It seems to me to be quite clear that the Treaty of 1861 was a cession of territory, which at the same time respected pre-existing rights of private ownership, and I hold that under it the foreshore round the island of Lagos became vested in the Crown, subject, however, to the then existing rights of riparian occupiers to use it for the purpose of access to the water, and for landing and embarking and mooring, and hauling up canoes.' [1] In this passage has been admirably summed up the native customary usages and rights in the foreshore to which the Lagos chiefs and other witnesses had deposed during the conduct of this case.

Mr. Johnson, the late Court Interpreter, who has been called in other proceedings as an expert in native law, said he knew of no rights below high-water mark. Mr. George, one of the witnesses for the Crown, professed to claim an unlimited right of reclamation, but he cannot be accepted as any authority. Ajayi, Chief Ojora, the senior of the White-Cap Chiefs, gave the most important evidence. . . . He stated that the foreshore belonged to the owner of the land, that is to say, the native owner of the land, for the distinction between ownership and the right to 'squat and eat', as one witness put it, is very clear to native mind. He went on to say that the foreshore was called 'Etisha', and that, if it is a place where a canoe lands, the person occupying the land will use the place, and that the 'Etisha' is neither land nor water by native law. . . . In re-examination, he was asked 'What rights has a man over the "Etisha"?' and said 'If his land comes down to the water's edge, and he has used it for a long time and anybody comes to interfere with him, he can stop him. He has a right to moor his canoe there and land there. If there is a passage along the "Etisha", anybody can pass there.' Questioned as to reclamation, he said 'Nobody would interfere with reclamation of land, even in deep water, if it does not interfere with our work. By this, I mean our fishing stakes. If it interfered with passing canoes he would be asked about it.

[1] With such a general statement compare this passage of Osborne, C.J. in the unreported decision in *Commissioner of Lands* v. *Kamajalodun* (1911), cited by Combe, C.J., *in Lieutenant-Governor of Southern Provinces* v. *Bakare Ajakaiye & 3 ors.* (1927), 7 N. L. R. 21, at p. 24: 'It is declared that the inhabitants of Okepa Village have the right to reside in the said village and to erect buildings therein for the purpose of carrying on the business of fishing and further that they have a right to use the land for drying nets and other purpose of fishing, and to farm within the bounadry cut at the time of the survey by Mr. George. But this does not confer the right to alienate any part of the land within the said boundary.' Okepa was a fishing village at Ikoyi, close by the sea.

It is impossible to fill it up so as to interfere with passing canoes.'
Idowu, Chief Eletu, propounded a theory that whoever owns the
land by the water owns the waterside, and his land extends to
where the water covers his head. But he had to admit that he had
never learnt this as a law, nor knew of any case about the 'Etisha'
in the native Courts, and I am unable to attach any weight to his
testimony on this point.[1]

The learned Chief Justice then remarked that the somewhat
slight evidence shows that there was no unlimited right of reclamation which would be at variance with the public right of fishery
in the waters of the lagoon and that, in any case, the matter was
res judicata, it having been held by the same Court, also sitting
with native assessors, in *Kasumu Giwa* v. *Amodu Akola*, on 11
February 1909, that there was no legal right of reclamation under
the local customary law, but there existed *ex necessitate* the right
of riparian grantees of land to use the foreshore for access to the
water, and for landing, embarking, and mooring and hauling canoes.

The Privy Council judgment in the case is also valuable for the
light it sheds on the elemental similarity between the local law and
other legal systems on the doctrine of accretion. In local, as in
English, law whenever the *de facto* boundary is the sea or an arm
of the sea, there is nothing to prevent the doctrine from applying
to such a case. The one condition for the rule to operate is that the
accretion should be natural and so slow and gradual as to be
practically imperceptible in its process.[2] Lord Shaw then drew a
line between this slow natural process of accretion and a conscious
artificial reclamation carried out by the riparian occupier of land:
'Artificial reclamation and natural silting-up are, however, extremely different in their legal results: the latter, if gradual and
imperceptible in the sense already described, becomes an addition
to the property of the adjoining land; the former has not this

[1] *Per* Osborne, C.J., at pp. 6 and 7 of 2 N. L. R. 1, reviewing local law as to
foreshore prior to the Cession.

[2] The law on the point is still more or less what it was in Justinian's day:
Institutes, Book II, Title I, s. 20: 'Praeterea quod per alluvionem agro tuo
flumen adjecit, jure gentium tibi adquiritur. Est autem alluvio incrementum
latens. Per alluvionem autem id videtur adjici, quod ita paulatim adjicitur, ut
intellegere non possis, quantum quoquo momento temporis adjiciatur.' In
similar vein is Blackstone's *Commentaries*, Vol. II, p. 261: 'As to lands gained
from the sea, either by alluvion, by the washing up of sand and earth so as in
time to make *terra firma*, or by dereliction, as when the sea shrinks back
below the usual water-mark; in these cases the law is held to be, that if this
gain be little by little, by small and imperceptible degrees, it shall go to the
owner of the land adjoining.'

result, and the property of the original foreshore thus suddenly altered by reclamatory work upon it remains as before, i.e. in cases like the present, with the Crown.' [1] And the following summary statement of principles emerge:

(i) The Crown is entitled to the foreshore including any reclaimed land but subject to the rights of adjoining land-owner or occupier to place and store things thereon, to erect buildings thereon, and generally to use such foreshore for other legitimate purposes.

(ii) Where a frontage owner reclaims, either by express or implied authority, any part of a foreshore [2] which is vested in another, be that other a private person, community of persons or the Crown, such a frontage owner should enjoy foreshore rights over and above those he possesses as a member of the public: *Lyon* v. *The Fishmongers' Companies*.

(iii) Accordingly, a reclamation of part of the foreshore by the Crown or by a third party does not affect the ordinary riparian rights of frontagers, so that these rights may continue to be enjoyed even though the land is no longer subject to the ebb and flow of the tide: *Marshall* v. *Ulleswater, etc. & Co.* (L. R. 7 Q. B. 166).

(iv) In estimating the amount of compensation to be paid, lands adjoining such a foreshore and any reclaimed area should be regarded as possessing not only the rights of navigation and otherwise in and enjoyable by the public at large, but also those special rights which become annexed, and therefore add value, to specific riparian lands: *Duke of Buccleuch* v. *Metropolitan Board of Works* (L. R. 5 H. L. 418).

It would appear then that the position of the Crown with regard to the Lagos foreshore has a universal application to the whole of the Nigerian foreshore, and may be regarded as similar to that of its relation to Nigerian land proper, viz. that the radical title is in the Crown but that it is subject to the immemorial rights of the natives as to which, as already pointed out, local expert evidence had been led in the case itself.

(ii) Beach Lands

In the case of a beach land, i.e. land with a water frontage, the general principle is that the Crown abdicates all control in favour of native customary idea of ownership. This is that beaches belong,

---

[1] p. 64 of 2 N. L. R.; also (1915), A. C.
[2] As to what is 'foreshore' for our present purpose, see Lord Shaw's definition at p. 56 of 2 N. L. R., i.e. 'land between high- and low-water marks at ordinary spring-tides'.

not to any particular family or household, but to the whole town or village community within the boundaries of which it lies. There are three reported cases on the point: the first one deals with the question of ownership in trading beaches in the Brass area, while the other two deal with the principles governing ordinary beach lands in Calabar.

In the case of *Chief Young Dede* v. *African Association Ltd.*[1] the Company claimed that they had bought the land comprising the beaches from King Koko under clause 7 of a Treaty of 1891. Under this arrangement no rent was charged for the use of the land but the king and his chiefs had agreed to receive comey and later on a portion of the export duty for which they had not only abandoned the slave traffic but also gave the traders the right to take water and to occupy land for the purposes of their trade. It was held by Osborne, C.J., in the Supreme Court at Lagos, on an appeal from the Divisional Court of the Eastern Province, that no fee simple of the beaches passed to the company under the treaty, since the real owners were the members of the community and not the king and chiefs of Brass, notwithstanding the payment to the latter of personal subsidies. The learned Chief Justice observed: [2] 'We consider that under the Commercial Regulations before referred to the firms trading in the river originally obtained the right of occupancy of the beaches so long as they continued to trade and pay comey, the ownership of the land remaining with the original grantors.'

Also, in *Efana Efana Henshaw* v. *Elijah Henshaw and ors. and Compagnie Française*,[3] the plaintiff, as head of the Henshaw family, sued for cancellation of an agreement for the lease of beach land made between the Compagnie Française de l'Afrique Occidentale and the Chiefs of Henshaw Town on the ground that the land in question was the property of his family. Webber, J., in the Divisional Court at Calabar found (i) that the plaintiff had never occupied the land concerned; and (ii) that under the local native law and custom beach land belongs to the town within the limits of which it lies, and not to any particular family. The learned judge said: [4] 'It has always been native law and custom that beach land belongs to the town and never to a particular family. The beaches of Duke Town are owned by the descendants of Etim Efiom, and Ekpo Efiom and the principal chiefs of the present four branches of Henshaw family have the control and disposal of them.'

[1] (1911) 1 N. L. R. 130.   [2] (1911), 1 N. L. R., at p. 142.
[3] (1927), 8 N. L. R. 77.   [4] Ibid., at p. 79.

Similarly, in *Offiong Egbo Archibong Bassey* (on behalf of family) v. *Chief Ntoe Eteta* (for self, chiefs and people of Akim Aqua Town),[1] the plaintiffs claimed, as grantees under native customary law of certain lands extending to the beach at Atimbo on the Qua river, two-thirds of the rents accruing from the subsequent lease by the defendants of the lands to certain European firms. Two pleas were entered by the defendants, namely, (i) that such portions of the lands as were 'beach lands' could not be the subject of such a grant, and (ii) that plaintiffs at most were entitled to only £10 a year by virtue of an agreement alleged to have been made by the head of the plaintiffs' family with the defendants. In a joint judgment delivered by the West African Court of Appeal sitting in Lagos by Kingdon, Petrides and Webb, C.J.J., it was held (i) that 'beach lands' could be the subject of a grant by the representatives of the community in whom the real ownership vested under native law; (ii) that the defendants were not entitled to grant leases of the beach lands previously granted by them to the plaintiffs; (iii) that, as the plaintiffs had, however, impliedly adopted the leases, the plaintiffs were entitled to an equitable share of the rents, in this case fixed at two-thirds of the total; and (iv) that the position was not in any way affected by the agreement alleged by the defendants. In reaching this conclusion the Appeal Court relied on the previous judgment of one of themselves, Webber, J., in a Divisional Court in 1915 and commented:[2] 'In his judgment, Webber, J., said "It is clear beyond doubt that the land was given to the defendant and his people to farm on, and it seems also clear that the permission to use the land extended to the beach. . . .".

Now these three cases indeed concern the Brass and Calabar areas of Eastern Nigeria, but, judging from the evidence adduced in the *John Holt Case* concerning the Lagos foreshore, there is no reason why the principles therein laid down should not apply to other areas of Nigeria. In fact, Osborne, C.J., who had a little earlier decided the *John Holt Case* regarding the foreshore also decided, on appeal, the *Chief Young Dede Case* on beach land; and Webber, J., who decided the *Efana Efana Henshaw Case* was also an associate judge of the West African Court of Appeal which many years later decided, on identical principles, the *Offiong Egbo Archibong Bassey Case*.

We may, therefore, summarise by saying that, while the Crown owns the Nigerian foreshore, subject of course to customary local rights therein, native law and custom still govern the principles of

[1] (1938), 4 W. A. C. A. 153. [2] At p. 155 of 4 W. A. C. A.

native ownership of beach lands which are regarded as the property of the contiguous community.

(iii) Finally, it is important to note that, under s. 20 of the Crown Lands Ordinance No. 7 of 1918, it is provided that any conveyance or lease under that Ordinance shall not, unless otherwise expressly provided therein, confer any right to the foreshore, or to the banks of any navigable waterway.

Also, under the Piers Ordinance No. 1 of 1916, no person shall erect or re-erect, alter or extend any pier except under a licence issued under the Ordinance (s. 3). For this purpose, a pier includes every pier or wharf of whatever description erected on or extending beyond the foreshore of the sea or of any tidal waters or extending into the water of any navigable inland waters. The Governor may cancel any such licence or order a pier to be removed by any holder of a licence, with compensation where necessary. The settlement of disputes as to the existence or the nature of the rights, both legal and equitable, of any person with respect to piers will be referred to the Supreme Court.

3. INLAND WATERWAYS AND RIGHTS OF FISHING, NAVIGATION, ETC. THEREIN:

We have seen that s. 3 (1) of the Minerals Ordinance, 1945, provides that 'the entire property in and control of . . . all rivers, streams and watercourses throughout Nigeria, is and shall be vested in the Crown. . . .'

Now this section, which is in identical terms with s. 3 (1) of the Minerals Ordinance of 1916, first came up for judicial interpretation in the now leading case of *Chief D. H. Braide & others* v. *Chief S. Adoki & others*.[1]

But before we go on to examine the decision in this case it seems helpful to consider the legal position before the Ordinance of 1916. Because of the elucidation of the principles of native law and custom and of English law in the case of *Charlie King Amachree* v. *Daniel Kalio and others* [2] there is probably no better starting point than a careful but brief analysis of its relevant facts. The case came before the Full Court as Lagos on an appeal by the defendants from the judgment of the Divisional Court sitting at Degema which had been delivered on 14 October 1913. It would appear that, in 1871, the Chiefs of Okrika signed, on board the H.M.S. 'Dido', lying in the Bonny river, a perpetual treaty of peace with

[1] (1931), 10 N. L. R. 15.   [2] (1914), 2 N. L. R. 105.

the Chiefs of New Calabar whereby the Okrika people secured the right to pass through and to make fishing settlements in any of the creeks belonging to the New Calabar.[1] In pursuance of this agreement the Okrikas started (i) to fish by casting nets in the New Calabar river and in the creeks and ponds being the small tributaries of that river and to fish near to the towns and villages of the said river and creeks; (ii) to erect huts and other temporary structures on the banks of the said river and creeks without the plaintiff's permission. Thereupon the plaintiffs sought (a) an injunction to restrain the defendants from doing these things; (b) £300 damages for what they had already done; and (c) any other equitable relief that might to the Court seem fit.

In delivering the judgment of the appellate Court, i.e. the Full Court at Lagos (made up of Speed, C.J., Webber and Ross, J.J.), Ross, J., made the following pertinent observations: 'These smaller creeks which shoot off from the main river and meander throughout the land occupied by the plaintiffs are, I think, the property of the owners of the land surrounding them, and I am satisfied that the defendants have all along paid tribute (however small), and asked permission to fish therein, and have thus admitted the right of plaintiffs to deal with the fishing in these small veins of the great artery, the New Calabar river. Now, the New Calabar river is the great water highway of that part of the country; it is *tidal* and has been used for years and years by the large vessels which run the trade between the towns of New Calabar, Okrika and other large towns and the sea.'[2] Having found these to be the facts, the learned judge continued: '(1) By the common law of England, the use of all tidal and navigable rivers for ordinary purposes, including fishing, is enjoyed alike by all the inhabitants of the country, so that even if King Amachree were still alive, or if he had been succeeded by some other king, *prima facie* he and his people would be amenable to that law. (2) This would have been the case even if it had been conclusively proved that the plaintiffs had a prior occupation and right to this large water highway. (3) Further, by all *natural law, the inhabitants of a country have an inherent right to the use of the elements that are common to all,* and in the absence of strong proof to the contrary, *I am of opinion from the evidence of*

---

[1] This treaty was not mentioned in the report of the case, though it might have been referred to in the Divisional Court. We first came to know of it only in the report of the case of *Chief D. H. Braide* v. *Chief S. Adoki* (1931), 10 N. L. R. 15 where the present case was also fully considered.

[2] Ibid., at p. 107.

custom and native law that this natural right to such use obtained in the New Calabar river.' [1] Ross, J., therefore held as follows:

(*a*) That the New Calabar people were not entitled to the exclusive right of fishing in the New Calabar river itself, as it was a great *tidal* waterway the use of which, for ordinary purposes (including fishing), was common to all the inhabitants of the country;

(*b*) That the creeks, tributaries of the river, running through New Calabar territory, were the property of the New Calabar people, who were entitled to an exclusive right of fishing in them; and

(*c*) That the Okrikas were not entitled to erect huts on their banks without permission or agreement of the New Calabar people.

Webber, J., declared an interesting 'peccavi' when he said: [2] 'I feel that my finding in the Court below, that the Respondents are entitled to the exclusive fishery in the New Calabar river cannot be maintained.' But he quite rightly warned that 'this principle of a common fishery in the open navigable and tidal rivers of the Protectorate referred to by my learned brother in his judgment, is based on no theory of ownership of the river beds by the Crown: it is a principle which must be maintained on the ground of public policy and of public interest, even if native law and custom are inconsistent with it.' Fortunately, native law and custom is at one with English and Roman law on the whole question, and the principles enunciated above are of universal application in Nigeria. [3]

With Webber, J's., *caveat* against any theory of Crown ownership of the river beds in our mind, we can now turn to the case of *Chief D. H. Braide & Ors.* v. *Chief S. Adoki & Ors.*[4] which arose on precisely the same facts as in the *Charlie King Amachree Case*, the only difference being that since the latter decision two further events had happened. These were (*a*) the enactment of the Minerals Ordinance of 1916; (*b*) the conclusion of a mutual agreement signed in August 1923 before the Resident of the Province according to which the Okrikas bound themselves to pay to the people of New Calabar an annual rent of ten shillings for each house or hut erected by them on the land covered by the Full Court

[1] (1931), 10 N. L. R., at p. 108. But the numbering in the passage, as well as the italics, is mine.

[2] At p. 110, ibid.

[3] For rights of fishing and navigation in Yoruba lands, see Ward Price, *Land Tenure* (1933), paras. 26 and 27.

[4] (1931), 10 N. L. R. 15.

judgment,[1] of 1914. It was, in fact, to enforce the payment of the agreed rent for the fishing huts erected by the Okrikas beside New Calabar waterways that the present action was brought. Let us now consider each of the two new factors separately:

(a) S. 3 (1) of the Minerals Ordinance, 1916, vests, as already stated at the beginning of this section, the ownership and control of all rivers, streams and watercourses throughout Nigeria in the Crown. The term 'watercourse' is defined in s. 2 of the same Ordinance as meaning 'Any channel whether natural or artificial which confines or restricts the flow of water.' The two terms 'river' and 'watercourses' together undoubtedly cover the tidal waterway known as the New Calabar river together with the network of creeks which branch off from it and connect it with other navigable rivers. Since all these rivers and creeks are *tidal*, the ownership by the Crown results in a common of piscary to be enjoyed by all the inhabitants of the country.

The legal effect of this Ordinance on the earlier decision in the *Charlie King Amachree* case was thus put by Berkeley, J., in the Divisional Court at Calabar: [2] 'The change is that claims to exclusive rights of fishing over definite tidal areas now give way to a general right of common fishery over the whole of the tidal waterways. . . . The people of New Calabar no longer own the beds of the rivers and creeks of New Calabar. Therefore, they no longer own any several right of fishery, which they can dispose of by contract, in the waters of these rivers and creeks. . . .' But he would be prepared to admit that, as riparian owners, the New Calabar people still own the banks of the rivers and creeks. Outsiders should therefore have no right to erect houses, fishing settlements, huts or other temporary structures on these lands of the New Calabar people merely because they enjoy, along with all the other people of Nigeria, a common of fishery in the tidal waterways lying within the territory of New Calabar.

(b) Berkeley, J., also held that the 1923 agreement must be taken to have bound the Okrika people to pay the agreed rents.

From these findings the appellants appealed to the Full Court at Lagos consisting of Kingdon, C.J., Webber and Butler Lloyd, JJ. The judgment of the Court was delivered by Kingdon, C.J., who held (1) that the Okrikas were entitled to go to the creeks and ponds, tributaries of the New Calabar river, from time to time and to fish; (2) that, for that purpose, they were entitled temporarily

[1] i.e. the Charlie King Amachree Case (1914), 2 N. L. R. 105.
[2] (1931), 10 N. L. R. 15, at p. 19.

to occupy lands abutting on the creeks, or islands in the creeks, and to erect thereon temporary huts and *to dry their nets thereon*, and temporarily to retain all the temporary huts already erected; (3) that, for all these advantages, they should pay yearly tribute to the New Calabar chiefs according to native law and custom.[1] To the extent to which the 1923 agreement had regulated the relationship between the parties with respect to 'any occupation of land or any erection of buildings' over and above what native law and custom would allow in such a case, the learned Chief Justice would not, however, interfere.

When, about two years later, the case of *Orku Sowa & Senabor* v. *Chief Jim G. Amachree* [2] came on appeal to the Full Court at Lagos, with Kingdon, C.J., Webber and Berkeley, J.J., as judges, the Court took the view that the rules of law on the subject had been settled in the 1931 case. Butler, J., who delivered the judgment of the appellate court, said: [3] 'The law on this point was settled by the Full Court in its judgment dated the 5th March, 1931, in the case of *Chief D. H. Braide* v. *Chief Samson Adoki*. This case established the right of all persons to fish within the tide-ways.'

The result of the cases and of the Ordinance (now of 1945, as later amended) would appear to be as follows:

(i) 'From time immemorial the people of Nigeria have enjoyed the right to fish the sea, with its creeks and arms and navigable rivers within the tides.' [4] But the beds of non-tidal rivers and creeks are owned by the community in whose territory they lie, as also the banks of all tidal waterways.[5]

(ii) The ownership by the Crown, in consequence of s. 3 (i) of the Minerals Ordinance (1945), implies that all tidal rivers and creeks are subject to a common of piscary to be enjoyed by all the inhabitants of Nigeria. 'The change is that claims to exclusive rights of fishing over definite tidal areas now give way to a general right of common fishery over the whole of the tidal waterways.' [6]

---

[1] For the similar Gold Coast custom of 'strangers' having to pay dues called 'Amandze' to 'natives', see p. 263 of H. G. Lemmon's *Public Rights in the Seashore*, London, 1934.

[2] (1933), 11 N. L. R. 82.   [3] Ibid., at p. 84.

[4] *Per* Berkeley, J., in (1931), 10 N. L. R. 15, at p. 18. It is useful to recall here the evidence of *Chief Ojora* (noted at p. 61) in *A.G. of S. Nigeria* v. *John Holt & Ors.* (1910), 2 N. L. R. 1, with respect to similar rights in Lagos waters.

[5] See also para. 21 (*e*) and (*f*) of Chap. IV of A. K. Ajisafe's *Laws & Customs of the Yorubas* (1924).

[6] Ibid., at p. 19.

(iii) The public rights in such rivers, streams and watercourses include: (*a*) the right to fish therein; (*b*) the right to occupy temporarily lands abutting on the creeks or islands in the creeks, and to erect temporary huts or other temporary structures thereon; (*c*) the right to dry their nets thereon and probably to pull up canoes and other fishing boats for temporary periods.

(iv) All the inhabitants of Nigeria also enjoy a right of free navigation in tidal and other large inland waterways.[1]

(v) Water may be taken from such rivers and creeks for all ordinary domestic purposes.

In all these cases, members of the public enjoy these normal rights subject to the sanctions of usage and reasonableness in accordance with the principles of native law and custom and the requirements of public interest.

Water on Crown Lands

By s. 19 of the Crown Lands Ordinance No. 7 of 1918, special reservations are made in favour of lands coming under that Ordinance. It is provided that no conveyance or lease of such lands shall, unless otherwise expressly provided therein, confer any right to the water of any spring, river, lake or stream other than such water as may be required for domestic purposes upon the land sold or leased.

4. UN-OCCUPIED LANDS

5. SWAMP AND GRASS LANDS [2]

For convenience we will treat these two headings together.

Now, leaving out for the moment a consideration of the indigenous theory that under the communal or collective ownership of land no land in Nigeria is without an owner, we shall direct our immediate enquiry into an examination of the legislation relating to the so-called unoccupied or vacant or waste land.

The principal enactment is the Public Lands Acquisition Ordinance No. 9 of 1917,[3] 'an ordinance to empower the Governor

---

[1] Note: A. K. Ajisafe, *The Laws & Customs of the Yoruba People* (1924), Chap. X, para. 25: 'On the lagoon, women are not allowed to ply a canoe. . . .' This would not, however, apply to, e.g., Ijaw women.

[2] 'The Government has dealt with swamp and unoccupied lands in the island as if they were Crown property': *Per* Winkfield, J., at p. 41 of (1911), 2 N. L. R. 1.

[3] Cap. 88 of *The Laws of Nigeria* (1923), Vol. I; the various later amendments will be mentioned presently.

to acquire lands when required for public purposes,' and it covers
both the Colony and the Protectorate of Nigeria. In s. 13 is contained the official definition of 'unoccupied lands':

'Land shall be deemed to be unoccupied where it is not proved
that beneficial use thereof for cultivation, or habitation, or for
collecting or storing water or for any industrial purpose has been
had for a continuous period of at least six months during the
period of ten years immediately preceding the publication of the
notice stating that such lands are required for public purposes.'

The first part of the same section lays down the principle that
no compensation is to be awarded by the Government in respect
of unoccupied lands as thus defined, whenever these are acquired
for public purposes. The Governor may acquire lands for any
public purpose for an estate in fee simple or for a term of years,
paying such consideration or compensation as he may think
proper.[1] Where lands so required for public purposes are the property of a native community in the Colony or Southern Provinces,
the recognised head chief of such community is given the power to
sell and convey the same for an estate in fee simple, notwithstanding any native law or custom to the contrary.[2] In all cases of dispute
as to compensation to be paid for and as to title to such lands
reference should be made to the appropriate Supreme Court for
final settlement.[3] Any compensation to be given for any lands or
any estate or interest therein or for any mesne profits thereof is to
be assessed by the Court according to the value of the lands (a) at
the time of service of notices, any improvements or works made
or constructed thereafter on the said lands being disregarded;
(b) where the value of the residue of the land acquired is enhanced
or likely to be enhanced by the acquisition of part only, the Court
may properly take that into consideration in making a settlement; (c) similar regard is to be had where such residue is or is
likely to be damaged by the acquisition of part only of the land.[4]
Owners of land intersected as a result of acquisition of adjacent
lands may insist on same being taken or acquired as well.[5]

Persons found in effective possession or in receipt of the rents
of such lands at the time of purchase or acquisition shall be
deemed to have been lawfully entitled thereto, but without

[1] S. 3 of the Public Lands Acquisition Ordinance, (see s. 15 later).
[2] S. 7, ibid.; also, s. 23 provides that such head chief shall distribute any
compensation so paid among members of the community or otherwise apply
it in a manner approved by the Governor.
[3] S. 10, ibid.   [4] Ibid., s. 15.   [5] Ibid., s. 16.

prejudice at any subsequent proceedings against such persons at the instance of any other person claiming to have a better right to such lands.[1] In any case the Government is fully discharged, to whomsoever payment has once been duly made.[2] But the mere fact of the service of a notice upon any person by the Governor with respect to any intended acquisition is not to be taken as an admission that the land in question is not Crown land.[3]

These provisions have been the subject of numerous judicial decisions which have helped to clarify the law.

The first of these is *William Lewis the Elder* v. *The Colonial Secretary* [4] where the question was first raised as to whether or not a certain piece of land in Lagos, belonging to the appellant and acquired by the Government under the provisions of the Public Lands Ordinance No. 8 of 1876, was 'unoccupied' within the meaning of s. 7 sub-s. 6 of that Ordinance. In the Divisional Court evidence had been led to show that the land was barren, had been once or twice planted with cassada with a view to cultivation, but had later been left to rot or for vagrant cattle to eat up. A flimsy fence had been erected which could not, however, prevent the incursions of goats. At the request of the Court the land was valued at £207 7s. 6d. or 1s. 3d. per acre. The Divisional Court then finally decided that no compensation should be paid to claimant as the land was 'unoccupied' within the meaning of the Ordinance. The appellant appealed to the Full Court consisting of Smalman Smith, C.J., Hutchinson and F. J. Smith, JJ., basing his appeal on three grounds: (1) that he had a valid title, supported by a written conveyance, to the land in question; (2) that land could not under any circumstances be considered 'unoccupied' when the claimant had a good title to it in fee simple and not a mere occupation or permissive title (otherwise s. 7 of the Ordinance would be inconsistent with s. 3); and (3) that the 'assessment' by the Court prior to its judgment amounted to an 'award' to him of the £207 7s. 6d., so that the Court could not later refuse to order its payment to him.

Hutchinson, J., in delivering the judgment of the Full Court, emphasised that 'effect must be given to the word "beneficial". It is not enough to have tried to cultivate the land; it is not enough to stick a few pieces of cassada in it and leave them to rot or for

---

[1] S. 21 of the Public Lands Acquisition Ordinance.
[2] Ibid., s. 22.   [3] Ibid., s. 31.
[4] (1891), 1 N. L. R. 11 (the whole report having been extracted from pp. 41 and 42 of *Lagos: Reports of Certain Judgments of the Supreme Court, Vice-Admiralty Court and Full Court of Appeal* (1884–1892). Colonial Office Library.

vagrant cattle to eat. If a man were to plant cassada, and find afterwards that the soil was so hard and barren that the cassada was not worth taking up, that would be no "beneficial use" of his land'. He therefore confirmed the judgment of the lower Court by holding that the land was 'unoccupied' and that the words 'beneficial use' mean beneficial to the user and not beneficial to the land.

The corresponding provision of the Public Lands Ordinance of 1903, i.e. s. 14 of this Ordinance, came in for review in the great case of *Amodu Tijani* v. *Secry. of Southern Nigeria*,[1] which is also valuable for the light it throws on the question of the ownership of palm and mangrove swamp and grass lands generally. The facts were that in November 1913 the Government proposed under s. 4 of the Public Lands Ordinance of 1903 to acquire lands the property of the community represented by the claimant, one of the land-owning White-Cap Chiefs of Lagos, and claimed compensation as the 'owner' of the whole area excepting such portion thereof as had been directly or indirectly alienated by deed or otherwise by the Oluwa family or held under Crown Grants as expropriated by the Government in 1900 and 1907. It having been decided by the Privy Council[2] that the claimant was entitled to compensation on the footing that he was transferring to the Governor the land in question in full ownership, the Divisional Court had to interpret s. 14 of the Ordinance which provides that no compensation should be awarded in respect of unoccupied lands.

A portion of the lands to be acquired consisted of palm swamp, mangrove swamp and grass swamp. With regard to these, the claimant proved that the inhabitants of the village on or adjacent to the land, from whom he regularly received tribute for the use they made of the lands in question, collected palm nuts from the palm swamp, caught mud fish and cut mangrove wood in the mangrove swamp. In addition, oil was extracted from the palm nuts and the oil was sold. Some of the mud fish were prepared for the market and sold, and the mangrove wood was converted into charcoal.

As regards the grass swamp, it was established that goats from the village grazed on it. The Divisional Court held that the swamp lands were 'unoccupied' within the definition in the Ordinance and that 'the Crown is under no obligation to pay anyone for unoccupied lands as defined'. In delivering his judgment on the section, Pennington, J., pointed out:[3] 'It seems to me that this

[1] (1923), 4 N. L. R. 18.   [2] (1921), A. C. 399.
[3] At pp. 22–3 of (1923), 4 N. L. R. 18.

section, whether in its original form or in its form in the 1903 Ordinance, is bound to work injustice if strictly applied to lands in and around Lagos and other large towns. I doubt not that there is still much land in Lagos which would come under this definition. The records of the Police Magistrate Court will show many cases of unoccupied land sold under s. 10 of the Public Health Ordinance. Again, all around Agege and up the line to Abeokuta there must be much land, not cultivated or used for habitation or for the purposes of industry for more than ten years, which must be quite valuable land for agricultural purposes. In many cases considerable sums have been paid for this land. It would hardly be just to take these lands without compensation. . . . I think therefore that the section wants some amending, but it is not for me to suggest the lines of such amendments.'

The claimant appealed to the Full Court where Combe, C.J., who delivered the judgment of that Court, observed that Pennington, J., in the lower Court, while satisfied that it would be unjust not to award compensation for the swamp lands which he had declared to be 'unoccupied', nevertheless gave the claimant compensation for the disturbance of the rights which he and his tenants had exercised over the mangrove swamp and palm swamp lands. Hence, with the learned judge's finding in the Divisional Court that whilst 'the *land* on which the palm-oil is made, the mud fish are smoked or dried, and the mangrove wood is converted into charcoal may be held to be used for such industrial purposes', nevertheless 'the swamp on which the nuts are collected, the fish caught and the mangrove wood is cut cannot be held to be used for any industrial purpose', Combe, C.J., in the Full Court, could not agree, since it appeared to him that Mr. Justice Pennington had placed 'a too narrow interpretation on the language of the section which, as we have stated, must be interpreted as widely as possible in favour of the claimant'.[1] The learned Chief Justice therefore held as follows:

(i) that s. 14, in so far as it sought to preclude the Court from awarding compensation to the owner of land acquired by the Crown unless the land shall have been occupied for certain specific purposes, may properly be regarded as to that extent, a confiscating section and ought therefore to be construed with almost a jealous regard for the interest sought to be confiscated; [2]

[1] (1923), 4 N. L. R. 18, at pp. 29 and 30.
[2] Compare the similar comment made by Waddington, J., upon the Public Lands Acquisition Ordinance (1917) in *Chief Commissioner, Eastern*

(ii) that the words 'beneficial use' means beneficial to the user and not beneficial to the land: *William Lewis* v. *The Colonial Secry.*, 1 N. L. R. 15.

(iii) that the swamp lands were not unoccupied lands in that claimant had proved that a beneficial use for an industrial purpose had been had of the palm swamp and mangrove swamp lands and that a beneficial use by the inhabitants had been had of the grass swamp land adjacent to the village on which the goats of the village grazed: [1] 'The villagers must have their goats and the goats must have some feeding ground, though very little may be sufficient. The grazing ground for the goats is a necessary part of an African village.' [2]

Combe, C.J., was, however, careful to give the warning that each case must depend on its own peculiar facts. If any piece of land in the country can be shown to have been put to only an intermittent use for the sole purpose of collecting wild products as and when they are ripe or ready for gathering, the Court may hold that such land is unoccupied, notwithstanding that the products collected are used in connection with an industrial purpose.

Principles of Assessing Compensation

When once it has been decided that the Crown must pay compensation to a private person, that is to say, that the land acquired is not unoccupied, the assessment of the proper amount to pay has been a matter of some difficulty.

Thus, in *Administrator of the Colony* v. *Thomas & George* [3] the Government acquired some land at Ebute Metta for public purposes and compensated the various holders at a standard rate with which the majority were satisfied. The two defendants, however, disagreed on the ground that they had seven years earlier paid a higher price than the Government's rate; stamped receipts were tendered showing that they had each paid £40 for their plots from one Mr. Gabriel Oshodi, as against the estimate of

Provinces v. *S. N. Onoye & Ors.* (1944), 17 N. L. R. 142, at p. 144: 'These statutory powers are powers of a very exceptional character, whereby an individual can be deprived of his property compulsorily; and proportionally exceptional care ought to be exercised to avoid their abuse.' The learned judge was dealing with a case of Government acquisition of land, partly Crown and partly private, in Onitsha.

[1] Ibid., at p. 32.

[2] Apapa village itself was covered by Crown Grants and so no compensation was paid for it; but there was for the one and a half acres not so covered.

[3] (1930), 10 N. L. R. 71.

£22 18s. 1d. or 1s. per square yard made by an officer of the Lands Department. It was held by Berkeley, acting C.J., that the measure of compensation should be the amount actually expended by the defendants in acquiring their holdings: 'I do not propose to assess the value of the defendants' holdings but merely the compensation which is proper for Government to pay in this particular instance to these two persons. I have no hesitation in saying that the fact that the defendants paid £40 each for their land must outweigh the opinion, however experienced, of the Lands Department as to its actual value, even though such opinion is supported by the fact that the defendants' neighbouring plot owners have acquiesced in the Department's assessment.'

A more instructive case, however, is *Commissioner of Lands* v. *E. F. A. Adeleye*,[1] which is important not so much for its facts (which were ordinary enough) but for certain *obiter dicta* regarding the principles to be applied in assessing compensation for a compulsory acquisition of land and also of any buildings thereon. The Government acquired some land in Lagos, along with the buildings on it, under the Public Lands Acquisition Ordinance of 1917.[2] The defendant disagreed with the Government valuation and, on reference to the Court under s. 10 of the Ordinance, the Supreme Court accordingly determined the proper amount of the compensation, Butler Lloyd, J., remarking: 'So far as I am aware these principles have not yet been the subject of judicial pronouncement in this Court and I therefore think it necessary to go into the matter at some length.'

According to him, the Land Clauses Acts applied to all cases of compulsory acquisition and their aim was to benefit the expropriated owner by generous compensation grants as well as awarding, under a practice which later grew up, an additional allowance of ten per cent. for compulsory acquisition. In 1919 a distinction came to be drawn between acquisitions of a purely private and commercial character and those by public authorities made in the public interest. The result was the supersession of the Land Clauses Acts by the Acquisition of Lands (Assessment of Compensation) Act, which governs all cases of acquisition by public authorities and the Government, expressly did away with the practice of paying ten per cent. as additional allowance for compulsory acquisition, while at the same time laying down the rule that the value of land should be 'the amount which the land if sold in the open market by a willing seller might be expected to realise'. The Nigerian

[1] (1938), 14 N. L. R. 109.   [2] Cap. 88 of *The Laws of Nigeria*, 1923.

Ordinance of 1917, with later amendments, was based on these principles and not on the earlier Land Clauses Acts. S. 15 of the Ordinance indeed asks the Court to assess compensation 'according to what it shall find to have been the value at the time of the service of notice of acquisition'.

Butler Lloyd, J., accordingly held that an allowance for compulsory purchase is not recognised by the Ordinance and cannot be claimed as a right. The Government may, however, still grant such an allowance in suitable cases, even if there is an express prohibition of same in any particular Ordinance.[1]

(i) *With regard to Land itself*, the learned judge then laid down this general rule: 'The principle to be applied in assessing compensation is in no way affected by the judgment in the case of the *Administrator of the Colony* v. *Thomas & Anor.*, *supra*, which merely laid down that the actual price paid for the land in question might be a better guide to its value than an expert estimate. . . . Now it is obvious that the best guide to an estimate of the value of land in any given neighbourhood is evidence as to the price at which actual sales in the locality have been made.'[2] Thus, a corner plot is always more valuable than one in a row, and the best condition for determining value is clearly by free sales in open market. In the case itself, there should be no comparison at all between the Campbell Street area (as to which compensation was to be made) and a place like Oko Awo or other similar districts because (*a*) figures for the immediate neighbourhood of the land in question were readily available, (*b*) the Government had carried out extensive improvements to the land around Oko Awo and (*c*) Oko Awo is much nearer the commercial centre of Lagos.

(ii) *With regard to Buildings on lands acquired*, he said: 'Coming now to the value of buildings on the land it appears to be necessary to lay down two principles: (1) The first of these principles is that in the case of a building some years old the fact that the cost of erection was at the time higher or lower than the present cost of erecting a similar building is entirely irrelevant to an enquiry as to its present value. If the former figure was higher the owner is so much the worse off, if lower he is the gainer by so much. (2) The second principle is that the present value of a building some years old is necessarily less than the cost of erecting a similar building

---

[1] e.g., although s. 49 (1) (*a*) of the Lagos Town Planning Ordinance No. 45 of 1928 expressly excludes such allowance, it is nevertheless paid in practice. See, however, the decisions in the next case.

[2] (1938), 14 N. L. R. 109, at pp. 110 and 111.

today by whatever amount it is proper to allow for depreciation in respect of its actual age. To put it another way, no one will pay as much for a house some years old as he would pay for a new one precisely similar.'

As applied to the case in hand, the agreed estimate of £800 as the cost of erection in 1927 less twenty-five per cent. depreciation was adopted in enabling the Court, after a full consideration of all relevant factors, to award £500 which was what the Government offered for the buildings. The Government's offer of 11s. a square yard for the land was also considered adequate. Under the proviso to s. 19 of the Ordinance, which says that whenever in disputes as to compensation amount the Court confirms the Crown's prior offer costs must be paid by the claimant, the plaintiffs in the present case were asked to pay the Government's costs in the action.

In the case of *Chairman, Lagos Executive Development Board* v. *Joye & Ors.*[1] the broad principles thus enunciated were applied to a slightly different type of problem of compensation for acquisition of land in the Idoluwo area of Lagos, this time by the Lagos Executive Development Board under s. 38 of the Lagos Town Planning Ordinance, 1928. The Board had offered £425 as representing the value of the land acquired and of the cubic capacity of the building upon it, with an addition of ten per cent. for compulsory purchase. The premises were let to rent-paying tenants and had been assessed by the Lagos Town Council at £100 per annum for rating purposes. This assessment was based on the rents actually collected by the claimant and not on the capital value of the property. The claimant, as the first defendant, desired compensation to be not less than ten years' purchase of the figure of the assessment for rates. The Board then took out a summons under s. 45 of the Ordinance for the Supreme Court to determine the proper amount of compensation. Butler Lloyd, acting C.J., held (1) that the rental value of premises cannot be made the basis of compensation in an over-crowded area like Lagos where rents are charged which are out of all proportion to the capital value of the property, and (2) that, in accordance with the provision of s. 49 (1) of the Ordinance of 1928 which specifically prohibits the inclusion of any additional allowance in respect of compulsory purchase, the Supreme Court could not and would not allow such additional amount to be included in the compensation estimate even though the Board had done so in order to obtain an early or

[1] (1939), 15 N. L. R. 50.

amicable settlement with the claimant. Accordingly, he fixed the compensation at £400, being the cost of the building at current prices less twenty per cent. for fifteen year's depreciation.

But whether the acquisition of land and buildings on it is by the Crown, that is, the Government, or by public authorities like the Lagos Town Council and the Native Administrations or even by local public corporations like the Lagos Executive Development Board, s. 13 of the Public Lands Acquisition Ordinance (1917) requires that such compulsory acquisition must be for 'public purposes'. What constitutes a 'public purpose' is stated *in extenso* in s. 2 of the Ordinance, but it is clear that the wide terms of this provision may have to be finally construed by the Court in doubtful cases. It is probably needless to state that the power to acquire land under the Ordinance does not derive from any claim to Crown ownership of Nigerian land; it is within the administrative competence of any civilised Government of any country, so long as reasonable compensation is paid to expropriated owners.

A case in which the Court has been called upon to decide what is 'public purpose' within the Ordinance is *Chief Commissioner, Eastern Provinces* v. *S. N. Ononye & Ors.*[1] Some twenty-five years earlier the United Africa Company had had leased to it for commercial purposes land at Onitsha, part of which was Crown land (under the Niger Land Transfer Ordinance already considered) and part of which, although contiguous, was not Crown land but had inadvertently been regarded as such through lack of a clear-cut boundary to the Crown lands under the Niger treaties. With a view to regularising the position, the Crown took steps to acquire this latter piece of land under the Public Lands Acquisition Ordinance; the Chief Commissioner for the Eastern Provinces therefore asked the Court:

(i) to determine the persons entitled to the land,

(ii) to estimate the amount of compensation payable, and

(iii) to grant to the Crown a certificate of title to the land.

Also, there was in addition to this land another piece included in the same proceedings for acquisition as a market site. *Held*: by Waddington J., in the High Court of Onitsha:

(i) that the acquisition of private land by the Crown for the mere purpose of granting a lease thereof to a commercial company was not a 'public purpose' within the Public Lands Acquisition Ordinance,

---

[1] (1944), 17 N. L. R. 142.

(ii) that the other piece of land included in the proceedings, being required for use as a local market, could be acquired by the Government as for a public purpose under the Ordinance, and

(iii) that, consequently, the issue of a certificate of title to the Crown must be refused with respect to the commercial lease but granted in the case of the market site.

It remains to consider the effect of the grant to the Crown of a certificate of title on the acquisition of land for a public purpose. In *Chief Ndoko* v. *Chief Ikoro and Attorney-General* [1] the plaintiff sought a declaration of title to land in Calabar as against the defendant. The Government had acquired the land from the defendant under the Public Lands Acquisition Ordinance and the Attorney-General was therefore joined as a party to the action. Acquisition under s. 21 of the Ordinance renders the Crown's title to acquired land no longer open to question in a court of law. The Attorney-General therefore applied to be released as a party. It was held by Webber, J., in the Divisional Court at Calabar that (1) the Government was entitled to demur at any stage of the proceedings and the Attorney-General should accordingly be discharged from the action; and (2) such discharge does not, however, affect the plaintiff's rights against the first defendant under the Ordinance.[2]

It would seem that despite this indefeasible title of the Crown, whether granted by the Court under the Public Lands Ordinance or acquired under some other arrangement like the Ikoyi Lands Ordinance (1908), the Crown may grant to the occupiers in possession at the time when the land became Crown land rights of continued habitation and user. In such a case compensation will be paid, on subsequent acquisition by the Crown, for disturbance of the occupiers' rights and other unexhausted improvements in circumstances analogous to acquisition of and compensation for lands in the Northern Provinces. In the consolidated action in *Lieutenant-Governor of Southern Provinces* v. *Ajakaiye and Laditan (as Heads of Iga Iduntafa) and Dosumu and Okoya (as nominated representatives of Onikoyi Family)*,[3] Governor Glover had permitted the inhabitants of a fishing village at Okepa to continue to occupy the land after its grant to the Crown. Under the

[1] (1926), 7 N. L. R. 76.
[2] See pp. 72-3, *supra*, for the provision of s. 21 (and its proviso) of the Public Lands Acquisition Ord., 1917.
[3] (1927), 7 N. L. R. 21; (1929), A. C. 679.

Ikoyi Lands Ordinance [1] the Crown wanted to define the boundaries of all private, and ascertain the areas of all Crown, lands at Ikoyi, and advertised a public notice for claimants to come forward for fresh Crown grants. One Kamajalodun, on behalf of the village dwellers, was granted a Crown certificate. This was confirmed in the unreported decision of Chief Justice Osborne of 7 September 1911, in *Commissioners of Lands* v. *Kamajalodun.* Now, when Government desired to acquire the village under the Public Lands Acquisition Ordinance, the defendants claimed for the first time that they were the absolute owners of the land in question. *Held*: by Combe, C.J., that the defendants could not sustain a claim to compensation as owners because (*a*) the Crown's title could not now be called in question; (*b*) the defendants had failed to assert a claim under the Ikoyi Lands Ordinance as previously advertised, (*c*) they were claiming as absolute owners and not merely as inhabitants; said Combe, C.J., 'It may well be that if the appellants are inhabitants of the village, the Government will be willing to compensate them as such, but this would now be done as an act of grace, and this Court can make no order in the matter'.[2]

Another courageous attempt to revive stale claims has recently been made by the Onikoyi Chieftaincy Family in the case of *Chief Secretary to the Government* v. *James George & 24 ors.*[3] In 1941, the Government wanted to acquire under the Public Lands Acquisition Ordinance, land in Lagos which was part of what Chief Onikoyi had in 1865 given to Governor Glover. Five Crown grants, giving grantees absolute title, were made to persons with respect to the land. When the Ikoyi Lands Ordinance took effect, the grantees were duly confirmed in their holdings, but no fresh survey or grant was issued as contemplated by the Ordinance. In 1941, twenty-three persons claimed compensation as holders or assignees of holders of Crown grants, and Onikoyi Chieftaincy family also claimed as against all the other twenty-four claimants. The Government therefore took out this summons to determine (*a*) who were entitled, and (*b*) amount of compensation. The Onikoyi family claimed (i) the right of reverter on the death in 1916 of the last survivor of the Hausa ex-soldiers to whom the land had been originally granted by Governor Glover; (ii) ownership of the

[1] S. 7 of which provides: 'All lands situated within the limits above described, to which no claim is made within the prescribed time, shall be deemed to be Crown lands thenceforward.'
[2] Ibid., at p. 24. This judgment was confirmed by the Privy Council in (1929), 9 N. L. R. 1.   [3] (1942), 16 N. L. R. 88.

land since the purported gift by Chief Onikoyi of the land to the Governor in 1865 had been originally without the consent of the Onikoyi family. Butler Lloyd, acting C.J., in delivering the judgment of the Supreme Court held: (1) that questions as to what were the intentions of the parties to the 1865 transaction or as to the legal effect thereof could no longer be raised in view of the terms of the Ikoyi Lands Ordinance (1908); and (2) that the owners of Crown grants approved under that Ordinance acquired an indefeasible title to the land covered by their grants: 'From that time on (i.e. 1908) there cannot be the slightest doubt that owners of Crown grants approved under the Ordinance acquired an indefeasible title to the land covered by their grants and the Crown to any land which remained unclaimed.' [1]

The competence of the Supreme Court of Nigeria to issue, under s. 28 of the Public Lands Acquisition Ordinance, certificates of title to the Crown in proper cases of land acquisition would seem to be very wide. This point once arose in *In the matter of Archibong Richardson Henshaw* [2] which came before the Full Court at Lagos on a case stated by Green, J., from Calabar as to whether or no the Supreme Court of Nigeria has jurisdiction to grant certificates of title under the Ordinance to land situate more than five miles from Calabar Court House, that is, outside the territorial limits defined by s. 24 of the Supreme Court Ordinance.[3] Speed, C.J., ruled that the Court had the necessary competence under s. 11 of the Public Lands Ordinance to issue a certificate to such lands, although outside the local limits of its jurisdiction, and that a certificate should be issued in that case.

Finally, under the new s. 3 (2) introduced into the principal Ordinance by the Public Lands Acquisition (Amendment) Ordinance No. 6 of 1945, all lands acquired by the Government under the Ordinance shall be deemed to be Crown lands subject to the Crown Lands Ordinance, even though the public purpose for which such lands have been acquired has failed or has afterwards been abandoned. This means that when once any land has been acquired by Government, it always remains Crown land, notwithstanding any later defeasance of the original public purpose.

---

[1] Such title will, however, now be subject to local law and custom as provided by The Crown Grants (Lagos) Ordinance No. 18 of 1947 already considered at p. 24.

[2] (1916), 3 N. L. R. 6.

[3] Chap. CXII of the *Laws of Southern Nigeria*.

In view of the repeated judicial strictures [1] on the harsh provision of s. 13 of the principal Ordinance of 1917 and because of the increased awareness of the nature of indigenous modes of user of land made possible as Government wants to obtain control over land required for or in connexion with planned rural development or settlement, s. 4 of this Amending Ordinance of 1945, repeals s. 13 of the Principal Ordinance in its entirety and substitutes this new s. 13 with regard to so-called unoccupied land and rights thereover:

13 (1) No compensation shall be awarded in respect of unoccupied land.

(2) Where any person or any community has, during the five years immediately preceding the publication of notice of intention to acquire, exercised any rights of fishing, hunting, grazing or the collection of uncultivated produce over unoccupied lands such exercise shall not have the effect of causing such unoccupied land to be deemed to be occupied but such person or community shall be entitled to compensation in respect of the rights extinguished by the acquisition and in default of agreement as to the amount of such compensation the Court may award such compensation as it deems reasonable and where such rights so extinguished were communal the compensation shall be paid into the revenue of the native authority concerned.

(3) For the purposes of this Ordinance land shall be deemed to be unoccupied land where it is not proved that the beneficial use thereof for cultivation, habitation, the collection or storage of water or for any individual purpose has been had for a continuous period of at least twelve months in the period of seven years immediately prior to the publication of notice of intention to acquire.

Provided that where any person proves that he has been settled on land otherwise unoccupied for a period of six months prior to such date with the intention of permanently residing thereon the area occupied by such person shall be deemed to be occupied land.

The principal changes effected by the new section are:

(1) There is provision for compensation for the extinguishment of rights, even of a rather precarious nature, over lands that would strictly have been regarded as 'unoccupied lands' under the former Ordinance. These rights embrace those of fishing, hunting,

[1] See Pennington, J., and Combe, C.J., at pp. 22 and 23 and 29–30 respectively of 4 N. L. R. 18; Waddington, J., at p. 144 of 17 N. L. R. 142 (dealt with on pp. 74–5 and 80–1, *supra*).

grazing and the collection of *uncultivated* produce. Where such rights were communal, on the acquisition of the land the compensation money goes to the treasury of the native authority concerned.

(2) The old requirement as to continuous beneficial user of such lands for a period of at least six months during the period of ten years immediately preceding the publication of the notice of intention to acquire is now reduced to one of a period of at least twelve months in the period of seven years immediately prior to the publication of notice of intention to acquire. One naturally recalls here Pennington, J.'s, complaint against what he described as the 'intolerable burden' of requesting occupiers of *rural* lands around Agege and up the line to Abeokuta and similar areas of the Southern Provinces to show that their lands were occupied in the sense of the old s. 13 of the Ordinance.

(3) The conception of 'occupied land' is now extended to cover an unoccupied land on which any person may have been settled for six months prior to the date of the publication of notice, so long as he can show that he intends permanently to reside thereon.

With regard to the principles of awarding compensation, s. 5 of the Amending Ordinance of 1945 repeals s. 15 of the Principal Ordinance and substitutes a new one which in effect introduces these two main changes:

(*a*) It contains an express prohibition of payment of the additional allowance of ten per cent. usually made on account of the acquisition being compulsory. This is in consonance with the rulings of Mr. Justice Butler Lloyd in *The Commissioner of Lands* v. *Adeleye* [1] and again in *Chairman, Lagos Executive Development Board* v. *Joye* [2] in both of which the learned judge had disallowed the ten per cent. additional payment.

(*b*) The proviso to the new s. 15 enacts that, in awarding compensation for the acquisition of any land which was already occupied by or on behalf of the Crown under a title less than a fee simple, no regard will be had to any increase in the value of the land due to any improvements thereto or other works constructed thereon by or on behalf of the Crown. This goes beyond the previous provision that improvements to land due to such Government activities should be used to abate the amount of compensation.

[1] (1938), 14 N. L. R. 109.
[2] (1939), 15 N. L. R. 50.
The two cases have been discussed at pp. 77 and 79 respectively, *supra*.

6. UNSETTLED DISTRICTS

This category is to be carefully distinguished from the one just considered. It is entirely a creation of statute, there being no parallel to it in the indigenous system of landholding. The governing provisions are contained in the Unsettled Districts Ordinance No. 34 of 1916, an ordinance giving power to the Governor to declare certain parts of the Protectorate to be unsettled districts and to appropriate them for other purposes relating thereto.

The Governor may, by notice in the Gazette, declare any portion of the Protectorate to be an unsettled district.[1] Areas so declared may not be entered by any person except (i) natives of the district itself, (ii) Public Officers of Nigeria and (iii) persons holding a licence or having a general authority granted by the Governor on security by bond or deposit of money to enter such a district.[2] Any non-native may be ordered by the Governor to remove from an unsettled district or may be permitted to stay on conditions,[3] and the Governor enjoys the same right to deport anyone acting contrary to the provisions of this Ordinance as he does under the Criminal Code of Nigeria.[4] The mere presence of a person in an unsettled district shall be a *prima facie* evidence of contravention of the Ordinance unless that person proves the contrary.[5] The penalty for any contravention is six months' imprisonment or a fine of £50.[6]

Under the powers vested in him by s. 2 of the Ordinance the Officer Administering the Government has by requisite notice [7] declared the following places to be unsettled districts: certain areas of the Adamawa and Muri Divisions of the Adamawa Province, and a large section of the Dikwa Division of Bornu Province, all being in the Northern Provinces of the Protectorate of Nigeria.

This declaration also says that 'all previous notices declaring areas in the Northern Provinces (including those portions of the Cameroons under British Mandate situate in the Northern Provinces) to be Unsettled Districts are hereby cancelled'.

We may note in conclusion that mining in 'unsettled districts' is forbidden by s. 14 of the Minerals Ordinance of 1945.

---

[1] S. 2 of the Ordinance.   [2] Ss. 3 & 4.   [3] S. 5.
[4] S. 7.   [5] S. 8.   [6] S. 6.
[7] 1933 Supplement to *The Laws of Nigeria*, on p. 863 of the Volume.

7. FOREST RESERVES

Under the Forestry Ordinance No. 38 of 1937 the Government is empowered to set apart certain areas of the country as forest reserves. The procedure is that a Reserve Settlement Officer is appointed to enquire into and determine all claims affecting the land to be acquired, it being the duty of the officer to treat each claimant separately and to arrive at a finding on each particular claim. If the officer rejects a claim an aggrieved plaintiff has a right of appeal to the Court; if he accepts a claim, however, it is for the Government to decide whether or not to acquire the holder's rights by putting into motion the machinery of the Public Lands Acquisition Ordinance. The Reserve Settlement Officer, as a Commissioner of the Provincial Court, should not go beyond recording the boundaries of the proposed forest reserve and all the particulars of claims alleged or rights preferred in respect of the land in question. Thus in *Re Oban Group Reserve* [1] the Reserve Settlement Officer demarcated the boundaries of the land to be acquired, marked out certain enclaves therein and proceeded to clear the rest of the area of its sparse population. He compensated the inhabitants by allotting to them similar holdings within the enclaves. It was held that he had misconceived his duties as a purely *judicial* functionary and had treated the whole matter as an *executive* task: the Ordinance gave him no power to arrange adjustments of the land and its occupant as part of his business of adjudication of claims. What he had in fact done on this occasion was only in the interests of the Forestry Department who wanted an area as free as possible from inhabitants.

The effect of such reservation is that no one may thereafter build a house or reside therein, turn the soil or take forest produce. The Government may, however, mitigate any or all of these restrictions as it wishes.

[1] (1931), 10 N. L. R. 24.

Chapter Five

INDIGENOUS SYSTEMS OF TENURE

---

1. *General Features.* 2. *Detailed Analysis of Rights in Land—Problems stated.* 3. *A Chief's Powers over Land:* (1) *The Chief as the Authority over Village Land;* (2) *The Chief as Family Head with respect to Land.*

---

1. GENERAL FEATURES

IN a country like Nigeria with so vast a land area and with such a diversity of tribes and cultural patterns it is obvious that no more than a broad outline of the general permanent features of indigenous systems of tenure can be attempted here. The reasons for this rather cautious approach are mainly two: (*a*) the local laws and customs with respect to land, in addition to being an unwritten law, vary from place to place in certain peculiar details; (*b*) the number of specialised studies of them is not large nor has there been any coherent, integrated account of the piecemeal but very able monographs and chapters hitherto written on the subject by sociologists, anthropologists and others.[1]

---

[1] Notable among such studies are: Ward Price, *Land Tenure in the Yoruba Provinces* (1933); C. K. Meek, *Law and Authority in a Nigerian Tribe* (1937); M. M. Green, *Land Tenure in an Ibo Village* (1941); C. K. Meek, *The Northern Tribes of Nigeria* (1925); C. K. Meek, *Tribal Studies in Northern Nigeria* (1931); C. W. Alexander, *Memorandum on the Subject of Land Tenure in the Colony & Protectorate of Southern Nigeria*, 1910; E. A. Speed, *Report on Land Tenure in Ibadan* (1916); Daryll Forde, 'Land, Labour & Diet in a Cross River Village', in *Geographical Journal*, July 1937; West African Lands Committee, *Minutes of Evidence*, Colonial Library, African 1047 (1912–14); N. Thomas, *Anthropological Report on the Ibo-speaking Peoples of Nigeria*, 6 Vols. (1913–14); Sir Donald Cameron, *A Note on Land Tenure in the Yoruba Provinces* (1933); Northern Nigeria Lands Committee: Cmds. 5102

But these field-workers, with few exceptions, are all too apt, probably from the necessity of their case, to treat their several areas of study as so many isolated social and political units and therefore to emphasize divergencies at the expense of such un-doubted similarities of concept and land usage as there are. On the other hand, the evidence which one gets from a comparative estimate of their studies, as also of the available data from judicial decisions, points to a large measure of common basic principles which underlie indigenous systems of tenure in various parts of Nigeria.

For our present purpose, which is strictly legal, we will attempt first a general statement of the main principles of land tenure, followed by a more detailed examination of the rules which the law reports as well as the specialised studies just referred to so far make possible.

There is probably no more convenient and authoritative starting point than the following general exposition of Viscount Haldane in the leading case of *Amodu Tijani* v. *Secry., Southern Nigeria* [1] in the course of his delivering the judgment of the Privy Council: [2]

'The next fact which is important to bear in mind in order to understand the native land law is that the notion of individual ownership is quite foreign to native ideas. Land belongs to the community, the village or the family, never to the individual. All the members of the community, village or family have an equal right to the land, but in every case the Chief or Headman of the community or village, or head of the family, has charge of the land, and in loose mode of speech is sometimes called the owner. He is to some extent in the position of a trustee, and as such holds the land for the use of the community or family. He has control of

and 5103 of 1910; S. F. Nadel, *A Black Byzantium* (1942); M. M. Green, *Ibo Village Affairs* (1947), Chaps. IV, XII and XIII; Sir Percy Girouard, *Memo. on Land Tenure & Land Revenue Assessment in Northern Nigeria* (1908) (Colonial Office Legal Folio 11714); Gollan (C.J. of Northern Nigeria), 'Notes on Land Tenure in Northern Nigeria' (*Journal of Soc. of Comparative Leg.*, Vol. 4, 1902, pp. 164–7); Raymond Firth, *Social Problems & Research in British West Africa*, Part II (A paragraph on 'Studies in Land Tenure'), (*Africa*, Vol. 17, No. 3 of July 1947, at pp. 173–4); J. S. Harris, 'Papers on the Economic Aspect of Life among the Ozuitem Ibo' (*Africa*, Vol. 14, No. 1 of January 1943, pp. 21 and 22).

[1] 1921, A. C. 399.

[2] At p. 404 (ibid.), cited from Rayner's, C.J., *Report on Land Tenure in West Africa* (1898).

it, and any member who wants a piece of it to cultivate or build upon, goes to him for it. But the land so given still remains the property of the community or family. He cannot make any important disposition of the land without consulting the elders of the community or family, and their consent must in all cases be given before a grant can be made to a stranger. This is a pure native custom along the whole length of this coast, and wherever we find, as in Lagos, individual owners, this is again due to the introduction of English ideas. But the native idea still has a firm hold on the people, and in most cases, even in Lagos, land is held by the family. This is so even in cases of land purporting to be held under Crown grants and English conveyances. The original grantee may have held as an individual owner, but on his death all his family claim interest, which is always recognised, and thus the land becomes again family land. My experience in Lagos leads me to the conclusion that except where land has been bought by the present owner there are very few natives who are individual owners of land.' [1]

This summary description, subject to the qualifications to be made presently, forms a useful basis for a more precise analysis of the situation. The general outline calls, however, for these special comments and amplifications:

(1) The first point arising from our quotation is that land is not ordinarily owned in fee simple by individuals, but by (*a*) a *community*, which usually embraces a congeries of kindred village-groups, or (*b*) a *village*, which is roughly made up of kin-groups

---

[1] This succinct outline of features of Nigerian tenure bears comparison with similar summaries by legal, as well as non-legal writers and investigators. See, e.g., C. W. Alexander, Commissioner of Lands, at p. 122–42 of *Minutes of Evidence* before the West African Lands Committee (Colonial Office Library, 13080 folio), particularly, paras. 3563–7; A. W. Osborne, Chief Justice of Southern Nigeria, at pp. 515–28 of *Minutes of Evidence* before the same Committee on Wednesday, 16 July 1913; paras. 14952–8; *West African Lands Committee's Report* (itself), paras. 88–101; C. W. Alexander, *Memo. on Native Land Tenure* (Colonial Office Legal Pamphlet, Vol. I, Folio No. 26 of 1910), particularly, paras. 1–16; Gollan, C.J., of Northern Nigeria, 'Notes on Land Tenure in the North', at pp. 164–7 of *Journal of Society of Comparative Legislation*, Vol. 4, 1902; A. K. Ajisafe, *Laws and Customs of the Yoruba People* (1924), especially paras. 4–9 of Chap. IV and Chap. IX (p. 27); C. K. Meek, *Law and Authority in a Nigerian Tribe*, (1937) pp. 100–4, 98; Sir Percy Girouard, *Memo. on Land Tenure in the North* (Colonial Office Legal Folio 11714 of 1908), especially paras. 2–26; M. M. Green, *Land Tenure in an Ibo Village* (1941), Chap. IV; S. F. Nadel, *A Black Byzantium* (1941), pp. 181–190, 200–1.

of families or extended-families forming a kind of local aggregate of 'communes', or (c) a *family* which, as the smallest social unit in the indigenous polity, is variously composed of a man, his wife or wives, their children, their grown-up sons and the wives and children of these, the man's brothers or close cousins and their wives and children.[1]

It is to be noted, however, that the real unit of land-holding is the family, and that the ascription of ownership of land to the community or the village is only accurate if viewed as a social aggregate. For, even within the community or the village, actual occupation and control are decentralised, so to speak, and the family, rather than the community or village, in fact exercise acts of ownership. The chief interest of the community or village in the land is the purely social and political one of maintaining group solidarity. The communal aspect of certain forms of social observance like ancestral worship, joint grazing of cattle by groups on some common grounds, etc., often imperfectly understood by some Europeans, has led to the erroneous idea that land is also jointly owned by the so-called village communities.[2]

(2) Secondly, the chief or headman of a community or village or the head of a family exercises a right of control over land as a trustee on behalf of the particular group he represents, and from him permission has to be obtained before grants of land are made whether to members or to 'strangers'.

(3) Thirdly, the essentially family character of land-holding is reflected in the facts (a) that grants to individual members of the group or to strangers leave the ultimate title in the family, (b) that land formerly held as an individual owner by a grantee under a Crown grant or an English conveyance devolves on his death upon all members of his family whose rights therein are recognised by local law and custom.

(4) Fourthly, a member of a community or family to whom land has been allocated by the head man cannot make any important disposition of his allotment without the consent of such a head or of elders of the community. That is, there is no right of alienation

---

[1] See, e.g., Meek, *Law & Authority in a Nigerian Tribe*, p. 88 (Ibos); C. W. Alexander, *Memo. on Land Tenure in Northern Nigeria, passim*; Meek, *Tribal Studies in Northern Nigeria, passim*; S. F. Nadel, *A Block Byzantium*, p. 30; *Ward Price*, para. 7 (Yorubas); M. M. Green, *Land Tenure*, Chap. II, para. 5.

[2] For a criticism of this assumption of Sir Henry Maine in his *The Origin and Growth of Village Communities in India* (1899), see A. S. Diamond's *Primitive Law* (1935), pp. 275-6.

inter vivos or by death, except such as local law and custom permits.

(5) Fifthly, wherever individuals now hold lands in their own right, as for example they do in Lagos, Abeokuta, Ibadan, Onitsha and Calabar, this is usually due to the importation of English ideas of land law wholly foreign to indigenous tenurial systems. This explanation of the phenomenon of individual ownership, like that of its congener—alienability of land, is only true in a broad sense; for even at the time of the British occupation of the country, the pressure of population upon land was already forcing the process of social change so that dealings in land in a crude economic sense had begun in certain crowded areas,[1] since subsistence economy was already proving unequal to the new demands of an increasingly complex society. We shall have occasion to deal with this point in a later chapter.

Our next task will be to attempt to delimit, so far as this is possible in the light of decided cases and other reliable sources, the exact scope and content of these generalised elements of Nigerian tenure. But before we go on to examine the somewhat tangled web of the social and economic organisation regarding land and the respective rights and obligations of chiefs, family heads and individuals (whether free-born, slave or stranger) it may be necessary to make a few preliminary observations on some of the terms and expressions commonly used by writers to describe indigenous systems of tenure.

'*Communal*.' We start, then, by observing that when land is said to be held in 'communal ownership', it is not in fact usually 'communal' nor is there any real 'ownership' of it, at least in the sense in which we ordinarily employ these terms in English law. In the first place, the relation between the group and the land they hold is invariably complex, since the rights of individuals and of the group with respect to the same piece of land often co-exist within the same social context. Lands described as communal often embrace both those in which individual members of the group hold clearly recognised rights and those over which no claim of right is ever asserted whether by groups or by individuals. In the second place, the term 'communal' has even been applied to lands like sacred groves and other fetish lands, market-sites, magico-religious grounds and houses, dumping grounds of the village, churches and

---

[1] See, e.g., T. R. Batten, *Problems of African Development*, Part I—'Land and Labour', pp. 25, 31–2; M. M. Green, *Land Tenure*, p. 36; C. K. Meek, *Land Law and Custom in the Colonies*, p. 300.

mosques and lands surrounding these—all of which are best described as 'public'[1] rather than 'communal'.[2]

'*Individual*.' Equally important it is to remember that 'individual' has been applied rather indifferently to parcels of land ranging from those over which only limited inalienable rights of user are claimed by individuals to those carrying absolute freehold titles. But to the extent to which individual rights exist only within the context of the wider claims of the group or kin, land-holding assumes a communal character under the supervisory or administrative authority of the head man.

Further, the communal nature of land-holding is again limited in at least two respects: (1) individuals are normally entitled to the products of the soil, the results of their own labour and exertion, and there is no collective claim to these; (2) the chief has no right, even under ancient customary tenure, of continuous control or detailed supervision over any land which has once been granted to a family, or to an individual, whose right of enjoyment and user cannot be lightly disturbed unless for good cause shown.

'*Ownership*.' Care must also be taken in applying the word 'ownership' to the complex scheme of relations between the Nigerian and the soil. Under the customary law of tenure there is no conception of land-holding comparable to the English idea of a fee simple absolute in possession.[3] The average occupier has something analogous to a possessory title which he, however, enjoys in perpetuity and which gives him powers of user and disposition scarcely distinguishable from those of an absolute freeholder, except that he cannot alienate his holding so as to divest himself and his family of the right to ultimate title. We will expand this in the proper place later.[4]

---

[1] In fact, they have been so described, e.g., by A. K. Ajisafe, op. cit., Chap. IV, para. 21 (*a*) (*b*) (*c*); C. K. Meek, *Law and Authority*, p. 100; W. Price, op. cit., para. 28; Nadel op. cit. p. 91.

[2] Of course, lands for grazing of cattle by mutual agreements between members of groups, etc., are often collectively held, particularly in rural areas.

On pp. 269–73 of A. S. Diamond's *Primitive Law*, the writer speaks of 'public property in land' as also 'communal property' and gives as illustrations 'passage-way, drawing of water, the taking of unused land, and hunting'. But from his later criticism of Maine on pp. 275–6, it seems clear that his views are in line with our own in this respect.

[3] Although, under the English law of Property, the Crown is the only true owner of land.

[4] These problems have been considered by the following among other observers: Lord Lugard, *Dual Mandate*, p. 316 ff.; Hailey, *An African Survey*, p. 834 ff.; Malinowski, *Coral Gardens and their Magic*, Vol. I, p. 379 ff.;

'Tribal.' Finally, one has to be wary of expressions like 'tribal tenure' for exactly the same reasons as those just advanced in the case of so-called 'communal ownership'. The unit of land-holding in Nigeria, as indeed throughout West Africa, is not the tribe, but the family. To speak, therefore, of *tribal* ownership or *tribal* tenure is to indulge in the popular fallacy of those writers like Sir Henry Maine who see in early as in modern agricultural communities only a rudimentary social organisation in which the conception of family property in land is a late arrival in history.[1]

It is, therefore, no less misleading to describe Nigerian land as in *tribal tenure* than it is to say that it belongs to *village communities*. If we must continue to use the more orthodox word 'communal', which is hardly less inapposite, we have to remember all the time that it is only accurate in the qualified sense already stated.

2. DETAILED ANALYSIS OF RIGHTS IN, TO OR OVER LAND—PROBLEMS STATED

We may now make some close study of the particular rights and obligations with respect to land of Nigerian (*a*) Kings, (*b*) Emirs, (*c*) Chiefs, (*d*) Village Headmen, (*e*) Family Heads, (*f*) Individuals (free-born), (*g*) Slaves and (*h*) strangers. There has been, so far as the present writer is aware, no systematic analysis by any previous writer on Nigerian land tenure of the respective powers and duties which these classes of people undoubtedly have regarding land, although the need for such more or less precise definition was not less urgent before.

R. Firth, *Primitive Economics of the New Zealand Maori*, p. 331 ff.; F. M. Keesing, *The South Seas in the Modern World*, p. 99.

[1] See, e.g., V. Liversage, *Land Tenure in the Colonies* (1945), where the learned author consistently describes colonial lands as under 'tribal tenure', 'feudal tenure', etc. (especially in Chaps. II, III and IX).

Similarly, C. W. Alexander, in his Memorandum on the subject of *Native Land Tenure in the Colony and Protectorate of Southern Nigeria* (Colonial Office Legal Pamphlet, Vol. I, Folio No. 26, 1910), after stating that the basic unit is family ownership goes on to say (in para. 1): 'It will probably be found, at any rate in the less developed regions of the Eastern and Central Provinces, that the ownership of land is vested in the whole village community whose powers have been delegated to a chief man assisted by a Council of Elders.' But, thanks to the researches of Meek, Daryll Forde and M. M. Green, we know what value to attach to this Mainesque postulate about Eastern Nigeria, even in 1910.

See, particularly, Miss M. M. Green's *Ibo Village Affairs*, Chap. IV, pp. 33–4.

It is not, of course, to be supposed that the institution of King-ship, Emirship and Chiefship is a universal concept in Nigeria. Sometimes, the final political and sociological authority over the land of a given community is called the Emir, as in the Northern Provinces; sometimes, he is called the King or Oba (or even Obi, as he is called in places like Onitsha, Agbor, Asaba and others), as in the Western and some Eastern Provinces; at other times, the administrative unit is the Council of Elders, as in certain parts of the Eastern Provinces wherever the political organisation is still so amorphous and the society still so atomistic[1] that the people have yet to attain the necessary social cohesion which alone makes pos-sible the existence of a unified, centralised authority like a para-mount chief or even a king.[2]

Miss M. M. Green has noted the absence of even a Council of Elders in the Eastern Provincial village of Umueke-Agbaja.[3] But she has also [4] described a ceremony of land-allotment by a conference of elders of the village at which the customary tributes were paid by the allottees of land. However rudimentary this might seem, it is submitted that the germ of the normal arrangement is there present. In the more politically developed Hausa and Yoruba areas as also in parts of the East, for example, in Calabar and Owerri, the central authority is permanent and fairly constant. In the less developed areas of the East, however, authority is vested perhaps in *ad hoc* bodies more or less inconstant but never-theless obeyed and recognised by the people.

It is thus clear that whatever the difference in nomenclature and in spite of the varying degrees of political and cultural levels of the several ethnic groups in Nigeria, there is a comparable uniformity, in essentials, of the privileges and responsibilities of the governing or administrative authorities over land and its use.

Certain Autocratic Rulers and the Land. We must also briefly

---

[1] But this may easily be exaggerated and inaccurate inference drawn therefrom. See Chubb's *Ibo Land Tenure* and a criticism of it by C. W. Rowling, in his *Notes on Land Tenure in Benin, etc.* (1948), para. 123.

[2] Mr. Temple, in para. 22 of Sir P. Girouard's Memoranda on *Land Tenure in the North*, op. cit., reported as follows: 'In cases where no such paramount chief exists, this power will invariably be found, I think, to have been vested in some kind of Council, and as far as native rights in land are concerned I cannot find that any radical difference exists between the customs obtaining in the pagan and in the Mohamnedan States. . . .'

[3] See her *Land Tenure in an Ibo Village*, Chap. IV, p. 6, and also her *Ibo Village Affairs*, pp. 33–4, 36.

[4] At pp. 13 and 14 of *Land Tenure in an Ibo Village*.

take account of the fact that in some very powerful kingdoms and
emirates certain autocratic rulers have sometimes arrogated to
themselves such absolute rights in or over lands properly belonging
to their people as amounted to virtual expropriation. Such, for
example, was the claim previously asserted by Bini kings (or, Oba)
over Benin land, with a corollary that wellnigh confused the
real nature of King Docemo's rights in Lagos land at the time of
the cession.[1] To this cause also has been due much of the misconception concerning lands in the Northern Emirates where it was
thought by British negotiators of treaties with the Emirs that these
local rulers in fact enjoyed such absolute rights in land under
Islamic law as virtually entitled them to convey the fee simple
therein to the Royal Niger Company.[2]

Fear of a re-assertion of such unwarranted claims by any
modern or future Nigerian ruler was expressed by the West
African Lands Committee during its sitting on Wednesday, 16
July 1913, when it suggested the passing by Government of protective legislation.[3] Chief Justice C. W. Osborne, however, replied
in his evidence before the Committee that he did not consider any
legislation was necessary.[4] It is a far cry from those days of uncertainty and ignorance of local land tenure to these when judicial
decisions and specialised studies have combined to increase our
knowledge of the real nature of the indigenous systems. No local
ruler, it is thought, would now prefer such a claim.

All this is not, of course, to deny the rights to land of these local
potentates which they might otherwise possess in virtue of their

---

[1] See Chap. II, p. 9, et seq., *supra.*

In this connexion it is noteworthy that paras. 348, 366, 368 and 372 of
Ward Price's *Land Tenure in the Yoruba Provinces* (1933) speak of all land in
Benin as ('belonging') to the Oba while at the same time stressing how he could
not deprive a subject of his land with impunity. A useful corrective is con-
tained in paras. 5, 6, 9 and 19 of C. W. Rowling's *Notes on Land Tenure in
Benin, etc.* (1948).

[2] See Chap. III, p. 28 et seq., *supra.*

Also, Lord Hailey, *An African Survey*, pp. 830–3, also p. 853.

It is understandable that in the halcyon days of Benin efflorescence in art
and native culture and in the almighty Hausa-Fulani dynasties of Sudanese
civilisation, such high-handed claims could have been asserted by the several
rulers whose hands would, no doubt, have been greatly strengthened by the
pride of conquest or by a superior alien culture superimposed upon the
indigenous stock. The Binis are said to have come from Ife.

[3] See Question No. 14956 on p. 528 of the Minutes of Evidence of the
Committee.

[4] Ibid., Questions and Answers Nos. 14957–8.

being heads of their respective ruling families whether as caretakers or as trustees, in the sense presently to be described for chiefs and other family heads. *A fortiori*, they may quite properly claim lands acquired by their individual exertions, at any rate in these days of budding individual ownership in many parts of the country.

Royal Estates. Before we leave these general remarks about the special relation to land of Emirs and Kings or Obas we must notice the related matter of what are called *Royal Estates.* These were formerly, and in some cases still are, lands attached to certain offices of State like those of the Emirs and some paramount chiefs in the Northern Provinces and of Kings or Obas and paramount chiefs in parts of the Southern Provinces where such offices exist, although in the latter areas the lands are usually called by the picturesque name of 'royal estates'. These estates are quite separate and distinct from lands held by the family as a whole, to which the king or chief also has the usual rights of a member.

The important feature of all these official lands is that they were permanently attached to the official head, to certain ruling houses and to important chieftaincies whether (1) by right of first occupation or of conquest, as in the case of royal families whose heads originally founded the new site or subjugated the former occupiers, or (2) as rewards by some conquering leaders to some henchmen or warriors for military services [1] or (3) to buttress the reputation of the overlords by endowing loyal sub-chiefs with gifts of lands for political reasons. In some cases again, the family or community bestowed houses and surrounding lands upon their head chief for the purely psychological purpose of enhancing his prestige and authority over the group.

But it is not strictly correct to describe these estates, as does Dr. Nadel in the case of the three royal estates of Nupe,[2] as implying 'absolute and permanent ownership'. While it is true that 'it implies more than merely the "administrative" control over family land that is vested in the family head', it does not connote any proprietary right in the living occupant of the throne such as an absolute owner normally enjoys. The office-holder had a sort of life estate descendible, not to his personal heir under customary law, but only to his official successor, whoever that might be.[3]

---

[1] Lord Hailey, *An African Survey* (1946), p. 853.

[2] See his *A Black Byzantium*, p. 198.

[3] For the Yoruba areas, see Ward Price's *Land Tenure*, op. cit., paras. 78, 80–82.

It seems that what are usually called 'stool lands' [1] on the Gold Coast compare well with these Nigerian 'royal estates'. In the West African Court of Appeal case of *Quarm v. Yankah II* [2] relating to the Gold Coast, Deane, C.J., in his judgment (in which the other two associate judges concurred), observed: '. . . the conception of the Stool that is and has always been accepted in the Courts of this Colony is that it is an entity which never dies, a corporation sole like the Crown, and that while the occupants of the Stool may come and go the Stool goes on for ever.' [3]

Along with this one may consider the remark [4] of Lord Haldane in the *cause célèbre* of *Amodu Tijani v. Secretary, Southern Nigeria,* [5] the Apapa land case in Lagos: 'Their Lordships doubt whether any really definite distinction is connoted by the expression "stool lands". It probably means little more than lands which the chief holds in his representative or constitutional capacity, as distinguished from land which he and his own family hold individually.' [6]

With respect to Sokoto Province Mr. Temple, as Administrative Officer in charge, reported as follows in 1908: 'Apparently, though there is no proof as yet available, certain areas of cultivated land are held by Emirs or their Courts. These in the past used to be worked by slaves. Some are probably attached to the office held, though it would appear that private and individual rights are asserted in others.' [7] Later still: 'The "gandu" or State farm goes with the office, and was formerly farmed with the free labour of villagers. Important Chiefs also have a good deal of personal chattels attached to their offices and these, like the *gandu*, descend to successive holders'. [8] Mr. Palmer's parallel finding in the case of Kano Province was: 'In the Hausa States there never were any regal lands till two years ago, except the emir's farm (say twenty acres).' [9]

---

[1] It should be noted, however, that on the Gold Coast, 'stool lands' are lands belonging to the community and are classified into the *two* types of (i) *Family* stool lands, and (ii) *Town* stool lands, each being made up of stool land proper and stool farm.

[2] (1930), 1 W. A. C. A. 80.

[3] The learned C.J. also cited J. M. Sarbah's *Fanti Customary Law*, p. 56.

[4] (1921), 2 A. C. 399, at p. 410.

[5] Idem.

[6] By 'individually' in this context His Lordship must be taken to mean 'corporately'.

[7] See p. 4, para. 2 of Sir Percy Girouard's Memoranda on *Land Tenure in Northern Nigeria* (1908).

[8] Para. 22, ibid.   [9] Para. 23, idem.

In the olden days, then, these so-called 'royal estates' were worked by slave-labour, with hamlets and sometimes whole villages planted over parts of the estates for the royal slaves' habitation, the heads of whom were usually given some other parcels of land for their private cultivation and sustenance. In such cases, the office-holder took all the produce. But very often these estates were left in the occupation of slaves, or of members of the particular royal house, or of other members of the village [1] or even 'strangers', all but the second category of whom had often to pay anything up to a third of the annual produce of the estate to the reigning overlord, keeping the rest for their labour in cultivation.[2] What was taken or left to the settlers on these estates depended on the whims and caprice of the particular occupant of the office at the time. The office-holder might abandon all claim to 'tithe' from the settlers on the estate and only require them to assist in keeping his house and land in good repair as well as helping by communal labour with the first annual cultivation; those who took part in this way were not paid as such, but they were invariably fed and entertained during the process.[3]

Change has, however, set in on the so-called royal estates. For example, many of them have been abandoned to various types of settlers and claims are no longer made by the royal or paramount overlords. The introduction of mixed farming on some of them has also altered the character of the occupation and the nature of services incidental to them. Subjects now frequently demand to be paid wages for such new species of services so radically different from the customary incidents of their tenure. Even where the estates are still under the control of the title-holder and no change has been introduced to alter the form of tenure, the people would now rather subscribe money towards the cost of hired labour in lieu of their traditional personal services.

An interesting point has been recorded by Dr. Nadel of a Nupe custom according to which, when land is 'given' to a 'stranger', fruit-bearing trees remain the property of the grantor who has the power to come on the land and collect the fruits even after the

---

[1] See para. 81 of W. Price's *Land Tenure in Yorubaland*, for an Ife incident in Yoruba-land where the then Oni of Ife felt obliged to disband a village which had sprung up on his official estate, members of which were using the Oni's name to oppress the people of Ife.

[2] Cf. S. F. Nadel, *A Black Byzantium*, p. 199.

[3] Cf. Ward Price's *Land Tenure*, para. 80, with S. F. Nadel's *A Black Byzantium*, p. 199, and the basic similarity of practice between Yoruba-land and Nupe-land in the North becomes obvious.

land has in this way changed hands. Thus, when, in 1936, the Government purchased the royal estate of the Etsu Masaba outside the Wuya gate of Bida as the site of the new official residence of the Emir, the land became Crown land but the family of the Etsu Masaba continue to collect the fruits of the trees thereon.[1]

Enough has now been said about royal estates except for one final word on Benin. It is significant that no actual system of royal estates has so far been specifically described for Benin by any writer. This is probably because the Oba's erstwhile claim to the whole of the land of Benin City as also to one-third of the country land [2] has made it unnecessary to appropriate any particular area as a 'royal estate' where the Oba has taken the entire Benin land to be his province. Nevertheless, the only royal house in Benin has always reserved lands of a description not dissimilar to those which we have just described for the North and other areas of the South.

By way of summary, then, we see that the Kings or Obas or Obis as well as the Emirs do not have a *de facto* proprietary title to the land over which they rule,[3] but that in the North as in many areas of the South certain lands referred to above as 'royal estates' were formerly attached to certain regal offices for political, military or sociological reasons and limited to the life of the holder at any one time. Concurrent rights of a miscellaneous character were sometimes enjoyed by members of the ruling house in these estates, and slaves and strangers were often settled upon them with or without payment of 'tithes'. Customary personal services of the villagers towards the cultivation and farming of the estates have in many cases now ceased to be rendered, and have even been commuted into money payments as the individual's share of the cost of any hired labour that might be employed by the overlord.

Apart from these royal estates and such other lands held by the family in which the head would naturally share, a natural ruler's role in land matters is thus the symbolic one of being the embodiment of the common consciousness of the people as the final administrative authority over land. His is a kind of sovereign oversight which does not connote ownership of the land. The theory is that the individual receives his allocation from his family head who derives his authority from the chief, who in his turn, has had

[1] S. F. Nadel, op. cit., pp. 199–200.

[2] See paras. 346 and 368 of W. Price, op. cit.

[3] Even on the Gold Coast, the king does not *own* the land of the State over which he enjoys paramountcy: Caseley Hayford's *Native Institutions*, p. 45.

delegated to him the supreme controlling power of the Oba or Emir. In practice the Oba or Emir or even the paramount chief is rarely consulted in the general minor dispositions of land held by the family. Such is the democratic if because also pluralistic basis of indigenous Nigerian society.

3. A CHIEF'S POWERS OVER LAND

The question we want to agitate now is not one of the general political powers and sociological role of the Chief as such but the more limited if specialised one of analysing the real nature and scope of a chief's customary rights and duties as regards land and its incidents of tenure. What we are going to say relates broadly to those common features of chieftaincy respecting land in Northern as well as in Southern Nigeria (wherever there is such an institution), and the judicial findings to be recorded later must be taken to represent what research, judicial as well as anthropological, has so far disclosed without any claim to comprehensiveness or finality.

Now, any legal consideration of the relation of a chief to the land must have two aspects: (1) the chief's general supervisory function over the village land as the authority allocating land to new families and to strangers; and (2) the chief's position considered as a family head with such ordinary rights in or over land as are enjoyed by the normal member of a family in addition, of course, to his special administrative status with respect to the whole land.[1] This functional dichotomy naturally involves some overlapping in so far as the chief's prerogatives in administering the land of the community as a whole bear a close similarity to those which he exercises over his own family land in his representative capacity. But it makes for clarity and convenience of treatment to state the *two* aspects separately: (1) the Chief as the Authority over Village Land; and (2) the Chief as Family Head with respect to Land.

(1) *The Chief as the Authority over Village Land*

In this connexion it is useful to remember that the chief derives by delegation, actual or implied, his authority from the paramount

---

[1] This role of the chief is again independent of and apart from his right to the so-called royal or other *ex officio* estates that may be attached to his particular post.

N.L.L.C.—9

chief of the particular district who again owes his own position to the ultimate authority of the King or the Emir.

The chief's task, then, is the allocation of land to the various families in the village or town through their respective heads and, where a family becomes extinct through failure of heirs or upon abandonment by former occupiers of the land, his is the duty to re-allocate it to new holders. In the interval between an allocation which has thus lapsed and the subsequent re-allocation by the chief, there is a clearly recognised right of reversion in the chief who, as the representative of the community, holds the lapsed land along with the general virgin, fallow and forest lands until fresh need arises for their disposal. For such allocations and re-allocations chiefs [1] formerly enjoyed and still sometimes enjoy rights to tribute in the form of part of the annual produce from the land, not indeed as a token of recognition of the chiefs' ownership of the land allocated but merely as an earnest of the grantee's *bona fides* to acknowledge that he is not himself claiming as owner, and also as an expression of his gratitude for the bounty thus conferred. These annual tithes are of course distinct from gifts of corn, palm wine, gin or other viands which invariably accompany any original grants of land all over Nigeria.

In some cases, it may be that one community having enough land and to spare agrees to settle another community on part of its vacant lands; when that happens, tributes in the form of tithes are for much the same reasons as those just stated usually demanded and paid by the 'guest' community to the 'host' community. These tributes are called 'ishakole' in Yorubaland,[2] 'akorhore' in Benin,[3] 'zakka' or 'dzanka' in the Northern areas; and, as we shall soon see, tributes or tithes are also paid in many areas of the East with chieftaincy systems or the usual Council of Elders.

These grants of land by chiefs to 'stranger' settlers were (and are) often made in perpetuity but inalienable and, where the amount of the tributes paid to the chiefs by the individual or group grantees had been large, rights of a proprietary nature have recently been claimed by certain donees who seem to have assimi-

[1] e.g. 'The Lagos chiefs, the landowners (e.g. Oloto, Ojora, Oluwa, etc.), each receive an annual tribute of 5s. per head from anyone who takes or settles on his land for farming purposes'.—A. K. Ajisafe, op. cit., Chap. IX, p. 27.

[2] As to whether 'ishakole' is Rent or Tribute, see pp. 197–9 later.

[3] The Benin equivalent of a chief is 'Enogie' and to him or the Village Council the 'akorhore' is usually paid.

lated the customary nominal dues to the position of purchase price
on account of the new economic values of land. No such land may
be re-assigned by the grantees without the prior consent and
approval of the chief and his council of elders. The right of short,
temporary lettings to others is often allowed to grantees in these
circumstances, but any long let or any important disposal of the
land requires the chief's formal sanction.

In addition to these tithes chiefs, when they make grants of
land whether to members of their community or to strangers,
sometimes reserve to themselves under the local law rights to
economic trees, as in Bida,[1] to game killed in hunting by the
allottees, and to fish caught in streams and rivulets flowing through
allocated lands, as in many areas of Nigeria.[2] But, normally,
grants to chiefs carry with them the rights of the grantees to the
trees, wells, rivulets and similar interests attaching to the land
allotted, although reservations are sometimes made in favour of
the original planters of economic trees or permanent crops. Again,
the chief's permission is sometimes required before certain trees
may be cut down or destroyed, at least in the early stages of
settlement.

Lands abandoned by previous occupiers may only be freely
re-allocated by the chief if they do not form sites of former houses
or if they were not formerly planted with economic trees or permanent crops. The existence of these would raise a presumption
that their owners might still wish to return to the land; strong
evidence is often needed to rebut the presumption. It seems that
the period of permitted abeyance during which previous occupiers
of land might be allowed to resume their occupation of it varies
with the locality; but Dr. Nadel's observation[3] with regard to
Nupe territory in the North is at one with Ward Price's[4] about
Yorubaland (including Benin) that non-user for a minimum period
of three years constitutes a valid ground for regarding the rights
of occupiers of land as having lapsed, so that the chief could often
make fresh allocations of it thereafter.

There remains to be considered the chief's right of eviction of
settled occupiers for grave political or criminal offences. Since the
original grant of land, whether to a local or to a 'stranger' family

[1] Nadel, op. cit., p. 187.
[2] e.g. A. K. Ajisafe, op. cit., Chap. IV, Nadel, op. cit., pp. 46–7.
[3] Nadel, op. cit., p. 186.
[4] W. Price, op. cit., paras. 86, 96, etc.; also, C. W. Rowling, *Note on Land in Benin, etc.*, paras. 20 and 41.

or community, must be taken to have been conditional upon the grantee's acceptance of allegiance to the Emir or Oba as well as upon continued good behaviour in consonance with the requirements of public order and welfare, it is only natural that a breach of such conditions should entail a forfeiture of what is after all the offender's mere right of occupancy. Another cause of forfeiture is the cesser of payment of the traditional tributes to the chief by the grantee, in as much as such deliberate with-holding is looked upon as a virtual claim to ownership on the grantee's part. It would seem also that the chief may take up and re-allocate lands granted to strangers but which are not being put to full or profitable use, though the extent of this right is at best indefinite; much would appear to depend on the circumstances of the case in any particular area.

But eviction or banishment for any proper cause does not ordinarily carry with it forfeiture of the offending grantee's right to his crops and other permanent improvements like houses, since these are the results of his own personal labour and exertion. All he has forfeited by his truculence or contumely is the right of occupation of the land, the only subject of the grant by the chief. Sometimes, even a banished allottee's land is allowed to remain in his family or in at least those of the family as have not sided with the offender. Confiscation of the entire land might result from the whole family or community being involved in the opprobrium of its head, though local ideas are extremely liberal in these matters and chiefs and elders rarely order a complete disestablishment of the whole group.

One other important function of the chief is the adjudication of land disputes as between members of the community over whom he holds sway. This is his internal juridical prerogative, buttressed by the co-operation and loyalty of the village elders. On the external side, the chief answers for his own group with other chiefs in the settlement of boundary disputes and in the demarcation of fishing and hunting rights of one community vis-à-vis another or other communities. In this way is maintained the social equilibrium so necessary to an orderly and peaceful enjoyment of the land. Thus it is also that the chief justifies his claim to tributes and other traditional perquisites.

The chief, therefore, has the style of a protecting authority and not that of the owner of the land. As the representative of his Emir or Oba, he allocates and re-allocates land to his people, and his consent is necessary to any important disposal of allotted lands, especially to 'strangers'. He receives tributes for his super-visory oversight, and may eject or evict grantees for good and sometimes bad reasons. The reversion of all lapsed or unoccupied lands is in him as the legal or juristic representative of his com-munity. Land once granted by a chief is to all intents and purposes beyond his care, so long as the grantee does not break any im-portant condition of his occupancy; therefore, as regards the general internal disposal of the allotted land as between the mem-bers of a group or family, the umpire is unsighted. This constitutes an important qualification of the chief's powers over land. He is neither more nor less than the caretaker, protector, administrator or trustee of the land which really belongs to his community. That is why the chief has no right to alienate such land without the consent of all the elders of the community.

(2) *The Chief as Family Head with Respect to Land (including an Ordinary Family Head)*

Let us note from the outset that the chief's role with regard to his own family land differs in no material respect from that of any other head of an ordinary family or extended family. It will, therefore, be convenient to describe the two together here; what follows then applies to both, so that much of what has just been said for the chief as the administrator of the land of the whole community equally applies to the chief considered as a head of a household. But, because chieftaincy and headship of a family do not often or necessarily coincide, there are a certain number of features in the land arrangement which are peculiar to the family head as such. We will for that reason proceed to give a brief description of these features.

A distinction must be made between town and country lands. Let us consider the latter first, as being more instructive from the point of view of the indigenous system.

Farmlands. In the villages or rural areas, the family head (who is not also a chief) usually has the right to take any as yet unappro-priated land in his district as family property, or he may ask his chief for additional land rendered necessary by the requirements of an expanding family. He would report to his chief or to the Emir or Oba the fact of any self-acquired land in order both to secure the chief as witness to the acquisition and to advertise the same to the community at large. The extent of the acquisition would depend upon the immediate needs of the family concerned but with due regard to the possible claims of others.

Where a family head requires land not for members of his household but for strangers (that is, people who are not native to the soil of the particular area),[1] he cannot take unappropriated land without the prior consent of the chief. The practice has almost always been that strangers would attach themselves to an influential person with whose family they would normally have been lodging for some period prior to a formal request being made on their behalf by their host. The head of the 'stranger' group could not normally go direct to the chief whose consent would often be given provided these conditions are satisfied: (1) the stranger should be of good report, (2) he should be ready and willing to obey the accepted social norms of the adoptive group and (3) he should have respect for and loyalty to the head chief as well as the elders of the community. Land so granted is held by the strangers in perpetuity in exactly the same way and subject to the like conditions of customary tenure as bind the members of the owner-occupiers themselves. The land rights and duties of the head of an adopted family or group are generally the same as those of any other head in the adopting group.

On important festive occasions the head of a land-owning family makes voluntary gifts of farm produce—yams, corn, palm-oil, palm-wine, gin, firewood and the like—to which all members of the family (including strangers on the land) would contribute, to his immediate administrative superior, the chief, who in turn would make similar presents to the supreme head—the Oba or Emir. Although the rendering of these services has never been obligatory, yet it has often been carried out for no other reason than that it is prudent to ensure the goodwill of the chief and of the Oba under whose rule the occupier lives.

A family head is, however, not customarily entitled, as is a chief, to regular presents of produce from members *per se*, although every member owes a social duty to help with the special economic requirements of the autonomous household on proper occasions. On the other hand, a family head, but not a chief, is in a stronger position to take over or re-allocate lands of adopted strangers on the ground of long non-user. It is doubtful whether he can turn

---

[1] Ward Price's definition of 'stranger' is: A stranger is a person who is: (a) Not a native by birth of the community. (b) One who does not wish to occupy communal land 'with the same rights and subject to the same obligations as are enjoyed by or imposed upon members of such community by the native law and custom regulating the rights and obligations of such members in relation to the lands occupied by them.'—para. 185 of *Land Tenure in Yorubaland*. But note and compare para. 253, ibid.

such strangers out of the family land previously allocated to them simply on the ground of the subsequent needs of members of his own family. Where the strangers' original occupation was understood to be temporary, it would seem that ejectment could be effected after a reasonable notice to quit. But where the intention at the time of the first grant by the family head was that the strangers should become part and parcel of the 'host' family, the occupation being then less precarious could not be easily disturbed without a very good cause shown. The grant of *virgin* land to strangers confers on them a rather more secure occupancy on the whole than does one of cultivated land. Whereas strangers may often plant permanent crops or reap palm trees on the former, they usually cannot do so on the latter.

It remains to add that, where the family land is plentiful and members of the family are yet too young and/or impecunious to receive and work separate allotments of their own, the family head is sometimes responsible for equipping these dependent members with farming tools and has, therefore, to provide them with the necessaries of life, if not also with its amenities, even such as they are under local conditions.

In disputes among family members about sharing farm produce like palm trees, as well as in cases of doubt as to the size and extent of individual holdings, the family head acts as referee. He also represents his family in all land cases whether against another family of the same community or against any other third-party (including the Government of Nigeria).

Townlands. As regards town areas, the position is, with minor variations, generally the same as in country districts. The main consideration here centres round the family house—usually a compound—sometimes a rectangular cluster of houses (as in many Yoruba urban and quasi-urban areas), sometimes a circular one (as in the normal Northern areas), but always with a gateway leading into the hollow centre. This compound idea is not now universal, especially in urban areas under the impact of new economic and psychological factors tending towards a partial break-up in traditional family life.

Excluding for the present a consideration of the detailed rules of inheritance according to which one has ultimately to settle who should be family head, it is sufficient to say here that heads of families are usually males but, in certain circumstances such as the absence of a senior male member or kin, females can be and are sometimes made family heads.

The primary duties of a family head briefly are: (a) the allocation and re-allocation of rooms to members of the household, for which, of course, no rents are payable, (b) the general supervision of the whole compound or house with regard to its proper use during the life-time of the individual occupiers, (c) the execution of major repairs due to fair wear and tear, including where applicable the painting, decoration and other worthwhile improvements, (d) the care of the younger members of the household and the provision for them of suitable accommodation within the precincts of the compound or house until they are old enough to have separate rooms of their own, either allotted to them on attaining majority if there are vacant rooms available then, or built by themselves (i) as additions to the main house or compound and (ii) independently of the latter should they decide at any time to set up house on their own. Where the family is sufficiently well-to-do, the family head (especially if he is also the founder or father of the household) often shoulders the responsibility of providing these extensions to the household at his own expense. In such a case, also, the head sometimes indulges in periodic acts of charity to the poor and even to strangers on temporary sojourn with the family.[1] Practice, however, varies from place to place, and it may be that a family head in some places will sometimes do more and sometimes less than what has been stated above.

The admission of non-members to this sort of compound depended on the strangers' good behaviour and amenability to the discipline and general well-being of the household. It did not entail the payment of tribute as in the case of similar occupation of farm-land. On the contrary, the privilege of being allowed to build rooms for himself therein usually secured to the stranger a measure of permanence which formed a kind of bulwark against arbitrary eviction by the family head.

Where, in such cases, eviction was justifiable, no compensation was paid in the case of the simpler types of mud-walled and thatch-roofed houses, but it would appear that, with respect to modern solid buildings, reasonable compensation should be payable to the evicted occupier. Mere temporary failure to occupy and use his rooms would not work a forfeiture. A clear intention to abandon

---

[1] Local idea of hospitality almost invariably dictates that the board and lodging of strangers on temporary stay with a family should be free. This is a universal practice in Nigeria. It may be that new economic standards might alter it in the course of time.

must be shown before the family head could give the vacated rooms to others.

If a non-member was permitted to build a house in the space around the usual family compound, as distinct from being allowed to build additional rooms within the compound itself, the family head could not usually evict him because of an ordinary quarrel between the host and the guest, nor could the head evict him for minor misconduct. If he became a positive nuisance to the 'host' family, the head chief and his council of elders would have to step in and expel such an undesirable member of the community. But, in this instance, compensation was normally paid for all the *separate* buildings he might have erected, even if built of mud and thatch.

Chapter Six

INDIGENOUS SYSTEMS OF TENURE
(continued)

*(Decided Cases illustrating and amplifying the Principles
stated in Chapter Five)*

---

1. *The Chief and the Land. The Chief as Trustee and Chief's Right
to Tribute. B. The Chief's Right of Revocation and Eviction. C. The
Chief's Right to Reversion. D. Other Matters relating to Chief's
Status. E. Family Head and the Land.*

L ET us now proceed to illustrate the outline of the general
principles of indigenous system given in the previous Chapter with a brief review of some judicial decisions. A useful
starting point would be to consider the attitude of the Courts
towards chieftaincy in its relation to land.

A. THE CHIEF AND THE LAND

The first important recorded case was *Sule Giwa & ors.* v.
Alashe.[1] This was an undefended action brought by the plaintiff, a
farmer, against the defendant, a White-Capped Chief of Lagos, for
seizing and converting plaintiff's property to his own use and for
entering the household of the occupants of the farm, breaking
down the fence for the purpose. Smalman Smith, C.J., in delivering
judgment, commented as follows: 'Such a position (i.e. of a chief)
only carries a certain social status and distinction among his fel-
lows, but no authority beyond that of any other private person.
More especially do I draw attention to this fact, inasmuch as

---

[1] (1891), p. 45 of *Lagos, Reports of Certain Judgments of the Supreme
Court, Vice-Admiralty Court & Full Court of Appeal* (1884–1892), delivered
on 15 May.

certain pretensions have recently been advanced by persons calling
themselves White-Capped Chiefs, to control over land in the lawful
and beneficial occupation of persons owing no rent or service to
them.'

This stricture is, however, to be confined to the arbitrary arrogation of power by the chief concerned and should not be taken as
covering the whole of the miscellaneous rights over land which a
chief undoubtedly enjoys under local law and custom. But the
learned Chief Justice's warning was timely and necessary in the
particular context, especially when one remembers that the very
act he was condemning is equally reprehensible under the existing
customary law of tenure. For the purpose of appreciating the real
nature of chieftaincy, however, the next case seems more helpful.

In *Adanji* v. *Hunvoo*,[1] in which an action had been brought by
the plaintiff in the case in order to establish his title to the chieftaincy of Fiyento of Badagry, the then Acting Chief Justice
defined [2] chieftaincy as follows: 'Now what is the chieftaincy?
I say without hesitation that it is a mere dignity, a position of
honour, of primacy among a particular section of the native community. . . .' The learned judge had a little earlier concluded that
it might be that chieftaincy carried with it by local law and custom
some or many rights and privileges which might be made the subject of an action at law; later decisions presently to be considered
will be seen to have clarified the nature of these rights and privileges of the chief.[3]

On the legislative side, s. 3 of the Interpretation Ordinance
No. 27 of 1939, gives this definition: ' "Chief" or "Native Chief"
means any native whose authority and control is recognised by a
native community, and "head chief" means any chief who is not
subordinate to any other chief or native authority.' This as a
definition is, to say the least, not explicit.

Nevertheless, it will be noticed from these judicial and legislative
statements that the chief's role with respect to land is not one of
ownership, but essentially one of political and social pre-eminence
over his particular community. This is not, however, to deny that
a chief may enjoy a dual capacity; his position of control and

---

[1] (1908), 1 N. L. R. 74.   [2] Ibid., at p. 78.
[3] In our case here, the Supreme Court held that the issue being just one of
mere title to chieftaincy was outside its jurisdiction under s. 11 of the Supreme
Court Ordinance. In the later case of *Wanta Dick* v. *Green* (1911), 1 N. L. R.
114, however, the Supreme Court entertained a chief's claim to the right to
receive payment of money, thus distinguishing at p. 115 *the Adanji Case.*

administration of community land, as well as his position as a land-owning individual in his private capacity. For example, in *Taiwo* v. *Sarumi*,[1] the Full Court at Lagos observed:[2] 'It seems to us that the Olofin of Isheri has been since the Egba Boundary Treaty, 1894, acting in a *dual* capacity, firstly as a chief in a district situated in a territory of the Egba United Government, and secondly as owning or controlling certain land outside the Egba boundaries and within the jurisdiction of this Court.' But it remains true that with respect to community land the chief is a kind of trustee or administrator.

We will next illustrate the main attributes of chiefly power over land:

The Chief as Trustee and Chief's Right to Tribute

These two inter-related questions were fully canvassed in the much-quoted case of *Amodu Tijani* v. *Secry., Southern Nigeria*.[3] The facts were that land at Apapa, on the mainland and within the Colony, belonged to the Oluwa Chieftaincy family. On its acquisition by the Government under the Public Lands Ordinance No. 5 of 1903, the question arose as to (1) the person or persons to whom compensation should be paid and (2) the basis on which it should be made and the title thereby conveyed by the payee or payees to the Crown. *Held*: by the Privy Council, (1) that, while the radical title to the land was in the Crown, the full usufructuary title vested in the chief on behalf of the community of which he was the head; (2) that, therefore, the proper person to whom compensation should be made was the chief as the representative of his community, among the members of which the compensation money should be distributed or for whose benefit it should be applied or used in such proportions and manner as the Native Council of the District in which the land is situated should determine with the sanction of the Governor (paras. 25 and 26 of the Ordinance of 1903). Viscount Haldane emphasised [4]: 'The chief is only the agent through whom the transaction is to take place, and he is to be dealt with as representing not only his own but the other interests affected'; (3) that compensation was payable on the basis that the chief, on behalf of his community, was transferring the land to the Governor in full ownership, and that for the purpose of payment of compensation at least, there was no practical distinction between 'stool' and 'communal' lands.[5] This transference of

---

[1] 2 N. L. R. 103.   [2] Ibid., at p. 104.   [3] (1921), 2 A. C. 399.
[4] (1921), 2 A. C. 399, at p. 408.   [5] 3 N. L. R., at p. 58.

the full ownership of 'communal' lands was, of course, the entire creature of s. 6 of the Public Lands Ordinance (1903), which their Lordships regarded as absolute in its terms when it provided: 'When the land required is the property of a native community, the head chief of the community may sell and convey it in fee simple, any native law or custom to the contrary notwithstanding.'

To the extent to which Speed, C.J., had held in the earlier case of *Oduntan Onisiwo* v. *Attorney-General of Southern Nigeria* [1] that the only right or title of the chief was 'merely a *seigneurial* right giving the holder the ordinary rights of control and management of the land, in accordance with the well-known principles of native law and custom, including the rights to receive payment of the nominal rent or tribute payable by the occupiers *and that compensation should be calculated on that basis and not on* the basis of absolute ownership of the land,' [2] Viscount Haldane's observation with respect to the learned Chief Justice's basis of compensation [3] may be thus summarised:

(i) Speed, C.J.'s, conclusion was based on a confusion between family and chieftaincy property,[4] since 'it does not appear clearly from the judgment of the Chief Justice whether he thought that any members of the community had any independent right to compensation or whether the Crown was entitled to appropriate the land without more'.[5]

'Their Lordships think that the learned Chief Justice in the judgment thus summarised, *which virtually excludes the legal reality of the community usufruct*, has failed to recognise the real character of the title to land occupied by a native community.' [6]

(ii) The learned Chief Justice had misunderstood 'the effect of the decision in the *Oduntan's Case*, 1908, which came before the Full Court, and in which compensation had been paid by the Nigerian Government on the basis of absolute ownership'. The relevant finding of Speed, C.J., in that case was: 'I am, moreover, quite satisfied that the suppliant is a son of a former Onisiwo, and is eligible for election to the title. . . . *He does not claim as Onisiwo,*

---

[1] (1912), 2 N. L. R. 77.

[2] All the italics in this quotation are the author's.

[3] But the rest of the learned Chief Justice's dictum here cited is otherwise unexceptionable.

[4] The land in the instant case is 'family' land occupied, however, by strangers who paid tributes to the head of the owning family who happened to be also a chief.

[5] (1921), A. C., at p. 402.

[6] (1921), 2 A. C., at p. 409.

but as head and representative of the family, and I have already expressed my concurrence with the finding of the Court below as to his right to sue on their behalf.' [1]

(iii) 'It follows that it is for *the whole of what he so transfers* that compensation has to be made.' This bundle of rights transferred by the chief includes the chief's own right to tributes from the occupiers, wherever such traditional tributes were normally paid before, but not otherwise; and for the deprivation of this right he must be compensated, not indeed by means of a separate award by the Court, but simply by means of any agreed sum out of the total amount granted. This, of course, would be additional to his proper share in the residue as a member of the community.[2] 'If he (i.e. a chief) is properly deriving tribute or rent from these allotments, he will have to be compensated for the loss of it, and if the allottees have had valid titles conferred on them, they must also be compensated. . . . In the case of land belonging to the community, but as to which no rent is payable to the chief, it does not appear that the latter is entitled to be compensated otherwise than in his representative capacity under the Ordinance of 1903. It is the members of his community who are in usufructuary occupation or in an equivalent position on whose behalf he is making the claim.' [3]

The right of the chief to receive tribute from stranger occupiers may sometimes be made the subject of an express agreement to pay rent as between two local communities. In *Chief Lulu Braid v. Chief Daniel Kalio* [4] the plaintiff, as representing the chiefs and people of Bakana (New Calabar), sued the defendant on behalf of the chiefs and people of Okirika on an Agreement of 1915 to pay rent for houses erected on certain village lands belonging to the Bakana people. The Divisional Court at Calabar gave judgment for the defendants on the ground that the claim was uncertain and that there was no consideration for the agreement. The Full Court, on appeal, set aside this judgment and ordered a re-trial because, said Combe, C.J., the lower Court, in requiring consideration for an agreement to pay tribute which the defendants were in any case

---

[1] (1912), 2 N. L. R. 77, at p. 80; the italics are the author's.

[2] Here one may recall the recognition of similar apparently shadowy rights by the payment of personal subsidies to, e.g. Docemo, Chief Young Dede, Emir of Sokoto, etc., under the various treaties of cession or lease of territory. Legally, the reservation to these local rulers of such personal annuities can be justified only on the hypothesis that they were meant to compensate them for loss of tributes over the lands.

[3] (1921), 2 A. C. 399, at p. 410.   [4] (1927), 7 N. L. R. 34.

bound to pay under the local customary law, had taken a wholly erroneous view of the position. No consideration is ever necessary under the indigenous system of tenure, and the liability of stranger occupiers to pay tribute or rent to their overlords cannot be taken away merely because a formal contract has also been entered into by them with a view to fixing precisely what the actual amount should be.

Similarly, with the permission of the Oba or Emir or other paramount chief, lesser chiefs or household heads may grant lands to refugees and other settlers on terms of payment of tribute or rent by the latter to their overlords. In a rapidly developing community difficulties are bound to arise if and when such payments are insisted upon by the descendants of the grantors from the descendants of the grantees who, after some generations, may have come now to look upon the land as virtually their own and the continued payment of tribute or rent as an unjustifiable imposition. Thus, in the very recent and celebrated case of *Ife Overlords* v. *Modakekes* (1948),[1] the plaintiffs claimed from the defendants 6 cwt. 1 qr. of cocoa or its equivalent (in this case, calculated at £18 2s. 6d.) representing the *ishakole* due from the latter to the plaintiffs in respect of the year ended 31 December 1947. The plaintiffs alleged that under an Agreement of 1886 the defendants through their predecessors undertook to pay yams and kola-nuts as *ishakole* to the plaintiffs' predecessors until the cocoa to be grown on their allotments should begin to bear fruits when each grantee of land must pay 1 cwt. of cocoa or its money equivalent to the grantors. This Agreement was not enforced until 1903, but it appeared that the defendants, who had been granted their lands some eighteen years previously, had paid *ishakole* of yams and kola-nuts for some eight years and that thereafter, when their cocoa trees began to yield, they had for ten years paid the agreed quantities of cocoa up to and including 31 December 1946. They then decided not to pay any more *ishakole*, which had now come to be looked upon merely as a voluntary but burdensome tribute. *Held*: by Hallinan, J., in the Supreme Court at Ife, confirming the findings of the Magistrate Court,

[1] 'The Daily Service', Wednesday, 22 December 1948, p. 1 ff. 'Judgment of the Supreme Court delivered at Ife by Hallinan, J., on Monday, 13 December 1948. In pursuance of the learned judge's advice that the parties should get together and effect an amicable settlement, the Oni of Ife summoned to his palace both parties who, however, failed to agree; the Modakekes still refused to pay any more *ishakole*.

(1) that *ishakole* was, even in ancient times, always based on agreement between grantors and grantees of land;

(2) that *ishakole* was in the nature of *obligatory rent*, not mere *voluntary tribute*, and was payable (whether as between individuals or as between families) by the grantees to the grantors; and that it was independent of any customary tributes which were payable at will on certain festive and other occasions;

(3) that *ishakole* must be distinguished from *Isin* which was always payable to the Oba as customary tribute in token of loyalty and fealty, and which never depended on any agreement;

(4) that the defendants must continue to pay the agreed *ishakole* to the plaintiffs, including the 6 cwt. 1 qr. or its money equivalent of £18 2s. 6d. as claimed by the plaintiffs in the case.[1]

Two interesting features of this famous case were: (1) the claim was not by the Oni of Ife on behalf of his people against the Modakeke settlers, but was between heads of family overlords and heads of family grantees. (2) The Oni's evidence in the case, expounding and delimiting the meaning and scope of *ishakole* and *isin* in relation to *rent*, questioned the correctness of the statement of principles in paras. 36, 85 and 117 of Ward Price's *Land Tenure in Yoruba-land* (1933) in so far as these say that *ishakole* is customary tribute, not rent, paid only on occasions, etc. The Oni pointed out that he himself was one of those consulted by Ward Price when the latter was collecting his materials for his Report which was afterwards published by the Nigerian Government.

The Chief's Representative Status

As we have seen, it is because, under Nigerian law and custom, the chief is not the owner of the land in the accepted English sense of the word, that we have denied the legal right of the chiefs to make treaties giving away Nigerian land as if they were the proprietors. This principle of the representative character of the chief with regard to the land of his community is of universal application in Nigeria. There are two sides to it: the negative and the positive, the former consisting in the chief's legal incapacity to treat the land as his personal property and the latter in the recognised rule that the chief is the legal representative of his community and that it is only through him that actions relating to land should ordinarily

---

[1] Compare the not dissimilar decision in *Chief D. H. Braide & ors.* v. *Chief S. Adoki & ors.* (1931), 10 N. L. R. 15, in which an agreement of 1923 between the people of New Calabar and the Okrikas was upheld on appeal to the Supreme Court. See also *Chief Lulu Braid* v. *Chief Daniel Kalio* (1927), N. L. R. 34.

be brought. Chiefs have all too often confused the two by claiming community lands as if they were beneficial owners thereof, merely because theirs is the right to bring a suit. Thus, in the famous *Amodu Tijani Oluwa Case*,[1] his original claim as beneficial owner of Apapa land had to be abandoned under correction by the Full Court at Lagos. In *Chief Omagbemi & ors.* v. *Chief Dore Numa*,[2] Webber, J., held in the Divisional Court at Calabar (at p. 19): 'Now the Olu never owned Jekri land as an individual. The land belonged to the community and the Olu was trustee. In him, as trustee, was vested the land.' To which Tew, J., in upholding Webber, J., on appeal to the Supreme Court at Lagos, added (at pp. 21–2): 'There is equally no doubt as to the position of the person holding the title of Olu Jekri with regard to the lands of the Jekri people. It was admitted by the first witness in the Court below, Chief Denedo, himself one of the plaintiffs, that the Olu held the land as trustee for the people and not as individual owner or on behalf of his family.' The case concerned land in Warri in Eastern Nigeria.

A necessary consequence of this trustee-beneficiary role of the chief over the land is that it is he who represents his community *vis-à-vis* another community in land disputes. Thus it was that, in *Nnaji Nwa-Ogaba* (for and on behalf of Akagbe Village) v. *Nnaman Nwa Okenwaeji* (for and on behalf of Akpugo Village),[3] a case concerning lands in the Udi Division of the Onitsha Province, the plaintiff, a kind of chief, sued the defendant (as another chief of his own community) in the Awkunanaw Native Court for (i) a declaration of title to the land in question, (ii) damages for trespass and (iii) an injunction. Similarly, in *Chief D. H. Braid & ors.* v. *Chief S. Adoki & ors.*,[4] the treaty of 1871 which secured to the Okrikas the right to pass through and make fishing settlements in any of the creeks belonging to New Calabar, had to be signed between the Chiefs of Okrika and the Chiefs of New Calabar.

It would seem, however, that if the chief on behalf of his community enters for valuable consideration into any negotiation, apparently valid and authorised, with a *bona fide* outsider, the members of such a group cannot be heard to say that his act was unauthorised. Thus, in *Secretary, L.T.C.* v. *Nowroudin B. Soule & Chief Aromire*,[5] during an interregnum in the Aromire Chief-

---

[1] (1921), 2 A. C. 399.   [2] (1923), 5 N. L. R. 19.
[3] (1944), 17 N. L. R. 117.   [4] (1931), 10 N. L. R. 15.
[5] (1939), 15 N. L. R. 72.

N.L.L.C.—10

taincy, one Yesufu Aromire acted as chief for about five years during which he sold two pieces of land *inter alia* to the first defendant. The parcels of land were later acquired by the L.T.C. and both defendants each claimed the compensation money. *Held*: that the proper person with a legal right to receive the compensation money was Yesufu Aromire, as representing the chief at the relevant time. The Court said (*a*) that the family knew of and impliedly consented to the deputy's dealing with the group land and the sale by him to first defendant was accordingly valid; and (*b*) that the second defendant's election was duly completed only *after* the particular transaction, and so he could not claim the money. But it is difficult to see why the compensation sum should not have been paid to the second defendant as the regular chief when the action was brought, since the money should, it is submitted, have been payable to whoever is the legal representative of the community at the material time. Surely the deputy, i.e. Yesufu Aromire, had surrendered his stewardship to the substantive holder of the office and the subsequent payment to him of the compensation money would seem to have entailed unnecessary duplication of function as of accounting.

Nevertheless, if a chief makes a clandestine arrangement under his ostensible authority which is not in fact properly exercised, his community may repudiate all liability thereby arising.

Thus, in *Aralawon* v. *Aromire & anor*.[1], the first defendant in his capacity as the acting Chief Aromire privately and without consulting the senior members of the Aromire family borrowed from the plaintiff the sum of £105 for the purpose both of completing the re-building of the chief's palace (called 'Iga') and of defraying the costs of chieftaincy law suits. As the money was not repaid, the plaintiff sued him both personally and in his representative capacity, joining the second defendant who had since become the substantive holder of the office. *Held*: that the first defendant was alone chargeable with the repayment, to the plaintiff, of the loan. In the circumstances, the community could properly repudiate liability.

B. THE CHIEF'S RIGHT OF REVOCATION AND EVICTION

A noteworthy case in which the chief's right to revoke the express or implied grant of an occupier and to evict him has been judicially recognised is probably *Idewu Inasa & ors.* v. *Saka Oshodi*.[2] In this

---

[1] (1940), 15 N. L. R. 90.   [2] (1934), A. C. 99.

case the Privy Council upheld the decision of the Supreme Court of Nigeria to the effect that the appellants' predecessor in title had lost his right, title and interest under local law and custom to that piece of land which he then occupied as a descendant of a domestic at Inasa Compound at Epetedo, Lagos, by selling and/or attempting to sell or otherwise dispose of a piece or parcel of land situate at Glover Street, which then formed part of Inasa Compound.[1]

It is not to be supposed that the chief's right of eviction is limited to a sale or attempt to sell part of the community land by an occupier. It covers all cases of an assertion of a right in or to the land which is inconsistent with the lawful rights of the chief. It extends, for example, to a case where, although the occupier had broken no customary condition of his occupancy of community land at Abonnema on the Owusara Road, the chief gave him notice to quit his holding on no other ground than that his continued occupation is against general family interest: *J. D. Manuel* v. *Chief Gladstone Bob Manuel*.[2] But the actual decision in the case itself denied the chief's right to evict, probably because the Court was not satisfied that the plaintiff's continued occupation was in fact against the interest of the group.

Another type of misconduct which would justify a chief in evicting was considered by the Full Court in *Chief Uwani* v. *Nwosu Akom & ors*.[3] In that case the appellants were headmen of four compounds of Aros who had settled at Ukpom in the Bende District of Owerri Province, with the permission of the respondent as representing the community to whom the land belonged. One Aro having sold or mortgaged his portion of the land (in this case, his farming rights) to another Aro, the respondent took proceedings to eject the people in all the four compounds. *Held*: by the Full Court, over-ruling both the Provincial and the Divisional Courts which had ordered the appellants to quit the land within two weeks, that the appellants should be allowed to remain on the land occupied by them on payment of an annual tribute of £15 to the respondent chief and his people. The Court was led to this conclusion since to hold otherwise would mean (1) the eviction

---

[1] See ibid., at p. 103: 'Now it is with the chief's rights . . . that the present litigation is concerned. These rights, whatever they may be, depend entirely on local law and custom. . . .' and in *Brimah Balogun* v. *Chief Saka Oshodi* (1931), 10 N. L. R. 36, Tew, J., remarked, at p. 51, that one incident of local tenure is the chief's 'right to evict any domestic for misconduct, and any attempt on his part to alienate without consent of family was regarded as such misconduct as made him liable to eviction'.

[2] (1926), 7 N. L. R. 101.   [3] (1928), 8 N. L. R. 19.

root and branch of some 310 Aros from their homes on the fifteen square miles of territory on which they had been permitted for fifty years by the people of Ukpom to build about 100 houses, and (2) the sacrifice by the Aros of some hundreds of cocoa and cocoa-nut trees (yielding an annual income of over £1,000), which they had been allowed to plant on Ukpom land. Combe, C.J., explained at p. 23: 'The payment of such tribute would be a yearly recognition by the community that the community represented by the plaintiff are the owners of the land, and will remove any fear that the owners may have that the Aro community may in future claim and establish that they own the land occupied by them.'

Again, an assertion of ownership of the land by strangers who have been permitted by the chief to settle thereon is sufficient misconduct to warrant their eviction, although on grounds of inconvenience as of equity such a right is in practice rarely exercised where there has been long occupation on the part of the grantees. Thus in *Ometa & ors.* v. *Chief Dore Numa*,[1] the plaintiffs' ancestors came to Warri from Agbasa Otun, and were permitted by the then Olu Itsekiri to settle on a small piece of land now known as Agbasa Village, for which they had paid tribute and performed services in return for the Olu's protection. *Held*: (by the Full Court at Lagos) that the plaintiffs on behalf of the Agbasa people had failed to establish their claim to ownership as against Chief Numa and his people and that, although that would ordinarily have entailed their eviction, they would nevertheless be left in occupation of the land 'provided the overlordship of the Olu of the Jekris was recognised'.[2]

Similarly, in *Iwok Owume* v. *Inyang*,[3] the appellant had been

[1] (1929), 9 N. L. R. 46.
[2] Incidentally, Webber, J., had in the Divisional Court (at p. 47, ibid.), adopted these statements of principles from the terms of settlement reached in 1921 between Chief Dore and Chief Olowu as to the position of Chief Dore and his powers as Olu in respect of land in his jurisdiction: (*a*) 'Where strangers require land as tenants or otherwise they can only have same with the approval of plaintiff (Chief Dore Numa) which cannot be unreasonably refused, and only the plaintiff or someone authorised by him can receive rents or tribute for any land.' (*b*) 'Where rent is received by the plaintiff from such strangers it must be shared equitably with any people who have been deprived of their occupation in whole or in part by reason of the grant to strangers.'
These enunciations of principles of customary tenure of land in Warri accord with our earlier exposition with regard to the role of chiefs over Nigerian lands. See pp. 101–9, *supra*.
[3] (1931), 10 N. L. R. 111.

for some time in occupation of a certain piece of land in Ikot Ekpene District of Calabar in the Eastern Provinces. He then alleged that he had bought the land outright from the head of the local community. *Held*: that he had not by his allegation so impugned his overlord's title as to render himself liable to eviction. But the appellant must, as a condition of continued possession of his holding, desist from making any further claim to ownership of the land.

If an adverse claim by an occupier to ownership of his overlord's land does not necessarily work a forfeiture of his holding, *a fortiori* a mere statement made by him in a judicial proceeding, to which the chief was privy (though not party), would not: *Chief Ashogbon* v. *Oduntan*.[1] The facts were that an action had previously been brought to eject the defendant's son from the property in question and the Court had ruled that the claim was unfounded. In giving evidence for his son the defendant had under cross-examination denied the chief's reversionary right in the land. It was finally held that a statement made by the defendant in such circumstances was not such misconduct as to render the defendant liable to eviction by the chief. Graham Paul, J., observed (at page 9):

'As regards the   question of what in native law and custom amounts to misbehaviour involving forfeiture of rights over land I cannot do better than refer to the Divisional Court judgment of Tew, J., in the case of *Saka, Chief Oshodi* v. *Aworan Inasa* (Suit No. 296 of 1925 in this Court).'

Dealing with this point Mr. Justice Tew said: 'The plaintiff himself and two other White-Capped Chiefs gave evidence as to the rights of domestics, to whom land has been allotted by the head of the family, and the terms upon which they and their successors in title occupy such land. They were agreed that such a person could be evicted for serious misconduct, such as burglary, making bad medicines, adultery, etc., and also if he attempts to alienate the land allotted to him. None of them was able to point to a case in which the strict native law had been enforced and a person had been evicted from the land which he occupied because of an attempt to sell it; but Chief Eletu Edibo recalled a case in which the offender, knowing that his conduct was about to be considered at a family meeting, had voluntarily quitted the land.

'The Chiefs stated that in their recollection the erring occupier had usually been treated leniently, and usually, on the intercession

[1] (1935), 12 N. L. R. 7.

of his fellow slaves or of some influential person, had been allowed to remain in occupation of the land.'

So wide has been the ambit of the Courts' equitable jurisdiction that not only has the chief been often precluded from lightly evicting ungrateful occupiers of land under his control but he has also been held to have no right to derogate from his grant. Nice problems have arisen on this score. For example, if a stranger occupier breaks some vital conditions of his holding, the chief can revoke his grant and evict him in proper cases. But what is the position if it is the chief or any other overlord that breaks his side of the bargain? Can the grantee treat the grantor's act of derogation as null and void or claim damages and obtain an injunction? The point fell to be determined in the following two cases. The first is *Offiong Bassey & ors.* v. *Chief Ntoe Eteta*,[1] of which the facts were briefly as follows: A predecessor in office of the defendant had, according to local law and custom, made a grant of certain lands extending to the beach at Atimbo on the Qua river to the plaintiff's predecessors. Part of these lands was subsequently leased by the defendant to European firms. The plaintiffs claimed to be entitled to a share of two-thirds of the rents from the lease since, once granted, the land remained in their effective occupation and immediate control, until they should forfeit their right to the holding. The defendant in the meantime therefore had no right to derogate from his grant by leasing part of the land already granted to the plaintiffs. The defendants, on the other hand, contended (1) that the part leased by them being 'beach lands' could not, under local law and custom, have been the subject of such a grant as that alleged by the plaintiffs because the defendant's ancestors had no right to alienate 'beach lands' to stranger occupiers; (2) that, by virtue of an agreement alleged to have been made between the head of plaintiff's family and a chief of the defendant overlords, £10 a year was all that the plaintiffs could get out of the £40 a year rent being paid by the firms. *Held*: by the W.A.C.A.: (1) that, in view of the judgment of a Divisional Court in 1915 deciding that as between these same parties permission to use the land extended to the beach, the present defendants' contention that 'beach lands' could not be the subject of a grant must be overruled; (2) that the defendant was accordingly not entitled to grant the leases in question, but that as the plaintiffs had adopted the leases, they should be entitled to an equitable share of the rents; (3) that in spite of the alleged agreement for £10 a year, the plain-

[1] (1938), 4 W. A. C. A. 153.

tiffs' share of the rents should be two-thirds. The reason for these conclusions may be discerned in the following passage of the judgment (at page 155):

'In the case of letting by a grantee to a stranger, whilst the strict rule of native law and custom is that such a letting entails forfeiture, in practice the Courts grant relief against such forfeiture usually upon the terms that the letting shall hold good and the grantee shall pay over to the grantor a proportion of the rent received, usually though not necessarily one-third. But no instance has been brought to our notice of a letting like those in the present case by the grantor, or his successors in title, in derogation of the grant made by him, and it may well be that the grantee, or his successors, would be entitled to treat such a letting as absolutely void. However, in the present case it is not necessary to give an opinion upon this point because the appellants, in effect, acquiesce in and adopt the leases but claim to receive an equitable share of the rents derived from them. We are of opinion that their claim cannot properly be based on native law and custom (as pleaded in para. 8 of the Statement of Claim), but that it should rather be regarded as one for money received by the respondents for the appellants' use.'

These three points stand out from the passage and deserve brief comments: (1) It would seem that the plaintiffs' share of the rents was fixed at two-thirds because, as we have seen, the defendant would under the customary law of land usually be given as tribute about one-third of the annual produce of the land occupied by the original grantees of it. (2) Therefore, their Lordships' view that the plaintiffs' claim 'cannot properly be based on native law and custom' would, it is submitted, not seem justified merely on account of the novelty of the claim. It is not inconsistent with principle that the defendant should be held to only one-third of the annual produce (be it money, rent, corn, kola or other) of the land already effectively granted to others and that those others should keep the remaining two-thirds. The result would have been the same, it is thought, if the land had been planted with crops instead of leased. It appears unnecessary, then, to import a *quasi-contractual* element into a local situation which can be fairly well met by applying the dynamic rules of customary law. (3) But a far bolder statement is the conjecture that if the plaintiffs had not adopted the lease they might have been entitled to declare it null and void and to evict the defendant's lessees. To the extent to which the point is not exactly covered by precedent, it may be that one is inclined to doubt the validity of such a development. But it is at least logical to assume that, if the overlord has no right to disturb the usufructuary occupation of the grantees who enjoy a perpetuity of tenure so long as they break no vital conditions thereof, any subsequent exercise of ownership in derogation of the grant must be frowned upon by law, whether local or English.

The second case is *Chief Etim & ors.* v. *Chief Eke & ors.*[1] The defendants' predecessors had permitted the plaintiffs to occupy certain of their lands in the Akpabuyo District of the Calabar Province until the grantees attempted to deny the grantors' title and were held liable to eviction. But the Full Court in 1915 commuted this into a fine of £10, and both sides effected reconciliation out of Court so that the plaintiffs continued in occupation. Later, the defendant grantors, without the grantees' permission, granted to a third party, a stranger to the locality, the right to enter upon and cut palm nuts on the land. In the event that happened this third party not only cut fresh palm nuts but also removed certain others cut by the plaintiffs, and did some other act which interfered with the plaintiffs' enjoyment of the land. Whereupon the plaintiffs claimed (i) a declaration that under the customary law they were entitled to a continued and undisturbed enjoyment of their holding; (ii) an injunction to restrain the defendant grantors, their servants and agents, etc., from further interference; (iii) damages against the third party for trespass in entering and cutting the palm nuts; (iv) an order for an account by the defendant grantors of all moneys received from strangers as rent or payment for the right to cut palm nuts and payment to them of *half* the amount so received. On the other hand, the defendant grantors claimed damages from the plaintiff grantees for having erected new buildings and planting permanent crops on the land without first obtaining their consent. The third party also sued the plaintiff for trespassing upon his right to cut palm nuts and for an injunction against its continuance. All the four suits were transferred from the Native Court to the High Court at Calabar which found for the plaintiffs in all their five claims and against both the defendants and the third party. The result of this judgment may be reduced into a number of propositions:

(1) That where a stranger occupier forfeits the conditions of his holding and so renders himself liable to eviction by the chief, the offence may be purged and condoned by, e.g., the imposition of a fine by the Court. We have seen that the payment by the grantees

[1] (1941), 16 N. L. R. 43.

of an annual tribute of £15 was ordered in one case (*Chief Uwani's Case*, page 119 earlier).

(2) That, once forgiven and restored to his former rights of occupation and of user, the chief as representing his community cannot subsequently treat the occupier as though the latter's occupation were now temporary and precarious, requiring the chief's prior consent to the doing of such things as the erection of new buildings and the planting of permanent crops.

(3) That it is, however, possible by the custom of a particular locality that the grantor continues to enjoy thereon certain rights *pari-passu* with the grantee—e.g. the grantor's right to continue to cut palm nuts on land already in the grantee's occupation. The grantees' admission of this right of the grantors in the case itself was presumably responsible for the former's claim to only a half of the proceeds of allowing a third party to exercise the right. This explains why two-thirds of the rents was awarded to the grantees in the *Chief Ntoe Eteta's Case* (where the grantors had no concurrent right to the user of the land granted), whereas only one-half was claimed in the instant case (where the grantors reserved such a right), which was acknowledged by the grantees themselves in their pleadings.

(4) That the same custom may also preclude the grantors from assigning part or all of their right to continued user of the land to a third party, a stranger to the locality in question. Perhaps such a usage derives from a condition of husbandry and an economic policy which regulated rights to land on the view that only the indigenous occupiers should or would want to do permanent farming and that strangers would simply 'come and go'. But in the altered circumstances, where strangers tend to settle and cultivate alien soils, it is understandable that the undesirability of such an arrangement should have earned the censure of Martindale, J., in the High Court at Calabar (at page 52) when he said:

'As a mere *obiter dictum* and without reference to this suit which is decided on other grounds, the view is held that severance of tenant's farming rights and the right to cut palm nuts over the same land is to be deprecated as being conducive to friction between the farmers and the palm-nut cutters and to the wholesale destruction of palm trees, and to the uneconomical working of the land. It is of interest that Tew, J., in *Yesufu Kugbuyi* v. *Odunjo* [1] held that only natives of the soil could reap palm fruits. That decision was, however, limited to that issue.'

[1] (1926), 7 N. L. R. 51.

Finally, the chief could evict occupiers of land for failure or refusal to pay tributes or render customary services. It is interesting to recall this passage from the judgment of Tew, J., in the Divisional Court at Lagos in *Sakariyawo Oshodi* v. *Moriamo Dakolo & ors.*[1]:

'In the case of *Ashogbon* v. *Jinadu Somade & Yesufu Oku* decided on 16 November 1885, Smalman Smith, C.J., upheld the action of a chief who had evicted tenants who refused the services due from them, and several White-Capped Chiefs who were asked for their opinion by the court agreed that the decision was in accordance with native law.' But this undoubted right of the chief must be limited to the case of those subject to his control and holding land mediately or immediately of him. There is no power of eviction in a chief over the land of anyone owing no rent or tribute to him. That was why, as we have seen at the beginning of this section, the same learned Chief Justice had so strongly deprecated the arbitrary arrogation of power by the chief in *Sule Giwa & ors.* v. *Alashe* (1891).

One more point deserves to be noted in conclusion. Granted that occupiers have forfeited their right and that the chief may now evict, we have to decide whether the chiefs' right of eviction relates only to the offending occupier(s) or whether it affects all of them. The point was first raised in an *obiter* of Combe, C.J., in *Chief Uwani* v. *Nwosu Akom & ors.*[2], already discussed (at page 22), as follows: 'It may be that the trivial offence committed by some members of the Aro community would render the whole Aro community liable to be ejected from the land, although I cannot but think that, if the question of the native custom was further investigated, it might be found that it is the persons who were parties to the offence and not the whole community who would be so punished.' That these judicial sentiments are an accurate forecast of what further investigation has revealed will be obvious when we turn to the later case of *Idewu Inasa & ors.* v. *Sakariyawo Oshodi.*[3] The result of the decision in that case seems to be that the chief can evict not only the offender but also such of his relatives as have supported or sided with him against the chief. Thus limited in scope the customary rule, in so far as it is not repugnant to natural justice, equity and good conscience, was given judicial sanction in that case. Their Lordships of the Privy Council said that they were not prepared to uphold the custom so far as it was stated to include a right to evict *all* the relatives; such an extension was unnecessary

[1] (1928), 9 N. L. R. 13.   [2] (1928), 8 N. L. R. 19.   [3] (1934), A. C. 99.

for the decision in that case.[1] They also warned that a chief should not proceed to eviction without obtaining from the court a declaration of forfeiture; failure to do that might entail his having very strictly to justify his conduct if in a subsequent proceeding his conduct should be called in question.

In carrying out his eviction right, even after the permission of the court, the chief should use no more force than is necessary to effect his purpose. Thus observed Kingdon, C.J., in the same case in the Supreme Court at Lagos,[2] at page 6:

'We agree with the judge in the court below that the modern method of moving the court for a formal declaration of forfeiture is to be commended and preferred, but we can find no authority for the proposition that a summary eviction by the overlord, using no more than reasonable force to accomplish same, is illegal. . . . We agree that where excessive force is used or damage to property has occurred the persons evicted are not debarred their remedy to proceed by way of damages for tort.'

C. THE CHIEF'S RIGHT TO REVERSION

It follows from the right, just considered, of revocation of the grant by the chief and the consequent eviction of the grantee, that there should be a reverter of lapsed land to the chief as the administrator of land. The principles were well stated in the leading case of *Chief Sakariyawo Oshodi* v. *Moriamo Dakolo*,[3] where an extensive compound was acquired by the Government under the Public Lands Acquisition Ordinance (Laws of Nigeria, 1923, c. 88), and the question arose as to who should receive the compensation money. Sakariyawo Oshodi claimed (1) the whole compound as paramount chief; (2) the compensation money in so far as it represented the value of the *courtyard* because, according to him, it did not fall within the title, of the various houses; (3) to be entitled to 'something' in virtue of his right to reversion in the community land. *Held*: by the Privy Council, as to (1) that their judgment in *Amodu Tijani* v. *Secretary of Southern Nigeria*,[4] effectively

---

[1] Cf. Hailey, *An African Survey*, p. 835: 'Even though the chief, in areas where centralised political institutions have developed, may have the right to evict a subject for misconduct or disloyalty, this is in effect only one aspect of a recognised political penalty; in many cases, indeed, the penalty might take the form of driving a man out of the community while leaving the land to his heirs.'

[2] (1930), 10 N. L. R. 4.   [3] (1930), A. C. 667.   [4] (1921), 2 A. C. 399.

negatived such a proprietary claim by a chief over community land; as to (2) that 'the courtyard was never in the actual possession of the plaintiff. It was used in common by all the inhabitants of the houses and must be considered as being held along with the houses as an undivided share' (page 670); as to (3) compensation must be paid for the taking away of the contingent right of the Oshodi Chieftaincy to the reversion of the land. To the extent to which the Appellate Court had denied compensation for such rights on the ground that, following the *Amodu Tijani's Case*, they 'are in embryo and may never fertilise', their Lordships of the Privy Council could not agree that 'This Court (i.e. the Privy Council) evaluate that contingent right at nil. . . .' All that the case decided was that the compensation payable for lands held as community lands under White-Cap Chiefs was to be paid to the White-Cap Chiefs as if their Lordships were giving them a fee simple right, but was to be given to them to be distributed among the usufructuary occupants whoever they were. *It did not deal with the rights of reversion.* Their Lordships therefore are of the opinion that *some portion* of the compensation money in this case should be allotted to the plaintiff in respect of his possible right of reversion; which is cut off for ever by the compulsory acquisition. . . . It is clear that the possible right of reversion on the failure of the family of any of the occupants, though not actually *elusory*, must be of *small value*. The case was then remitted back to the judge on the spot 'in order that the Court below may allot such portion of the compensation money to the Chief as represents in their view the value of the possible rights of reversion'.

Nor must it be supposed that these principles apply only to Lagos lands held under White-Cap Chiefs. Their universality was emphasised by their Lordships in these words (page 668): 'The general character of the title of natives to lands in Lagos was examined by the Board in the case of *Amodu Tijani* v. *Secretary, Southern Nigeria*. . . . That case had to do with community lands held under the White-Cap Chiefs; but the general principle was held to apply to other lands not held by White-Cap Chiefs in the subsequent case of *Sunmonu* v. *Disu Raphael* [1] at page 884, where this was expressly stated.' [2] Then followed this remarkably

---

[1] (1927), A. C. 881.

[1] The statement referred to runs thus: 'Their Lordships are aware that that was said of the title of the White-Cap Chiefs. Their title was the question in that case, *but the principle applies generally.*' (1927), A. C., at p. 884.

E.g. para. 7 of the defence in *Ometa* v. *Chief Numa* (1929), 9 N. L. R. 46,

definitive pronouncement: 'In general terms what the law comes to is this. The paramount chief is owner of the lands, but he is not owner in the sense in which owner is understood in this country. He has no fee simple, but only a usufructuary title. He may have some individual lands which he occupies himself, but as regards other lands they are occupied for his household, i.e. before the abolition of slavery for his slaves. These various occupiers have the right to remain and to transmit their holdings to their offspring, but in the event of the family of an occupier failing and being extinct, the chief has a right to reversion.' This passage has become classic in the history of land tenure in Nigeria, and has since been frequently cited in later cases.[1]

Thus, in *Ramotu Otun & ors*. v. *Osenatu Ejide & ors*.[2] at page 125, a chief had put certain domestics or slaves in occupation of a compound and, years later, when the chief or his descendants had ceased to evince any active interest in the compound or its occupiers, the head of the household had obtained a Crown Grant with respect to the land but without thereby making any proprietary claim thereto. Some members of the household later still claimed to be entitled to alienate portions of the compound occupied by other members thereof on the ground (1) that the chief and his descendants had ceased to claim tribute from or exercise any other act of ownership over the compound, and (2) that the Crown Grant had so effectively put an end to the chief's right of reversion and thereby vested the absolute property of the compound in the household head that the plaintiff's members had lost all right to go on living on the land even during good behaviour. *Held*: by Kingdon, C.J., that cesser of interest on the part of the chief or his descendants in the compound or its occupiers did not affect the rights of the occupiers under customary law, and (2) that a Crown Grant could affect neither the reversionary interest of the overlord chief and his descendants nor of the right of other occupiers of the compound. The learned Chief Justice cited the passage just quoted from Viscount Dunedin's judgment in the *Moriamo Dakolo Case* as evidence of the judicial attitude to chief's rights (including that of reversion) and also several passages from other urges the contention that under native law and custom the lands in occupation by the Asbasa people revert to the defendant chief for the reason that the plaintiff as tenant has denied and contested the title of his landlord.

[1] See, e.g., *per* Kingdon, C. J., in *Ramotu Otun* v. *Osenatu Ejide*, 11 N. L. R., at p. 125; also, *Idewu Inasa* v. *Oshodi* (1934), A. C., at p. 102; (1934), 11 N. L. R., at p. 10.

[2] (1932), 11 N. L. R. 124.

judgments on the courts' interpretation of the legal effects of Crown Grants made to slaves in occupation of chieftaincy lands:

In 1904 the case of *Sanusi Alaka* v. *Jinadu Alaka* [1] decided that:

'When land has been given by a master to the headman of his household in trust for all the household, and the headman has obtained a Crown Grant of the property in his own name, he holds it as trustee for the household; and a member of the household has sufficient interest in the property to oppose its sale for the debt of another member of the household.'

In 1918 in the course of his judgment in the case of *Amodu Nasa* v. *Seidu Ajetumobi & ors.* (printed at page 76 of the Record of Proceedings in the Privy Council in the *Dakolo Case*) Ross, J., said:

'It is a very well-known fact in Lagos that at the time when Crown Grants were first issued the masters of slaves would place a slave at the head of the compound, and it was nearly always the custom that this head slave would be instructed by his master to apply for a Crown Grant, and there are numerous cases where a slave has applied and a Crown Grant issued to him in his own name, he being the man to whom the administration of the Compound was entrusted by his master.

'These Courts have, time after time, refused to hold that land granted under such circumstances is the family property of the grantee in whose name the grant is made to the exclusion of the other members of the household of the original master of the grantee.'

The learned Chief Justice then relevantly finished off (at page 127): 'When an Arota was settled by his master in a compound, he acquired for himself and his descendants a right to live there in perpetuity subject to good behaviour. It is unthinkable that that right should be lost simply because the overlord's descendants cease to take any interest in the Arota or the compound.' But although the chief's right of reversion remains unaffected either by his indifference (and that of his successors or descendants) to the grantees of land or by the issue to the latter of Crown Grants yet statute might expressly negative the reversionary right of the chief which he holds on behalf of the community. In the case of *Chief Secretary to the Government* v. *George & 24 ors.* [2] (already considered earlier [3] in another, though not very dissimilar, connection), the then Chief Onikoyi had, at the request of Governor Glover, granted land for farming and settlement to certain Hausa

[1] (1904), 1 N. L. R. 55.   [2] (1942), 16 N. L. R. 88.   [3] p. 82, *infra*.

ex-soldiers. But, not long after, certain Crown Grants, purporting to convey an absolute interest to the grantees, had been issued to them and, when the Ikoyi Lands Ordinance (Cap. 91) came into effect in 1908, these grants were exhibited and approved but the land was not resurveyed nor were fresh grants issued as contemplated by the Ordinance. The last survivor of the Hausa grantees from the chief died in 1916. In 1941 the Nigerian Government wanted to acquire land covered by five of these Crown Grants under the Public Lands Acquisition Ordinance and the question was as to whom compensation should be paid. The Onikoyi Chieftaincy claimed as against some twenty-three others the compensation money on the ground of his right to the reversion on the death of the last survivor of the grantees from the chieftaincy. *Held*: by the Privy Council, confirming the decision of the W.A.C.A.,

'(i) that, since the Onikoyi Chieftaincy had failed to put in a claim under the Ordinance of 1900, the grantees had, under s. 7 thereof, acquired an indefeasible title to the land in question,

'(ii) that, in the Privy Council judgment in the *Bakare Ajakaiye & ors.* v. *Lieut.-Governor, Southern Nigeria*,[1] the Onikoyi Chieftaincy had failed to raise the issue of reverter although part of the land now being claimed was involved in that case. It is hard to take seriously a point raised nearly eighty years after the event, especially as it is raised by the successor in title of the grantor whose authority he now seeks to impeach.'

It is nevertheless clear that nothing short of statute can deprive a chief of his right to the reversion. For example, allotments to stranger occupiers, even if made at the request of the Government of the day, are still governed, as between the grantees and the land-owning chieftaincy, by the customary law of land tenure. Thus, in *Chief Oloto* v. *John*,[2] some parcels of chieftaincy land were given to Governor Glover for allotment among certain refugees from Egba-land. Some of these allotments were, however, not taken up, and the then chief permitted people of Ishan to occupy the vacant ones. The Ishan later abandoned the land but the plaintiff chieftaincy did not resume occupation or make fresh allotments. About 1934, the defendant built upon this land, and claimed to be its fee simple owner for the reason that the right of reverter had become extinguished by the re-allotment of the land to the Ishan people and by the chief's failure to resume occupation after the allottee's subsequent abandonment. *Held*: by the

[1] (1929), A. C. 679.   [2] (1942), 8 W. A. C. A. 127.

W.A.C.A., that the chief's right of reversion remained intact, since there could be no question of any resumption of ownership by the chieftaincy whose *ultimate* title to the land could not be impaired by any grant to strangers who had since abandoned their holdings. But the legal nature of a Government allotment of land in such circumstances was only precisely determined in the slightly later case of *Chief Oloto* v. *Williams & anor.*[1] There, under the Glover Settlement scheme the defendants' ancestors had had allotted to them as Egba refugees in 1868 part of the plaintiff's land (at Ebute Metta) placed at Government disposal for the purpose of settling refugees. The chieftaincy now claimed a right of reversion in the land but the defendants contended that the Glover allotments conferred upon the allottees an absolute title in the nature of Crown Grants and that, in any case, the plaintiff was estopped by acquiescence in the defendants' family's long possession. *Held*: by Butler Lloyd, J., in the Supreme Court at Lagos,

(1) that all that the Glover allotment to the allottees gave was only a right of occupation according to local law and customary, and no more than this had been inherited by the defendants from their ancestors;

(2) that the chief's right of reversion could not be extinguished either by lapse of time or by acquiescence in another's dealing in the land;

(3) that the reversionary right could not, however, be exercised by the chief to oust those in present occupation, since his long acquiescence would then become a relevant factor to take into account. The learned judge gave two reasons for thus holding in favour of the chief's right of reverter:

(1) 'The allottees were *ex hypothesi* refugees and may well have been expected to return to their native country when the conditions which had caused them to leave were removed.

(2) 'Governor Glover's policy was to issue Crown Grants purporting to convey a fee simple to almost any applicant who could show possession of a portion of land. If it was intended that these allottees should take a similar title surely he would have issued Crown Grants instead of the flimsy *tickets* which is all they were provided with' (page 30).

It would thus seem that Crown Grants could confer an indefeasible title upon the grantee, but not tickets of allotment; with the result that the chief's right of reversion might be lost in the first case but not in the second. But our previous analysis of

[1] (1943), 17 N. L. R. 27.

the legal effects of Crown Grants [1] shows that titles acquired thereunder cannot, under the local customary law, be of such an absolute character as to deprive the chief of his right to reversion. The fuller realisation of this fact has led to the passing of Ordinance No. 19 of 1947 (para. 4) and Ordinance No. 21 of 1947, both of which now provide for the chief's right of reversion in spite of any previous Crown grants of land in Lagos.

D. OTHER MATTERS RELATING TO CHIEF'S STATUS

We have seen so far that the chief as trustee or protector can allocate land as well as revoke its grant, can receive tribute or rent and eject from the land for good cause, and has a right of reversion as the juridical embodiment of the community. He represents his own community in its dealings with another community or with other third-parties (including the Government). But, again as we have seen, he cannot employ community land to satisfy his own private wants. Thus, in *Adesola* v. *Giwa*,[2] judgment was obtained in 1929 against Chief Oloto in his personal capacity and property belonging to the chieftaincy was sold under a writ of *Fi-Fa* to satisfy the judgment. The purchaser could not get possession and therefore brought an action for a declaration of title thereto. *Held*: by the Supreme Court at Lagos that the plaintiff purchaser had bought a nullity, since the right, title and interest in the property were those of the Oloto Chieftaincy family.[3] Here the action for possession was resisted by members of the chieftaincy family, but the result is the same where it is a third-party suing for such a sale to be set aside. In *Momo* v. *Igbo & anor.*,[4] the plaintiff was in possession of the chieftaincy land at Ebute Metta which he had bought in 1938 and since let to tenants. The first defendant had in 1940 obtained a judgment against Chief Oloto in his personal capacity and sold under a writ of *Fi-Fa* the chieftaincy land to the second defendant who succeeded in obtaining possession of the property. The plaintiff sued to set aside the sale to the second defendant. *Held*: plaintiff was, as against the second defendant, entitled to possession of the property, not indeed by the strength of his own title but merely because as between two adverse possessors the first in time prevails. Moreover, the plaintiff's title, though unsupported by any deed of conveyance, was well-established and

---

[1] See pp. 24–5, 52–3, *supra*.   [2] (1942), 16 N. L. R. 92.
[3] See also *Kuti & ors.* v. *Salako & anor.* (W. A. C. A. 1679 of April 1942).
[4] (1942), 16 N. L. R. 94.

might be upheld as a valid purchase from the chieftaincy family
if the point was ever litigated; whereas the defendant derived his
possession from the circumstance that chieftaincy land had been
treated as the personal property of a chief, a clearly much weaker
position than that of the plaintiff's direct purchase from the
chieftaincy family.[1]

Even where the plaintiff has derived his title from a supposedly
defective source and has re-purchased the property under a writ
of *Fi-Fa* in the mistaken notion that the judgment creditor or his
assignee might thereby obtain a better title than his own, the sale
may be set aside in his favour. In fact, it was so set aside in
Abraham v. *Chief Oluwa*,[2] where the plaintiff Lodge had bought a
piece of land from one Savage who had himself bought it in 1883
from a holder of a Crown Grant but without a properly executed
deed of conveyance. The defendant, thinking that the land in
question was that of Chief Oloto, advertised its sale under a writ of
Fi-Fa. The plaintiff put up a caution notice but, as the defendant
nevertheless proceeded with the sale, the plaintiff purchased the
land for £68 as the highest bidder, under the mistaken idea that
he had either a defective title or no title at all. He later learnt that
his original title was good and then sued this action for the recovery
of the price of £68 from the defendant. *Held*: by the Supreme Court
that the plaintiff could recover. Here, the land was erroneously
thought by the judgment creditor, a chief, to belong to Chief
Oloto, the judgment debtor, who, as it eventually turned out, had
no kind of connexion whatever with the property in question.
This fact distinguishes this case from those we have just been considering, in which the issue has been that land held by a chief on
behalf of a community cannot be attached for the chief's personal
debts or liabilities.

E. FAMILY HEAD AND THE LAND

The decisions so far considered, while illustrating mainly the
nature of the chief's legal position with respect to community land,
also cover in a general way the case of a family head *qua* family
head. But there are, as between the two, some differences of detail
that deserve notice.

Who is Family Head? As pointed out previously, the proper
person to manage the family land is the oldest male member
thereof whether he happens to be the first-born[3] or, if the first

---

[1] See *per* Butler Lloyd, J., at p. 95.   [2] (1944), 17 N. L. R. 123.
[3] *Lewis* v. *Bankole*, 1 N. L. R. 81.

child be a female, he comes next and so is the oldest male child.[1] If the first-born female, however, happens to be a strong and influential character or if there are no other male members of the family old or pushful enough to assert a claim to the headship, such a senior female may be elected family head: *Rebecca Taiwo* v. *Sarumi*[2] (in which the plaintiff had brought an action on behalf of herself and as head of the family of Chief Taiwo). And Government recognition of such an election is not necessary provided it has been made in accordance with local law and custom.

It must not be supposed that the senior male member of the family is invariably and inevitably the family head, because the family can by a unanimous resolution decide for good cause who should be family head. Thus, in *Inyang* v. *Ita & ors.*[3], Berkeley, J., held that it was within the discretion of the members of a family to choose the person who should be head of their house. The plaintiff had protested that, as the eldest surviving male member of the Ewa Ekeng family at Calabar, the election of another member as the head was contrary to local law and custom, asserting that he was head of the house, without the necessity for an election, because he was the senior male member of the family. Berkeley, J., roughly summarised the position in the following words (at page 85):

'Before the Government came to Calabar and established law and order, it is certain that the headship of a house belonged as of right to the senior male member of that house. But he took it at his peril. If he failed to find support within the family only two courses were open to him. Either he went into exile or else he stayed and was put to death. In either case the succession to the vacancy devolved on the next senior male, if he chose to take it up. . . . Thus we see, even under a system of *strict primogeniture*, the will of the family functioning as an important factor in placing a man in the headship, and in maintaining him there or ejecting him therefrom. (Moreover, it has been common ground throughout this trial that it was quite possible for an exiled head to return. The one condition precedent to such a return being that he made his peace with the family.) His return was sanctioned or refused by

[1] *Ricardo* v. *Abal* (1926), 7 N. L. R. 58; though in this case, as pointed out by Tew, J., at p. 59, *ibid.*, the eldest female child's right of priority of choice in the event of a partition of the family property, remains unaffected. See further the later Chapter on Succession and Inheritance.

[2] 2 N. L. R. 103.

[3] (1929), 9 N. L. R. 84.

democratic suffrage, not by autocratic decree. It is obvious that, even *before* the advent of the Government, the theory of election, though in a very rudimentary form, was already inherent in the family system of the Efik people of Calabar.' [1]

Finally, the family head may be nominated as such by the last deceased holder on his death-bed, and his wishes are almost always respected. This right of the last preceding head may, since the introduction of Wills into the country, sometimes be exercised under his will instead of being orally declared *ante mortem.* Thus, in *Sogbesan & ors.* v. *Adebiyi,*[2] the testator appointed a brother to be the head of his (the deceased's) family and directed that he should act in all family matters under the direction, control and advice of the testator's mother and aunt. The appointment was held valid. Apart from any such express appointment, however, younger brothers of deceased heads of families usually succeeded to the family headship under the ancient and, it would seem, many modern systems of land tenure.

An interesting case in which an appointment by a testator of his eldest son as the family head has been held to imply, in the absence of any express provision in the will to the contrary, the customary duties and prerogatives of the head is *Abusatu Balogun & anor.* v. *Amodu Ayinla Balogun.*[3] There it appeared that the testator, a very wealthy person, was in the habit of looking after all the younger members of the family as well as entertaining strangers and feeding the poor on certain occasions. He appointed the defendant as head under his will but omitted to make him due allowance for the additional expense of caring for the children and of entertaining strangers. *Held:* by W.A.C.A., that his appointment entitled him to the £10 reserved to him out of the income of the estate by the family and the executors (but excluding the two plaintiffs who contested the allowance) towards meeting these demands. The following propositions of Butler Lloyd, acting C.J. (as he then was), were adopted [4] in the judgment of the Appellate Court:

(1) That the customary head of a family has duties of an onerous nature in connexion with family ceremonies, the maintenance of the family house and of the needy members of the family, and hospitality to strangers;

(2) That he is entitled to reimburse himself for expenditure in

---

[1] Cf. W. Price, op. cit., para. 44.   [2] (1941), 16 N. L. R. 26.
[3] (1935), 2 W. A. C. A. 290.
[4] By Aitken, J., at p. 294, and by Barton, J., at p. 305.

connexion with these duties from family resources in his control or failing such resources by contributions from members of the family;

(3) That in the present case the executors made the allowance complained of to the head of the family for the purpose of reimbursing him for expenditure of this nature;

(4) That the allowance has been spent in the manner intended.

Rights and Duties of Family Head. These are much the same as those of the chief in land matters. Indeed, many of the cases discussed in that connexion concern actions litigated by chiefs sometimes *qua* chiefs and sometimes as family heads. The head of the family is, like the chief, a trustee beneficiary of family lands.[1] Actions affecting family land are, as in the case of chiefs with respect to community land, brought by family heads as legal representatives and beneficiary-trustees. In *Aregbe & ors.* v. *Adeoye & anor.*[2] the action was brought by the family heads of Eweino Court, a compound in Lagos, praying that the defendants be restrained from building houses on an adjacent piece of land over which they had hitherto exercised by local law and custom such a degree of control as to entitle their families, as owners and occupiers of the houses in the compound, to the use and enjoyment of the surrounding open space. The headmen could under customary law grant permission to other people to occupy temporarily part of this open space, and they did permit one Labinjoh to erect a shed on part thereof, since such a structure interfered but little with their use and enjoyment of the land. But the plaintiffs in the instant case were non-suited by the Supreme Court, over-ruling the Divisional Court, because instead of basing their claim on local law and custom they had claimed a prescriptive right of user—a concept of English law.[3]

But if the headmen, who normally have the right to protect family land, cannot or will not bring a necessary action, a member of the family can. In *Bassey* v. *Cobham & ors.*[4], the first defendant claimed the absolute ownership of a piece of swamp land which he alleged had been previously given by the then head of the Cobham family (his mother's husband) to his deceased mother

---

[1] See *Bassey* v. *Cobham & ors.* (1924), 5 N. L. R. 90.

[2] (1924), 5 N. L. R. 53.

[3] The headmen could, of course, bring a fresh action to restrain the defendants from interfering with their undoubted rights under local law and custom.

[4] (1924), 5 N. L. R. 90.

who had subsequently reclaimed it. This claim was contrary to the
local law of land tenure according to which no one could be absolute owner of part of family land even if such a one had reclaimed
it from the swamp. The plaintiff, who was not the family head,
brought an action to dispute this claim of the first defendant
against the family land. The first defendant denied the plaintiff's
right to bring the action. *Held*: that, since the head of the family
is as regards family land in a position analogous to that of a
trustee and since the members of the family are beneficiaries, any
member may assert a right to its protection if the head neglects or
refuses to do so.

Now, the same rights of grant of land and of its revocation, of
ejection as well as of reversion, inhere in the family head even as
they do in the chief. An attempt by a member of the family to
alienate part of family land without the prior consent of the family
head and other elders may work a forfeiture of the individual's
holding. In *Kadiri Adagun* v. *Fagbola*,[1] the head of the Olorogun
family was held entitled to eject the defendant member of the
family when the latter mortgaged his allotted portion to a third
party who proceeded to advertise the property for sale and so
enabled the family to become aware for the first time of the
defendant's illegal dealing with his allotment. Kingdon, C.J.,
observed (at page 111):

'When the head of a family allots to a member of the family a
portion of the family land for him to live on, that member becomes
entitled to occupy and enjoy that portion during good behaviour,
but he does not become the owner of the land as against the family
and he cannot alienate it without the consent of the family; if he
does so, his action amounts to misbehaviour and he can be treated
by the family as having forfeited his right to occupy the land and
be ejected.'

It follows, therefore, that if the family head may eject a free,
sanguine member of the family for condition broken, he may
with greater justification evict a slave member or the descendants
of one. Accordingly, in *L. B. Onisiwo* v. *Gbamgboye & ors.*,[2] the
defendants, who were the descendants of an ancestor of the
plaintiffs, granted a thirty years' lease of their overlords' family
land without the prior consent of the head of that family. *Held*: by
the W.A.C.A., affirming the Supreme Court at Lagos, that the

[1] (1932), 11 N. L. R. 110.
[2] (1941), 7 W. A. C. A. 69. Sub-nom. *L. Buraimo* v. *T. Bamgboye* (1940), 15
N. L. R. 139.

defendants-appellants' misbehaviour constituted such a challenge to their overlords' rights to the family land as under local law and custom to involve forfeiture of their allotments. But it may be that a short lease in similar circumstances would not work such a forfeiture.[1] It must, however, be noted that this rule that the family head can evict an occupier for serious misbehaviour is a concept purely of the indigenous system of land tenure, and should not be confused with the very different rights of a landlord over his tenant under English law. Accordingly, when the plaintiff in *Bashua* v. *Odunsi & another*,[2] attempted to evict his monthly tenant under English law, by a confused appeal to local law and custom, it was held that he could not act otherwise than in consonance with the terms of the tenancy agreement between him and his tenant—'a native customary law by which the denial by a tenant of the landlord's ownership of the premises extinguishes the tenancy cannot apply to a tenancy by the month at a monthly rent which was not proved to be a native customary tenancy.'

Although, in olden days, slaves or domestics were assimilated to their overlord's family household, they still retained a measure of individuality which normally gave them full control over their *personal* property. Since they must depend on their overlord for land they could not obviously own lands of their own. The family head, while retaining the reversion in land granted to former domestics, cannot claim any ownership in their personal property. As Butler Lloyd, J., said in delivering the Divisional Court judgment at Calabar (at page 65) in the case of *In Re Offiong Okon Ata:*[3]

'Personal property acquired by slaves is in their absolute disposition subject to the ordinary rules of law as to dealings with it, and to hold that the mere fact of the slave continuing to reside on the communal property confers any rights whatever on the head of the house in respect of personal property would be very largely to render nugatory the provisions of the Slavery Abolition Ordinance; and to import a native custom to that effect would be contrary to natural justice.'

Similarly, in *Martin* v. *Johnson & anor.*,[4] the first defendant claimed, as against the plaintiff next of kin, to be entitled to the

[1] The judges of W. A. C. A., at p. 70. But how short must be such an innocent alienation by persons in the position of defendants is not indicated by the learned Appellate judges. Every case must be considered on its own facts. [2] (1940), 15 N. L. R. 107.
[3] (1930), 10 N. L. R. 65. [4] (1935), 12 N. L. R. 46.

grant of letters of administration of a deceased's personal estate on the ground that the deceased's father was a slave of the house of which the first defendant had then become head. The deceased died intestate in 1934 at Buea in the Cameroons under British mandate. *Held*: that, since the abolition of slavery in Nigeria, the head of the family no longer has any right in or over the personal property of slave members of the family.

Accountability of Family Head. The final point we want to make here concerns the extent to which the head of a family is accountable to the family for his dealings with family property. We may take it that he, like the chief, cannot use family land or its proceeds for his own purposes. If family property is attached for his debts the creditor gets nothing and the transaction is absolutely void. Equally important is it also that he makes no major disposal of family property without consulting the senior members of the family. This is a useful device of customary law to check the family head from possible mis-use of his powers over the family land. But, *quaere*, whether transactions engaged in for the benefit of family land by the family head without necessary consultations are, with regard to third parties, merely voidable, and not void? On principle such dealings by the acknowledged legal representative of the family should be only voidable, especially if the family land stands to benefit thereby.

But, where what the family head has done has been speculative or reckless or surreptitious, he will be liable for it personally. Hence it was that, in *Aralawon* v. *Aromire & anor.*,[1] the first defendant as the acting family head was held personally liable to refund the loan he had taken, without family consultation or consent, from the plaintiff for the purpose of prosecuting speculative litigation and rebuilding the official residence of the chief of which he was the then occupant. Carey, J., very pertinently summed up thus (at page 91):

The head of the family undoubtedly has power to bind the family in routine matters, but before borrowing appreciable sums of money, disposing of, or charging family property, etc., except possibly where he acts in an emergency for the benefit of the family, he must consult the senior members of the various branches of the family and get their approval.[2]

---

[1] (1940), 15 N. L. R. 90.
[2] Cf. J. M. Sarbah's *Fanti Customary Law*, at p. 78: 'If the family therefore find the head of the family misappropriating the family possessions and squandering them, the only remedy is to remove him and appoint another

If the family head has, however, acted properly and fairly with respect to his dealings with the family land so that he can count on the support of the majority of the members of the family, he will not be compelled to render accounts to a dissident minority. Thus in *Kosoko* v. *Kosoko & ors.*[1], the plaintiff claimed as against the defendants an order of the Court for an account of all the rents and mesne profits of the family property which the defendants as trustees had managed for about forty years before action brought. The local law did not require the keeping of accounts so long as there had been no definite breach or abuse of the manager's trust; the defendants had accordingly kept no accounts until shortly before the suit was brought. *Held*: that the plaintiff, having left Lagos and deliberately absented himself from the family meetings for over thirty years, could not then on his return claim an account of the concerted dealings of the trustees with the family land. Here the place of the usual family head acting alone was taken by the head with a council of senior members acting jointly; and that seemed to have made the plaintiff's case against them so much weaker, as also was the fact that only one other member supported the plaintiff. Carey, J., wound up in these words (at page 132):

'Furthermore I am not satisfied that the plaintiff, who apparently is not supported by his brothers and sisters, has any rights in the circumstances disclosed, as a solitary individual to demand from the head of a large family who has the support of the family behind him, except for one other member, an account of the family's dealings with the family property, unless he can point to a definite delinquency amounting in effect to a breach of trust by the family representatives.'

instead; and although no junior member can claim an account from the head of the family or call for an appropriation to himself of any special portion of the family estate or income therefrom arising, yet the Customary Law says they who are born or they who are still in the womb require means of support, wherefore the family land and possessions must not be wasted or squandered.'
—Cited, with approval, by Mitchelin, J., in delivering the judgment of W. A. C. A. in *Nelson* v. *Nelson* (1932), 1 W. A. C. A. 215, at p. 216. In this case some of the children of a deceased native brought an action for an account against a brother of theirs who had been appointed by the deceased, on his death-bed, to look after their interests in his estate. *Held*: that an action for an account lay against him as he was not the head of a family, as that term is understood in the customary law of the Gold Coast, but a 'caretaker' for his brothers and sisters.

[1] (1936), 13 N. L. R. 131.

Chapter Seven

INDIGENOUS SYSTEMS OF TENURE
(continued)

A. The Juridical Nature of Rights of Individuals in Land. B. Capacity to hold Land—Special Cases of. C. Individual Rights in the Cameroons. D. Conditions of Cesser of Individual Rights in Land.

A. THE JURIDICAL NATURE OF THE RIGHTS OF INDIVIDUALS IN LAND

T HE right of an occupier to his land under the customary tenure of land is usually described as 'usufructuary' but this term, though convenient and highly suggestive, is not very accurate. For, whereas the Roman usufructuary normally enjoyed only a species of *jus in re aliena* (i.e. right over the land of another) and was in any case bound to return his holding unimpaired to the *dominus* of the land at the end of a fixed period or at his death, the Nigerian occupier's [1] interest in or right over the land of his community or family partakes of the nature of part-ownership enjoyable, at least in theory, in perpetuity and not subject to many of the pettifogging restrictions [2] which were the inevitable incidents of any form of servitude such as was a usufruct.

[1] We are not, of course, here dealing with the special cases of slaves or strangers to whom a portion of family land might be given with or without conditions. Our immediate concern is with the right of a normal occupier of land as a member of a land-owning family.

[2] What these were would become clear to anyone who might care to compare the following account of the Nigerian occupier's rights to land with that of his Roman counterpart in any standard textbook on the subject—e.g. Moyle, *Institute of Justinian*, 1931 Impr., pp. 221–4; Buckland, *A Manual of Roman Private Law* (2nd edition), pp. 162–5.

The very early development of the conception of *absolute* ownership of land in Rome, in contrast with the Greek idea of *relative* ownership,[1] makes the Roman usufructuary a strange bed-fellow of the Nigerian occupier; the latter's interest is not, as was invariably that of the usufructuary, in any sense alien to the ultimate ownership of the land. The Nigerian occupier's rights are indeed relative with respect to those of the other members of the family whose welfare, which is the community's, is the only limiting factor.

The more detailed analysis which we are about to attempt will, it is hoped, bring out more clearly the technical inaccuracy of describing the Nigerian occupier of land as a usufructuary, from whom he is, of course, at first scarcely distinguishable.

An attempt to delimit the exact scope of the rights of the individual in the family land is at once fraught with the difficulties inherent in the very nature of the hitherto largely undifferentiated complex of land rights. Now, if one grants that the normal occupier is not strictly a usufructuary of the land, the question is: What, then, is he? We have to examine *four* closely integrated questions:

(A) Does he hold a separate and individual share or an 'undivided share'[2] in the family land allotted to him? This naturally involves the further and related question as to whether his interest is *real* or *personal* property.

(B) Is his right to the land a pure *life interest*, or is it *hereditary*?

(C) Can his title be regarded as really *proprietary* or as merely *possessory*?

(D) Or, in terms which English law has made familiar, shall we consider him as enjoying a joint tenancy or a tenancy in common?

Now, under the traditional system land could in the first place be acquired by an individual in one of four ways:

(i) A man might have taken some yet unappropriated land for himself;

(ii) He might, as a welcome stranger to a land-owning family,

---

[1] See Vinogradoff, *Historical Jurisprudence*, Vol. II, Chap. X, p. 198: 'As to the problem under discussion, Rome developed the conception of absolute property for the citizen—the *dominium ex jure Quiritium*—while Athens worked out a conception of *relative* property rights.' (Also, pp. 197–229 *passim*.)

See also, Hunter, *Introduction to Roman Law* (9th edition), pp. 69–70; Lee, *Roman Law* (pp. 162–3, 166–7).

[2] This expression is not here used with the strict particularity of s. 34 L. P. A. 1925 and its transitional provisions. Its special meaning will become clear as we proceed.

have been granted land by the head of the family, subject to the latter's right of reverter;

(iii) It might be an out-and-out gift to him of virgin land by a family having more land than it actually needed; or

(iv) A man might, as a member of a family, inherit a share of family land, the ownership being of course still in the family.

Also, town-land for building purposes might often be given outright to an individual, whether or not he was a stranger. To our list may be added the type of interest acquired by an individual on a partition of a formerly jointly-owned land.

But, in every case, at the death of the original grantee the land would at once become family land in the hands of his children and other relations. Even when land has been acquired by an individual in fee simple under English forms of conveyance, it has been held that such land became, with respect to his children, family land on the death of the owner, testate or intestate.[1]

It is at this point, then, that we are confronted with the basic problem of finding out the precise legal nature of the right of the individual in the family land. Unfortunately, the requirements of social cohesion implicit in the kinship basis of tenure have obscured or obviated the need for a clear formulation of principles regarding the rights of the individual in land. So long as every member of the group had enough land for the limited needs of a subsistence economy, which used to rule and still largely rules the indigenous system of tenure, the older generations of Nigerians did not trouble themselves over-much about any abstract theories of the nature of individual rights.

We have, therefore, to fall back upon such principles as can be extracted from judicial decisions if we are to formulate any reasonably intelligible rules according to modern notions and usage. Let us now try to consider the four problems we have posed above by reference to their judicial treatment.

The earliest important case is *Lewis & ors.* v. *Bankole*,[2] where a man, Mabinuori, having acquired certain plots of land about 1868 died in 1874, leaving twelve children the eldest of whom was a woman although the oldest son, Fagbemi, succeeded their father as the family head in their father's house. There were three pieces of land forming the estate of Mabinuori. Fatola, Oduntan and Odubi, three of these original twelve children of Mabinuori, had been granted some adjacent land and houses (later known as

---

[1] See *Jacobs* v. *Oladunni Bros.* (1935), 12 N. L. R. 1.
[2] (1909), 1 N. L. R. 82.

Fatola's Compound) by their father during his life, while the other children lived with him in the main residence (the Mabinuori Compound) up to his death; also, some members of the branch families of the three children living apart from Mabinuori had later been allotted houses and rooms in the main building. The children of these three children of Mabinuori as plaintiffs contended that (1) Mabinuori Compound was family property to which all the descendants of Mabinuori were equally entitled, and (2) they (the plaintiffs) had (i) a right to be consulted before the family compound was leased or otherwise dealt with; (ii) a right to share in any rents or profits accruing from dealings with the family compound; (iii) a right to build on any unoccupied part of the family compound; and (iv) a right of ingress and egress. In short, they claimed as grandchildren to be entitled to the joint-ownership of the land in dispute as tenants in common having equal shares [1] with the defendants, direct children of Mabinuori, who, on the other hand, asserted, by reason of the fact that they had always resided with their father in the compound, a claim to something analogous to individual absolute ownership of their several allotments which they had enjoyed for over thirty years before action was brought.

Speed, Acting C.J., in refusing in the Divisional Court to 'throw the property into the melting pot of an acrimonious family feud', favoured the defendants' claim to individual absolute ownership of their allotments in the Compound, and held: 'On the ground therefore that by tacit mutual arrangement and acquiescence of all parties extending over a number of years these various properties have been separated and come to be considered as separately owned, I find on this issue in favour of the defendants.' [2] The plaintiffs appealed to the Full Court which reversed this decision, remitting the case to the Divisional Court to take fuller evidence of Lagos law and custom and then either give a fresh judgment or state a case for the opinion of the Supreme Court.

At the resumed Divisional Court hearing on 29 June 1909, White-Capped Chiefs Ojora, Eletu Odibo, Oloto and Onitana and war-chief Ashogbon gave evidence as expert witnesses. [3] Osborne, C.J., then held, with reference to the issues with which we are

---

[1] *Per* Osborne, C.J., at p. 88, (1909), 1 N. L. R. 82.   [2] Ibid., p. 87.

[3] It is interesting to record here that, thanks to the plaintiff's witnesses from other parts of Yoruba-land, the Lagos customary law was found by the Court to be generally the same as those of other Yoruba areas. (See pp. 102–3, ibid.)

here immediately concerned, that: (1) all the branches of the Mabinuori family had a right to be consulted before family property could be leased or otherwise dealt with; (2) rents from a lease should be divided in equal shares between the respective branches, regard being had to property received by any of the founder's children during his life-time; (3) the different branches of the founder's family would be represented *per stirpes* on the family council, each branch having one vote; (4) grandchildren of the founder, the plaintiffs in this case, had no inherent right to build in the family compound without the prior consent of the family council; (5) normally, members of a family who do not reside on the family property have no general right of ingress and egress, but have a right of entry to attend family meetings, and, if members of the family council, a right of entry to inspect the state of repairs; such rights must, however, be exercised so as not to interfere unnecessarily with the quiet enjoyment of the occupants.

Two important principles we may deduce from this interesting case are (1) that the grandchildren of a founder of a family do not in Yoruba-land usually enjoy the exact plenitude of rights in family land which his immediate children have; (2) that the individual allottee of family land enjoys anything but an absolute fee simple estate in his holding. This latter principle would seem to have been the basis of the decision of the West African Court of Appeal when in *Oshodi* v. *Balogun & ors.*[1] it was held that no absolute estate in fee simple could pass to a purchaser for value to whom part of the Oshodi Chieftaincy family had been conveyed by a descendant of a domestic in the Oshodi Compound. It was pointed out that the same result would follow if the conveyance had been by any other member of the family, since no individual allottee of family land has an absolute fee simple in his share.

It will be observed that in *Lewis* v. *Bankole* the main issue was the determination of the rights of *non-resident* grandchildren of the founder of the family in the family house. We must supplement our information there with a brief reference to the almost identical findings on the rights of *resident* members *per se* in *Thomas* v. *Thomas & anor.*[2] where, in an action between members of a family for sharing rents of leased portions of the family house, Butler Lloyd, J., in the Supreme Court held as follows: 'Now so far as I can gather from the existing decisions, the rights of members of a

[1] (1936), 4 W. A. C. A. 1; (1936), 2 A. E. R. 1632; followed in *Oshodi* v. *Imoru & ors.* (1936), 3 W. A. C. A. 93.   [2] (1932), 16 N. L. R. 5.

family with regard to a family house are (1) to reside in it; (2) to have reasonable ingress and egress; (3) to have a voice in its management; and (4) to share in any surplus of income derived from it after necessary outgoings have been met; and if these rights are infringed they can come to this Court, which will enforce them by partition and/or sale if necessary.' [1] The two main additions to our knowledge appear to be: (a) the individual member's right of residence and (b) his right to apply to the Court for partition or sale. We shall take each of these points in turn.

Right of Residence. As to the right of residence we may quote two illustrative passages from two other decisions:

Thus observed Tew, J., in *Ricardo* v. *Abal*: [2] 'Each party so interested has *the right to live* on the property and the right to come to the Court to ask for partition (see *Lopez* v. *Lopez*, 5 N. L. R. 47) and that is the whole extent of his or her individual interest. That interest would pass to his or her children under native law and custom, but in no case to anyone who was not of the same blood, and consequently not to his or her wife or husband.'

And Kingdon, C.J., in *Adagun* v. *Fagbola*: [3] 'When the head of a family allots to a member of the family a portion of the family land for him to live on, that member becomes entitled to occupy and enjoy that portion during good behaviour, but he does not become the owner of the land as against the family and he cannot alienate it without the consent of the family.'

Thus, in *Miller Bros.* v. *Ayeni*,[4] the appellants sought to attach the interest of the respondent judgment debtor in certain family property, and the latter's brothers successfully resisted the appellants' claim on the ground that their brother had no separate and alienable interest in the family property which the appellants could seize in satisfaction of their debt. Van der Meulen, J., delivering the judgment of the Supreme Court, observed that although their father had bought the land under a conveyance of 6 October 1899, yet on his death intestate the children held undivided shares in common under local customary tenure, and *not* as tenants in common under English law.[5]

---

[1] (1932), 16 N. L. R., at p. 5.   [2] (1926), 7 N. L. R. 58, at p. 59.
[3] (1932), 11 N. L. R. 110, at p. 111.
[4] (1924), 5 N. L. R. 40; applied in *Jacobs* v. *Oladunni Bros.* (1935), 12 N. L. R. 1.
[5] Van der Meulen, J., pertinently added at p. 42, ibid.: '. . . it may also be pointed out that under the principles governing the English law of property they could not on an intestacy have inherited this property as tenants in common.'

A similar result was reached on substantially the same facts by Berkeley, J., in the Supreme Court decision of *Majekodunmi* v. *Amodu Tijani* [1] where the learned judge emphasised: 'There is nothing to show that these allotments were intended to or did create a separate and alienable estate in the persons to whom they were allotted. . . . In the course of his evidence he (the plaintiff) stated that some of the family land remained unallocated. But this in itself is sufficient to show that no partition has taken place, but merely a series of allotments for occupation according to native custom.' [2]

The point of the difference between tenancy in common by English property law and the customary common tenancy of local tenure was well brought out in *Caulcrick* v. *Harding & anor.* [3] The facts were that the plaintiff, as the husband of one of the three daughters of a deceased intestate, claimed a one-third share of the land in virtue of his wife's right, although the wife had since died. Tew, J., held that the father's death intestate created a customary common tenancy by which no one member had any separate estate apart from the whole: 'The plaintiff's claim is really based on the argument that Agnes Caulcrick could have disposed of her one-third interest in the property by will, and that, as she died intestate, this interest passed as personalty to the plaintiff. This argument is entirely fallacious for it rests on the assumption that the three daughters of Labinjoh were tenants in common in the meaning which that term has in English law.' [4] The learned Judge then cited *Miller Bros.* v. *Ayeni* [5] as authority for the proposition that 'a tenancy in common was a tenure unknown to native law', and concluded: 'The customary tenure recognised by native law and custom as arising in such a case has not the essential characteristics of a tenancy in common strictly so-called, in that it gives no right of alienation.' [6]

For this reason, Butler Lloyd, J., held in the Supreme Court judgment of *George & anor.* v. *Fajore* [7] that, where a testator

---

[1] (1932), 11 N. L. R. 74. But in the somewhat unsatisfactory case of *Saibu* v. *Igbo* (1941), 16 N. L. R. 25, it was held that the interest in house property of a judgment debtor who was in the position of a tenant in common was attachable under a writ of Fi-Fa.

[2] (1932), 11 N. L. R. 74, at p. 75.

[3] (1926), 7 N. L. R. 48.

[4] (1926), 7. N. L. R. 48, at p. 49.

[5] (1924), 5 N. L. R. 40.

[6] (1926), 7 N. L. R., at p. 49.

[7] (1939), 15 N. L. R. 1.

devised his land to twelve named persons 'their heirs and assigns for ever *as tenants in common*[1] without any power or right to alienate or anticipate the same or any part thereof', the use of the words 'tenants in common' did not alter the fact that the testator intended the property to be held in accordance with local customary law of tenure, so that the defendant in the case, the testator's widow, could not claim her son's interest upon his death without issue.

At this stage, it is instructive to note the interesting corollary from the nature of local customary common tenancy which Graham Paul, J., drew in *Taylor* v. *Williams & anor.*[2], to the effect that a devise by a testatrix of her undivided share in a family property, *even where the devise was to her own son*, was null and void, since under local law and custom she could not dispose of her 'unliquidated' interest whether by will or otherwise. This at once raises the issue as to whether the individual's right in the family land is or is not an estate of inheritance which he or she can leave to her children as she chooses. It is clear from this judgment that the individual has no such right and that his or her issue must look to the customary rules of tenure for their rights. We may quote the following definitive words of the learned judge in full, as they throw a flood of light on the whole problem of the individual's right in family land. He said: [3]

'It has been for long settled law in this Court that a member of a family in these parts cannot alienate his or her undivided share in the family property, and in the case of *Ogunmefun* v. *Ogunmefun & ors.* (N. L. R., Vol. X, page 82) it was specifically held following the earlier cases that a testatrix could not devise by will her undivided share in her father's land. . . . In my view *the basis of all decisions on this point is not that it was a stranger to whom the alienation was being made but that there was not in the member of the family any right or interest of which he or she could dispose.*'

Then he continued:

'Until there has been partition, that is until the family structure, with all its incidents of native custom, has been broken up, it seems to me that the correct view is at any moment that the ownership of the family property is vested in the whole family as trustees for the whole family. *Each individual member of the family has in addition vested in him or her what may perhaps be described as a*

[1] Italics are the authors.

[2] (1935), 12 N. L. R. 67; see also *Davies* v. *Sogunro & ors.* (1936), 13 N. L. R. 15.

[3] (1935), 12 N. L. R., at p. 69. (The italics are the present writer's.)

*right of user during his or her life. That individual right of user is
to my mind purely and simply a life interest.* On the death of the
individual that interest reverts to the whole family though by
reason of the user enjoyed by the deceased individual during his or
her life, the family will generally permit his or her children to have
among them the same user as their parent had if the circumstances
of the family and of the property admit.' [1]

With the latter part of this passage may be contrasted Viscount
Dunedin's following statement in *Oshodi* v. *Dakolo & ors.*: [2]
'These various occupiers have the right to remain and to transmit
their holdings to their offspring, but in the event of the family of
an occupier failing and being extinct, the chief has a right of reversion.' If all that Viscount Dunedin meant to say was that the
individual's right of transmission of his share to his offspring is as
according to local law and custom, issue can hardly be joined on
the point. The truth is that there is no individual estate of inheritance (in the fullest sense) in an undivided family land, but the
children are not necessarily left to the whim and caprice of the
family head with regard to their right of succession to their father's
share therein. In short, the individual's share is not an absolute
life interest.

Before we turn to a consideration of the issue of partition and
its consequences, there are two more points to record. One is the
possible distinction that one might make between land rights
acquired by the individual by purchase in more recent times and
rights enjoyed by the individual in family land under the indigenous
system of tenure. Thus, in *Chief Eyo Ita & ors.* v. *Asido*,[3] in which
the plaintiffs had sought a declaration of title to land at Ikot
Esion in Calabar, Webber, C.J., in delivering the judgment of the
West African Court of Appeal, remarked: 'It is indubitable that
if the learned Judge had found in favour of a sale of the land a
grant of declaration of title conveying a fee simple was inevitable
but he does not appear to have discriminated between rights in the
acquisition of native land by purchase and rights acquired under
native law and custom—*the former being* proprietary *rights and
the latter* possessory *rights or rights of occupancy.*' [4] Much the
same language was used by Osborne, C.J., in *Lewis* v. *Bankole* [5]

[1] (1935), 12 N. L. R., at p. 70.
[2] (1930), A. C. 667, at p. 668.
[3] (1935), 2 W. A. C. A. 339.
[4] Ibid., at p. 340. (The italics are the author's.)
[5] (1909), 1 N. L. R. 82

when he said: [1] 'Nothing in this judgment will affect the *possessory* rights of those members of the family who were actually living in the family compound when this writ was issued, or who had houses or rooms which they were then entitled to occupy for residential purposes.'

The other matter to be noted is the distinction made between the individual's inalienable right in the family land as such and his alienable one in any structure such as a building which he may super-impose on the family land (with, of course, the consent of the family) by his own personal exertions. This seems to go on the analogy of the right given to the individual by customary law to formerly unappropriated land first cultivated by him or to crops planted by him on existing family land. There would seem to have been no direct Supreme (or Higher) Court decision on the point, but in a case at Iperu in the Ijebu Province of Yoruba-land,[2] one Desalu owed a debt to one Coker and the Supreme Court issued a write of Fi-Fa to attach the judgment debtor's interest. A successful interpleader summons was allowed to other members of the family who claimed that the land, but *not* the house erected by Desalu thereon, was their family property. The Court, therefore, held that only the house could be attached, as it was the only thing which Desalu could claim as his absolute property.

Right to Partition. With regard to the individual's right to demand partition [3] of the family land, this is usually granted where disputes as to occupation rights or as to the sharing of net rents from leasing family property cannot be amicably settled among the family members themselves. But the elders in former times and now the Courts would exercise a discretion as to what might be best in the interest of the family as a whole in ordering partition or sale of the family land. The mode of carrying out partition under the local law has been thus described by Chiefs Eletu and Ashogbon as expert witnesses in the case of *Ricardo* v. *Abal*: [4] 'The Council of the family, or of neighbours, as the case might be, would divide the property into two or more parts, as required, and

---

[1] (1935), 2 W. A. C. A. 339, at p. 106; see also *per* Viscount Haldane in *Amodu Tijani* v. *Secretary, S. Nigeria* (1921), 2 A. C. 399, at p. 410.

[2] See para. 320 of Ward Price's *Land Tenure in the Yoruba Provinces* (1933). For the general uncertainty of Native Courts' decisions and of local witnesses in such a matter as the nature of the individual's rights, see paras. 316–21 of the same Report.

[3] See p. 147, *ante*.

[4] (1926), 7 N. L. R. 58.

the eldest child, whether male or female, would take the first choice.' [1]

In this case both plaintiff (a female) and defendant (a junior male, who however became the family head) agreed to partition, and the only dispute was as to the order of choice. The Court held that the priority of choice rested with the plaintiff as the eldest child, irrespective of sex. The same principle of equality and impartiality of the Yoruba law of tenure was up-held by the Divisional Court in *Sule & ors.* v. *Ajisegiri* [2] where it was ruled that partition must be equally between those entitled to it, regardless of sex.[3] Even an illegitimate (illegitimate, that is, by English law) son has been held entitled to a share of his father's land on the latter's death intestate.[4] In *Chairman, L.E.D.B.* v. *Ashani & ors.*[5] it was decided that a partition of family land by a deed of agreement, which differed from a scheme under the testator's will, was valid even though some of the beneficiaries were minors at the date of partition; the proper representatives of the minors had consented to the subsequent agreement on behalf of the minors. They were free to impeach the partition in a court of law as soon as they attained their majority; instead, they continued years later to take benefits under the partition.

But the court will not order a sale or partition of family land if none of the individual's customary rights enumerated above [6] is infringed. That was why the Supreme Court refused in *Thomas* v. *Thomas* [7] to grant to the plaintiff member of a family his prayer for a sale or partition on the mere ground that the family head had not allowed him a share of the net rents, which were proved to be nil, accruing from a lease of portion of the family property. Similarly, where in *Bajulaiye & anor.* v. *Akapo* [8] the parties to the action agreed that partition was impracticable, Butler Lloyd, J., refused to order a sale or partition of family property for no better reason than that some of the interested parties desired to turn the

[1] *Per* Tew, J., at p. 59, ibid.
Compare also (1) the Lagos Chiefs' evidence as to the principles of partition at pp. 96–8 and 103–4 of *Lewis* v. *Bankole* (1909), 1 N. L. R. 82; (2) M. M. Green, *Land Tenure in an Ibo Village*, pp. 13–14.
[2] (1937), 13 N. L. R. 147; see also *Andre* v. *Agbebi*, 10 N. L. R. 79.
[3] Hence *Lopez* v. *Lopez* (1924), 5 N. L. R. 47, was doubted.
[4] *Davies* v. *Sogunro* (1936), 13 N. L. R. 15.
[5] (1937), 3 W. A. C. A. 143.
[6] See pp. 146–7, *supra*.
[7] (1932), 16 N. L. R. 5.
[8] (1938), 14 N. L. R. 10.

family property into cash. The first plaintiff did not wish, and had not asked, to live on the premises. The defendant, on the other hand, was willing for the plaintiffs to share in the occupation of the premises or alternatively in the rents derived therefrom, but did not want the property to be sold.

The guiding principle for the family council or the court seems to be a consideration of what in a given situation is best in the interest of the family as a whole. Butler Lloyd thus explained the institution of 'family house': [1]

'The purpose of the institution is, as its name implies, to provide a place where members of the family can reside if they so desire and, so long as that purpose is still capable of achievement, I conceive that it would be wrong for the Court to order the sale of property subject to this form of tenure.' Further light was thrown on the subject by the judgment of Carey, J., in *In the matter of the Estate of Edward Forster* [2] where property left under a testator's will was held to be intended as 'family house' under the local law of tenure. He observed that the institution of 'family house' among the Yorubas is designed as a permanent residence set apart by the father of a family for occupation, during and after his decease, by his wives and children. It cannot therefore be sold by any of the children who, if male, have the right to reside with their mothers, wives and children therein and, if female, are entitled to reside therein until marriage or thereafter on deserting or being deserted by their husbands. To mortgage or sell the family house, the consent of all those thus entitled to reside therein must first be obtained. [3]

But, on the principle of what is best for the family as a whole, the Court would nevertheless order a partition or sale of family land, although a trust deed by which the land was devised by a testator forbade it. [4]

Now, in almost all the decisions we have been considering in this Chapter, the judges have insisted on two factors as conditions precedent to the alienability of a member's interest in family land:

---

[1] (1938), 14 N. L. R. 10, at p. 10; see also *Olawoyin & anor.* v. *Coker* (1892), 16 August: (Law Reports (Colonial), Nigeria A) in the Colonial Office Legal Library—(claim for partition of house and land in Shopono St., Lagos).

[2] (1938), 14 N. L. R. 83.

[3] Ibid., at p. 86. To realise the universality of these principles throughout Yorubaland, see, e.g. para. 298 of Ward Price, op. cit.

[4] *Giwa & ors.* v. *Otun & ors.* (1932), 11 N. L. R. 160. But it was clear from the Trust Deed in question that the testator intended it to be governed by English law.

(*a*) prior consent of the family, and (*b*) partition of the land, where possible and authorised either by the family council or by the court.

It would seem to be implicit in such a statement that with family consent or by partition the individual acquires a separate and absolute estate in his share. The first noteworthy pronouncement is that of Chief Eletu Odibo in his evidence in *Lewis* v. *Bankole* [1] when he declared: 'I agree with the Ojora except on one point. If the compound is divided it will no longer be a compound, and each one will have authority in his own portion.' One would hesitate to deduce from this any clear principle of an absolute property being vested in the individual member by partition.

A much more intriguing case is *Oshodi* v. *Balogun* [2] in which the West African Court of Appeal held that a purchaser from or through a descendant of a domestic of the Oshodi family could not acquire a fee simple absolute estate in the portion of family land purported to be thereby conveyed to him. But Lord Maugham, in his Privy Council judgment which virtually confirmed that of the W. A. C. A., warned: [3] 'To prevent any misconception it seems desirable to state that the present decision is not based on any doubt as to the possibility of a title equivalent to a fee simple being obtained as the result of a sale of family lands with the general consent of the family.' He then cited Lord Dunedin's judgment in the *Dakolo Case* and proceeded: [4] 'The last sentence above quoted means only that the chief as contrasted with the family as a whole has no fee simple. The dispute was in fact between the chief as plaintiff and the occupants as a body as defendants. No question as to the extent of the family title arose.'

It would appear from the concluding words of the latter quotation that what their Lordships of the Privy Council were conceding was that the family as a whole could have the fee simple in the family land, which could be made over to a purchaser with necessary consent; but that the chief or family head as such had no independent fee simple of his own in the family land as against other members. We are still left with the question as to whether, on partition or with family consent, this fee simple of the family, can be regarded as split into as many parts as there are eligible family members, each such part being an absolute estate in itself

[1] (1909), 1 N. L. R. 82, at p. 97.
[2] (1936), 4 W. A. C. A. 1; (1936), 2 All E. R. 1632.
[3] Ibid., at pp. 6 and 1638 respectively.
[4] Ibid.

capable of alienation or attachment for debt? If we hold with Chief Eletu Odibo in *Lewis* v. *Bankole* [1] and with Graham Paul [2] in *Taylor* v. *Williams & anor.* that partition breaks down the family structure with all its incidents of customary tenure, it is possible that an absolute separate property enures to the individual on a partition of family land. This point was expressly laid down by W. A. C. A. in the recent case of *Balogun* v. *Balogun & ors.* [3] where the seven surviving children of one Okolo Balogun by deed partitioned the whole of their father's property in Lagos into well-defined portions. The plaintiff-appellant claimed, as against the defendants-respondents' contention, that the property was in spite of partition still family property, that he had an absolute title to those portions of the partitioned property which he had acquired by and in consequence of the partition. *Held*: by the West African Court of Appeal that a partition of family land, with the consent of all members of the family, conferred on each member an *absolute* property in his partitioned portion.

What is not so clear, however, is the nature of the interest which an individual can alienate to a purchaser (including in this term a mortgagee and the like) where only the family consent has been obtained to the transaction but no partition has yet taken place of the family land. Since in such a case the family structure remains intact, it would appear that the portion alienated from the undivided whole cannot be a fee simple, unless indeed such family consent to the deal is to be interpreted as equivalent to a partial partition as between the individual's interest so transferred and the remaining block left in the family. In this connexion we may note that where part of family land is given to a member thereof for his occupation, it still remains family property although he may have improved it by, for example, clearing some bush or reclaiming a swamp thereon. Thus, in *Bassey* v. *Cobham & ors.* [4], Webber, J., in the Divisional Court at Calabar held that, on a careful consideration of the evidence of local assessors on customary tenure, the act of reclaiming swamp land does not confer any special property in the land reclaimed on the individual who reclaims it as against the corp oratetitle of the family. The learned Judge said:

[1] (1909), 1 N. L. R. 82.

[2] See pp. 149–50 earlier; see also *per* Kingdon, C.J., in *Balogun* v. *Balogun & ors.* (1943), 9 W. A. C. A. 78, at p. 84.

[3] (1943), 9 W. A. C. A. 78; see also *Chairman, L.E.D.B.* v. *Ashani & ors.* (1937), 3 W. A. C. A. 143.

[4] (1924), 5 N. L. R. 90.

'But I premise by stating that the assessors were unanimous in this opinion that no individual member could acquire absolute ownership of family land in the sense of a fee simple with rights of alienating and selling. This is established law for which there is abundant authority.' [1]

For the individual to acquire anything in the nature of an absolute property in his allotment it would seem to be essential that the family through their proper representative should make it quite clear that the member has had thereby conferred upon him an absolute title. Merely being allowed to act, for however long a period, as if he were the owner of the family land would not give him any separate and absolute right thereto. Consequently, where a Crown grant had been made to a person with respect to his family land, Viscount Haldane, delivering the judgment of the Privy Council in *Sunmonu* v. *Disu Raphael*,[2] held that the individual concerned must be presumed to have taken the Crown grant on behalf of his family and that he could not acquire by exclusive possession of the family property a separate and individual title to it against the other members of the family.

Another, but not unrelated, type of problem is that occasioned by an attempt on the part of an individual to convey his undivided share of family land to a purchaser by means of a modern deed of conveyance in which he represents himself as a fee simple owner. In *Adagun* v. *Fagbola*,[3] Kingdon, C.J., decided in a Supreme Court judgment that a recital in a deed of gift of part of family land by a member which described him as the fee simple owner of his allotment was void as against local customary tenure. The purported conveyance was a nullity.

Summary

We may now summarise our answers to the questions [4] posed at the outset of this enquiry as follows: The individual member of a family may acquire an absolute property in land by (*a*) the appropriation of as yet unoccupied or uncultivated virgin land; (*b*) being given, with the consent of his family, an absolute interest in an allotted portion of the family land; (*c*) accepting an out-and-out

[1] (1924), 5 N. L. R. 90, at p. 92. The learned Judge then cited five decisions covering the period 1909–22.

[2] (1927), A. C. 881; see also the W. A. C. A. judgment to the same effect in *Larki* v. *Amokor & ors.* (1933), 1 W. A. C. A. 323, where it was ruled that long-continued possession of family land on the Gold Coast by a family head would not give him individual ownership of it.

[3] (1932), 11 N. L. R. 110.   [4] See p. 143, *supra*.

gift from another land-owning family having surplus land; and
(d) becoming a holder of a piece of land in consequence of the
partition into specific and identifiable lots of what was formerly
family land.

Land acquired by an individual in any one of these ways becomes, under the local system of tenure, family land at the death
of the first occupier. The interest of each member of a family in
the family land is neither strictly usufructuary in the Roman sense,
nor is it a tenancy in common or a joint tenancy according to
English land law.

Again, it is not *proprietary* in the sense that it carries such a
complete power of disposal as is enjoyed by an English fee simple
owner of land; it is equally inaccurate to regard it as merely
possessory, for the occupier ordinarily enjoys a degree of freedom
of user which a fee simple owner might envy.

It is also clear that the Nigerian occupier of family land is not a
life-tenant of his holding such as is his opposite number in an
English settlement, and he would be the first to admit that his
interest is not fully hereditary although he would quickly add that
his offspring could not be lightly disinherited from his own allotment
by the surviving members of his own family. And, to the extent
to which his interest may come to an end for any of the reasons we
shall give later,[1] it seems that he holds a kind of fee conditional
or even fee determinable, which, however, is peculiarly indigenous.

Individual's Rights in Farm Land. The principles so far considered
relate chiefly to town or urban lands, but the broad elements apply
equally to agricultural or farm lands. Every member of a farming
family is entitled to have his own allotment, may cultivate it and
plant what he likes in it, may cut down or burn or destroy anything
growing on it, and may dig or bore holes in it or fill up any existing
openings. Any member who is desirous and capable of working
effectively a piece of land has the right to demand his own portion
from the family head. Even where part of the family land is being
worked on a co-operative or communal basis by a group of kins-
men, the products of their cultivation are generally owned individually and are very often separately barned or garnered.

The allottee cannot sell his allotment and may not mortgage it,
but he can pledge it or the crops on it for debt. He cannot permanently alienate it, though he can temporarily give its use to
strangers without family approval. Subject to performing all his
obligations under the customary law, he enjoys definite security of

[1] See pp. 164–171, *infra.*

tenure. But he is not an absolute owner of his share as against the ultimate family title.

The offspring of a deceased cultivator can and do succeed to their father's allotment which is shared out among them according to customary rules.

These broad principles seem fairly common to all three regions of Nigeria.[1] Such variations of details as exist are due to differing cultural levels reflected in local methods of husbandry.

It is thus clear that the type of communal land-holding, with largely undifferentiated rights, which is to be found in pastoral or nomadic communities, cannot be properly attributed to more settled and agricultural communities such as are to be found in Nigeria. When, therefore, Lord Hailey wrote: [2] 'Rights to land have the character of a privilege based on membership of a community, entitling every member to the beneficial use of the community lands, whether for grazing, hunting, collecting fruits, or cultivating, rather than of a right over specific areas identified with the holder', the learned writer must be read subject to the warning notice issued by Dr. F. M. Keesing whose researches among the Pacific communities had led him to the conclusion that the usual kind of land tenure in agricultural communities was for 'living sites and cultivations around villages to be very precisely defined as to what families or individuals had authority over them and as to who could use them. . . . Nowhere was there any complete collectivism or communism such as some theorists have postulated for the primitive world.' [3]

This corrective, though issued in connexion with Pacific land-holding, applies with equal force to Nigeria. Mere absence of clearly defined boundaries does not affect the specific nature of individual or family holdings.[4]

---

[1] Compare the very similar accounts contained in the following: W. Price, *Land Tenure in Yoruba-land* (1933), paras. 50–93; A. K. Ajisafe, *Laws & Customs of the Yoruba* (1924), Chap. IV, paras. 4–8; C. W. Alexander, Memorandum on *Land Tenure in Southern Nigeria*, paras. 6, 8, 11–16; M. M. Green, *Land Tenure in an Ibo Village*, pp. 33–4; Chap. IV, *passim*; C. K. Meek, *Law & Authority in a Nigerian Tribe* (*Ibo*), pp. 100–4; Sir Percy Girouard, Memorandum on *Land Tenure in Northern Nigeria* (1912), para. 22, *et passim*; S. F. Nadel, op. cit., pp. 181–8; Forde and Scott, *Native Economics of Nigeria*, pp. 64–7, 78–80, 88–91, 120–2.

[2] Hailey, *An African Survey* (1945), p. 830.

[3] Keesing, *The South Seas in the Modern World*, p. 98.

[4] See, e.g., W. Price, op. cit., paras. 41 and 54; M. M. Green, op cit., Chap. IV; Sir P. Girouard, op. cit., para. 2; C. W. Alexander, op cit., para. 6; S. F Nadel, *A Black Byzantium*, p. 183.

B. CAPACITY TO HOLD LAND—SPECIAL CASES OF

It seems necessary to say a few words at this stage about the land rights of women, minors, strangers and slaves or domestics, all of whom constitute in Nigerian, as in English or any other, legal system, a special category of individuals subject to certain incapacities with respect to land-holding. Let us consider them *seriatim*.

(a) A Woman's Right in Land

This must be considered according as the woman is either married or unmarried. An unmarried daughter has, like her brother, the right to live in her father's house subject to all the normal incidents of local tenure; but, since a woman does not actually undertake to cultivate land in a subsistence economy, she is not usually given any farm-land in the general allotment. But if she can show that she can employ labour to cultivate a piece of land, she may be given some portion of the family holding. Marriage of the woman to a man, whether belonging to the same tribe or locality or not, does not give the man any automatic right over such a land which on her death devolves upon her children. It will, however, be held by her husband as trustee for the children during the latter's minority.

Moreover, a married woman may be given land by her father on marriage or she may be 'shown' one by her husband.

The nature of the right which a woman may hold in land depends upon the farming practice of the particular locality. It may be that she is allowed only to plant minor food crops in the spaces between her husband's major crops, as is the case in most of the Eastern provinces.[1] It may be that, in the South as in the North, women do not have to contribute food crops towards the maintenance of the autonomous household.[2] It has even been recorded that among certain South-Eastern people of Nigeria the men merely clear the bush for the actual farming by their wives.[3] In some areas women may also hold direct right in land by purchase

---

[1] M. M. Gree⁻, *Ibo Village Affairs* (1948), pp. 33–4; 97; *Land Tenure in an Ibo Village*, Chap. IV, *passim*.

[2] Forde and Scott, *Native Economies of Nigeria* (1946), pp. 66–7, 78–9, 122–3.

[3] C. K. Meek, *Land Law & Custom in the Colonies* (1946), p. 159, footnote 4, citing G. I. Jones's unpublished studies on the area.

or pledge through a male proxy, and she can personally lease land.[1]

With respect to urban areas, we have seen that on a partition of family house priority of choice is with the eldest child, irrespective of sex;[2] and that male and female share equally, regardless of sex.[3] To the extent to which certain *dicta* in *Lopez* v. *Lopez*[4] would suggest that female rights in the family house are less than those of males, *Ricardo* v. *Abal*[5] has cast doubt upon their correctness.

But it has been held in *Oloko* v. *Giwa*[6] that where rooms in a house are allotted to wives by the family head, the latter do not acquire any separate and absolute property in such rooms which have been granted for their life only. Nevertheless, in *Oluremi Johnson* v. *U.A.C., Ltd.*[7] where the intestate, deceased owner of certain land left a widow (married under the Marriage Ordinance 1916) and children, the Divisional Court at Lagos held that under the English Statute of Distribution the widow's one-third share in the property could be attached by the defendant company. It is not, however, uncommon for the children of the same mother to claim their deceased mother's apartment as their own by right of inheritance.[8]

[1] See for general comparison: A. K. Ajisafe (for the Yorubas), op. cit., Chap. IV, paras. 9 and 10; W. Price (for the Yorubas), op. cit., para. 99; C. W. Meek, *Law & Authority in a Nigerian Tribe (Ibo)*, p. 203; D. Forde, *Land & Labour in a Cross River Village*; M. M. Green, *Land Tenure in an Ibo Village*, Chap. IV; Sir P. Girouard, Memorandum on *Land Tenure in Northern Nigeria*, para. 26; G. W. Rowling, *Notes on Land Tenure in Benin, Kukuruku, Ishan and Asaba Divisions* (1947), paras. 50 and 99.

[2] *Ricardo* v. *Abal* (1926), 7 N. L. R. 58.

[3] *Sule & ors.* v. *Ajisegiri* (1937), 13 N. L. R. 147.

[4] (1924), 5 N. L. R. 47.

[5] (1926), 7 N. L. R. 58; also *Andre* v. *Agbebi & ors.* (1931), 10 N. L. R. 79, which was preferred by Butler Lloyd, J., in *Sule* v. *Ajisegiri* (1937), to *Lopez* v. *Lopez*.

[6] (1939), 15 N. L. R. 31 (a Supreme Court decision).

[7] (1936), 13 N. L. R. 13.

[8] See the judgement in *Oloko* v. *Giwa* itself.

Also, *per* Kingdon, C.J., in *Otun & ors.* v. *Ejide* (1933), 11 N. L. R. 124, at p. 129: 'There remains to consider the special case of the second plaintiff who, admittedly, is not in actual occupation of any part of the compound. He claims to have a right to occupy at any time, at his will, that portion which his mother occupies; and I think the well-established native custom clearly goes so far as to give him that right. There is nothing, so far as I know, to indicate for how long or for how many generations such a right continues to subsist when it is not exercised, and I need not come to any decision upon that question in the present case, but I might point out that an indefinite continuance of the right would eventually lead to impossible confusion owing to multiplicity of titles.'

In the same way, it has been held that, on the death without issue of a son having an allotment in the family house, his mother has no right to his portion, although the son's own wife has.[1]

(b) Rights of Minors

Infants, that is, those who have not reached the age of puberty *or married*, cannot directly hold land, since they cannot usually fulfil the customary law requirements of effective use (in the case of farm-land) or of having separate apartments allotted to them (in the case of family house). This incapacity of the minor to hold land does not mean that he or she cannot have any right to or interest in land; it only implies that an adult relative, usually the father or the senior brother, will hold it for the minor on trust until the attainment of puberty or so soon as the minor is capable and ready to cultivate or use the land profitably.

These principles would seem to be of fairly general application to all parts of the country.[2]

(c) Land Rights of Strangers and of Slaves (or Domestics)

Most of the ordinary rights of use and enjoyment of land which the member of a family possesses can also be enjoyed by non-members such as the slaves of the household and strangers to the family. But from the inclusive nature of the family or community holding of land, these categories of individuals do not in certain respects enjoy the plenitude of powers of disposal which the normal family member does; for example, a stranger may have to pay his overlord some tribute for his holding and may be forbidden to plant permanent or economic crops on the land allotted to him. A family member is not normally so restricted.

A good deal depends, however, on the mode of adoption of the slave or the stranger and the degree of his assimilation with the adopting family or group. Where the slave or the stranger is of good behaviour and is acceptable to the family and to the local community as a whole, he is often allowed to enjoy almost absolute rights with respect to his holding. Thus, in *Sanusi Alaka* v. *Jinadu Alaka & anor.*[3] the plaintiff had issued execution against certain

---

[1] *George & anor.* v. *Fajore* (1939), 15 N. L. R. 1.

[2] See, *e.g.*, (*a*) W. Price, op. cit., paras. 50 (6) and 99; A. K. Ajisafe, op. cit., para. 9 (Chap. IV); Sir P. Girouard, op. cit., para. 26; M. M. Green, *Land Tenure in an Ibo Village*, Chap. IV. (*b*) *Lewis* v. *Bankole* (1909), 1 N. L. R. 82 (the whole judgment; children and grandchildren); *Davies* v. *Sogunro* (1936), 13 N. L. R. 15 (illegitimate child's rights); *Saibu* v. *Igbo* (1941), 16 N. L. R. 25 (posthumous child's rights).   [3] (1904), 1 N. L. R. 55.

lands at Epetedo in Lagos and the claimant, one Aminu Ekri, claimed to be entitled to a share thereof. It appeared that the lands concerned were originally granted by one Chief Oshodi to one Oguntusi, one of the domestics of Oshodi, in trust for all the slaves of Oshodi. The defendant in the case was a fellow slave of Oguntusi but the claimant failed to prove that he or his father was. It was nevertheless clear that the claimant was a slave or at least a slave's slave of Oshodi, whether or not he was contemporary with Oguntusi. *Held*: by Nicoll, C.J., delivering the Supreme Court judgment, in these words: [1] 'I am satisfied on the evidence that the land in question was given by Oshodi to the head man of his household in trust for all his (Oshodi's) household. The appellant was clearly a member of his household, whether as son or slave or slave's slave is immaterial. As such therefore he has sufficient interest to oppose the property being sold for the debt of another member of the household.' This judicial recognition of the right of a slave to bring an action to prevent the unauthorised alienation of family land granted by an overlord to the domestics of his household illustrates the extent of the land right of assimilated slaves, very much like the identical right of an ordinary member of a land-owning family which we have noted above [2] in *Bassey* v. *Cobham & ors.*

An interesting side-light of the *Alaka Case* was the series of affirmative answers of certain Lagos Chiefs to the following questionnaire of the judges of the Supreme Court:

(1) If a man bought a slave and that slave had an under-slave and the master sold the slave, is the under-slave the property of the master? [3]

(2) Has the master any right over his slave's slaves? [3]

(3) Has the head-slave any more rights in the master's house than the under-slave?

(4) If the master wants to provide a compound for his household, would that compound belong equally to all his slaves?

The general rights of occupation and user of land allotted to the slave have been the subject of many judicial pronouncements to which we have had occasion to make passing references. [4]

---

[1] (1904), 1 N. L. R. 55, at p. 56.   [2] See p. 155, earlier.

[3] Now subject, of course, to the Slavery Abolition Ordinance: *In re Ata* (1930), 10 N. L. R. 65.

[4] See, e.g. *Idewu Inasa* v. *Oshodi* (1934), A. C. 99, generally; *Ashogbon* v. *Oduntan* (1935), 12 N. L. R. 7, esp. at p. 9; *Buraimo* v. *Bamgboye* (1940), 15 N. L. R. 139.

If, as we have seen in *Bassey* v. *Cobham* and other cases like *Oshodi* v. *Balogun*,[1] a family member does not normally hold an absolute estate in his portion of family land, *a fortiori* a slave cannot do so whether with respect to his own family title or as against the title of the overlord family. It follows that a slave cannot alienate his interest, for example, by mortgage: *Erikitola* v. *Alli & ors.*[2] (mortgage of Onilegbale family land by a descendant of a domestic and subsequent purported sale of same by the mortgagee held invalid). A slave's attempt to alienate without due authorisation involves such a misconduct as to warrant forfeiture of his interest, though some other penalty might be inflicted according to circumstances.[3] We have partially examined these in Chapter VI and shall soon have something again to say on the subject here when we deal with the conditions of terminating the land rights of individuals in the family land.

Strangers. Let us note one final point with respect to strangers. Where a stranger's occupation of part of family land has sufficiently crystallised, the Court will protect his right by the grant of a limited or qualified injunction against disturbance.[4]

C. INDIVIDUAL RIGHTS IN THE CAMEROONS

The land rights so far considered relate roughly to the three regions of Nigeria proper. We may now illustrate the essential basic similarity of principles of land-holding in the Cameroons to those already described by taking the case of *Wokoko* v. *Molyko*.[5] The facts may be set out *in extenso* : There was a dispute between two villages of Buea which, as the units of social life, were cultivated in common by the inhabitants who enjoyed the right to build dwelling houses thereon without the chiefs' permission. Strangers could not, however, build or settle thereon without the local chief's authority first sought and obtained. While under the German Empire the Cameroons had been organised into a series of 'reservats' for the settlement of the local communities of which the two villages in question were typical. As between the various 'reservats' there was complete freedom of movement for the

[1] (1936), 4 W. A. C. A. 1 (p. 146, earlier).
[2] (1941), 16 N. L. R. 56; also *Akeju* v. *Chief Suenu & ors.* (1925), 6 N. L. R. 87 (a slave of Onikoro family could not alienate family land without authorisation).
[3] *Ashogbon* v. *Oduntan* (1935), 12 N. L. R. 7.
[4] *Umana* v. *Ewa* (1923), 5 N. L. R. 24.
[5] (1938), 14 N. L. R. 42.

inhabitants who were treated, and looked upon one another, as members of one compendious community. The Wokoko people started to build dwelling houses on the more sparsely inhabited Molyko land and the latter objected on the ground that the two 'reservats' had made the two villages mutually exclusive land areas. The Wokoko people denied this. Two cross actions were brought in a Native Court with a District Officer as President, and an appeal was made to the Resident and further to the High Commissioner who finally ruled, under s. 36 (2) of the Native Courts Ordinance, 1933, that the entire proceeding should be re-heard by the High Court which held: (1) that the 'reservats' had, under local customary law, become established as inter-dependent communities and that both Molyko and Wokoko were part and parcel of an undifferentiated whole; (2) that every individual of the Wokoko village, like every other inhabitant of the Molyko, had become an indigenous villager of both and the other villages of the reservats in Cameroons so as to be entitled to the site occupied by him or on which he had built his dwelling house. Pearson, J., in the High Court at Buea, said:

'Now by native custom—as proved by the first witness, Chief Enderly, District Head, Buea—any member of a village community can build a house anywhere he likes on the communal village land, without reference to the village head, but if a stranger desires to build in the village, he must apply to the village head and present a pig to him. Before the advent of the German administration each village was a distinct community. The Germans, however, on establishing reservats, treated all the inhabitants of a reservat as one community for all purposes. This system has been accepted by the inhabitants. . . .' [1]

Mr. C. W. Rowling's recent study [2] confirms these principles of local tenure and their primary similarity to those obtaining in the other parts of Nigeria.

D. CONDITIONS OF CESSER OF INDIVIDUAL RIGHTS IN LAND

It remains now to state shortly the various conditions on the happening of which the land right of the individual determines under local tenure. From a consideration of what has been said in this and the two preceding chapters it would seem reasonable to

[1] (1938), 14 N. L. R. 42, at pp. 43-4.
[2] *A Study of Land Tenure in the Cameroons Province*, duplicated, p. 37. Govt. Printer, Lagos (1948).

infer that, on the happening of any one or more of the following events, the land right or interest of the individual ceases:

1. By express surrender or release;
2. By abandonment;
3. By failure of effectual occupation or user;
4. By alienation or attempted alienation;
5. By denial of the title of the land-owning family;
6. By refusal or failure to pay the customary dues or render the customary services;
7. By 'bad behaviour' to the chief or to the family head.

We will briefly consider each in turn.

1. *Express Surrender or Release*

An individual, who finds his portion of the family house or land inadequate for his personal requirements owing to the concurrent claims of the other members of the family or of his own increasing offspring, may by arrangement with his chief or head of family surrender his holding into the general family pool or release it to some particular member or members of the family. Usually, he is able to acquire new lands on his own in any of the ways described above [1] and so set up house with his own sub-family. Where land is plentiful and the local economy is still at the subsistence level, this type of voluntary self-denying ordinance is practicable and necessary as the enlargement of the land-holding group increases the pressure on the land. The practice will, however, be rare in areas where land has acquired special economic values and where there is not enough land for everybody. It may be that such a condition would entail a demand for sale or partition of the family or group land.

2. *Abandonment*

This occurs when the land-occupier vacates his holding for an unreasonably long time and does nothing to show an intention or exercise of continuous occupation. Generally, the continued existence on a farm-land of permanent crops or of economic trees like palm trees and cocoa and, on a town-land, of houses originally firmly built, is taken as an indication that the absent occupier intends to return to it ultimately. But the question is: How long a period of absence would suffice to extinguish the occupier's right and so enable the chief or family head to re-allot the abandoned portion to other members? As we have seen, [2] the requisite period

[1] p. 143–4, *supra*.   [2] See pp. 103, earlier.

varies with the locality, depending upon the particular type of the husbandry practised in each; but it seems that three or more years' continuous abandonment would, in the absence of extenuating circumstances, often extinguish the previous occupier's right.

Thus in the case of *Otun & ors.* v. *Ejide*,[1] Kingdon, C.J., after upholding the claim of the second plaintiff to 'a right to occupy at any time, at his will' the portion of a family compound previously occupied by his deceased mother, as being in accordance with local law and custom of Lagos, went on to question whether some kind of time-limit should not be set to such a claim: 'There is nothing, so far as I know, to indicate for how long or for how many generations such a right continues to subsist when it is not exercised, and I need not come to any decision upon that question in the present case, but I might point out that an indefinite continuance of the right would eventually lead to impossible confusion owing to multiplicity of titles.'[2] Had his Honour come to a decision upon the question of length of continuance of the claimant's right, we might have been happier.

On the other hand, the question of what constitutes abandonment under Efik custom has been judicially considered in two cases. In the earlier one, *Baillie & ors.* v. *Offiong & ors.*,[3] the people of the town of Ikot Offiong were, by a 1913 judgment, declared to be entitled to the exclusive occupation of certain land in that town subject to the right of certain strangers, of whom the plaintiff Baillie was one, to remain in undisturbed occupation of the area then being used by them. In 1917, Baillie left this site and his house subsequently fell down. In 1920, the defendants entered on the land and claimed the right to resume possession. *Held*: by the Supreme Court (1) that there had been no abandonment of his site by Baillie who proved to the Court's satisfaction that his apparent inactivity over the previous three years or so had been due to illness and that he had always had the intention to resume his occupation of his compound; (2) that even if the local customary law requires an individual, who had been permitted to build a house on another's family land and who had let the house fall down, to obtain fresh permission of the grantor of the land before rebuilding, such a rule clearly could not apply to Baillie's case because his portion of the town land had been granted, not merely for the purpose of building a house, but for the purpose of occupation generally in which sense it had hitherto been used.

[1] (1933), 11 N. L. R. 124.   [2] Ibid., at p. 129.   [3] (1923), 5. N. L. R. 28.

Also, in *Eyamba* v. *Holmes & anor.*,[1] Berkeley, J., in the Divisional Court at Calabar held that the first defendant, the daughter of a deceased grantee of the plaintiff's family land, could not be said to have abandoned occupation merely because a lodger—one Moore—had been allowed to occupy two rooms and a parlour in the house built thereon, since the rest of the holding was still occupied by members of the grantee's family.

3. *Failure of Effectual Occupation or User*

One almost invariable condition of land-holding under the indigenous system is the requirement that land granted to a family or to an individual shall be put to beneficial use. This over-riding postulate of a valid occupancy also underlies the restriction which local customary law places on the acquisition of land by any individual beyond his immediate needs or what he can usefully cultivate. It ensures fairness of land distribution which is so vital to social polity and economic well-being.

An individual or family, therefore, who fails to maintain his building or part of a building or who neglects to cultivate effectually his farm plot, runs the risk of having his allotment or so much of it as he has failed to use taken away from him and given to more necessitous individuals. Any prostitution of much-needed land, especially if it be fertile, is regarded as an anti-social act.

But much would depend upon the circumstances of each particular case; for example, upon the locality, the occupation or farming habits obtaining therein, and any other factor or factors relevant to the individual's failure to use his occupation properly.

Under this head, too, must be considered the issue of a misuse of one's holding, including the use of it for purposes other than those for which the grant has been made. In the *Eyamba* v. *Holmes* case just considered, evidence was led to show that under Efik custom a grantee would forfeit his occupancy if he used his allotment for unauthorised or contrary purposes. It would seem to imply that purely agricultural land should not be converted into a building site or dwelling houses turned into pig-sties, without the consent of the grantor. The rule would, it is submitted, apply with greater force to stranger occupiers than to family members, but even the latter must respect the collateral but by no means lesser claims of the other members whose holding may be prejudicially affected by any wanton use of his portion by one of their number.

[1] (1924), 5 N. L. R. 83.

4. *Alienation or Attempted Alienation*

On the well-established principle that family or community lands are inalienable under Nigerian indigenous system of tenure, any alienation or executed attempt to alienate by an individual occupier works, at least in theory, an automatic forfeiture of his interest; though in practice the alienation, rather than the alienor's right (especially if that of a family member), is usually forfeit.[1]

The word 'alienation' in this context must, according to Butler Lloyd, acting C.J., in *Buraimo* v. *Bamgboye*,[2] be 'used as having an extended connotation and must be taken to include any transaction by which rights in the property are transferred to a stranger'. The transaction involved in an alienation that would entail a forfeiture might be a sale, a mortgage, a lease, or, *semble*, an unauthorised dealing *inter se* by individuals of a group grantee of land. We may briefly take the following cases as illustrations:

Sale. Thus, in *Miller Bros.* v. *Ayeni*,[3] the other members of the family were held entitled to object to one of their number alienating his interest through its attachment for debt by his judgment creditor, unless with the family consent or on the partition of the land. Such a transaction, if allowed, would amount to an unauthorised sale of family land and would be contrary to customary law of tenure.

Mortgage. In *Adagun* v. *Fagbola and anor.*[4] a member of the Olorogun family, who had granted a mortgage of the portion of family property allotted to him for his use and occupation, was held to have thereby forfeited his holding. *A fortiori*, a domestic or a descendant of one or a brother of the wife of a former head of the Onikoro family who mortgaged his allotment, was held in *Akeju Chief Obanikoro* v. *Chief Suenu & ors.*[5] to have forfeited his right

[1] See, generally, *Ashogbon* v. *Oduntan* (1935), 12 N. L. R. 7, *per* Graham Paul, J., at pp. 8 and 9.

[2] (1940), 15 N. L. R. 139, at p. 141; a little earlier, Butler Lloyd had observed: 'From these and a number of other judgments of this Court, some of which have been cited in the present case, the clear principle emerges that the rights of the holder under Native Law and Custom are limited to occupation during good behaviour and do not include the power to alienate without the consent of the family and further that the attempt to alienate without such consent will involve the forfeiture of those rights.'

[3] (1924), 5 N. L. R. 40; see also the other cases cited on pp. 155–8, *supra*, and *Shoti* v. *Paul & ors.* (1933), 11 N. L. R. 120.

[4] (1932), 11 N. L. R. 110.

[5] (1925), 6 N. L. R. 87.

to continued occupation, Van Der Meulen, J., remarking:[1] '... therefore in whatever capacity Kuti joined the Onikoro family I am convinced that he was then only given this property for him and his family to reside upon so long as they should properly conduct themselves towards the head of the Onikoro family.'

Lease. In *Onisiwo & ors.* v. *Gbamgboye & ors.*[2] the grant to a stranger of a thirty years' lease by an occupier (to whose ancestor, a portion of family land had been allotted for occupation under local law and custom) without the consent of the overlord family was held by the West African Court of Appeal to effect a forfeiture of the occupier's right.

Intra-mural Dealings by Members of a Group-Grantee of Land. It would seem from *Chief Uwani* v. *Nwosu Akom & ors.*[3] that a mortgage or sale of his farming right by one member of a group grantee of family land to another member of the same group might work a forfeiture.

5. *Denial of Title of Land-owning Family*

What constitutes a denial is a question of fact in each particular case. Thus a stranger occupier's false allegation that he had purchased the land granted to him for occupation under local law and custom has been held not to amount to such a denial of the landowner's title as to involve forfeiture.[4] But in *Oloto* v. *Dawuda & ors.*[5] the Full Court at Lagos held that the defendants, as occupiers of part of the Oloto family land, forfeited their right thereto when, upon being asked for rent, they claimed ownership of their allotment under a deed of assurance which extrinsic evidence showed was not intended to pass any absolute property in the land to the defendants.[6]

6. *Refusal or Failure to acknowledge Grantor's Ownership*

Since the main object of paying the customary tributes or rendering the traditional services—which latter are becoming more and more increasingly rare nowadays—is merely to acknowledge that the stranger occupier is not, and does not claim as, owner, refusal or

[1] (1925), 6 N. L. R. 87, at p. 90.

[2] 1941), 7 W. A. C. A. 69.

[3] (1928), 8 N. L. R. 19.

[4] *Iwok Owune* v. *Inyang* (1931), 10 N. L. R. 111.

[5] (1904), 1 N. L. R. 58.

[6] Similarly, in the first part of the judgment in *Chief Etim & ors.* v. *Chief Eke & ors.* (1941), 16 N. L. R. 43, the denial of the title of the first defendant's father by the plaintiffs was held to work a forfeiture of their rights, though only a fine of £10 was imposed on that occasion.

cesser of either would imply a challenge to the grantor's title, and might therefore work a forfeiture. In practice, of course, a fine is often imposed upon, or some sort of rent fixed against, the ungracious grantee: (i) *Chief Etim & ors.* v. *Chief Eke & ors.*[1] (ii) *Chief Uwani* v. *Akom & ors.* (1928), 8 N. L. R. 19.

7. *'Bad Behaviour' to the Chief or to the Family Head*

It is not easy to define in precise terms the complex of social norms a violation of which might entail forfeiture of the individual's right to his holding. At best we can only illustrate the general principles by classifying the available data into a number of propositions. Even within a given community what constitutes 'bad behaviour' must vary with prevailing codes of conduct and the peculiar circumstances of the case in hand. But these are relevant factors:

(i) Serious misconduct such as burglary, adultery with any wife of the household, unreasoning insolence or truculence towards the head or chief, would all seem to have the effect of rendering the recalcitrant occupier liable to forfeit his right: *Ashogbon* v. *Oduntan* (1935), 12 N. L. R. 7, esp. at page 9.

(ii) But 'a possibly angry or confused answer of an old man exasperated by cross-examination in the course of an unfounded litigation brought against his son' was held not to amount to bad behaviour on the part of the occupier towards a chief as family head who was privy, though not party, to a previous suit in which the occupier's son had been held not liable to ejectment by the chief. The occupier's right could not be terminated on account of such a statement in a judicial proceeding, even though it amounted to a denial of the family's reversionary right in the property concerned; the occupier's evidence might conceivably be an erroneous view of the particular tradition.

(iii) Equally, a mere extravagant boast of absolute ownership of his portion of family land by a member, however much it might annoy the chief or head of the family, would incur any other penalty except forfeiture of the individual's right to his holding: *Manuel* v. *Manuel* (1926), 7 N. L. R. 101.

(iv) Though, if the individual's occupation of a portion of family land is against general family interest, the same may be terminated in proper cases: *Manuel* v. *Manuel* (1926), 7 N. L. R. 101; *Per* Webber, J., at page 102: 'There can be no question as to the legality of the occupation under native law and custom from the

[1] See the preceding footnote for reference; also, pp. 120-7, *supra*, generally.

moment of entry, and freedom from the payment of rent. There is, however, a vast difference in the tenure of a member of a family occupying family land for dwelling purposes and that of a member of a family occupying land for purposes of trade. In the former case the land is practically inalienable provided the usual native law as to conduct or abandonment are not transgressed, but as to land given for business purposes, different considerations apply, and it is quite within the native rule to add a condition to the terms of the tenancy that it can be determined if the family require the land. Such a rule could not justify the head of a house in determining the tenancy on his mere *ipse dixit* that the family required it.'

Family interest, and not a refusal by the occupier to pay rent for such commercial use, may, however, determine the occupancy.

But there was no evidence of family interest in the case itself. The occupier merely denied having annoyed the chief by his extravagant boast that ten years' possession of land gave the occupier the ownership of the land in question. There was accordingly no forfeiture.

(v) It would appear also that an honest misconstruction of the terms of an agreement between grantor and grantee, without more, would not operate to forfeit the grantee's right to land, though it might entail some other penalty: *Chief Braid & ors.* v. *Chief Adoki & ors.* (1931), 10 N. L. R. 15; *Ometa* v. *Chief Dore Numa* (1929), 9 N. L. R. 46.

(vi) Finally, we may cap our illustrations with a Lagos case of 1892, *Sheffi* v. *Williams*,[1] where it was held that a female member of a family had forfeited her right to the occupation of her portion of the 'family house' when she had brought her husband to reside therein without the previous consent of the family head.

(vii) On the whole, the authority to evict for bad behaviour would seem to be stronger in the case of the founder or 'father' of the family than in that, for instance, of a senior brother as head with respect to his collaterals. Age, personal status and influence naturally enter into the situation as additional factors, but these are by themselves inconclusive.

Relief against Forfeiture. The circumstances in which the Court would grant relief against forfeiture in the case of the individual are the same as those already outlined in the case of groups on pages 120–127 above, and we need not repeat them here.

[1] Lagos: Reports of Certain Judgments of the Supreme Court, Vice-Admiralty Court and Full Court of Appeal (1884–1892). Law Reports (Colonial). Nigeria A; Colonial Office Legal Library in London.

Chapter Eight

ALIENATION OF LAND (INTER VIVOS)

(i) Gifts of Land. (ii) Pledge (or Pawn). (iii) 'Borrowing' of Land.
(iv) 'Leases'. (v) Leases, Mortgages and Sales—Southern Provinces
—Northern Provinces—The Colony and Certain Other Areas.
A. Certain Problems affecting Sale of Land. B. Some Problems
relating to Mortgage and Lease of Land

THERE is perhaps no other principle more fundamental to the indigenous land tenure system throughout Nigeria than the theory of inalienability of land. Various reasons have been advanced for this. It is said by some that the notion of inalienability derives from a religious or magico-religious attitude towards the land regarded as a sacred trust of the living undertaken in memory of the dead.[1] Some, again, postulate a myth of the original ancestor [2] according to which the common origin of the members of a community renders inconceivable the giving away of ancestral land to non-autochthonous individuals or groups. This looks like a slight variant of the first proposition. A third, and more plausible, hypothesis asserts that community and family land has been held inalienable from a desire to preserve it for the requirements of the owning group, past, present and future.[3] This is a simple socio-economic device to protect the interests of present and future generations of the group, as otherwise the living might fritter away the contingent interests of their progeny; and the

[1] See, e.g., C. K. Meek, *A Sudanese Kingdom*, Chap. X; Nadel, op. cit., pp. 232 and 237–8; C. K. Meek, *Land Law & Custom in the Colonies* (1946), pp. 151–2, 162; E. S. C. Handy, *The Religious Significance of Land* (Royal African Society, 1939, Vol. XXXVIII, pp. 114–23).

[2] See, e.g., M. M. Green, *Land Tenure in an Ibo Village* (1941), Chap. III, pp. 5 and 6; W. Price, *Land Tenure in Yoruba-Land* (1933), para. 105.

[3] See, e.g., W. Price, op. cit., paras. 104, 225; L. P. Mair, 'Modern Developments in African Land Tenure,' *Africa*, July 1948, pp. 184–9.

reference to the dead in this context is, similarly, to the duty incumbent upon them when alive not to compromise the rights of the present occupiers; it is not based on any religious or mythical theory.

Thus, para. 91 of the West African Lands Committee's Report reads; A third principle [of land tenure] is that land is considered as still the property of the original settler, and thus as belonging to the past, the present and the generations to come. This idea was thus put by one of the Chiefs of Ijebu-Ode: 'I conceive that land belongs to a vast family of which many are dead, few are living, and countless members are yet unborn.' [1] There have been a number of judicial *dicta* in support of this view, of which the following one in the dissenting opinion of Chief Justice Kingdon in the Supreme Court at Lagos in *Balogun & ors.* v. *Oshodi* [2] is typical: 'In passing I wish to refer to one point in connection with the question of changing the law which should not be overlooked. I refer to the rights of future generations. Under native customary tenure an individual cannot alienate the land he occupies, consequently the rights of his descendants are safeguarded and cannot be realised by him. But once the tenure becomes fee simple, the rights of generations yet unborn can be sold and the proceeds squandered by the present generation. This alone should, in my opinion, make the Court slow to implement, in the exercise of its equitable jurisdiction, the actions of persons who have selfishly sold or purported to sell the fee simple of land previously held under native customary tenure. The equities are not all on one side.' [3]

But strict as has been the traditional system of tenure against the principle of alienation, certain forces, economic no less than sociological, have for very long been at work to temper its rigour even within the context of a purely subsistence economy of land usage. Whatever the supposed theoretical justification of the notion of inalienability may have been in any particular local community, the people of the fertile regions around Lake Chad have for long been buying and selling parcels of land among themselves; and the same is true of certain other pagan tribes in the

[1] Colonial Office Legal Library (London). Folio 13080, dated April 1917 and published along with the Committee's Minutes of Evidence.

[2] (1931), 10 N. L. R. 36, at p. 58. It is interesting to add that, in consonance with this general view of the learned Chief Justice, the West African Court of Appeal reversed the majority decision in the Supreme Court at Lagos. See (1936), 4 W. A. C. A. 1.

[3] Cited in full in *Balogun* v. *Balogun* (1943), 9 W. A. C. A. 78, at p. 83.

North.[1] In the Emirate of Dikwa in the Cameroons under British mandate, a class of land known as 'firki' has also for some time been the subject of sale on account of the labour involved in its first cultivation.[2] The effect on land of influx of strangers into the Cameroons has recently been described as acute and in need of stricter control by the local authorities.[3] The pressure of population on the land in Ibo-land and the consequent pledging and borrowing of land have been noted by many writers.[4] With regard to the Colony and the adjoining areas, we have had occasion to note various judicial statements to the effect that the influx of slaves from Sierra Leone as well as European contacts have served to introduce the practice of alienation into Lagos. Thus, Osborn, C. J., in *A.-G. of Southern Nigeria* v. *John Holt & Co.*[5] ascribed the new vogue of alienation to the abolition of the slave trade in 1852 and the consequent influx into Lagos of liberated slaves from Sierra Leone since that date; and in *Lewis* v. *Bankole* [6] the same learned Chief Justice had observed: 'The idea of alienation of land was undoubtedly foreign to native ideas in the olden days but has crept in as the result of contact with European notions, and deeds in English form are now in common use.'

These three broad principles emerge from the foregoing considerations: The first is that, under the traditional system of tenure, land was originally (and is still largely) inalienable. The second is that certain factors soon set in, acting as a kind of solvent to the rigid rule against alienation and thus producing the granting, pledging and loaning of land—all of which are more or less natural adaptations of indigenous notions to new situations. The third is that, in certain areas of the country and under certain conditions, alienation by sale, lease and mortgage is now recognised in the light of more modern economic and social facts.

Let us now briefly consider the main features of each of the three earlier modes of land transfer, viz. gift, pledge and loan.

---

[1] C. K. Meek, *Land Law & Custom in the Colonies* (1946), pp. 150 and 300.

[2] C. K. Meek, ibid., p. 23.

[3] See C. W. Rowling, *A Study of Land Tenure in the Cameroons Province*, Duplicated, p. 37, Govt. Printer, Lagos (1948).

[4] e.g. J. O. Field, 'Sales of Land in an Ibo Community', a letter to *Man*, Vol. XLV, No. 47 of 1945; M. M. Green, *Land Tenure in an Ibo Village*, Chap. IV, 'Ibo Village Affairs', pp. 33–4; L. T. Chubb, *Ibo Land Tenure*, Gaskiya Corporation, Northern Nigeria, 1948, p. 97; G. C. I. Jones, 'Agriculture & Ibo Village Planning' (*Farm and Forest*, Vol. V (1945), pp. 9–15).

[5] (1910), 2 N. L. R. at p. 3.

[6] (1909), 1 N. L. R. 81, at p. 83.

(*i*) GIFTS OF LAND

This is an out-and-out transfer by the grantor, having enough land to spare, to the grantee or grantees who usually enjoy perpetuity of tenure subject to good behaviour. The procedure of making the grant is by no means uniform in all details throughout the country, but the general outline is the same and is briefly as follows.[1] The chief, or the family head as the case may be, will either go in person, or delegate someone else on his behalf to go, with the intended grantee in site of the parcel of land the extent of which is roughly demarcated sometimes by placing a mound of earth at each of the four corners and sometimes by planting some trees in the same positions as evidence of the boundary. Then kolas are split, gourds of wine are drunk and other viands taken in celebration of the occasion to which those present are expected to be witnesses in any future dispute, since the customary law is unwritten.

The nature and extent of the rights thus acquired by a grantee of the land will doubtless vary according as the land is cultivated or uncultivated, town-land or farm-land, or according to the nature of the husbandry practised in any particular locality. If uncultivated, that is, virgin forest land, the grantee takes everything; if cultivated, it may be that a right to reap crops or cut things like palm nuts will be reserved to the previous occupiers by whose labour such species of produce have been grown. Again, while the grant of farm-land often attracts tributes in the form of voluntary annual presents of produce, that of town-land hardly ever entails more than customary respect and courtesy issuing from the grantee to the grantor. The reason that both virgin forest land and town-land are thus exempt from any continuing obligation on the part of the grantee, while cultivated and farm lands are not, is the value which indigenous ideas attach to the products of human effort, as the legitimate monopoly of him who does the spade-work; if there are no unearned fruits to be gathered by the grantee, as in the case of town-land for building purposes, no further obligation should accompany the transfer of the land in question to the grantee.

But the conditions attaching to gifts of land must depend on

[1] The ceremony here outlined appears to be common to North, East and South of Nigeria; W. Price, *Land Tenure in Yoruba-land*, paras. 116 and 117; S. F. Nadel, *A Black Byzantium*, pp. 188–9; M. M. Green, *Land Tenure in an Ibo Village*, Chaps. IV and V, *passim*; A. K. Ajisafe, op. cit., Chap. IV, paras. 13 and 14.

what has been agreed between the parties and the relevant customary rules. Thus, in *Odu* v. *Akiboye* [1] the plaintiff claimed damages
for defendant's unlawful reaping of the palm trees on the land
granted to defendant by plaintiff's father. Evidence was led to show
that in the Popo area as well as in the West District of the Colony
in the Awori region, only those native to the soil could reap palm
trees and that a gift of land did not ordinarily carry with it all
rights of unconditional exploitation by the grantee. The plaintiff's
claim was, of course, limited to the eighty bundles of palm kernels
reaped by defendant subsequently to warning by the plaintiff;
the defendant's right to the land itself was not called in question.
The defendant's claim to a right concurrent with that of the plaintiff
to reap the trees failed. On the other hand, in *Chief Etim & ors.* v.
Chief Eke & ors.[2], it was held (1) that grantees of land in Calabar
were entitled to occupy the land granted and to exercise a concurrent right to cut palm nuts together with the grantors; and (2) that
a stranger to the locality could be restrained by injunction, at the
suit of the plaintiff-grantees, from cutting palm nuts thereon under
a collateral agreement with the grantors. Martindale, J., said:
'It is now settled law that once land is granted to a tenant in
accordance with Native Law and Custom, whatever be the consideration, full rights of possession are conveyed to the grantee.
The only right remaining in the grantor is that of reversion, should
the grantee deny title or abandon or attempt to alienate. The
grantor cannot convey to strangers without the grantee's permission any rights in respect of the land.' [3]

We have also noted Dr. Nadel's observation that in Nupe country palm trees are usually held by the chiefs and other family
heads to whom rights to the trees may have been transferred. Even
younger men of the locality are disentitled to have palm trees;
and strangers are in no better position with respect to trees on the
land given to them.[4]

The absence of written evidence of a grant of land under the
traditional system was adequately provided for by the requirement
of publicity which accompanied it. But wherever population

---

[1] (1892), Judgment of Smalman, C.J., on 19 August, appearing on pp. 19
and 50 (Appendix C) of Lagos: Reports of Certain Judgments of the Supreme
Court. Vice-Admiralty Court and Full Court of Appeal (1884–1892)—Law
Reports (Colonial), Nigeria A. Colonial Office, London.

[2] (1941), 16 N. L. R. 43.

[3] Ibid., at p. 50.

[4] S. F. Nadel, *A Black Byzantium*, pp. 188–9; cf. W. Price, *Land Tenure in
Yoruba Province*, paras. 39, 35, 281.

density increases and land acquires a commercial value, disputes are bound to arise over titles thus acquired. While the practice still prevails in purely rural or agricultural areas, land grants in urban or town areas are now commonly made in writing, which again brings in its train its own peculiar problems. Thus, in *Oloto* v. *Dawuda & ors.*[1], a document, purporting to be a deed of gift, was executed by a landlord in favour of his tenant who had complained that certain third parties had been interfering with his possession. The document was only to protect the grantee against trespassers and was not intended to affect the existing relationship between grantor and grantee who continued to pay rents even after the execution of the deed to him. The grantee later claimed that the document meant what it said that he was entitled to an outright gift of the land in question. *Held*: that, in spite of the language of the deed, extrinsic evidence was admissible to prove the real understanding between the grantor and the grantee, since by the ancient local law of Lagos there was no absolute alienation of land and very strong evidence would be required to warrant the Court coming to a conclusion contrary to custom.

But this finding does not mean that no absolute gift of land was possible in former times. With the consent of the whole family land could be and was given outright to strangers as well as to group members in need of land. Otherwise, it would be difficult to explain, for example, how it is that the Oshodi chieftaincy family could ever claim an unconditional proprietary interest in the much-litigated Oshodi compound which was originally granted to the immigrants by a White-Cap Chief of Lagos. Berkeley, J., thus commented on the question in *Balogun & ors.* v. *Oshodi*[2]: 'The land belonged to the family and no portion of it could be alienated by any individual member to a stranger. But even at that time the land could be alienated to a stranger with the general consent of the family. Otherwise Oshodi Tappa could not have obtained a title from the White-Cap Chief to whose family he was himself a stranger.'

Finally, gifts of land cannot now be lightly impugned on the ground that, contrary to the vogue of drawing up all kinds of documents in land transactions, a grantee of land has no written evidence of his particular claim. If the customary notoriety necessary to a valid gift could be otherwise proved, there would be

[1] (1904), 1 N. L. R. 57.
[2] (1931), 10 N. L. R. 36, at p. 45.

no lack of judicial support for the grantee's claim.[1] An interesting case on the subject is *Bintu Alake* v. *Awawu*[2] in which plaintiff had claimed an account of rent and mesne profits in respect of two properties, one of which the defendants claimed to have been given to him by the mother of both plaintiff and defendant. The plaintiff contended that any such gift should be declared invalid for non-compliance with the Statute of Frauds, 1677. *Held*: by the Supreme Court, affirming on appeal a Divisional Court judgment, that (1) there was sufficient evidence before the Divisional Court to support the defendant's claim to the gift of the land; (2) the application of the Statute of Frauds to land transactions by illiterate people in Nigeria must depend on the circumstances of each case, but that there was no special circumstance in the instant case to justify the application of the Statute so as to invalidate the gift alleged and proved by the defendant. The result of this case is that a gift of land in Nigeria need not be supported by a note or memorandum in writing which is normally required by s. 4 of the Statute of Frauds, 1677 (now s. 40 of the L.P.A., 1925) in England.

(*ii*) PLEDGE (OR PAWN)

Pledge (or Pawn, as it is sometimes inaptly called) is a kind of indigenous mortgage by which the owner-occupier of land, in order to secure an advance of money or money's worth, gives possession and use of the land to the pledge creditor until the debt is fully discharged.[3]

An English mortgagee's rights against a defaulting mortgagor are (1) to sue on the personal covenant, (2) to foreclose in proper cases, (3) to sell the land under certain conditions and (4) to enter into possession, which is rarely done (at least since the Law of Property Act, 1925) because of the rather strict liability to account imposed on the mortgagee who goes into possession of the

[1] So held, in connexion with a gift of land on the Gold Coast, by the West African Court of Appeal in *Kwakuwah* v. *Nayenna* (1938), 4 W. A. C. A 65.

[2] (1932), 11 N. L. R. 39.

[3] The West African Court of Appeal, *per* Mitchelin, J., i n *Adjei* v. *Dabanka & anor.* (1930), 1 W. A. C. A. 63 at pp. 66–7, thus stated the nature of a pledge:

'It is an essential of a native mortgage that possession of the mortgaged premises should be given to the mortgagee at the time when the transaction takes place between the parties. This is made clear from the following passage which appears in Sarbah's Fanti Customary Law at p. 261:

' "Mortgage or rather pledge of land is a transaction in the presence of witnesses, the possession of the land pledged being given to the lender of the money." '

mortgaged land.[1] Under the indigenous system, however, the pledge creditor obtains possession of the land from the very inception of the deal and also enjoys the usufruct of the land for as long as it is considered necessary to give the pledge an equivalent credit. The pledgee may be restricted to the usufructuary enjoyment of only those trees or crops planted on the land by himself since taking possession of it, or he may be permitted to exercise all the powers of an owner-occupier. In the latter case, if he plants permanent or economic trees like kola, palm or cocoa trees on the pledged land, he is usually not allowed any compensation for improvements when the time comes for him to vacate the land on payment of the debt or satisfaction of the credit by the pledgee's exploitation of the land. Since the whole original arrangement does not envisage a permanent state of affairs, this custom is understandable. Indeed, only the crops are sometimes pledged, the land remaining in the occupation of the pledgor. This occurs mostly in palm-oil, kola- or cocoa-growing areas.

Pledge Perpetually Redeemable. But since there is generally no prescriptive right to land under the indigenous system, a pledgee can never obtain the absolute ownership of the pledged land, for however long the debt may remain unpaid. One cardinal principle of the local pledge system is its ultimate redeemability; indeed, one may say that its underlying assumption is: once a pledge, always a pledge. And cases have been known where the grandchildren of the pledgor finally pays their ancestor's debt on the family land and redeems it from the pledgee's living descendants.[2] This heritability of the pledged land has given rise to some perplexing problems, among which is the difficulty of knowing, after two or more generations, what the actual arrangement between the original parties really was, especially after all evidence of its original provenance shall have been lost. Another and equally complicating factor is the right, recognised in some areas, of the re-pledging by the pledgee of lands already pledged to him; or, the land may be pledged to one person while the trees thereon are pledged to

[1] See ss. 85–120 of L.P.A., 1925, especially ss. 99–103; and Cheshire, *Modern Real Property* (5th edition), pp. 610–26.

[2] C. W. Alexander, Memo. on *Native Land Tenure in the Colony and Protectorate of Nigeria* (1910). Colonial Office Legal Pamphlet, Vol. I, Folio No. 26, paras. 9, 10 and 24; W. Price, op. cit., paras. 69, 93, 106, 107, 137, 203, 204 and 259; A. K. Ajisafe, op. cit., para. 12 (Chap. IV); M. M. Green, *Land Tenure in an Ibo Village*, Chap. IV (para. 1) and Chap. V; J. S. Harris, 'Papers on Economic Aspect of Life among the Ozuitem Ibos' (*Africa*, Vol. XIV, pp. 12–23).

another. A prescriptive right to the land is often claimed by the pledgee's descendants and the all-important factor of effective occupation and user has generally inclined the local elders and the Courts to award the land to the long-entrenched occupier.[1]

In *Kuahen* v. *Avose* (1889),[2] the plaintiff sought to eject the defendant from the possession of certain palm trees at Gedu in the Badagry area of the Colony. It appeared that, for the purpose of raising funds to pay tribute due from the people of Gedu to one Omitutu, King of Appa, the palm trees in question had been pledged in the alleged sum of 1,360 bags of cowries (the equivalent of £340 in English money) by the defendant's great-grandfather (one Ayidemo) to the plaintiff's father (one Saba). The annual produce of the palm trees was estimated at £12 a year, while the highest tribute payable was only £9 a year. For about thirty years the palm trees had been farmed by the pledgee and his descendants. It seemed incredible that so large an amount as £340 or 1,360 bags (nearly equal to forty years' tribute) should have been paid by Saba, particularly since the payment of the tributes ceased altogether with the death of the recipient, Omitutu, which took place eight years before the death of Saba (the pledgee), and Ayidemo (the pledgor) died during the lifetime of Omitutu. *Held*: by Smalman Smith, C.J., (1) that where palm trees are given in pledge for money advanced on the security of the crops, the amount of the produce so realized shall be taken into account, and some portion of it be set aside each year against the original debt. In the course of years the debt would be paid off, and the palm trees would be redeemed and might be reclaimed by the descendants of the original pledgor; (2) that, as whatever money might have been advanced by the pledgee in the instant case must have been repaid many times over, the descendants of Ayidemo (the pledgor) and Avose as representing the people of Gedu were entitled to resume possession of the palm trees. The learned Chief Justice considered as 'unjust and inequitable and opposed to natural justice' a custom alleged by the plaintiff according to which the pledge was entitled to 'farm the trees and hold them until the original debt be paid, giving and rendering no account of the

[1] In *Agbo Kofi* v. *Addo Kofi* (1933), 1 W. A. C. A. 284, the West African Court of Appeal held that lapse of time is no bar to recovery of land pledged on the Gold Coast.
[2] The reference is the same as that in footnote (1) on p. 176; see also pp. 16 and 17 of the Report.

value of the produce, which in this case amounted to more each year than the amount paid as tribute'.

In support of this finding of the Court and against the plaintiff's allegation of custom one has only to recall these concluding words of paragraph 97 of the West African Land Committee's Report already referred to: 'He (i.e. the individual holder) can, however, pawn it or the crops upon it for debt; but the pawnee must evacuate the premises when the debt is liquidated, and native custom is impatient of attempts on the part of the pawnee unduly to prolong occupation.'

Nigerian Moneys. It is perhaps fitting to observe briefly here that the mention of 1,360 bags of cowries in the case just considered is an important reminder of the fact, all too easily ignored or not generally known to the outside world, that even before the advent of Europeans in Nigeria there were certain indigenous media of exchange, however crude and rudimentary these might be or seem, which were the local means of expressing their economic evolution from the barter stage to the stage of notional or convertible exchange. Cowries [1] and manillas were two species of local money survivals into modern times; the former eventually petered out only about two decades ago and the latter was abolished by legislation last year (1948). The importance of this digression into ancient Nigerian monetary system is the effect this must have had on the various local modes of transferring rights over land and the consequent transition, thus facilitated, from that period to the modern European economic ideas.

Let us return to our consideration of the redeemability of pledged land. The court seems on the whole to favour a kind of 'equity of redemption' in the pledgor and his descendants, even if no documentary evidence is available, so long as it is still possible to identify (*a*) the land, (*b*) the parties to the pledge and (*c*) the original purpose or understanding behind the transaction. Thus, in *Orisharinu* v. *Mefun*,[2] the plaintiff was held entitled to exercise his right to redeem farm-land pledged to the defendant under local customary tenure, although defendant unsuccessfully attempted to thwart the plaintiff's right by appealing to the decision in *Bintu Alake* v. *Awawu* [3] to the effect that parol evidence

---

[1] But *cowries* are said to have been originally imported into Nigeria from the East Indies: see pp. 122 and 273 of Sir Alan Burns's, *History of Nigerai* (4th edition).

[2] (1937), 13 N. L. R. 187.

[3] See footnote 2, p. 178, above.

is admissible to explain the real nature of the original transfer, and so he had vainly hoped to deny the pledge.

Similarly, in *Ben Warri* v. *Onwuchekwa*,[1] the defendant signed a document whereby he secured his house at Aba in the Eastern Provinces to the plaintiff for £45, providing therein that the plaintiff 'is authorised herein to sell the house pledged and secured to him'. On failure to repay the £45, plaintiff sued as on a promissory note and disregarded the pledge side of it, and a Magistrate Court upheld his contention. The defendant appealed to the High Court on the grounds (1) that the document was a local form of mortgage or pledge, and not a promissory note; (2) that the document was inadmissible in evidence because it was not registered in accordance with the Lands Registration Ordinance, 1924. The High Court upheld the defendant on both grounds.

(iii) 'BORROWING' OF LAND

The practice of 'borrowing' land is fairly wide-spread in Nigeria. Owing to the 'shifting' or 'fallow' system of agriculture it is naturally to be expected that a family head, whose family land reserve is in fallow and therefore has no spare land to meet the interim demands of rising adolescent members of his household, would approach neighbours or other members of the community for a temporary loan of the needed land. Such a land loan is only valid for the period of fallow, usually two to seven years at the most,[2] and is thereafter returnable to the lender on terms. It is obvious that no cash or permanent crops may be grown on the land by the borrower as the harvesting must necessarily take place long after the customary period of the loan shall have expired. This feature distinguishes borrowing or loan of land from other forms of temporary grant of land of a more permanent character which we shall next be considering.

As regards the consideration for the loan, there is no one common standard. The more cordial the relationship between the lender and the borrower the more probable it is that no more than a small token is demanded in mere acknowledgment of the lender's ownership. In less propitious circumstances a more substantial *quid pro quo* is often involved; this normally takes the form of

---

[1] (1940), 15 N. L. R. 111.

[2] Much depends on the periods of fallow allowed in any particular agricultural district. E.g. Dr. J. S. Harris (see footnote 2, p. 179, above) has noted four to sixteen years as the period among the South-Eastern Ozuitem Ibos. Different periods still might apply in the more arid North.

annual payment of a fixed percentage of the produce from the borrowed land. Dr. Nadel has noted that while payment in kind is still recognised in the less sophisticated Trans-Kaduna side of Nupe-land, a premium of 8*d*., 2*s*. and even 6*s*., according to the quality of the land, is paid in advance followed by a further payment of the annual produce or its equivalent in the more commercially sophisticated Cis-Kaduna region of the same Nupe country.[1] In some places the consideration may consist in the rendering, by the borrower to the lender, of farm-work in lieu of the usual annual produce. In all cases of failure to work the land borrowed effectually, the loan may be called off and the borrower accordingly dispossessed, with a refund of the initial deposit if that has in fact been paid.

Sometimes growing trees, economic and other, pass with the land to the borrower; at other times, the trees and the land on which they grow are lent separately, giving rise to complications particularly where the borrowing has not been re-called after two or more generations. For, although loans of land are by their nature often intended as short-term leases, they are sometimes not called in on the expiration of the agreed periods due either to the intervening death or migration of the lender and the general inertia of his successors to reclaim the land in due course. The borrower or his descendant continues, of course, to work the land on the original terms. Long occupation, especially if accompanied by the payment of the annual dues falling into desuetude for an unreasonable length of time, might be tantamount to ownership in the borrower or his heritors. This is the same problem as we have come across in the case of Pledge and as we shall have occasion to note presently in the case of Long Term Leases and implied purchases.

We have a useful illustration in the Bida Court case recorded for Nupe by Dr. Nadel:[2] A claim to recover the possession of two pieces of farm-land, one of which had been lent by A's grandfather and the other by A's father. It appeared from the evidence that the annual dues had not been claimed by A's family for a long time, although the borrower and his family continued to farm the lands and had come to look upon them as their own. The local court held that A could recover the land lent by his own father but not that lent by his grandfather! The reason given was that the former did not show such culpable acquiescence as was

---

[1] *A Black Byzantium*, pp. 185; 190–2; cf. W. Price, op. cit., paras. 184, 254.
[2] Ibid., p. 191.

involved in the latter. Here is a tacit recognition by customary law of a right in the nature of title by prescription.

(*iv*) 'LEASES'

While 'borrowing' represents a kind of short-term lease granted by one having extra land to another in order to relieve that other's temporary shortage due to fallow, leases under this head cover long-term grants of land not necessarily connected with fallow. Thus, the usufruct of farm-land may be granted to a lessee for life or for an indefinite period on the basis of the payment of annual rental partly in cash and partly in kind. Leases ostensibly granted for life are sometimes inherited by the descendants of the original grantee, with or without the grantor's permission; and although the grantor has a right to revoke the grant on the death of the grantee, unless his permission to renew the tenancy is sought at once by the grantee's descendants, nevertheless the grantor very often continues to receive the agreed rentals from the grantee's successors without further ceremony.

Again, the long-term lessees of land are on occasions given such complete power of exploitation of the land, including the power to sublet or assign, as to amount practically to ownership of it. The rent may be fixed, not by reference to any cash payment, but by means of a share of the produce of the land by the grantor with the grantee. This is sometimes known as the Metayer system.

It is thus possible for these species of transferred land rights, i.e. leases for life and for an indefinite period, to give rise to disputes and confusion after the memory of the original bargain shall have faded and witnesses to the transaction have long been dead. The tendency is for the descendants of the first lessee to claim that the land had been bought outright by their progenitor and for the descendants of the original lessor to assert that only a tenancy had been conferred in the first instance. Endless litigation has very often resulted, particularly since land has acquired a commercial value in many parts of the country.

'*Kola*' *Tenancies*. What has been called Kola Tenancies in certain areas of East Nigeria aptly illustrates the type of confusion that has arisen. Under this form of tenure land-owners would grant unwanted portions of their land to grantees (loosely described as tenants) for a kola or other token payment and sometimes for no consideration at all. The rights of the grantees were practically the same as those of owner-occupiers in respect of user and occupation and of any disposal short of complete alienation. The special feature of this tenure is, however, the invariable practice of the grantees to make further grants of their holdings to others for consideration in money or in kind far more substantial than they themselves had had to pay to the owner-grantors. These latter or their successors, alarmed at the new enhanced value of the lands they had granted more or less in a charitable or humanitarian spirit, would suddenly awake to the commercial possibilities of their erstwhile acts of bounty and then assert claim to the ultimate ownership of the lands in question. No account seemed ever to have been taken of possible improvements to the lands through the labour and expense of successive occupiers, whether as lineal descendants or as assignees of the original grantees.[1]

The spate of interminable squabbles and of consequent bad blood caused such wide-spread disruption of the social polity among agricultural no less than urban communities of Onitsha town and other areas of the Southern Provinces that the Government of Nigeria was compelled to pass The Kola Tenancies Ordinance No. 25 of 1935. This ordinance provides in s. 1 for 'the extinction of certain holdings of land commonly called kola tenancies'. In s. 2 is contained the following definition of 'a kola tenancy': 'a right to the use and occupation of any land which is enjoyed by any native in virtue of a 'kola' or other token payment made by such native or any predecessor in title or in virtue of a grant for which no payment in money or in kind was exacted.' Where a tenant of such tenancy or any predecessor in title of the tenant has granted interests in the land to any person for a consideration other than a token payment and where the payments in cash or kind received by the tenant confer on him a more substantial benefit than the grantor might have reasonably anticipated as likely to accrue to the tenant, the grantor is entitled to apply for the extinction of the tenancy concerned. A tribunal, constituted by the Resident of the district and two local assessors, should determine the amount of compensation payable by the tenant to the grantor who is given power to recover possession of the land on the tenant's failure to pay; the grantor must himself pay to the tenant an assessed amount as compensation for the tenant's improvements, if any, to the land. At the end of five years from the date fixed by the tribunal for payment by either side, the tenant shall be deemed to have all the grantor's rights in the land automatically vested in him. There is a right of appeal to the Supreme Court from a decision of the tribunal.

[1] See G. T. Basden, *Niger Ibos*, Chap. XIX, pp. 265–6.

Laudable as the aim of this Ordinance appears to be in attempting to extinguish the anomalous incidents of this form of tenure, it is not free from certain difficulties of its own. The Ordinance seems to crystallise the apparently dubious rights of the grantor by giving him a chance to profit by an enhanced value of a piece of land regardless of (*a*) the real nature of the grant at the time of its original provenance, and this might very well have been an out-and-out gift of the land; (*b*) the state and quality of the land on its first hand-out; (*c*) the grantor's long lack of enthusiasm to assert even a token claim of ownership until now that the land has become so valuable a commodity.

(*v*) LEASES, MORTGAGES AND SALES

No attempt will be made under this head to describe the principles of leases, mortgages and sales according to English Law, for which one must consult one of the standard English works on the subject.[1] But an effort will be made to examine into some of the more notable results of the impact of European ideas upon the indigenous system. In particular, the processes of change and the adaptations of immanent concepts to new economic and social habits of land usage are interesting reflections of the state of flux in which dealings in land stand today in many urban and semi-urban areas of Nigeria.

Many interesting problems of land alienation have arisen in various parts of the country and a few typical cases will be briefly discussed before we go on to study the case-law on the issues involved.

Let us take first the *Southern Provinces*:

(*a*) *Abeokuta.* In Abeokuta, for example, sales of land have been going on for over eighty years now and they were sufficiently notorious in 1913 to warrant the passing of an Order-in-Council (which repealed an Order of 1903) which limited mortgages and sales of land to dealings between Egbas only while all leases to non-Egbas must have the approval of the Alake-in-Council. The relevant provisions of this Ordinance (No. 1 of 1913) are:

s. 2: 'From and after the coming into operation of this Order-in-Council it shall not be lawful for any person seised of land within the territories of Egba-land to sell, mortgage, assign or in any way incumber the whole or any part of such land to any person who shall not be a native of Egba-land, and any sale, mortgage,

---

[1] e.g., G. C. Cheshire, *Modern Real Property* (5th edition); Goodeve and Potter, *Modern Law of Real Property* (1929).

assignment or incumbrance made contrary to this provision shall be absolutely null and void.

s. 3: 'From and after the coming into operation of this Order it shall not be lawful for any proprietor or owner seised of any land to lease the same to any person not native of Egbaland without the sanction of the Alake and Council.'

Because of the loose definition of 'native of Egbaland' certain evasions of these Ordinance provisions later occurred and sales were made to non-Egbas; the position is further attenuated by a declaration said to have been made by the Oni of Ife that 'no Yoruba man should be regarded as a "stranger" in any of the various sections of the race'.[1]

In 1922, certain educated elements petitioned the Alake to grant facilities to individuals and families to obtain written titles to their lands and to enable those desirous of leasing, mortgaging and selling their lands to do so without let or hindrance. The Alake and Council acceded to the request if limited to town-lands in Abeokuta and other trading centres, recommending to the Nigerian Government that *agricultural* lands should be preserved against acquisition by foreign capitalists. Sir Hugh Clifford, the then Governor, pointed out in his forwarding memorandum to the Secretary of State for the Colonies that the right of foreclosure, even in the case of town-lands, should not be granted to European mortgagees since that would be contrary to s. 3 (*a*) of the Native Lands Acquisition Ordinance (1917).

In 1925, the Secretary of State for the Colonies finally agreed that, while crops might be mortgaged, no agricultural land could be leased, mortgaged or sold in the Egba Division. In town areas, house property not forming part of the normal family compound could be mortgaged, but only an Egba should be permitted to purchase the land on foreclosure of the mortgage. There was to be a local Registration Office for the recording of these land transfers in the Egba Division. Some attempts at drafting rules of Registration were made in 1929 and again in 1938, but nothing concrete has so far emerged from these.

In 1933 Sir Donald Cameron, commenting on Mr. W. Price's *Report on Land Tenure*, thought that Nigerians should be allowed to deal freely with land, town as well as farming, but that farming land should not in any case be made attachable for debt. Farming lands should never be mortgaged to aliens, though crops could. Governor Cameron would allow aliens to foreclose for

[1] See W. Price, op. cit., paras. 250–3.

non-payment of the mortgage debt or to purchase non-farming lands attached for debt, but in neither case should aliens acquire more than a lease for a reasonable term, which is all they can obtain under the Native Lands Acquisition Ordinance (1917). This is a definite advance upon the 1922 and 1925 position, but the recommendations have so far been put into cold storage.[1]

(b) *Ibadan.* We can deal more briefly with Ibadan, the largest city in West Africa. In 1903, a public notice [2] was issued by the Bale and Council of Ibadan claiming (1) that all the land of Ibadan Division was vested in the chiefs of the district and (2) that only the Bale and Council could grant valid leases thereof and to them payment of the rent should be made. If this was intended to deprive private owner-occupiers of land of their customary law rights therein, it must be regarded as invalid. As customary overseers of land, the Bale and Council possess undoubted rights of administration and control of land use, including the right to declare or modify rules of customary tenure, but that is far from saying that the Bale and Council could claim rents from private leases. For equally good reasons one must doubt the validity of the Native Court Rule of 1918 which provides that 'strangers' in occupation of '*communal*' (as distinct from '*family*') land must obtain a formal lease from the Court with the subsequent approval of the Resident. Now, while the Rule itself mentions specifically 'communal' lands (of which there were hardly any left even in 1918), in practice it has ever since been applied to govern leases of privately owned lands, with the result that leases are still issued and rents demanded by the Ibadan Native Administration.[3]

(c) *Ijebu-Ode, Ondo, Ife, Oyo, Benin.* All these other areas have had their own problems in varying degrees of intensity and forms of adaptation to the new demands of land usage. But the processes of change have been conditioned by the stage of development each has attained and the influence of outside forces quickening the pace and moulding traditional concepts. On the other hand, in all of them certain limited rights of transferring land for money values are recognised, and many are the problems awaiting solution. Instead of the old magnanimity of giving surplus lands away to needy neighbours or 'strangers' one notices a growing com-

---

[1] For a detailed account of these matters, see W. Price, op. cit., paras. 247–63, and pp. 138–46.

[2] Ibid., paras. 183 and 184.

[3] Ibid., paras. 185–96 for further details regarding these leases, and 'The Speed Commission Report' in paras. 188–97.

mercial sense with regard to land for which money rents are now demanded, unless perhaps the grantees happen to be blood relations.

Thus, Mr. Ward Price has recorded how on the borders of the Colony (i.e. parts of Abeokuta, Ijebu-Ode, etc.) lands planted with cocoa were being sold about 1933 for £3 and two bottles of gin per acre. Sometimes the price of farm-lands for sale was based on the number of trees which in one case was reckoned at one shilling per cocoa-tree of a few years' growth.[1]

(d) *Eastern Region*. Nor is this phenomenon of changing concepts in land values confined to the Yoruba regions of the Southern Provinces. For example, Dr. J. S. Harris [2] stated that among the South-Eastern Ibos pledges and sales are now widely recognised, purchase prices being twice the amount for which the land could be pledged; in 1938, parcels of land capable of growing 2,000 yams were being pledged for 30s.; the purchase price would, of course, be £3. 'Indeed, the native farmers never refer to their farm-land in terms of size but in terms of how many yams a given tract of land can produce—a far more reliable measure. The unit of measurement is 100 yams. Rentals of land are based upon this measurement. . . . The rental fee itself depends upon two major factors: (1) the general price level in Ozuitem at the time which, in turn, is directly influenced by the selling price of palm produce, and (2) the degree of friendship or relationship which exists between the rentor and rentee.' [3]

Mr. J. O. Field in a letter to the journal, *Man*, entitled 'Sales of Land in an Ibo Community',[4] has described the following characteristics of land sales at Nnewi in the Onitsha Province of Eastern Nigeria:

(a) Apart from sacred groves, markets, etc., which are held communally, lands in Nnewi are now held by sub-families and individuals whose interests in the land are 'more than a heritable usufruct for he may alienate it temporarily by letting it out at a rental or by pledging it and may in certain circumstances . . .' alienate it outright by selling it and when so doing he may act on his own without obtaining the consent of, or even consulting, his family or anybody else; (b) the one final test of an outright sale

---

[1] See W. Price, op. cit., para. 254.

[2] 'Papers on the Economic Aspects of Life Among the Ozuitem Ibos': *Africa*, Vol. XIV, pp. 12–23.

[3] Idem, pp. 21 and 22.

[4] See *Man*, Vol. XLV, No. 47 of 1945.

is whether or not a goat has been killed on the land. If no goat has been killed, the transaction cannot be other than a pledge of the land. Sales may expressly reserve to the vendors an interest in the economic trees growing on the land; (c) land may not be sold outright to a stranger; any such purported sale would give only a redeemable pledge; (d) when land is sold in Nnewi the vendor nevertheless retains a right of pre-emption at double the original purchase price provided, of course, that the purchaser is willing to re-sell at the same or any other price as he himself has paid for it; (e) sales of land were unknown in Nnewi in ancient times but are now fully recognised. 'The custom has not arisen through the importation of alien ideas of land tenure for the Nnewis have had little, if any, opportunity of coming in contact with such ideas. It appears to be a custom that has arisen spontaneously as a result of economic circumstances.'

We have already noted [1] that, under the Native Lands Acquisition Ordinance No. 32 of 1917 (and its later amendments), the utmost title that a non-national of Nigeria can acquire in the Southern Provinces is a leasehold for ninety-nine years, although the Nigerian Government had in a number of cases in the past permitted to certain 'aliens' absolute rights in land outside the Colony area. The Ordinance also provides that mortgages by a Nigerian to a non-Nigerian should receive the formal approval of the Governor—in effect, of the local authority of the district in which the land is situate.

S. 3 of the Ordinance is these terms:

(a) No alien shall acquire any interest or right in or over any lands within the Protectorate from a native except under an instrument which has received the approval in writing of the Governor.

(b) Any instrument which has not received the approval of the Governor as required by this section shall be null and void.

S. 4 provides that it shall be unlawful for any alien or for any person claiming under an alien to occupy any land belonging to a 'native' unless the right of the alien to occupy or authorise the occupation of the land is evidenced by an instrument which has received the approval of the Governor (or his delegate) in writing; any default is punishable by fine or imprisonment or both.

An illustration of the judicial attitude to these sections of the Ordinance is afforded by the West African Court of Appeal decision in *Eyamba & 3 ors.* v. *Kouri.*[2] There the appellant sought

[1] Chap. II, above.   [2] (1937), 3 W. A. C. A. 186.

(*a*) to recover possession of a piece of land valued at £140 on the waterfront at Calabar in the Eastern Provinces and (*b*) the removal by the respondent of the buildings thereon. By a deed dated 1 May 1923, three members of the Eyamba family leased the land in dispute under the Native Lands Acquisition Ordinance to the third plaintiff, a Syrian then doing business at Calabar; on 25 May 1923 the lease was duly approved by the then Lieutenant-Governor. It was an express term of the lease that the lessee should erect on the land leased buildings worth not less than £300, and the third plaintiff had actually erected at the date of the action buildings of over £2,000 and by a series of advances paid rent up to 1942. In pursuance of a judgment of Calabar-Aba High Court against the third plaintiff, a writ of *Fieri Facias* was issued and both the land and the buildings thereon were seized in execution. The defendant purchased both for £2,900 and received a Certificate of Purchase dated 21 February 1936. But before its issue to the defendant, the plaintiffs brought this action, contending that while the purported sale of the buildings to the defendant was valid, that of the land (as an assignment of the third plaintiff's rights in the unexpired term created by the lease) was contrary to ss. 3 and 4 of the Ordinance and was therefore invalid. The plaintiff accordingly claimed recovery of the land. *Held*: by the West African Court of Appeal that s. 3 applies only to acquisition of land from a 'native' of Nigeria and as all that was there transferred was a Syrian's right, the section could not apply. The defendant could therefore retain both the leased land and the buildings.

Northern Provinces. As regards the North we have considered some of the problems in Bida, as outlined by Dr. Nadel. According to 'Land Survey in Kano Emirate' by Captain D. F. H. MacBride,[1] land may be pledged for money loan in Kano and the right to cultivate may be assigned to another person indigenous to the district; but no alienation by sale is allowed, and if the Emir hears of any sale he orders a refund to the payer who is nevertheless allowed to continue in possession. But the practice of assigning land rights for an indefinite period bears a close resemblance to complete alienation of the land.

Also, farmers might pay anything like 10,000 to 20,000 cowries as tribute to the *seriki* of a town or unit, but they would not on that account enjoy any right to alienate the land by sale or mortgage; and though the language of sale was often used, it is clear, wrote Mr. Palmer about Kano in 1908, that there was no such

[1] A contribution to *Journal of the Royal African Society*, April 1938.

thing as between emirs and tenant-occupiers.[1] Referring to Yola Province Mr. Barclay wrote: 'A man may not sell his land but may give it away.' [2]

The Maliki Code of the predominantly Moslem North does not recognise in a grantee of land any right of an absolute character. At any rate, the indigenous system is so dynamic as to have tempered, if it had not absorbed, some of the vagaries of the Maliki rules on the subject of the alienation of land rights.

At the Annual Conference of Chiefs in 1939, the Sultan of Sokoto, the recognised leader of all the Moslems of Northern Nigeria, as well as the Emir of Zaria, asserted the inalienability of farm-lands as a principle of indigenous tenure in their districts and stated that the sale of land was permitted only in certain limited areas and, then, with the formal approval of the appropriate local authorities in special cases. Also, a decision was reached that, whenever 'fragmentation' under the Moslem law of inheritance would lead to uneconomic subdivision of land or encourage insanitary conditions, the sale of farm-lands should be permitted so that the proceeds could be shared by those normally entitled. MacBride's observation in the study already referred to was that mergers of many formerly separate plots would appear to be counteracting the effects of fragmentation, at least within the last ten years.

The Land and Native Rights Ordinance No. 1 of 1916 (with later amendments) now governs the tenure of land in the Northern Provinces and to it and to the Regulations made thereunder must be referred all questions of lease, mortgage or sale of land rights in this part of Nigeria. The main provisions for our present purposes (for we have considered the whole legislation more fully elsewhere [3] are as follows: s. 10 provides that subject to the provisions of s. 11 and to the terms and conditions of any special contract the occupier shall have exclusive rights to the land the subject of the right of occupancy against all persons other than the Governor. S. 12 provides that *except as may be otherwise provided by the regulations in relation to native occupiers,*[4] *it shall not be lawful for any occupier to alienate his right of occupancy,* or any part thereof *by sale, mortgage, transfer of possession, sublease or bequest or otherwise* [4] *howsoever* without the consent of the Governor first had and obtained, and any such sale, mortgage,

---

[1] Sir Percy Girouard, Memoranda on *Land Tenure in Northern Nigeria* (1908) (Colonial Office Legal Folio 11714), para. 23.

[2] Ibid., para. 26.   [3] See Chap. II, earlier.   [4] The italics are mine.

sub-lease, transfer or bequest effected without the consent of the Governor, shall be null and void.' The power to approve assignments has since been by delegation vested first in the Lieutenant-Governor of the Northern Provinces and later in the Local Authority and the Resident.

Under the Governor's power to make Regulations for governing the transfer by sale or otherwise of rights of occupancy, it is now provided that, in the case of 'native occupiers', the consent of the district headman and the approval of the head chief are necessary to any sale, transfer or bequest by one occupier to another of the same district, unless there is some local law or custom to the contrary. Where the proposed sale, transfer or bequest is to a 'stranger' to the locality concerned, the consent of the head chief backed by the Resident's approval is essential. There is machinery for appeals from Native or local Courts to the Supreme Court.[1]

A case of some interest on these provisions is *Martins* v. *Molade & 2 ors.*,[2] where the defendant, Molade, held a plot of land, under a Certificate of Occupancy, in Zaria in the Northern Provinces. He purported to assign his right of occupancy to Rolfe, one of the claimants, who later erected buildings on the land and therefore sought in this action to resist the plaintiff, Martins, who had subsequently obtained a judgment against the defendant and had accordingly proceeded to levy execution on the buildings. The plaintiff maintained that the buildings were the property of the defendant since the Land and Native Rights Ordinance provides that 'all buildings on the plot shall be the property of the occupier'. The Divisional Court held that the plaintiff could not levy execution on the buildings inasmuch as the defendant had as occupier of the land and, therefore, owner of the buildings sold them to the claimant Rolfe. The Full Court at Lagos, reversing the Divisional Court judgment, held that the sale of the buildings was valid only as between the vendor and the purchaser and could not affect the right of a third party, such as a judgment creditor, to regard any buildings on the plot as the property of the occupier within the meaning of the Ordinance. Petrides, J., delivering the Supreme Court judgment, said:

'As Molade had purported to sell the land to Rolfe and Rolfe, relying on that purported assignment had erected all the buildings on the land, it is perfectly clear that Molade would be estopped as against Rolfe from denying that Rolfe was the true owner. . . .

[1] See Appendix II for the texts of the Ordinance and of the Regulations.
[2] (1930), 9 N. L. R. 53.

It is true that a person who has contracted to sell real property is in a sense a trustee of it for the purchaser but that trust can only subsist against the vendor and cannot be asserted against a third party. . . . I do not think that there was any agreement to sell land in this case. All that Molade could dispose of was a right of occupancy in the plot, and that he could only dispose of with the Lieutenant-Governor's permission. That permission not having been obtained and Rolfe not having become the registered owner of the plot before execution, it seems to me that he cannot enforce against the execution creditor, who was a stranger to the agreement of sale by Molade to Rolfe and apparently had no notice of it, any equities he may have had to the property in the hands of Molade.' [1] Thus, non-registration by Rolfe at the date of execution of his occupancy right bought from Molade who remained the registered occupier gave the judgment creditor (the plaintiff) the right to Rolfe's buildings.

Similarly, the plaintiff in *Logios* v. *Attorney-General of Nigeria*,[2] a case concerning a plot of land in Kano, was held *obiter* disentitled to create an equitable mortgage on his contingent right of occupancy in favour of a creditor of his. He had not at the material date actually obtained a Certificate of Occupancy nor had he got the usual permission from the Lieutenant-Governor when he purported to assign his inchoate right.[3]

Summary

We therefore arrive at a situation in which dealings in land as between the indigenes of a district are still governed by the local rules of customary tenure, but as soon as an exotic element enters into the transaction, such as when one of the parties to the contemplated transfer of land rights happens to be an alien or even a 'stranger' Nigerian, the provisions of either the Native Land Acquisition Ordinance (Southern Provinces) or the Land and Native Rights Ordinance (Northern Provinces) become at once operative.

Desirable as might be the original Government idea to protect the unsophisticated Nigerians against a wanton alienation of their lands which is their only source of wealth, it would seem that while the existing restrictions should continue in the case of non-Nigerians acquiring land rights in both Provinces, the analogous

---

[1] (1930), 9 N. L. R. 53, at pp. 55 and 56.   [2] (1938), 4 W. A. C. A. 162.
[3] But the case itself turned upon the issue of agency as between the absent plaintiff (in England) and his solicitor in Nigeria.

discrimination against Nigerians acquiring lands from areas of the country other than their own places of birth could, with proper safeguards such as at present exist as between two local inhabitants transferring their land rights, be abolished. There is probably about as much justification in the Government wanting to save Nigerians from themselves as there can be in allowing non-Nigerians to acquire in the Colony area rights in Nigerian lands of an absolute character.[1] The growing economic development of the country no less than the pressing need for the creation and fostering of a Nigerian national solidarity further reinforces the argument for the desirability of a uniform set of rules on the subject of land acquisition by all Nigerians irrespective of their ethnic or linguistic or geographical location in the country, so long as reasonable checks and balances are provided against unscrupulous exploitation.

The Colony and Certain Other Areas. It remains to consider certain special features of land tenure which reflect the impact of English property law upon the indigenous system, in particular the latter's re-action to the modern conceptions of sale and mortgage of land in the Colony proper as well as in other progressive areas beyond. While sales, leases and mortgages follow the normal English rules, the land itself is very often still deeply rooted in the traditional family or community. Notable exceptions occur, however, in some areas where the individual ownership of land has developed or is developing; in such cases no serious problems arise, as sale or mortgage follows fully the rules of English Law. But in those numerous instances of purported alienations of ancestral lands some interesting situations call for comment.

A. CERTAIN PROBLEMS AFFECTING SALE OF LAND

(1) *Alienation without Family Consent Ineffectual.* From the theory that family or group land could be given away with the unanimous consent of all the important members of the family or group, we infer that, with the transition from a subsistence to a money economy, family land can and has in fact been sold to meet certain economic contingencies of the whole family or group. The first issue that falls to be determined is as to whether the lack of

---

[1] At the recent Session of the Nigerian Parliament, the Legislative Council, the Governor in his Presidential Address promised, inter alia, to review the Nigerian Youth Movement and others' agitation against acquisition by aliens of absolute land rights in the Colony district.

consent to a sale of a vital member of the family makes the alienee's title *void* or merely *voidable*. This question first came before the Court in *Aganran* v. *Olushi & ors.*[1] where, in March 1902, family land in the Badagry district was sold by Chief Ajope, the head of the family, to the defendants, Olushi and certain others. The consent of some important members of the family had been obtained, but not that of the present plaintiff, another important member whose approval was necessary to the sale. When the plaintiff drew the attention of his family to the irregularity a family meeting was immediately summoned at which a compromise was reached that the plaintiff should receive £5 out of the purchase money as an acknowledgment of his claim. Soon afterwards the plaintiff changed his mind and notified the withdrawal of his ratification of the sale; this implied the virtual rejection of the £5 offer as well. The plaintiff took no further step in the matter, not even when the purchasers had later to defend in a court suit their rights to the land against trespassers, and a compensation of £24 was then awarded. In 1905, however, the plaintiff brought this action claiming from the defendants recovery of possession on the ground of the invalidity of the sale to them, without his consent, of the land in 1902. The Full Court held, Pennington, J., dissenting, that (1) the sale of family land without the consent of all the necessary members thereof is invalid under local law and custom, but it is *voidable* and not *void*; (2) that the plaintiff's conduct in the circumstances of the case itself estopped him from suing to set aside a sale which it had taken him so long to impugn and which the purchasers had no reason to know had ever been challenged until the plaintiff brought this action.

But if a family member purports to alienate any portion of the family land without the consent or approval of the others, the purported alienation is a nullity and the purchaser from him has a *void* and not merely a *voidable* title. It is on this principle that all the cases of attempted sale or mortgage of portions of family land by an unauthorised member thereof have been held to be void transactions. In *Ajose* v. *Harworth and ors.*,[2] for instance, a part of family property at Ebute Metta was sold by Obalade, a member of the family, in 1916 to Cole, and no deed of conveyance was executed but a receipt was given for the payment of the price. In 1919 Cole sold the land to Oguntuyi and a deed was executed in

[1] (1907), 1 N. L. R. 66; see also *Oshodi* v. *Balogun* (1936), 2 A. E. R. 1632; *Marks* v. *Bonso*, 3 W. A. C. A. 62.
[2] (1925), 6 N. L. R. 98.

1921. In 1922 Oguntuyi in his turn sold the land to Ajose, the present plaintiff, also by means of a deed of conveyance. But, while all these transactions were going on, the other members of the family had in 1917 deeded all their rights to Obalade who had in 1920 mortgaged the entire land to Harworth. On the mortgage instalments going by default Harworth exercised his right of sale and Oshilaja bought the land at a public auction in 1924. Neither Harworth nor Oshilaja knew anything about Obalade's previous alienation of part of the land or the subsequent chain of sales thereof. The plaintiff, Ajose, on the strength of his own title acquired in 1922, sought in this action to set aside both the mortgage of 1920 to Harworth and the subsequent sale of Oshilaja in 1924.

Held: (1) that since the sale by Obalade to Cole in 1916 had been made without the consent and approval of his family, it was invalid and, accordingly, Ajose as one deriving title through Cole had no legal title to the land in question; (2) that the subsequent surrender by the other family members of their rights in the land to the original vendor Obalade could not validate the prior invalid alienation by Obalade of his then unliquidated interest in the family land; (3) that Harworth, having obtained the legal title as a purchaser for value without notice of any adverse claim against the land at all material times, could pass a valid title to Oshilaja whose right to the land was therefore upheld. The great moral of this case seems to be that a sale of part of family land by a member without *prior* family consent would give the purchaser nothing, and, *a fortiori*, all those claiming through the latter. Equally, any subsequent acquisition of absolute interest in such land would not have any retro-active effect so as to validate what was previously improperly alienated by him. But, *quære*, whether this means that in no case whatsoever will a subsequent ratification by the family validate a previous improper alienation by a member?

(2) *Invalidity of Sale without Consent of Infant.* It has been shown in the preceding chapter that an infant can have an interest in land though this is usually held on his behalf by the head, or by an adult member, of the family. On account of this incapacity he is not often considered important enough to be consulted when the question of disposing of part or the whole of family land is contemplated; but his exclusion from participation in the transaction does not affect his undoubted right to his share, in due course, of the family land or of the proceeds of it if it has in fact changed its form.

A case in which this point incidentally arose was *Onade & anor.*
v. *Thomas*,[1] where a man died intestate, leaving three children,
one of whom was an infant. The two adult children completed an
uncompleted sale of a portion of the family land which their
father had negotiated with the plaintiff, and in 1916 executed a
deed of conveyance of the land, covenanting for themselves and on
behalf of the infant for grant of an easement to the purchaser
covering a common passage adjoining the land sold. In 1917 both
vendors without reference to the infant sold the other half of the
land to the defendant purporting to convey the land to him with an
exclusive right to the easement of the passage previously granted to
the first purchaser. The defendant proceeded to obstruct the latter
in his use of the passageway and the plaintiff brought this action
to vindicate his prior title to it. The defendant argued that since
the infant was not a party to the 1916 deed of conveyance to the
plaintiff, the sale to the plaintiff was invalid and so must be his
claim to the easement of passage.

Held: (1) that the non-participation of the infant in the first
grant was not fatal to the validity of the sale to plaintiff whose
title should be stronger than that of the defendant, to whose deed
of conveyance the infant was equally not a party; so long as the
interest of the infant was preserved under the sale, the sale
was valid; (2) that the exclusive right reserved to the defendant
in his conveyance which was subsequent to that of the plaintiff
was, as a derogation by the vendors from their own grant,
void against the vendors as well as third-parties in the plaintiff's
position.

(3) *Plea of 'Caveat Emptor' in Sale of Family Land.* Another
type of problem fell to be considered in *Owo* v. *Kasumu*:[2] the
defendant as judgment creditor of one Sunmonu issued a writ of
Fi-fa against the latter's plot of land at Oko Baba (at Ebute
Metta). The plaintiff as the highest bidder paid £60 to the defendant, but, being unable to get possession of the land, sued the
defendant for refund of the purchase price. The defendant gave
no covenant for title and the conditions of sale contained an
express warning to intending purchasers to investigate the title;
there was no misrepresentation, innocent or fraudulent, by the
defendant. *Held*: that the plaintiff could not recover on the principle of *caveat emptor* even if the inability of the plaintiff to get
possession of the land had been due to the fact that it was an unauthorised alienation of family land by the judgment debtor. On

1 (1932), 11 N. L. R. 104.   2 (1932), 11 N. L. R. 116.

the other hand, in *Ajike* v. *Tamakloo & anor.*[1], the plaintiff was the purchaser of land attached by the first defendant in satisfaction of a judgment against the second defendant who, however, in a later consent judgment obtained against him by the plaintiff admitted that he had never had or claimed any right, title or interest in the property in question. Thus far, the purchase money had been paid to the Sheriff for payment into Court, pending the result of the litigation. The plaintiff therefore claimed refund of the purchase price, but the first defendant counterclaimed it for himself on the ground that, as there was no covenant for title given by the second defendant, the doctrine of *caveat emptor* applied to bar plaintiff's claim to refund. *Held*: by Graham Paul that (1) there was a mutual mistake of fact on the part of both auctioneer and purchaser that the second defendant had some right, title or interest in the property supposed sold; (2) the contract of sale was to that extent void; (3) the plaintiff was entitled to the refund of his money. The learned judge thus distinguished the *Owo Case* in these words:

'But the principle of *caveat emptor* has been held in *Sopido* v. *Coker & ors.*[2] not to apply to a purchaser of land advertised as about fifty acres when it was only twenty-two acres in area; the sale was set aside by the Divisional Court, in spite of the fact that the particular purchaser had subsequently to the advertisement and in pursuance of it been taken round the boundary by the vendor's agent, the auctioneer. All the cases quoted in the judgment where the principle of *caveat emptor* was applied against the purchaser were cases where the purchaser had accepted a conveyance; and in all these cases that fact was expressly regarded by the Court as important. . . . Here there is as yet no acceptance by the purchaser of a conveyance or of a certificate of purchase under the Rules of Court *ad hoc*. For that reason alone I consider I would be justified in not applying to this case the decision in *Clare* v. *Lamb* (1875, L. R. 10 C. P. 334). Similarly, in *Owo* v. *Kasumu*, (1) the money in that case had actually reached the hands of the judgment creditor; (2) it was never suggested in argument in that case that the sale was void or voidable because the seller and the purchaser were not *ad idem* in the essentials of their contract.' [3]

The result of the two cases would appear to be that if the judgment debtor's interest in the land purported to be sold formed part

---

[1] (1935), 12 N. L. R. 62.   [2] (1932), 11 N. L. R. 138.
[3] Ibid., pp. 64–5. The numbering in the latter part of the quotation is the author's.

of family land so that the purchaser of it under a writ of *Fi-fa* cannot get possession of the land, the purchaser will not be able to recover the purchase price if already paid to the judgment creditor, so long as there has been no actual conveyance and therefore no covenant for title. But, if the judgment debtor has no right, title or interest in the land being sold by the judgment creditor on the mistaken view that the debtor has, then the purchaser has nothing to pay for and can recover his money provided it has not been paid to the judgment creditor.

(4) *Sale of Land by Illiterate Persons.* Again, apparent sales of land may be set aside by the Court, especially where the alleged vendor is an illiterate person who does not fully grasp the import of the transaction or of whom a literate purchaser seeks to take advantage in circumstances bordering on sharp practice. In doing so the Court has tended towards a relaxation of the ordinary rules of evidence required in such cases, as we have seen in the case of *Bintu Alake* v. *Awawu* [1] where a gift of land by an illiterate was held valid although there was no written evidence of it as required by the Statute of Frauds which the Court was not prepared to allow plaintiff to invoke in that case. However, in *Okoleji* v. *Okupe*,[2] the Supreme Court itself invoked the Statute of Frauds in order to save an illiterate woman plaintiff from a literate moneylender defendant. The facts were briefly as follows: the defendant was in possession of the title deeds of plaintiff's property which he alleged to have been sold to him for £54 by the plaintiff who, however, contended that the transaction was a loan to her upon the security of her title deeds. The plaintiff offered to pay whatever amount the Court should find due from her to him in respect of the redemption of her property by him from the Lagos Building Society, Limited, which had originally threatened sale before she approached the defendant for the loan. The defendant sought an order of the Court for her to execute to him a proper deed of conveyance of the property in question, producing as evidence of the alleged sale a receipt by an auctioneer for £4 being his 'commission and expenses on purchase price of £54', and which was on the face of it a document between the alleged purchaser and the auctioneer. It was admitted, however, that the alleged sale had been by private treaty and not by public auction. *Held*: by the Supreme Court (1) that, in a case of an alleged sale of land by an illiterate woman to a literate registered moneylender, the provisions of the Statute

[1] See pp. 177-8, earlier.
[2] (1939), 15 N. L. R. 28.

of Frauds should be invoked; (2) that the auctioneer's receipt tendered in evidence of the alleged sale by the defendant was not a
memorandum in writing within the meaning of the Statute since
an auctioneer's implied authority to sign as the purchaser's agent
does not exist where, as was admitted in the present case, the sale
is otherwise than by public auction; (3) that the woman borrower
was entitled to have back her title deeds on payment of the moneylender's estimated amount of the loan. Graham Paul made this
pertinent observation; 'In my opinion the Court should be more
willing to hold that the Statute of Frauds is applicable in Nigeria
in a case where it is pleaded by an illiterate against a literate
party.' [1]

(5) *Sale Affected by Particular Custom*. Sometimes, an out-and-
out sale of land may be subject to pre-existing rights of others
thereover. We have noticed that in the Awori country, in Nupe and
in certain parts of Yoruba-land, a custom exists whereby the land
itself might be given away to 'strangers' but only the indigenous
people of the particular locality could reap the palm trees growing
thereon. [2] An extension of the same principle occurs in *Kugbuyi* v.
Odunjo. [3] There the plaintiff had purchased a certain piece of land
in the Awori country while the defendant, a sitting tenant on the
land at date of the purchase, continued to plant crops and collect
palm nuts on the land after its purchase by the plaintiff. The latter
thereupon brought an action of trespass against the defendant,
claiming damages therefor. The learned trial Judge, Tew, acting
C.J., had, in pursuance of the previous judgments by Pennington,
J., in *Alli Tinubu* v. *Seidu Jabita Williams* and *Salami Ajikpo* v.
Oseni Falade & Anor. (both decided on 24 February 1919), as well
as Tew's, J., own judgment in *Fabunmi Sule Larinde* v. *Disu
Adebiyi & ors.* (Suit No. 10 of 1925 decided on 11 May 1925),
held that in accordance with the established Awori custom the
right to reap palm trees was confined to 'natives of the soil' and
that the rights of a purchaser of the land in question were subject
to the right of a previous tenant to remain on the land as tenant
under local law and custom. Also, Tew, acting C.J., had taken the
point in *Fabunmi Sule Larinde's Case* that the tenant, in the absence of any authority to the contrary, was entitled to continue to
reap the trees after the purchase. But when his attention was in the
present action drawn to the decision in *Odu* v. *Akiboye* (1892) with

[1] (1939), 15 N. L. R. 28, pp. 29–30.
[2] See pp. 175–6, earlier.
[3] (1926), 7 N. L. R. 51.

which he confessed he was not previously acquainted, the learned Acting Chief Justice finally decided that the defendant tenant must be regarded as a trespasser with regard to the reaping of the palm trees. But this finding was silent on the question of the presence of the tenant on the land itself. Should not this formal repudiation of his shadowy right to remain on and cultivate the land sold carry with it also an *ipso facto* annulment of his tenure which is an inconvenient burden on the absolute estate of the purchaser in the land? It is submitted that, subject to any clear contract between the purchaser and such a tenant, the sale of land under this form of tenure should, on the analogy, if not the authority, of this case, be regarded by the Courts as putting an automatic end to any sitting tenant's subsisting rights over the land sold.

(6) *Principle of Quicquid Plantatur Solo, Solo Cedit.* The Roman Law doctrine of *Quicquid plantatur solo, solo cedit* is a principle of English, as of Nigerian, property law. Like many another empirical rule of social regulation of a specific legal situation, the concept of the accession of a building or other structure to the land built upon is reasonable, convenient and universal. If A builds on B's land, even with A's materials, the land and the building belong to B on the principle that the accessory belongs to the principal thing. Whether the Nigerian idea would follow all the Roman implications of the maxim we need not stop here to consider. It is better to confine ourselves here to so much as has been vouchsafed to us, in the absence of any other data, by the case of *Francis* v. *Ibitoye*.[1] The plaintiff in that case had paid the sum of £26 as a deposit towards a proposed contract of sale of land between the plaintiff and the defendant vendor. The contract of sale was, after a consent judgment, abandoned. The plaintiff nevertheless built a house worth £120 on the defendant's land at Ebute Metta without the latter's knowledge, leave or licence. The plaintiff then sued the defendant in this action for the total sum of £146, representing as to £26, the deposit paid on account, and as to £120, the cost of his erection of the house. *Held*: that (1) the plaintiff could recover the £26 as on a consideration that had totally failed because the contract of sale of the land was never carried out, but (2) that the principle of *Quicquid plantatur solo, solo cedit* applied to bar the plaintiff's claim to the cost of the building on the defendant's land without the latter's authority or ratification. *Quære*: Whether the plaintiff would have been entitled to have pulled down the building and taken away his materials? He should be able to do

[1] (1936), 13 N. L. R. 11.

that, it is submitted, if he would pay adequate compensation for any damage done to the defendant's land in the process.

Ownership of Land as Distinct from that of Things Thereon. It is, however, important to bear in mind that all the known customary systems of land tenure in Nigeria make a clear distinction between the ownership of land and the ownership of things *either* attached to or built on it *or* otherwise growing on it. The land may be owned by a whole community or by a family or by an individual while 'strangers' to the land or even a member of the land-owning group may be permitted to build a house or grow crops on it. This follows logically from the indigenous idea that, except in the rare cases of individually-owned parcels of land due to first cultivation, land is usually owned by a community or family. Therefore, all surface accretions to it by the labours of others normally belong to the latter provided the activities have had the sanction of those entitled to give it on behalf of the land-owning group.

In *Moore* v. *Jones* [1] the plaintiff claimed to be entitled to the ownership of a house built on another's land and sued the defendant, who was then residing in the house, for possession and damages. The Divisional Court decided that the plaintiff's ownership of the house had been established but that the question of damages concerned the previous occupant and not the present defendant, while the question of possession necessarily involved the ownership of the land on which the house stood.

The above are some of the problems that have arisen in connexion with the alienation by sale of family or group land and it is possible that others will come to light in the course of this difficult period of transition and, therefore, of deep social, economic and political changes through which the country is now passing.

We will next consider, very briefly, the problems relating to mortgages.

B. SOME PROBLEMS RELATING TO MORTGAGE AND LEASE OF LAND

Here we are chiefly concerned with the adaptation of the indigenous system to English forms of mortgage and the problems to which this gives rise. We have already noted some of these in the two preceding Chapters when we discussed the nature of the rights of the individual in the family land: e.g. (*a*) we have observed, in a number of cases of which *Adagun* v. *Fagbola* [2] is typical, that any

[1] (1926), 7. N. L. R. 84.   [2] (1932), 11 N. L. R. 110.

attempted *mortgage* by a family member of his unliquidated share in family land is null and void, so that the unfortunate purchaser of such property gets nothing: (*b*) similarly, a lease for a long period, say thirty years, of part of family land by an individual member occupier of it without his family consent is void and both the offending member and his tenant forfeit their rights thereto: *Onisiwo & ors.* v. *Gbamgboye & ors.*[1]

It remains to note in conclusion two cases which are of interest, not because they have any direct bearing on the indigenous land tenure, but because they reflect the sometimes indirect operation of the latter even in land transactions ostensibly governed by English property principles:

(1) *Mortgage or Conditional Sale?* In *Seidu Olowo* v. *Miller Bros.*[2] the Court had to interpret a document which the Nigerian plaintiff contended was a mortgage of his property to the defendant English firm which insisted that it was a conditional sale. It was proved in evidence and admitted by the plaintiff that the document, itself anomalous in form as in phrasing, provided that the plaintiff could at any time within a fixed period of five years redeem his property on repayment of the amount of the loan (£2,400) to the defendant firm and that, on such redemption, the defendant firm should be granted a lease at a rent not exceeding £150 p.a. It was further provided that failure by the plaintiff to redeem within the stipulated period should vest the absolute ownership of the land in the defendant firm. The plaintiff failed to redeem in time but soon afterwards offered to repay the total amount of the loan and recover his property which he argued was no more than security for the loan—a mortgage; he therefore claimed an equity of redemption. The Court held that the large amount of the loan and certain affirmations of the plaintiff during his cross-examination in Court led it to form the impression that a conditional sale, and not a mortgage, was originally contemplated by the parties. The document in question would, if the plaintiff's allegation be accepted, be a very unorthodox type of a mortgage instrument. But the plaintiff might very well have put forward the argument in the genuine, though unexpressed spirit of a local form of redeemable pledge to which no time limit ordinarily applies and which can never become the property of the lender or pledgee. This is an important aspect of the case which deserves the careful

[1] (1941), 7 W. A. C. A. 69; sub. nom. *Buraimo* v. *Bamgboye* (1940), 15 N. L. R. 139, in the Supreme Court at Lagos.
[2] (1911), 3 N. L. R. 99.

attention of the Court when called upon to interpret ambiguous or
inexpertly-phrased documents between parties one of whom is a
Nigerian illiterate or semi-literate. The attitude of the Court in
the present instance is a little difficult to reconcile with that it
took in such cases as *Bintu Alake* v. *Awawu* and *Okeleji* v. *Okupe*
to both of which we have referred above.[1]

   (*ii*) *Severance of Joint Tenancy by Equitable Mortgage.* The
second case concerns an issue which transcends the immediate precincts of Nigerian property law. The novel issue in *Ipaye* v.
Aribisala [2] was: Did the creation by a joint tenant of an equitable
mortgage of his share sever the legal joint-tenancy? The difficulty
of the case was that there existed no exact precedent for it whether
in English or in Nigerian land law. Let us first look at the facts:
the plaintiff, Musa Abiodum Ipaye, and his brother, Sakariyawo
Falade, became joint tenants under their mother's voluntary
settlement the deed of which was in Falade's custody. After
Falade's death it became known to Ipaye (his brother) that Falade
had deposited the title deed with the defendant as security for a
loan of £30, thus creating an equitable mortgage of Falade's share
in the estate. The plaintiff neither knew of nor consented to
Falade's deposit of the title deed with the defendant; indeed,
Falade got someone to impersonate the plaintiff and sign himself
in the plaintiff's name at the bottom of the loan agreement, thereby
representing to the defendant that the co-joint tenant was agreeable to the use he (Falade) was making of the title deed. On these
facts the Divisional Court held that there had been no severance
of the joint-tenancy, that the plaintiff's right of survivorship
operated to vest the entire legal estate in him alone, and that the
defendant should accordingly return the title deed to the plaintiff.
The defendant then appealed to the Full Court which unanimously
reversed the Divisional Court judgment and ordered the plaintiff
to hand the title deed back to the defendant with costs.

   Petrides, J., after citing *Short* v. *Stone* (1710), 91 E. R. K. B. 146,
and *Re Pollard's Estate*, 142, E. R. (1863), 161, as instances of a
legal mortgage held to effect a severance of a joint-tenancy, confessed to some difficulty in the case before him when he said; [3]
'I have had some doubt whether an equitable mortgage will constitute a severance of a joint tenancy in the same way as a legal
mortgage undoubtedly does, as the effect of a legal mortgage is to

---

[1] See pp. 178 and 200, *supra*, respectively.
[2] (1930), 10 N. L. R. 10.
[3] Ibid., at p. 12.

vest the legal estate in the mortgagee whereas an equitable mortgage does not pass the estate to the creditor.' The learned Judge
then found support for his decision, that the defendant should have
back the title deeds from the plaintiff, in Jessell's, M.R., dictum in
Carter v. *Wake* (1877), 4 Ch. D. 605, to the effect that 'where there
is a deposit of title deeds the Court treats that as an agreement to
execute a legal mortgage, and therefore as carrying with it all the
remedies incident to such a mortgage'. Nor was Kingdon, C.J., any
the happier about the unique situation with which the facts of the
case confronted him when he proceeded to observe: '*Whether or
not an equitable mortgage has the same effect appears never to have
been decided.*' [1] His Honour then went on: 'If this is the principle,
and I think it is, it appears to me to apply with equal force to an
equitable mortgage as to a legal mortgage; and the two should, in
my opinion, stand on exactly the same footing in this respect. The
present case appears to me to be a very good example of the
soundness of the reasoning. One joint tenant was able to raise
money on his share because the lender did not imagine that he
would lose his security by the death of the mortgagor. Had he
envisaged such a possibility it is extremely unlikely that he would
have lent the money. . . . I am of opinion therefore that one of two
joint tenants by giving to a third party an equitable mortgage of his
share severs the joint tenancy.' The learned Chief Justice then ruled
that the title deed must be returned to the defendant by the plaintiff
because then the defendant had as much right to the possession of
the deeds as the plaintiff; and on the principle of *Potior est positio
possidentis*, the defendant was entitled to retain possession of it.

In reaching this result possible hardship to the joint tenant and
the mortgagee of his interest seemed to have weighed very much
with the court and, in the absence of any clear authority on the
point, the precedent was there established that an equitable mortgage of his interest by a joint tenant creates a tenancy in common
as between him and his co-owner so as to enable him to dispose of
his share as he pleases. The mortgagee from him also gets thereby
valid security for his money and can assert a right to the mortgagor's share as against the co-owner of the legal joint-tenancy.
This case, if we may say so, ought to be more widely known.

Conclusion

Apart from these special problems, then, the modern rules of
law governing cases of leases, mortgages and sales are the same

[1] (1911), 3 N. L. R. 99, at p. 13. (The italics are the author's.)

as those of English Law for which one must consult the standard English works dealing with these matters.

Native Authority Ordinance of 1945. A recent Ordinance, the importance of which for the future of land law and custom in Nigeria cannot at present be fully assessed, is the Native Authority (Control of Lands—Amendment) Ordinance No. 73 of 1945. It provides that in addition to the subjects enumerated in the principal Ordinance, the various Native Authorities may make rules relating to the use and alienation of interests in land in their respective districts. The following are among the special things they can do: (*a*) the control and use of whatever remains of communal lands and of family lands, and such control may be general or limited as to specific forms of cultivation; (*b*) the control of mortgages of land; (*c*) purchases or sales of land may be made subject to the Native Authority's approval; (*d*) the control or prescription of the size and extent of communal and family lands over which any individual may exercise rights; (*e*) the regulation of the allocation by the chiefs and family heads of communal and of family lands.

In similar vein is the earlier Native Authority (Amendment) Ordinance No. 3 of 1945 which inserts into the principal Ordinance a further Section (29A) which confers powers on Native Authorities to declare and, if necessary, modify what in their opinion is 'native law and custom'. If these powers are intended to enable these bodies to make the local customary law keep pace with the social facts of any particular situation, it is thought that such a desirable end would be better secured if the courts are allowed to take care of the natural evolution of indigenous rules and customs. The normal judicial process of taking the expert evidence of local assessors and arbitrators reasonably ensures that due regard is had to existing laws and customs which are upheld or rejected according as they conform, in a given situation, to the over-riding requirements of equity and good conscience.

The provisions of Ordinance No. 73 of 1945, so strangely reminiscent of those of the Bale of Ibadan and Council of 1918 which we have discussed above, can only lead to a multiplicity of land rules and customs far more numerous and divergent than would be desirable for the progressive development of the country. The true line of approach should be the encouragement and fostering of uniformity, so far as possible, of principles of land usage and practice in Nigeria.

Chapter Nine

SERVITUDES, EASEMENTS, PROFITS AND RESTRICTIVE COVENANTS

Servitudes. Easements (in Local Tenure). Profits (in Local Tenure). Restrictive Covenants.

I N the preceding Chapter we have discussed the various modes in which an individual or a group of individuals can, under the indigenous system as well as under English law, acquire substantial rights in or over the land of another whether by borrowing, pledge, leasing, mortgage or sale. Here we want to consider how far there exist in the Nigerian land tenure system, ancient and modern, qualified rights of an absolute character which one person can be said to enjoy over the land of another.

SERVITUDES

In Nigeria, as elsewhere, the principle of an owner-occupier sharing the enjoyment of his surplus lands with his less fortunate neighbour extends to the crops and other produce, especially where the neighbour has had a bad harvest or is otherwise unable to meet the normal needs of his household. Even if no such domestic need arises, it is possible for the man with more land than he can fully or profitably cultivate to allow his neighbour occupier to use the unwanted portion for growing crops. The general terms are often mutually agreed between the parties, including the fixing of the consideration, the nature of the use to which the land may be put, and the condition of the termination of the arrangement.

Sometimes, an owner-occupier of land may grant to another a right only to cut palm trees or collect other fruits from trees and plants growing on the land, but the land itself remains in the owner's possession and under his control. Such a right may be gratutious or for value.

Instead of one such right being given to just one licensee, two or more concurrent rights to the same or different types of the land's produce might occasionally be found. One person might be given permission to farm the land for food crops and another to cut the palm nuts thereon at the same time. Where the respective spheres of influence of the two have not been properly defined, complications set in. Some such issue arose, as we have seen, in *Chief Etim & others* v. *Chief Eke & ors.*[1], where the defendants' predecessors granted land in Calabar to the plaintiffs' predecessors for occupation and farming under local law and custom. Later, the defendants granted to a third party, who was a stranger to that locality, the right to cut palm nuts on the land. Martindale, J., awarded damages to plaintiffs for trespass by the third party and granted the injunction asked for by the plaintiffs, forbidding any further interference by the defendants and their agents with the plaintiffs' occupation and enjoyment of the land under customary law. The learned Judge then remarked: 'As a mere *obiter dictum* and without reference to this suit which is decided on other grounds, the view is held that severance of tenant's farming rights and the right to cut palm nuts over the same land is to be deprecated as being conducive to friction between the farmers and the palm-nut cutters and to the wholesome destruction of palm trees and to the uneconomical working of the land.' [2]

Another species of right which an owner-occupier of land may grant to another is permission to build on his farm- or town-land. The buildings or structures in such cases are generally of a temporary nature so that they can be easily removed when the grant expires. The parties often arrange their own terms which, of course, condition the servitude.[3] Often, the permission to build houses results in the stranger-occupier not being any longer subject to ejection unless for serious crimes.

PROFITS

Rights of fishing in the ponds or streams lying in another's land as well as the rights of navigating the same and of carrying away therefrom water for domestic purposes are common. Rights also exist of collecting fire-woods or of trapping animals like rabbits, hares, and so on, on another's land.

[1] (1941), 16 N. L. R. 43.   [2] Ibid., at p. 52.
[3] See A. K. Ajisafe, op. cit., paras. 16–19 of Chap. IV.

The digging of gravel for building and other purposes and the felling of uneconomic trees and thatch for houses and barns are also matters of every day occurrence in the rural areas of the country.[1]

EASEMENTS

Again, certain footpaths separating two farm-plots or buildings or building sites are generally regarded as affording public or private rights of way, according to their location and width. It is not uncommon for owner-occupiers of lands to allow their neighbours rights of access across their lands to such neighbours' own lands lying beyond, if that is convenient and agreeable to the occupier of the servient tenement and is considered indispensable to the proper enjoyment of the other occupier's dominant tenement. Such rights often arise as the result of express agreement, but prescriptive claims of various kinds are frequently made to rights of way. Where legal and customary rights are all too often largely undifferentiated and, in the absence of written evidence, personal witnesses to such transactions eventually die out, memories of the actual rights granted or refused grow dim over the years and much confusion might result. But the practical insistence on the claimant's showing positive, apparent and long user of the right now being asserted tends to discourage clearly bogus claims.

Moreover, there is in favour of the public a general right of way over lands adjoining rivers or streams, especially if these serve also as the sources of water-supply for domestic purposes. A definite right of free passage exists over all public thorough-fares since ancient times, for certain highways have from time immemorial become well worn by travellers and traders making long journeys along established routes. Towns and villages are often connected by a network of high-roads and footpaths, which are generally maintained by the joint labour of contiguous villages at fixed intervals. No one individual or body of individuals has a right to obstruct its free use by the public. The members of it used to resort to many forms of self-help to prevent or remove an obstruction.

Thus, in *Obasa* v. *Baruwa & ors.*[2], an ancient highway, the Agege Ipaja road, on the outskirts of Lagos, had in or about 1916 been by the plaintiff widened, with the consent of the landowners through whose land the road passed, so as to make it fit for motor traffic and had since spent money on repairing and improving it. To reimburse himself the plaintiff placed a gate across the entrance

[1] A. K. Ajisafe, op. cit., Chap. IV., para. 20.   [2] (1931), 10 N. L. R. 104.

and collected tolls from vehicles using the highway until the commencement of the present action, 1931, when the defendants broke down the toll-bar. The plaintiff sued them for trespass to the gate and for an injunction. Butler Lloyd, J., in the Divisional Court in Lagos, held (1) that the plaintiff had no right to collect tolls on a public highway, or to obstruct the highway with a toll-bar; and (2) that the defendants were within their rights in abating the nuisance. This finding, it is submitted, is in consonance with the indigenous rule on the subject which is the same as English law on which the learned Judge based his argument: 'I am perfectly clear that the plaintiff had no right to collect tolls on this road. The only tolls known to the common law are tolls traverse and tolls thorough, both attributable to a grant or presumed grant from the Crown; the former being payable to the original owner of the lands, the latter to the person being liable to repair the highway. There is no suggestion of a Crown grant here and the plaintiff is neither the owner of the land nor under any liability for repairs.' [1]

Under the local customary law, only the rulers can collect tolls through their appropriate officers in charge of town or village gates.[2]

Some Local Cases of Easements under English law. We saw in *Onade & anor.* v. *Thomas* [3] how certain vendors of two adjoining pieces of land in Lagos sold the first plot to the plaintiff with an easement covering a common passage between that plot and the second one which was later sold to the defendant with an exclusive right to the same easement; and how the second grant was held void on the principle that 'a grantor cannot derogate from his grant'.

In *Opeifa & anor.* v. *Lawal* [4] the main point was that the plaintiff's action had been misconceived. The plaintiffs sued damages for trespass which consisted of (*a*) the defendant's cutting down trees and building a brick boundary wall on the plaintiffs' land; (*b*) the erection by the defendant of a dwelling house on defendant's land which immediately adjoined the plaintiffs' and the interference of the house with the plaintiffs' easements over the defendant's land. It was held that an action of trespass does not lie in respect of an interference with a mere easement and that the plaintiffs must fail in their action. The plaintiffs were no doubt entitled to an easement of light over the defendant's adjoining land and would evidently have succeeded if, instead of bringing an action in trespass, they had sued for the disturbance of their easement.

[1] (1931), 10 N. L. R. 104.
[2] See A. K. Ajisafe, op. cit.
[3] See p. 198, earlier.
[4] (1934), 12 N. L. R. 11.

Next, we must note the rather novel features of the law of easements considered in the important Privy Council judgment in *Attorney-General of Southern Nigeria* v. *John Holt* [1] which we discussed in another connexion at some length in Chapter Two. The respondents claimed the following two species of easements over land reclaimed from the sea washing Lagos foreshore: (*a*) an easement over part of the land for the purpose of storing thereon coopers' stores, casks, trade goods and produce; and (*b*) an easement for jetties erected on another part of the land. The Attorney-General, on behalf of the Crown, did not object to the claim of easement for the jetties, but maintained with regard to the easement of storage that such an easement was unknown to the law. Lord Shaw, delivering the judgment of the Privy Council, held: [2]

'Their Lordships see no reason why upon the first point a right of easement should be exclusive of the storage claim. The law must adapt itself to the conditions of modern society and trade, and there is nothing in the purposes for which the easement is claimed inconsistent in principle with a right of easement as such.' This principle is of general application, and was so treated in the House of Lords in *Dyce* v. *Hay* ((1852), 1 Macq. 305) by Lord St. Leonards, L.C., who observed: 'The category of servitudes and easements must alter and expand with the changes that take place in the circumstances of mankind.' [3]

But the Crown's further contention was that the nature of the respondent's right in the peculiar circumstances of the case could not in any case amount to an easement as commonly understood in English law. The respondents had earlier on admitted that the land in question was the property of the Crown, although they had throughout been using the land in the various ways already described under the innocent belief that the land was their private property. How, then, argued the Crown, could they as owners of the land claim to have acquired and enjoyed an easement over the same land? It is of the essence of an easement that there must be a servient as well as a dominant tenement and that both should be in the hands of two different fee simple owners.

But as the Crown had itself acquiesced in the respondents' use and occupation of the land for an unreasonably long time, the respondents' right in the manner already stated should not be

---

[1] (1915), A. C. 599.

[2] Ibid., at p. 617; also 2 N. L. R. 1, at p. 66.

[3] See Professor G. C. Cheshire's comments on this case in his *Modern Real Property* (5th edition, p. 236).

disturbed, a kind of irrevocable licence by the Crown being presumed in their favour.

As a final point, it should be noted that rights in the nature of servitudes, easements and profits may be expressly reserved as well by statutes as by private agreements. Thus the occupier's exclusive right of occupancy 'against all persons other than the Governor' under the Land and Native Rights Ordinance of 1916 is expressly made subject to existing easements and roads of access to neighbouring lands by s. 10 of the Ordinance which provides as follows:

(1) Every right of occupancy shall be subject to any easement affecting the land at the date of the grant of the right of occupancy.

(2) The holder of a right of occupancy shall, if required by the Governor, allow a road of access over the land the subject of his right of occupancy to any person occupying land which is so situate that such road of access is, in the opinion of the Governor, reasonably required.

(3) The person requiring a road of access shall pay to the holder of the right of occupancy in respect of the land to be traversed compensation in respect of any growning crops or improvements damaged or destroyed by the construction of the road.

(4) In the event of the holder of a right of occupancy and the person desiring or using a road of access over the land the subject of such right of occupancy being unable to agree as to the direction or width of the road of access or as to any matter in connexion with the construction, repair or use of the road or as to the amount of the compensation to be paid in accordance with the provisions of sub-s. (3), any of the parties concerned may appeal to the Governor who may appoint any officer to determine the matters in dispute, and the decision of such officer shall be binding on all persons concerned.

RESTRICTIVE COVENANTS

We have seen, when discussing the customary law on pledge, 'borrowing' of land, and traditional forms of leases,[1] that the indigenous system of tenure has always recognised various types of restrictions as to the kind of use to which land may be put under these modes of alienation *inter vivos*. The nature of the restriction imposed in any particular case would be dictated as much by the form of arrangement, whether this is a pledge or a land 'borrowing' or a customary lease, as by the circumstances of the parties to the transaction. The obligation imposed might be that no

---

[1] See pp. 175-186, *supra*.

permanent crops be planted on the land subject to the arrangement or that purely farming-land should not be turned into arable or even that the grantee should not reap certain specified fruits (usually palm nuts) from trees growing on the land—in each case with or without the grantor's or the grantor's family's consent.

It is therefore but natural that with the introduction of development estates more modern forms of restriction as to the user of the new houses should be imposed, in much the same way as these are being imposed in more developed countries. Thus, in the *Chairman, L.E.D.B.* v. *Belo Raji* [1] there was imposed by the plaintiff Board a restrictive covenant to the effect that 'the land [is] to be used for residential purposes only'. The defendant began to hold prayer-meetings on the premises attended by many friends from outside, and the plaintiff contended that the house was thereby being used as a mosque and that that was a breach of covenant. The defendant argued that he used only the sitting-room 'to perform his holy devotions together with members of his family'. It was, however, proved in evidence that in the defendant's original building plan 'a prayer hall' was included. It was held by W. A. C. A. that there had been a breach by the defendant of his covenant under the lease.

On the other hand, parties may enter into *positive* covenants as part of their dealings in land, and this may take the form of requiring the tenant to do some act or thing designed to enhance the value of the land. The covenant may be that certain species of crops shall be sown and cultivated or that farming-land shall be turned into arable or into one growing cash crops; or, in urban or residential areas, the tenant may be required to build houses or other erections often to certain specifications, or to maintain existing buildings and carry out some specified repairs. For instance, in *Onwuta* v. *Niger Co. Ltd.*[2] the defendants covenanted to erect on land leased to them by the plaintiff certain buildings to the value of £1,000 within six months of the commencement of the lease. The defendants failed to fulfil the covenant but the plaintiff continued to accept the rent for three years afterwards, and then sued the defendants for breach of covenant and for recovery of possession of the land. It was held that the plaintiff was entitled to re-enter because, although he had waived his right to recover possession during the period he was accepting rent, the waiver terminated when he gave oral notice and refused further rent, the oral notice being deemed sufficient to terminate the lease for the continued breach of covenant.

[1] (1939), 5 W. A. C. A. 137.   [2] (1926), 7 N. L. R. 79.

Chapter Ten

INHERITANCE AND SUCCESSION (ALIENATION ON DEATH)

A. The Yoruba Rules of Inheritance. B. The Ibo Rules of Inheritance. The Calabar Rules of Inheritance. C. The Rules of Inheritance in the Northern Provinces. Inheritance in the North and the Maliki Code. D. Variation of Customary Rules of Inheritance: (i) By a Dying Declaration or by Family Verdict; (ii) By Christian or English Marriage; (iii) By Will. E. Ordinances and Statutes Relating to Succession.

IN discussing the customary rules of inheritance of property it is necessary to keep these two principles in mind: (1) that, as a result of the unwritten nature of the indigenous law and custom, the inheritance of property is governed by traditional canons of descent and not by *wills*, unless, of course, a person has expressly made a will or married according to English law, when other considerations will apply. Inheritance is, therefore, normally determined by the customary rules whenever a person dies without having made a will or married under English law. There is accordingly no need to divide the customary rules of inheritance into testate and intestate, terms which we shall, however, have occasion to consider when we come to deal with the problems raised by the making of wills of family or group lands by individuals. (2) That, because of the pluralistic tendency of social norms and concepts, especially in the matter of land usage, there is a constant inter-play between tenure and inheritance. In such a situation, therefore, there is bound to be a measure of overlapping in stating the principles of either. Thus, in discussing the nature of the rights of individuals, we have had to consider, *inter alia*, problems of allocation and of partition, of the heritability or otherwise of the individual's right in family land, of what constitutes 'family property' and of the individual's right therein. But it is possible and reasonable to treat inheritance apart from pure tenure and, by a shift in emphasis, concentrate in the present Chapter strictly on the rules peculiar to inheritance and succession as such.

It is proposed (a) to set out such evidence as there is of the main customary rules of inheritance in each of the three principal regions of Nigeria, noticing as we proceed some important variations wherever these occur; and (b) to formulate in a systematic whole the scattered strands of the laws and customs. We shall next consider the extent to which the traditional rules have been and are being modified or altered by (i) certain evolutionary processes, (ii) the introduction of Wills, (iii) marriage according to English law, (iv) certain Statutory enactments.

Unlike the matrilineal systems which obtain in some other colonial areas,[1] the Nigerian systems of succession are predominantly patrilineal and patrilocal. There were and probably are, it is true, a few isolated cases of matrilineal inheritance; indeed, the patrilineal principle not infrequently embraces, as a kind of secondary or supplementary inheritance, a matrilineal counterpart. But the patriarchal remains the standard pattern of succession throughout the country.

Again, the patriarchal arrangement may range from the practice, on the one hand, of *Primogeniture* (as in Bini, Nupe and some other areas of the North),[2] according to which property is inherited by the eldest son to the exclusion of all others, to that of *Ultimogeniture* (as among the Marki group of the Verre[3] in Northern Provinces), according to which inheritance is exclusively by the youngest son, on the other. We shall later deal at somewhat greater length with these features.

Let us now study the main body of evidence relating to the Yorubas, the Ibos and the Hausas, and compare and contrast the relative principles of succession and inheritance. We employ here the three ethnic names only in a generic sense.

A. THE YORUBA RULES OF INHERITANCE

We may conveniently begin our examination of the evidence here with our old friend, *Lewis* v. *Bankole*,[4] in which, it will be

---

[1] e.g., the Gold Coast, Malaya.

[2] See W. Price, op. cit., paras. 274–5; *Per* Berkeley, J., in *Inyang* v. *Ita & ors.* (1929), 9 N. L. R. 84, at p. 85; Nadel, op. cit., p. 88.

[3] C. K. Meek, *Tribal Studies in Northern Nigeria* (1931), Vol. I, p. 415.

[4] (1909), 1 N. L. R. 82; for the facts of this case see pp. 144-5, *supra*.

remembered, the following propositions relevant to succession among the Lagos Yorubas were laid down by the Full Court:

(i) When the founder of a family dies, the eldest surviving son called the 'Dawodu', succeeds to the headship of the family with all that that implies, including residence and the giving of orders in his father's house or compound;

(ii) On the death of the eldest surviving son, the next eldest surviving child of the founder, whether male or female, is the proper person to succeed as head of the family;

(iii) If there is going to be any important dealing with family property all branches of the family must be consulted, and representation on the family council is also *per stirpes* according as there are wives with children.

(iv) The division is into equal shares between the respective branches, regard being had to any property already received by any of the founder's children during his life-time.

(v) The founder's grandchildren only succeed to such rights as their immediate parents had in the family property.

(vi) The founder's compound or house is usually regarded as the 'family house' which must be preserved for posterity.

In thus upholding the existing rules of inheritance with the help of Lagos chiefs and other witnesses from outside Lagos, Osborne, C.J., remarked: [1] 'That the present Lagos customs are modifications of the original Yoruba customs there is little reason to doubt; and the evidence as to those Yoruba customs is of undoubted value, as showing how far the general principles remain intact in Lagos, and how far they have been modified to meet present requirements.' [2] After observing that the eldest surviving son is the proper person to succeed the deceased founder of a family, the learned Chief Justice continued: 'This seems to be *a well-established rule both in Lagos and in other parts of Yorubaland. It is after the death of the Dawodu that we begin to find variations; according to the plaintiff's witnesses, by Yoruba custom the other sons of the founder of the family are taken in turn, and then the sons of the Dawodu and other son's sons, the headship being ever kept in the male line.* One explanation of this rule is that

[1] (1909), 1 N. L. R. 82, at p. 102.

[2] Compare W. Price, op. cit., para. 5: 'Whatever their degree of advancement now, however, it seems highly probable that there was only one ancient system of land tenure for all the sections of Yoruba-land and that any variations which may have occurred locally established themselves later than "ancient" times.'

the women on marriage go and live with their husbands; another is that a woman is only "part of a man". . . . On the other hand the view of the Lagos chiefs is that it is the eldest child, whether male or female, who becomes head after the Dawodu.' And in the case before him His Honour saw no reason why the female plaintiff should not become the family head since the chiefs appointed by the Court to go into the matter described her as appearing to them 'gentle and intelligent and capable, in fact, she should be the mother and the guiding head of this family'.[1] This requirement of mental and cultural competence as a pre-requisite to the family headship, like the patriarchal principle itself, will be met with again when we come to deal with rules obtaining in the Eastern as well as the Northern regions of the country.

As a complement to the foregoing principles it is necessary to examine a few more cases in which other aspects of the customary rules of inheritance have been considered by the Courts.

We should next consider the rights, if any, of surviving parents in their child's property, as against brothers and sisters of the whole or half-blood. In *Adedoyin* v. *Simeon and ors.*,[2] the plaintiff was the mother of a woman who died intestate (i.e. under customary law) and without issue. The defendants were the deceased's surviving three half-sisters, all four of them having inherited from their common father an estate the subject of this action. The three defendants claimed the whole estate on the ground that their deceased sister's share had lapsed into the residue for their benefit. This plea also amounted to the claim of a right of survivorship as if all four sisters had held the estate on an English joint tenancy. The plaintiff, the deceased sister's mother, disputed the three sisters' contention and claimed to be entitled to her daughter's share of the property. *Held*: that, under Yoruba law and custom of inheritance, the mother must take her deceased daughter's share to the exclusion of the deceased sisters of the half-blood. The judgment is, however, of more general interest on account of the recorded evidence of certain important witnesses to the Yoruba customary rules of inheritance which will therefore be reproduced here:

'I have had the advantage of having the opinion of Chief Obanikoro, Chief Ojora, and Mr. Wilson the Interpreter in this Court, and I find that they are all agreed that under native law and custom in Lagos, and throughout Yorubaland, the personal property of Comfort Ajayi would on her death pass to her mother and

[1] (1909), 1 N. L. R. 82, at p. 103.   [2] (1928), 9 N. L. R. 76.

to her mother alone. In reply to questions put by the Court, Chief Obanikoro stated:

(1) If a child dies leaving personal property, *her father being dead but her mother alive*, the property will pass to the mother, *provided the child has no brother or sister being children of her mother*.

(2) If the *father is alive as well as the mother* the property would be shared between the father and the mother, although the father would generally invite the mother to take the whole.

(3) If the *father had been alive as well as the mother and also a brother and sister of the child by the same mother* the property would be divided between the brother and sister and *the parents would take nothing*. Half-brothers and half-sisters being the children of a different mother would not take any share. It makes no difference if the personal property was given to or left to the child by her father.

These answers both Chief Ojora and Mr. Wilson agreed were correct statements of native law and custom *throughout* Yorubaland.' [1]

But it should not be inferred as a general rule that a mother can always inherit the share of her child who has died intestate and without issue. Thus, in *George & anor.* v. *Fajore*,[2] the defendant was the widow of a testator whose surviving executors were the plaintiffs. It appeared that the testator had left real property in Lagos to twelve named persons, one of whom was the widow's son who had been allotted a portion of the premises by the executors. This son died in 1931, leaving a widow and a son who also died in 1936. After her grandson's death, the defendant took possession of her son's allotment, to recover which the plaintiffs then sued this action. It was held (1) that succession to the testator's devised property was in the circumstances of the case governed by local customary law under which a mother could not acquire any interest upon the death of her son and failure of his issue: (2) that, in any case, the defendant could not succeed in the absence of proof of the death of her grandson's mother (i.e. her son's widow) who would be preferred to the defendant grandmother. Two important results of this case seem to be: (*a*) a mother cannot inherit her deceased child's allotted but not yet partitioned share of the family property; (*b*) there is here a tacit recognition of a widow's claim to her deceased husband's allotted portion; at least, to such of his rights thereto as are recognised under local law and custom. One

---

[1] (1928), 9 N. L. R. 76.   [2] (1939), 15 N. L. R. 1.

short reason for this exclusion of the testator's widow in such a case is probably that she already has her own apartments in her husband's house which she can retain for her life; another is that succession to a deceased member's portion of the family land is by customary law given to that member's child or children, if any. On this analysis, the implied recognition in the above case of the deceased son's widow's right to his share of the family property would appear to be doubtful, for she would have had her own rooms during her husband's life-time and from these no one could have lawfully ejected her for her life—unless, of course, she merely intended to continue living in the common apartments previously occupied together with her deceased husband. If she should decide to leave her husband's house after his death, the apartments would no doubt revert to the head of the family for necessary re-allocation or otherwise.

Under customary law, a husband cannot ordinarily inherit his deceased wife's share of her family property. This follows logically from the well-known principle that no one member of the family has any separate and alienable estate in the family property to which a stranger to the family can succeed on that member's death. Rules of inheritance apart, local sentiments would frown upon the idea of a scape-grace husband aspiring to a share in his deceased wife's family's property. Thus, in *Caulcrick* v. *Harding*,[1] property was left by a man to his three daughters, one of whom was the plaintiff's deceased wife. The plaintiff husband claimed a one-third share of the property in virtue of his deceased wife's right to such one-third share. Tew, J., held that the plaintiff had no such right as the family property was, under local law and custom, inalienable. It was not an English tenancy in common.

Another aspect of the customary law of inheritance is illustrated by *Andre* v. *Agbebi*[2] in which the question arose as to the succession to the property of a deceased intestate who had left him surviving two minors, one of whom was an uterine brother while the other was a half-sister born to his father in lawful wedlock with another woman. The issue to be decided then was whether the deceased's half-brother by the same mother or the deceased's half-sister by the same father was the proper person to inherit his estate. Webber, J., observed:[3] 'I am inclined to the opinion that the trend of the decisions is in favour of the uterine brother succeeding to some share of the inheritance. On the other hand I cannot disregard the evidence of a chief who lays it down that the deceased's

[1] (1926), 7 N. L. R. 48.   [2] (1931), 10 N. L. R. 79.   [3] At p. 80.

father's family is entitled to inherit.' The learned Judge, therefore, held that both the uterine brother and the half-sister must succeed to the inheritance in equal shares. In the present case the evidence of Chief Amodu Tijani as to succession was that 'if a child leaves property the family on his father's side will inherit'. But the case is different where the child has inherited the property from his or her mother who has herself inherited it from her own family. This point will become clear from a consideration of the next case.

Thus, in *Idewu* v. *Hausa & ors.*,[1] a man, Idewu, died in 1895, leaving three daughters, one of whom died intestate before the allocation of the land to the three branches, but the deceased daughter's third part was given to her surviving son, Belo, who through his father collected rents therefrom until his death in 1923. Belo's father thereupon claimed to succeed to his son's share, alleging a previous partition of Idewu's land in virtue of which his son had acquired a separate estate in his own portion capable of devolving upon him (the father) as next-of-kin. The plaintiff, on behalf of herself and other members of the Idewu family, invoked local law and custom whereby on the death of a man intestate without issue, family property inherited from his mother reverts to the mother's family. It was decided by Carey, J., that, in the absence of partition to Belo, the onus of proving which was on Bello's father who alleged it, Belo's allotment should revert on his death without issue to Belo's mother's family and not to Belo's father.

On the question of partition of the family property we have observed in *Sule & ors.* v. *Ajisegiri* [2] that the tendency is to hold that the children now take equal shares regardless of sex, thus in effect disregarding *dicta* in *Lopez* v. *Lopez* [3] that female rights in family property might be different from those of males. When *Lopez* v. *Lopez* came up on appeal to the Supreme Court, Combe, C.J., after stating that in the olden days the rights of daughters differed from those of sons and that the position had not changed up to the date of his judgment, continued: [4] 'However that may be, females undoubtedly have rights and the Court must have jurisdiction to make such order as may be necessary to protect a female in the enjoyment of her rights. . . . A case might arise in which an order of partition would be the only effective means of ensuring

[1] (1936), 13 N. L. R. 96.
[2] (1937), 13 N. L. R. 146, and see Chapter Seven, earlier.
[3] (1924), 5 N. L. R. 47.
[4] Ibid., at p. 51.

that a female and her issue shall live on her father's lands without being disturbed by other members of the family, and I can see no reason for holding that the Court could not order partition in such a case.' The occasion here envisaged arose in *Sule & ors.* v. *Ajisegiri* where the plaintiffs claimed partition and sale of six properties which had been left to their mother and the defendant, their mother's brother, as part of the undistributed estate of their grandfather. The defendant asserted that as a male child he was entitled to a larger share than the plaintiffs' mother, but Butler Lloyd in the Divisional Court held that the plaintiffs were entitled to demand partition in right of their mother and that the division of the property or its proceeds must be equally between their mother and the defendant, without regard to sex.

So inexorable in their operation are the rules of customary inheritance that land acquired by an individual as absolute private property, whether purchased with his own money or obtained as such in consequence of partition of family land, devolves upon his children as family property under the customary law of succession. Thus, in *Ogunmefun* v. *Ogunmefun*,[1] the plaintiff's grandfather died intestate, leaving a fee simple estate to his children only two of whom, however, survived him with issue. The plaintiff's mother was the sole surviving child of her father when she purported to devise by will her share of the estate. It was held that the purported devise was invalid, as until partition plaintiff's mother's succession rights were inalienable by her under the customary rules of inheritance which must be taken as governing the form of land tenure left by the intestate grandfather. The plaintiff, therefore, succeeded to his mother's share to the exclusion of the intended devisees.

Enough has now been noticed of the judicial findings as to the customary rules of inheritance and succession. Let us see next the extent to which these may be qualified or supplemented by evidence from other available sources. And, for this, one naturally turns in the first place to A. K. Ajisafe's little book on *The Laws and Customs of the Yoruba People*.[2] There the writer asserts the patrilineal principle of succession, but believes that goods and land of a deceased person are shared and distributed according to rank, title or age, the eldest taking the largest share and the other children's shares follow in a descending order of magnitude. While

[1] (1931), 10 N. L. R. 82.
[2] Published in 1924 by George Routledge and Sons Ltd., London; see Chap. IV, paras. 5, 11, 23–7 on Yoruba rules of inheritance.

adopted children cannot inherit from their adoptive parents, slaves of good behaviour who had also spent much money on behalf of the family on certain ceremonial occasions formerly could inherit, probably because as the writer has observed else-where [1] a slave who had lived for some time in his master's com-pound and behaved well was considered a member of the family; but in modern times only blood relations can inherit. One other important observation made by the writer is that bequests of both movable and immovable property might be made or promised by the deceased before his death and these would normally be respected and carried out afterwards. This would seem to be a kind of *donatio mortis causa* of the deceased's goods or an *ante mortem* oral declaration calculated to institute or disinherit a particular person in the matter of succession to land.

Something similar to this last point has been recorded [2] by W. Price in his *Land Tenure in the Yoruba Provinces* to which we must now turn for a more extended treatment of the subject of succes-sion rights. On the whole the general pattern of the rules of in-heritance as outlined above is much the same as that described by Mr. Price in this his Report.[3] prepared by him in 1933 as an Administrative Officer, to the Government of Nigeria. It is, how-ever, useful to make a note of certain peculiar features there recorded.

Firstly, the successor to the family-headship was usually the next younger brother of the deceased head, so chosen because he was the eldest male of the senior branch of the family. It was only when there was no such younger brother of the deceased that the deceased's eldest surviving son succeeded to the family headship; and it was a short step from this to hold that the eldest son should generally become head whenever his uncle was younger than he. A younger brother might supersede his senior eldest brother as the family head on the ground of ability or intelligence, 'the choice being confined to those descended from a common father through males'. If there were no males, the eldest female member would succeed. All these seem so reminiscent of the canons of descent which we have seen laid down above in *Lewis* v. *Bankole*, with the exception of the deceased's younger brother's priority of succession over the eldest surviving son. That this was also the ancient customary rule in Lagos is clear from these interesting passages

[1] Op. cit., Chap. I, para. 3.
[2] Cf. W. Price, op. cit., para. 46.
[3] See, on the whole subject, paras. 44–52.

which occurred in the judgments of Smalman Smith, C.J., first
In re Hotonu (*deceased*) (1892).[1]: 'Under the native custom as
applicable to this case, the eldest brother of the deceased succeeds
to the whole of the property of the deceased including his wives
and his personal property and is not in any way called upon to
account for the personal property so received, but may distribute
it or dispose of it much as he pleases, controlled only by the moral
obligation of doing right in the eyes of his relatives and friends';
and, again, in *Omoniregun* v. *Sadatu* (1888): [2] the eldest son
succeeds to the land in the place of his father for his own benefit
and for that of the family. The children and wives have the right to
live in the house. The widow who takes another husband loses her
right. The son has no right to sell the land or house for he holds
it in trust for the family. In order to sell he must consult the elders
of the family (his father's brothers) and his own brothers who must
give their consent. If there be no son or male issue the elder brother
succeeds and if he be dead then the younger brother and so on.
If all the brothers be dead, the land descends to the elder brother's
male children; if they be dead, not to their issue (if any), but to
the issue of the younger brother. Females cannot inherit land,
they can only have the right to stay in the house. A female has no
right to bring her husband to live in the family house, but she does
not lose her right to return to it by marriage. Her children have
the right.

In case of personal property—the eldest son takes charge of
the house and the personalty is divided among collaterals (uncles
and aunts). Among the Mohammedans, the male takes two parts
and the female one part. Among the Yoruba heathen male and
female share according to age, except the eldest son who comes
first. The personal property follows no special or particular rule of
distribution, all the relatives or collateral branches sharing with
children, although not of right. It has become the custom to share
some portion of the personal property with them.

Secondly, the potential head of the family might be displaced
in the inheritance for shirking the responsibilities of headship or
because the late head had requested, on pain of incurring his
everlasting wrath even in death, that he be expressly excluded
therefrom. If the nature of the victim's offence to the departed

[1] At p. 18 of 'Lagos: Reports of Certain Judgments of the Supreme Court,
etc. (1884–1892)'—Law Reports (Colonial), Nigeria A. Colonial Office
Library, London.
[2] At p. 15 of the same Report.

head be heinous enough to warrant the carrying out of such an injunction, the family would execute it.[1]

Thirdly, to land individually owned by a deceased, in ancient times as now, the eldest son always succeeds his father as the head of the family. On a division of the land and the permanent crops thereon, the deceased's brothers, whether of the whole blood or of the half-blood, are entitled to a share, as are his sisters, if willing. The children of the deceased will then divide the remainder of the farm-land or house among themselves, the eldest taking the largest share and each of the other children having more than each of his uncles. This last point is in substantial agreement with Mr. A. K. Ajisafe's statement above. The deceased's daughters are entitled to their shares which are heritable by their own children. But, although widows are given living apartments for their lives, they cannot as a rule inherit their deceased husband's land. Young children usually wait till puberty before being given their shares. If the deceased dies without issue, the nearest relative inherits his land and, if a woman, her husband's family can in no circumstances inherit the land.

Fourthly, in order to meet local or domestic requirements some families at Ibadan arrange that, if the eldest son dies in his father's life-time and the next eldest son happens to be of the same mother with him, such next eldest is (to avoid unnecessary jealousy) passed over in favour of the next eldest son by another mother. Another Ibadan practice of a more general nature occurs where the deceased was a title holder, when only a younger half-brother (i.e. of the same father but of a different mother) of the deceased succeeded to the titled head of the family in preference to the deceased full brother.[2] But, even at Ibadan, the old laws of inheritance have been undergoing some recent modifications, whereby sons claim to inherit their father's property to the exclusion of their father's younger brothers. The eldest son now steps into his father's shoes. This is as it should be.[3]

Fifthly, there is a general rule at Abeokuta that the eldest son cannot succeed his father as head of the family so long as an uncle, who may be much younger or less capable than he, is alive.[4] But if this be taken with the growing practice of children acquiring relatively absolute and individual ownership of their portions of

[1] W. Price, op. cit., paras. 46 and 47.
[2] See, op. cit., paras. 51 and 65.
[3] Para. 182.
[4] Para. 272.

family-land, which the writer has described in the preceding paragraph, and again the duty postulated of a man to pass on to his children what he has himself inherited, which the writer has described in the following paragraph, it would seem that the alleged rule cannot be an unmitigated canon of descent.

There are no important modifications of the normal pattern of the laws of inheritance recorded for Ondo, Ijebu and Oyo Provinces.[1]

Sixthly, in Benin there exists the doctrine of primogeniture according to which the right of succession to property, town-land as well as country-land, belongs exclusively to the eldest son of a deceased person. The rights of the younger children to their father's house are very precarious and, if their eldest brother refuses to let any of them stay on, they must ask the Oba for fresh lands for themselves. The eldest son may lose his enviable prerogative by neglecting properly to perform his father's funeral obsequies. If there is no son or if the eldest son dies without issue during his father's life-time, a daughter will succeed as head of the family until she can have a son, through the now largely discredited practice of entertaining in her father's house suitors who can inherit the property.[2]

But, thanks to the recent researches of Mr. C. W. Rowling in his *Notes on Land Tenure in the Benin Province*,[3] the following qualifications to Mr. Ward Price's statement must be made: (1) the strict rule of primogeniture would seem to be limited in Benin to (a) the house in which the deceased father had himself lived and (b) title-houses which must necessarily go to the eldest son; (2) of all other houses, apart from these, the younger children may claim their shares, nor can they be lightly excluded even from their father's house of residence over which the eldest son holds complete sway; (3) although it would seem that this Benin doctrine of primogeniture apparently rules out the question of a 'family house' which the Yoruba system [4] of joint inheritance by all the deceased's children makes possible, yet sufficient sanctity and inviolability are secured to the father's house to make it impossible for the eldest son to sell the house over the heads of the other children or, in effect, to treat it as if it were his own privately-acquired, absolute property: an appeal case (Oba. A 340/1946) in the Oba's Court, for example, upset a sale by the family head on

---

[1] Op. cit., see paras. 235, 326–7, 339.   [2] Paras. 374 and 375.
[3] Govt. Printer, Lagos (1948)—Paras. 18, 22–4, 36, 49, 65 and 99.
[4] W. Price, op. cit., para. 60.

the ground that other members with the right to live there had not been consulted.[1] There were two other appeal cases before the Chief Commissioner in which a partition of house property with the consent of the eldest son had been regarded as an accepted modification of Bini custom, though it is not clear whether if the eldest son objects to partition it can nevertheless be ordered on the precedent of these cases.[2]

No serious exception can be taken to this doctrine which seems hard on the younger children of the family, seeing that an exact parallel existed among English landed families until abolished [3] in 1925 by the Administration of Estates Act 1925, section 45. With the influx into Binin of Yoruba elements and their system of equality of succession rights, a better acquaintance with English property ideas and, above all, increased social and economic activities of the people themselves, it is to be hoped that the rule of primogeniture will be in increasingly bad odour with the rising generation and so hasten the dawn of the day of its abolition. It is significant that while the Ishan and Asaba Divisions of the Benin Province follow the main Benin rule of primogeniture, there exists in the Kukuruku Division of the same Province a dual system of matrilineal and patrilineal inheritance operating at the same time. The wife remains a member of her own family and, on the husband's death, the children take his estate with them to their mother's family.[4]

One more point to note in connexion with the Benin rules of inheritance is the one which has to do with the custom, by no means universal but nevertheless seriously asserted in some places, of limiting or attempting to limit succession to the house property of strangers (i.e. non-Binin Nigerians) to only the children of such strangers as are born to them by Bini women. This inequitable practice has met with Government opposition and it is not likely to be persisted in.[5]

B. THE IBO RULES OF INHERITANCE

In describing the Ibo customary laws of inheritance we may very well start with Onitsha, if only because of its historical and

[1] C. W. Rowling, op. cit., para. 18.
[2] C. W. Rowling, op. cit., 23.
[3] See Cheshire, *Modern Real Property*,(5th edition), pp. 808 and 812.
[4] See C. W. Rowling, op. cit., paras. 49, 65 and 99.
[5] Ibid., paras. 23 and 36.

ethnic link with Benin with which Onitsha shares the rule of primo-geniture. Succession is by the eldest surviving son of the deceased, to the exclusion of all others; and much of what we have said about the Benin law of inheritance applies with equal force to Onitsha the people of which are said to have migrated originally from Benin.

Perhaps the only High Court decision on Onitsha law of succession was that in *Nwugege* v. *Adigwe & anor.*[1] where the plaintiff claimed that, as the Okpala of the family of Ngbo Ogbuefi (deceased), a woman, he was the proper person under local law and custom to administer the deceased woman's estate. The defendant, on the other hand, asserted that he had a better right by virtue of the fact that his late father had married the deceased woman according to local law and custom. Each party had three chiefs ready to give evidence as to the local rules applicable to the case. At the close of the plaintiff's case both counsel agreed that the six chiefs should at that stage sit in Court together and give their respective answers to questions of customary law to be put by counsel. From the unanimous answers of the chiefs to the questions put to them the following propositions of Onitsha law emerged: [2]

(1) On the death of a married woman property which she had acquired before her marriage goes to her own family and not to her husband or his family, but movable properties acquired by the wife before marriage, if taken by the wife to her husband's house, go to the husband or his family on her death.

(2) Property acquired by a married woman after her marriage goes to her husband on her death.

(3) Where a man marries a woman who has a house and lives with her as man and wife in that house, it goes to the wife's family on her death.

'This last proposition,' said Graham Paul, J., 'I cannot accept as a proposition of native custom as in laying it down the chiefs explained that under their custom it was unheard-of that a man marrying a woman should live with her in her house. It is obvious that the native custom could not provide for a set of facts unknown to native law.' The learned Judge accordingly held that the defendant was the proper person to administer the deceased woman's estate in right of his father.

Now, if the principle underlying the above propositions of Onitsha rules of succession be compared with that behind the rules already stated above for the Yorubas in the three cases of

[1] (1934), 11 N. L. R. 134.   [2] Ibid., at pp. 134-5.

Caulcrick v. *Harding, Andre* v. *Agbebi* and *Idewu* v. *Hausas & ors.*[1], it would be found that there is not much difference between the two. It may be that later judgments might reveal divergencies, but in the present state of our knowledge it would be wise not to speculate.

As to the succession rules among the Ibos generally, we may state the following available evidence:

According to Mr. G. T. Basden, 'personal property descended to the eldest son as heir or, failing a son, to the eldest brother or male relative'.[2] This looks like the pure patriarchal principle of the Yorubas which we have observed.

The same patrilineal system has been described for the Yako by Professor Daryll Forde [3] and for the Ozuitem Ibos by Dr. J. S. Harris.[4] Both state also that the deceased's sons inherit their father's lands as well as any other land that might have been pledged to him before his death. And land rights acquired by a woman either by purchase or on pledge, both through a male proxy, are inherited by her sons to whose male descendants the succession is restricted. If the woman's sons are too young at her death, her husband holds the land as trustee until they are old enough to take it up. As a rule, land cleared or otherwise acquired by one person is inherited jointly by the descendants who usually have particular areas allotted to them at the general distribution following the man's death. Dr. Meek's findings in the Owerri district agree generally with these principles, and he also says that, after a co-operative clearing of the bush by a patrilineal kin group, the land is shared out according to seniority and each member's plot becomes his permanent family property inheritable by his sons.[5]

Miss M. M. Green says that in Umueke Agbaja the inheritance of land is by a man's sons and, if the man dies without issue, his younger brother of the same mother, if there is one, will inherit him: 'In the first place a man holds his land in common with the other members of his land-owning group. At the time of his death it will not pass definitely to his sons or other heirs but will continue as the common property of the group of which they form a

[1] See pp. 220-1, *supra*.

[2] *Niger Ibos*, Chap. XIX: 'Land Tenure and Inheritance', at p. 268.

[3] 'Land and Labour in a Cross River Village', *Geographical Journal*, Vol. XC (1937), pp. 24-51.

[4] 'Papers on the Economic Aspects of Life Among the Ozuitem Ibos'. *Africa*, Vol. V, No. 14, pp. 12-23; 302-334 (1943-4).

[5] *Law and Authority in a Nigerian Tribe* (1937), pp. 102-4.

part. It is only when the children of the group increase and grow up and marry that the need of dividing up the land will make itself felt. In the second place when the division is agreed upon it will be done publicly and ceremonially by the elders of the village according to the rules of inheritance.' [1] In another place [2] she writes: 'Clearly, matriliny pays a considerable part in Ibo society. Descent and succession are patrilineal, marriage is patrilocal and a man inherits from his father. But the matrilineal principle is there asserting itself both legally and emotionally.' The writer warns that the fact that people will often refer to themselves or others as children of a particular mother may lead one to suppose that descent is matrilineal, whereas the society itself is patrilineal in spite of the horizontal alignments involved in the practice of exogamy.[3]

The principles of succession to titled family headship follow more or less the pattern noticed in the case of the Yorubas at Ibadan,[4] while the regard paid to mental and physical qualities in a family head, also already observed among the Yorubas, has been discovered among the Ibos of Umueke.[5] The value of this rather extended treatment of the rules of inheritance of a comparatively small village lies in the fact, admitted by the writer herself, that the main rules apply to other Ibos as well: 'Here the situation will be described chiefly with reference to the village of Umueke Agbaja. But in the main it seems to hold good over much of Ibo country.' [6]

Calabar. This area of Eastern Nigeria is important and distinct enough to deserve a separate, though brief, treatment.

The local customary rules of inheritance would seem to be substantially the same among the people of Calabar as those we have so far noted among the Yorubas and the majority of the Ibos. The eldest surviving male member of the family succeeds as head, and the succession may be automatic or subject to election at a family conclave after the death of the previous family head. So much was decided in *Inyang* v. *Ita & ors.*[7] by Berkeley, J., who, however, incidentally observed that 'the succession to the vacancy devolved on the next senior male, if he chose to take it up. . . .

---

[1] *Land Tenure in an Ibo Village* (1941), pp. 13 and 14.
[2] *Ibo Village Affairs* (1947), p. 161.
[3] Ibid., at p. 16.
[4] Cf. *Ibo Village Affairs*, pp. 69–70 with pp. 225–6 herein.
[5] See *Ibo Village Affairs*, pp. 72–7.
[6] Ibid., p. 153.
[7] (1929), 9 N. L. R. 84.

Thus we see, even under a system of *strict primogeniture*, the will of the family functioning as an important factor in placing a man in the headship, and in maintaining him there or ejecting him therefrom.' [1] There is here, it is submitted, an obvious difficulty: either the system is one of 'strict primogeniture'—in which case the eldest surviving son of the deceased takes to the exclusion of all the others—or, it is not. To say that the succession of the head depends on the consenting will of the family, even if that will is expressed 'by democratic suffrage, not by autocratic decree', is in terms to contradict the very principle of primogeniture as it is commonly understood in property law.

Indeed, the learned Judge's reference to primogeniture is, if we may say so, particularly unfortunate as it is as unnecessary to the actual decision which he rightly reached in the case itself as it is most likely to mislead one into thinking that such a system as we have attributed to Benin and Onitsha in fact exists in Calabar. Fortunately, when we recall the express disavowal of any power in the family head arbitrarily to eject a member of the family in *Manuel* v. *Manuel* [2] and again the findings that a family head in Calabar as elsewhere is a mere trustee and that all the members are beneficiaries of the family property in *Bassey* v. *Cobham & ors.*[3], we can dismiss Berkeley's, J., incautious reference to primogeniture as an inaccurate *obiter*.

It is, therefore, safe to say that the Calabar law and custom of inheritance follow the patrilineal principle which is not, however, of the primogeniture type.

C. THE RULES OF INHERITANCE IN THE NORTHERN PROVINCES

There are two preliminary observations we should make before going on to the evidence: they are (1) that the customary rules of succession are expressly excepted from the provisions of the Land and Native Rights Ordinance No. 1 of 1916 (as later amended); [4]

[1] (1929), 9 N. L. R. 84, at p. 85.   [2] (1926), 7 N. L. R. 101.
[3] (1924), 5 N. L. R. 90.
[4] S. 14 and Irving's *Titles to Land In Nigeria*, p. 346 (para. 41).

S. 14 of the Ordinance reads: 'The devolution of the rights of an occupier upon death shall be regulated, in the case of a native, by the native custom existing in the locality in which the land is situated, and in the case of a non-native, by the English law governing the devolution of a lease for a term of years: Provided that a right of occupancy shall not be divided into two or more parts on devolution by the death of the occupier, except with the sanction of the Governor.

(2) that the Moslem law of succession under the Maliki Code has been largely absorbed into the indigenous system of property inheritance. We shall indicate in appropriate places what modification to this statement may seem necessary later.

In Sir Percy Girouard's *Memorandum on Land Tenure, etc., in Northern Nigeria* [1] occurs this passage culled from the Report of Mr. Barclay, an Administrative Officer for Yola Province:

'A woman cannot inherit land, but her husband or father can give her land during his life-time provided she has servants to work it. A death-bed gift of land to a woman is not recognised. In the case of a man dying without male issue a wife or daughter may apply to the chief of the village to be allowed to take over his land, and, if she can show she is in a position to cultivate it, the land is given to her.

'The sons of a dead man divide his land equally between them. If one, or more, of such sons is a minor, the eldest son acts as trustee for him until he is of an age to be able to take over the land himself. In the case of all the sons being minors an uncle or other relative acts as a trustee until they are of age. In the event of a minor having no relatives the court appoints a trustee for him. A minor, however, can take possession of land if he has sufficient servants to work it for him. No man may occupy more land than he can cultivate.

'. . . As far as I have been able to ascertain, land tenure among the pagans is exactly the same as among the Fulanis, all land being vested in the paramount chiefs.' [2]

There is a close similarity between this general description and those given by the other Administrative Officers for Kano, Sokoto, Muri and the other areas of the North. It was thus possible for the collator of the various Reports, Sir Percy Girouard (the Governor), to conclude in his Summary of Conclusions, in Part IV of the Memorandum, that there was no difference between the pagan and the Moslem system of tenure and that both of them were patriarchal. [3]

Dr. Meek in his *Tribal Studies in Northern Nigeria* has made a number of interesting anthropological studies of many tribes in the Northern Provinces. Thus, among the Bachama and the Mbula tribes, [4] the basis of inheritance is patrilineal in the sense that the

---

[1] Published as Colonial Office Legal Folio No. 11714.

[2] Para. 26 of the Memorandum.

[3] See the Memorandum, para. 3, on p. 26; also pp. 26 and 27 generally; and Irving's *Titles to Land in Nigeria*, pp. 342–3, para. 30.

[4] Vol. I, pp. 15 and 16.

eldest son (in the absence of a brother of his father) inherits his father's spear, shield, bow and arrow and also the compound (if he is old enough); all other property such as horses, goats, clothes and cattle are heritable by the father's sister's son. But the writer notes that a tendency has set in against the custom of matrilineal succession and the people now argue that the whole of a man's property should be heritable by his sons alone; in many instances, the man himself would before his death declare publicly that his property should be inherited by his eldest or some favourite son or sons only and that his sister's son should be disqualified on some such pretext as that he had been disrespectful to his uncle.

Again, among the Chamba [1] the normal rule of inheritance is that a man's property passes to brothers by the same mother or to his sister's sons; the sons do not inherit anything except what the father's brother or the sister's son, as the case may be, is willing to give them.

But, generally, among the Verre tribe [2] as among the Longuda tribe [3] of the Adamawa Province, the customary law of succession to property is *matrilineal* according to which a man's children are entitled to inherit from their maternal uncles but not from their father. Conflict is bound to arise when, for example, a man from a tribe practising the matrilineal form of inheritance marries a woman from another tribe with the patrilineal system: the children of the matrilineal father have no claim to their father's property, whereas the children of the patrilineal wife have no claim to their maternal uncle's property. Happily, among these Verre and Longuda tribes, as among the Bachama and Mbula noted above, matrilineal inheritance is being rapidly abandoned as contrary to modern requirements and notions. The process of disintegration would seem to be in the three stages of (a) repudiation of the absolute authority of the mother's group as regards the custody of her children born into another group, (b) followed by a period of transition in which the children's grouping becomes bilateral and (c) this in due course becomes purely patri-potestal. [4]

Primogeniture. Among the Marki group [5] of the Verre tribe also is found the custom of *Ultimogeniture*, whereby inheritance is by the youngest son. This is the familiar 'Borough English' of English property law which was abolished in England only in 1922 by the Law of Property Act of that year. [6]

[1] Vol. I, pp. 395–401.   [2] Vol. I, pp. 415–16.
[3] Vol. II, pp. 346–7.   [4] Vol. II, p. 557.
[5] Vol. I, p. 415.   [6] Cheshire, op. cit.

For the Nupe in the middle belt Dr. S. F. Nadel describes the system of inheritance as patrilineal, also observing that the old rule of primogeniture prevalent in the pre-Fulani era [1] has given place to the more modern democratic idea of joint succession with the eldest son succeeding his father. This eldest son is succeeded by his classificatory younger brother who is the man next in seniority of the same generation until, after that generation is exhausted, the succession falls to the eldest son of the eldest brother who is the most senior member of the next generation.

Succession in the paternal and in the maternal lines supplements each other, the sons naturally inheriting the manly property rights of the father while daughters inherit their mother's; but as in Nupe women neither own nor work land, succession to land is entirely patriarchal. The requirement of personal competence in the family head, which we have noted for both the Yorubas and the Ibos, is also here emphasised. [2] In the otherwise strongly patrilineal society of the Nupe the writer has chanced upon only one obscure and small village with a matrilineal succession to chieftaincy. [3]

Inheritance in the North and the Maliki Code. Dr. Nadel records [4] how the people of Nupe now tend to adopt, as against local customary rules, the Moslem rules of inheritance by which real and personal property of a deceased father goes to his sons in equal shares. The customary rule requires that their deceased father's younger brother should succeed him as the sociological father of the deceased's children in addition to retaining his physiological paternity over his own sons. This arrangement, primarily intended to keep agricultural lands within the paternal line and to conserve it for future generations, while good in its own way, has far less appeal for the rising generation impatient of the trammels of tradition and anxious to grasp the new economic opportunities afforded by a fair share of the land for all. The dangers of excessive sub-division of the land—for the Moslem rules are ideal only for moveable property—which have started to confront more developed communities in other areas of the North have yet to make themselves felt in Nupe.

Thus, at the 1939 Conference of Northern Chiefs, it was decided that the Native Authorities should be empowered to order the sale of agricultural lands, the proceeds being distributed equally among the legatees. This was found necessary because of the undesirable 'fragmentation' to which the Moslem law of inheri-

---

[1] *A Black Byzantium*, p. 88.   [2] Op. cit., pp. 29–32.
[3] Op. cit., p. x (Introduction).   [4] Op. cit., p. 173.

tance has led, with resultant unhealthy surroundings and over-crowding in many areas. In 1940 the Conference further decided that Native or Local Authorities should have a discretion to set a minimum limit to the extent of permitted sub-division of agricultural lands in their respective districts.

A similar problem might have arisen out of the modern practice, among the Yorubas and others, of partitioning lands and houses among the children of a deceased parent, but for the early development of the practice of the courts to order sale in all cases where partition is neither possible nor desirable. It is suggested that the Courts in the North, and not the Local Authorities, should be allowed to exercise all the discretion relating to these matters which were at the 1939 and 1940 Conferences assigned to the Local authorities.

D. VARIATION OF CUSTOMARY RULES OF INHERITANCE

As already observed at the outset, the customary rules of inheritance and succession may be displaced in one of three ways: (i) by some contrary oral dying declaration of a deceased owner or family-head, or by a unanimous verdict of the family council after the death of the former head; (ii) by the marriage according to English law of an owner-occupier or founder of a family; and (iii) by express provisions in a will.

As to (i) we need not say more here than we have already said in various places earlier.[1] Suffice it to add that such express displacement of the member from the member's succession is not of frequent occurrence, since very good reasons should exist for the invocation of the custom, or it would be set aside by the court as contrary to 'justice, equity and good conscience'.[2]

Items (ii) and (iii) require a somewhat fuller examination:

(ii) *Marriage according to English law* normally operates to displace the customary local law of inheritance in the case of the children of such a marriage. There are two categories of marriage to consider here but with hardly any difference in legal effects so

---

[1] See e.g., pp. 223, 224–5.

[2] On the Gold Coast custom of *Samansiw*, J. M. Sarbah in his *Fanti Customary Law* writes at p. 82 as follows: 'Death-bed dispositions known as Samansiw seem to be recognised not so much because of any assumed right to make such a disposition as because from feelings of affection, respect or even superstition, the last wishes of the deceased are considered to be entitled to weight among the members of his family.'—Cited bv Mitchelin, J., in *Nelson* v. *Nelson* (1932), 1 W. A. C. A. 215, at

far as succession to property by the issue of either form of marriage is concerned: (a) Marriage by Christian rites and (b) Marriage under a Marriage Ordinance. We are assuming under this heading that the property-owning spouse has died intestate. Cases where the spouse has, in addition to the Christian marriage, also made a will, will be considered under (iii) below:

(a) *Marriage by Christian rites.* The *locus classicus* on the subject is *Cole* v. *Cole* [1] in which one J. W. Cole, born in Lagos, left Lagos in 1864 for the sister colony of Sierra Leone where he married according to Christian rites one Mary Jemina Cole by whom he had in 1866 an only son, Alfred Cole, who was a lunatic. J. W. Cole died in 1897, leaving his wife, his son and a brother A. B. Cole who brought this action for a declaration that, in spite of his brother's marriage by Christian rites in Sierra Leone, the succession to the deceased's estate must be governed by the customary rules of inheritance and not by English law. A Marriage Ordinance had been passed in Lagos in 1864 which dealt only with marriages solemnised within the Colony and, as J. W. Cole's marriage had been contracted outside the Colony and Protectorate of Nigeria (namely, in Sierra Leone), the marriage did not come under it. If the Ordinance of 1864 did not apply, then the Statute of Distribution would not also apply since it too related only to marriages solemnised within the Colony. On appeal from the judgment of Rayner, C.J., in the Divisional Court that the devolution of the estate must be governed by local law and custom merely because all parties were Nigerians, Griffith, J., in delivering the judgment of the Full Court held that the marriage of the deceased by Christian rites negatived the application of the local customary law of inheritance. Accordingly, the English law of succession applied to disentitle the plaintiff brother of the deceased from succeeding to the inheritance which must legally fall to the son of the marriage:

'By the Common Law of England the eldest son is the heir, no matter whether he is a lunatic or not, and I am of opinion that the defendant Alfred Cole must be declared the heir of the deceased. The widow's rights to dower and to one-third of her husband's personalty follows.' [2]

It must not, however, be supposed that the local law and custom of inheritance would invariably be displaced by English law because of the mere fact that a Christian marriage had supervened. Circumstances might arise in which the customary rules might be

---

[1] (1898), 1 N. L. R. 15.   [2] Ibid., *per* Griffith, J., at p. 22.

preferred to the applicable English law. Thus, in *Smith* v. *Smith*,[1] one John Gustavus Smith, a Lagos man, married in 1876, again in Sierra Leone, according to the rites of the Church of England. He died in Lagos, to which he had since returned with his wife, in 1917, leaving his widow and three children. The widow collected rents on part of the family house and otherwise managed it until her death. All three children lived together in the house which they used as family property since their father's death. The defendant at one time needed money and got the plaintiffs, his sisters, to agree to execute a deed of mortgage in 1922 which recited that they were all three tenants in fee simple of the property. Later, the defendant wanted more money and asked his sisters for a second mortgage, which was refused. The defendant then claimed for the first time that succession to the property must be governed by English law because of their parents' marriage in Sierra Leone by Christian rites. It was held by Van Der Meulin, J., (1) that, although the fact that Nigerians have married in accordance with the rites of the Church of England raises a presumption that they intend that their lives, their actions and their property should be regulated by English law and standards, this is not conclusive evidence of such an intention; (2) that the Court should, in deciding the question, always be guided by a consideration of the position in life occupied by the parties as well as their conduct with reference to the property in dispute; (3) that, guided by these principles, it would be inequitable that the devolution of the property in dispute in the present action, should be governed by the English law of inheritance. The learned Judge thus distinguished *Cole* v. *Cole*: 'The defendant has contended that the effect of that decision is to lay it down as a binding rule that when parties have been married according to the rights of the Church of England their property must devolve according to the English law and not according to the native law and custom. I have carefully perused that decision and I am unable to find that any such general rule is laid down thereby. I do not consider that the case goes further than to decide that in such cases it might be inequitable for the native law and custom as to succession to property be applied.'[2]

But even on this liberal interpretation nice questions of succession are bound to arise where, for instance, an intestate first contracts a local customary form of marriage and later goes through a Christian one, and vice versa. As an illustration of the first problem, let us consider *Adegbola* v. *Folaranmi & ors.*[3] where the

[1] (1924), 5 N. L. R. 102.   [2] Ibid., at p. 104.   [3] (1921), 3 N. L. R. 81.

plaintiff, as the daughter by local form of marriage of one Johnson deceased, claimed to be entitled to succeed to the property of which her father died intestate. It happened that her father had, after the birth of the plaintiff, been sold into slavery in Trinidad (British West Indies) where during about forty years' stay he had married one Mary in a Roman Catholic Church of which Johnson had since become a member. Three years after the marriage, Johnson returned with Mary to Lagos and was received in the Roman Catholic Church there. His former wife by local marriage and his daughter, the plaintiff, were both still alive at Awe where Johnson had left them, and the daughter used to visit her father in Lagos. In 1900 Johnson died intestate, and Mary Johnson continued to live in his house until she herself died in 1918, leaving by her will the house to the first defendant as her executor. Before the daughter brought this action her mother died, but it is not known whether she died before or after Johnson. Combe, C.J., in the Supreme Court, held, affirming the decision of the Divisional Court, that (1) the presumption on the facts of this case must be that Johnson and Mary had contracted in Trinidad a valid Christian marriage which the Courts of Nigeria must recognise; (2) the Christian marriage, although subsequent to the local customary marriage of which the plaintiff was the issue, was valid despite the provision in the Marriage Ordinance of 1884 that 'no person can in Nigeria contract a valid Christian marriage if he is married to any other person under native law and custom', since that Ordinance was enacted after Johnson's Christian marriage to Mary in Trinidad before 1876 at least; (3) accordingly, the English common law, and not the local customary law, must govern the succession to Johnson's property in Lagos and, therefore, the first defendant was entitled to it under the will of Mary who was entitled under English law to inherit Johnson's property. The daughter by the prior customary marriage got nothing.

The converse case occurred about six years later in *Haastrup* v. *Coker*.[1] There, one Haastrup had in or about 1848 married by Christian rites one Christiana in Sierra Leone. On his return to Nigeria he had subsequently succeeded to some chieftaincy in the Provinces and married a number of women by local custom. He died intestate in 1901, leaving two children by the Christian marriage and nine by the local marriage. In 1911, one of the two children of the Christian marriage took out Letters of Administration of the deceased's estate and in 1917 she conveyed part of the land

[1] (1927), 8 N. L. R. 68.

to the defendant. The plaintiff, one of the nine natural children, purporting to sue on behalf of all the surviving children of Haastrup, sought to set aside this sale and asked for a declaration that the land devolved upon all the deceased's said children under local customary law. Petrides, J., held in the Divisional Court (a) that, following *Cole* v. *Cole*, the English common law must on account of the Christian marriage prevail over the local customary law of inheritance; (b) that it was immaterial whether the parties to the Christian marriage did or did not actually profess the tenets of the Christian religion at the time of the marriage because, as the learned Judge pointed out, 'the decision in *Cole* v. *Cole* was based, not on the fact that the parties to the marriage were Christian natives, but on the fact that they had gone through a marriage by Christian rites'.[1]

The second part of the decision had been provoked by the plaintiff's ingenious argument that the subsequent local customary marriage by their deceased father must be taken to have invalidated the prior Christian marriage in Sierra Leone, so that succession to their father's property should then be subject to the customary rules of inheritance. Moreover, their father's subsequent mode of life supported his allegation, the plaintiff added, that their father had later abandoned his Christian beliefs, in consequence of which both Christian and pagan rites were performed over his funeral. A weapon of some weight in the plaintiff's armoury, but ineffectual whether as a weapon of attack or of defence in his plight, was *Asiata* v. *Goncallo* [2] in which a Nigerian Moslem had been taken to Brazil as a slave and had there married a Moslem woman, first in accordance with Moslem rites and then in a Christian Church with Christian rites. Griffith, J., held that a contract which a Christian marriage would ordinarily imply was clearly not to be implied in such a case as the present, as it is clear that the parties obviously intended by their precedent Moslem ceremony to marry and live as Moslems and that it was their fortuitous presence in a Christian country (Brazil) that made them go to Church for the subsequent ceremony which alone they considered would give their new status State recognition. As it happened in the case itself, the husband, on return with his wife to Lagos from Brazil where they left behind their two daughters, took on another woman by whom he had other children. It was further decided that the children of both sets of marriages were entitled to succeed to the intestate estate of their father under the Moslem law applicable to such a case.

[1] (1927), 8 N. L. R. 68, at p. 70.   [2] 1 N. L. R. 41.

This decision, taken along with that in *Smith* v. *Smith*, shows that the principle of *Cole* v. *Cole* is not so much a question of the form of the particular rites observed for the marriage in question being Christian as one of the avowed intention of the parties themselves having regard to their personal circumstances at the time when the marriage is celebrated and their understanding of the nature and consequences of the particular marriage contract. Petrides', J., dictum cited at the end of the last paragraph but one would seem to require, it is respectfully submitted, some qualification to this effect.

(*b*) *Marriage under a Marriage Ordinance.* For the Marriage Ordinance (1914) to operate to vest the wife, children or other eligible relations of the husband with the right of succession to property, the property must be a freely disposable estate of inheritance at the deceased owner's death intestate. In the case of umpartitioned family property in which a husband has an interest with other members of his family, it follows that no wife of a marriage under the Marriage Ordinance can claim a right to inherit her deceased husband's interest therein, apart, of course, from such rights as local customary law gives her. The children of such a marriage will succeed to their father's allotment, not indeed by virtue of the marriage under the Ordinance, but in right of their being inheritors by blood under local customary rules of inheritance. Thus, in *Sogunro-Davies* v. *Sogunro & ors.*[1], the plaintiff claimed from the defendants, members of her deceased husband's family, her husband's share of his family property from a distribution of which she, as the legally married wife of the deceased under the Marriage Ordinance, had been excluded by the family. It was held that the deceased husband left behind him no separate estate in the family property which the plaintiff, his widow under the Marriage Ordinance, could inherit: 'The children of the deceased Alfred Falade, if there had been any, would have taken by birthright because they were of the blood. . . . They inherit as members of the family not by virtue of any estate left behind by their father.'

The case would have been different if the property being claimed by the widow had been a specific, partitioned lot acquired as such by her husband in his lifetime or, *a fortiori*, absolute estate of his own. The point fell for consideration in *Johnson* v. *United Africa Company, Ltd.*[2] The owner of certain real property in Lagos had died in 1926 intestate, leaving him surviving a widow (married under the Marriage Ordinance) and four children. Under a

[1] (1929), 9 N. L. R. 79.   [2] (1936), 13 N. L. R. 13.

judgment for £285 7s. 6d. against the widow for goods sold and delivered to her, the defendant sought to attach her interest in the property, and the eldest son of the marriage took out an Interpleader Summons claiming that the widow had no attachable interest in the property on two alternative grounds: (a) that by reason of the marriage of their parents under the Marriage Ordinance 1914, s. 16 of the Supreme Court Ordinance should enable the Court to apply the Administration of the Estates Act 1925 to the devolution of their father's intestate estate, or (b) that, in view of their collective treatment of the property as family property since their father's death instead of selling it and sharing the proceeds, succession to it should therefore be governed by the local customary law of inheritance. It was held by Butler Lloyd, J., in the Divisional Court (1) that under s. 36 of the Marriage Ordinance (1914) the property of the deceased must be distributed according to English law as it stood at the date of the Marriage Ordinance; (2) that the Administration of Estates Act, 1925, did not apply; (3) that the widow's one-third interest of the property under the Statute of Distributions was attachable. His Honour said: 'In the recent case of *Taylor* v. *Taylor* (Suit No. 127 of 1934) the West African Court of Appeal held explicitly that the Administration of Estates Act 1925 does not apply in Nigeria, and s. 36 of the Marriage Ordinance expressly declares that in circumstances such as the present real property of which the deceased could have disposed by will shall be distributed according to the law of England relating to the distribution of personal estate, any native law or custom to the contrary notwithstanding. This Ordinance obviously speaks from the date of its enactment, namely, 1914, at which date the law in force in England was the Statute of Distributions which gave one-third to the widow and two-thirds to the children.'[1]

It was held in *Administrator-General* v. *Coker* [2] that Letters of Administration could be granted to a divorced widow on behalf of her eleven-year-old daughter on the death intestate of her ex-husband, to whom had previously been awarded the custody of the child. The marriage had been under the Marriage Ordinance 1914, but had been dissolved in 1940. One Michael Stephen Akitoye Coker, a relative of the deceased father, was accordingly appointed to act with the widow until the child came of age.

That the mere fact of marriage under the Marriage Ordinance does not of itself make English law applicable to govern succession

[1] (1936), 13 N. L. R. 13, at p. 80.   [2] (1942), 16 N. L. R. 111.

to the property of a deceased husband intestate, unless the property of which he died possessed was disposable by will, was emphasised in *Davies* v. *Sogunro & ors.*[1] There the plaintiff was the illegitimate son of one Alfred Sogunro Davies who had died entitled to a share of his own deceased father's estate of which there had been no partition up to the date of Alfred Sogunro's death intestate. Alfred Sogunro had also married under the Marriage Ordinance. The plaintiff claimed an account and payment to him of the share of his grandfather's estate to which he was entitled under the customary rules of inheritance. The defendants, receivers of the grandfather's estate, contended that by virtue of s. 36 (*a*) of the Marriage Ordinance the whole property of Alfred Sogunro (including the share of his grandfather's property) must on his death intestate be distributed according to English law. *Held*: by Graham Paul, J., (1) that since Alfred Sogunro had no right to dispose by will of his share in his father's estate, the provisions of s. 36 (*a*) of the Marriage Ordinance did not apply; (2) that the devolution of that share must be governed, not by English law, but by the local customary law of succession. *Haastrup* v. *Coker* and *Cole* v. *Cole*[2] were both distinguished by the learned Judge on the ground that in both the property in question was the freely disposable, absolute estate of the deceased whereas in the present case the property in question at the death of the deceased intestate still formed part of the deceased's inalienable family property.[3]

In *Coker & ors.* v. *Coker & ors.*,[4] a grandfather, who had married by Christian rites, devised in 1883 his absolute fee simple estate to his two surviving sons, Samuel and Benjamin, for 'the use of my children's children for ever', although there were no grandchildren when he died in 1890. This devise was *ipso facto* void for remoteness and, therefore, Samuel and Benjamin took the property as if their father had died on an intestacy. Each of them later contracted a marriage under the Marriage Ordinance and died in 1917 and 1910 respectively, each leaving legitimate as well as illegitimate children surviving him. The plaintiffs, the illegitimate children of both Samuel and Benjamin, sued the defendants, the

---

[1] (1936), 13 N. L. R. 15.   [2] See pp. 236–8, earlier.

[3] Ibid., *per* Graham Paul, J., at p. 17: 's. 36 is quite clear in its terms. It only applies the English law of succession to the personal property and real property of which a deceased intestate (who had been married under the Ordinance) might have disposed by will. Alfred Sogunro Davies' share of his father's estate could not have been disposed of by will and therefore s. 36 of the Marriage Ordinance does not apply at all to this case.'

[4] (1943), 17 N. L. R. 55.

legitimate ones, for partition or sale of this undisposed-of property of their grandfather, which had therefore become the common family property, according to local customary law of inheritance. Brooke, J., in the Supreme Court, held that the intestate estate of a Nigerian who contracted a Christian or civil marriage came, as regards succession to property, under English law, so that the illegitimate children could not claim. The point of the distinction between this case and *Davies* v. *Sogunro & ors.* would appear to be that in the latter the grandfather had never contracted a Christian marriage which the grandfather in the former had done; and although there was there an intestacy, the two children of the grandfather's Christian marriage took their father's undisposed-of estate under English law by which the devolution of the same property upon their own children must be governed under their marriages in accordance with the Marriage Ordinance. The property had not descended to Samuel and Benjamin as customary family property to which their own children, legitimate as well as illegitimate, might have been entitled. Samuel and Benjamin took the property under English law, not as family property. That was not the situation in *Davies* v. *Sogunro* where the property continued to be family property even after the immediate father of the plaintiff had died.

We will now consider how as stated above [1] the customary rules of inheritance may be displaced by express provisions in a will where a Nigerian died having made a will.

(iii) We have noted at the beginning of this chapter that the modern customary law of inheritance among the Yorubas is that the eldest son succeeds to his father's property as the family head on behalf of the other children, and that the practice is increasingly against the deceased father's younger brother succeeding to the position. We have also noted latterly that a deceased founder of a family may by oral declaration before death institute or exclude a particular individual as his successor to the family headship. If this variation to the succession can be made orally, it is only to be expected that it can and will be made by will now that wills are proving a popular innovation among urban and other literate persons. Even where the deceased has been silent as to the succession, the family may at a subsequent meeting appoint who should be family head and what should be their 'family house', if either of these has not before been settled or established. Thus in *Thomas* v. *Thomas* [2] the decision to treat a house as a ' family house',

1 See p. 235, *supra.*   2 (1932), 16 N. L. R. 5.

which was reached after the family founder's death, was upheld by the Supreme Court as properly connoting what that expression normally implies under local customary law. In *Sogbesan & ors.* v. *Adebiyi* [1] a trustee devised his real property in Lagos to certain trustees upon trust to hold the same as 'family house', and also appointed his brother to be 'the head of the family', directing that he should act in family matters under the control, advice and direction of the testator's mother and aunt. The beneficiaries under the will wanted to know whether the term 'family' in this clause of the will was intended to include the testator's brothers and sisters as well as his children or whether it referred only to testator's children. It was decided by the Supreme Court that the will as a whole made it clear that the testator intended the word 'family' to include his brothers and sisters and their descendants as well as his own children. Butler Lloyd pointed out that this case is an illustration of the difficulties which are only too likely to arise where a legal document in English form is used to create an interest unknown to English law but which nevertheless has a well-understood meaning in local law and custom; and, believing that it would be contrary to customary law 'as well as to good sense to appoint a person who himself is given no interest in the family property to act as head of the family, a position which involves the management of that property', the learned Judge decided the case as already stated.

On the other hand, in *Balogun* v. *Balogun & ors.*,[2] a testator by his will appointed his eldest son as head of the family and directed him to perform certain duties including the care of the stripling members of the family and the giving of charities to the poor, but without making any specific allowance for these onerous disbursements. It was held by the West African Court of Appeal that, in view of the fact that the testator had made a consistent and repeated use of the expression 'native law and custom', the various provisions of the will must in the absence of any express statement to the contrary be taken to be intended by the testator to be governed by local customary law; consequently, the allowance of £10 made to the eldest son to discharge the duties of his office under customary law was rightly made.

What really constitutes a family house as an indigenous institution and the condition under which the Court will or will not order its partition or sale will next be considered in a number of decisions, of which the most instructive is *In the Estate of Edward*

[1] (1941), 16 N. L. R. 26.   [2] (1934), 2 W. A. C. A. 290.

Forster.[1] The testator in that case made the following bequest of his house; 'I leave and bequeath my present dwelling house to the whole of my family or blood relative and their children's children throughout and cannot be sold for any debt or debts that may be contracted by any of them, but at present the house should be occupied by my grandson Nath and my son Edward subject to the approval of my executors or otherwise. . . .' The house was nevertheless ultimately sold by an order of the Court and the question was as to who were entitled to participate in the share of the proceeds. Carey, J., held (1) that the bequest did not, as had been objected, contravene the rule against perpetuities, nor was it void for uncertainty; (2) that the testator's intention was to make his dwelling house 'a family house' according to Yoruba custom; (3) that, consequently, those entitled to share in the proceeds of its sale were those of his descendants who were entitled under local custom to reside in the premises at the time of the sale. Then, Carey, J., after carefully studying all the evidence of local custom submitted to him, found as follows: [2]

'A family house (in the custom of the Yorubas of Lagos) is a residence which the father of a family sets apart for his wife and children to occupy jointly after his decease. All his children are entitled to reside there with their mothers and his married sons with their wives and children. Also a daughter who has left the house on marriage has a right to return to it on deserting or being deserted by her husband. No one has any chargeable or alienable interest in the family house. It is only with the consent of all those entitled to reside in the family house that it can be mortgaged or sold.'

The institution of the 'family house' is thus the Nigerian counterpart of the English settlement, the aim of both being to keep the property in the family for as long as possible. That being so, the Court would be slow in ordering partition or sale of the family house if the interests of all concerned would thereby be prejudiced. But if partition or sale appears to be the only means of doing justice between the parties or if there is a unanimous consent of all the family members, the Court will order it. Thus, in *Giwa & ors.* v. *Ottun & ors.*[3] a Trust Deed declared that the grantees of certain property were to hold as joint tenants and tenants in common and that the property was not to be sold without the written consent of all the beneficiaries. On a dispute arising between the parties the Court ordered sale as the only solution. In *Jacobs* v. *Oladunni*

[1] (1938), 14 N. L. R. 83.   [2] Ibid., at p. 86.   [3] (1934), 11 N. L. R. 160.
N.L.L.C.—18

Bros.[1], a testator devised his property to all his four children 'to remain and be retained as a family property in accordance with native law and custom'. The defendants attached the property under a writ of *Fi-fa* issued against three of the four children, and the fourth child interpleaded that the property being family property under local customary law should be released from the attachment. It was decided (1) that the devise did not constitute the devisees 'tenants in common' under English law and (2) that the facts (*a*) that the testator had acquired the particular property under a conveyance in English form of the fee simple and (*b*) that he made a will in English form, did not prevent the property in the devise becoming 'a family property under native law and custom' as effectively as if the children had succeeded to it on intestacy, and (3) that the property must be released from the attachment.[2] Similarly, in *George & anor*. v. *Fajore*,[3] a devise by will to twelve named persons 'their heirs and assigns for ever as tenants in common without any power or right to alienate or anticipate the same or any part thereof' was held to be subject to local customary law, notwithstanding the use of the English expression 'tenants in common'.

But where the clear and definite intention of the testator as gathered from the will as a whole is that English law should govern the devise, the Court will carry out his wishes as expressed therein. In *Branco* v. *Johnson* [4] the testator devised certain real property in Lagos to trustees 'to let the same and collect the rents and to distribute the balance equally' among his children and after their death among their children *per stirpes*. The testator then continued: 'I desire and declare that my said houses shall never be sold.' It was proved in evidence that the property was always let to tenants during the testator's life-time. The plaintiffs claimed as co-owners, residuary devisees and/or life tenants under English law which, they alleged, should govern the inheritance. The defendants contended that the real intention of the testator was to create family property under local law and custom by which the succession to the property should be determined. Baker, acting C.J., held that, as it was the rents from the property and not the property itself which were the subject-matter of the bequest and as the bequest itself followed closely the English form, the law of England should apply and the property should be sold. It is quite clear that the properties concerned were not bequeathed by the testator

---

[1] (1935), 12 N. L. R. 1.   [2] But see *Saibu* v. *Igbo* (1941), 16 N. L. R. 25.
[3] (1939), 15 N. L. R. 1.   [4](1943), 17 N. L. R. 70.

to his children as family house, as was the position in the cases we have just been considering above. Had that been the case here, local customary law would have applied to govern the devise.

When Customary Succession cannot be affected by a Will. It follows then that once property is held to be family property, no member of it has any separate and inalienable interest therein which that member may dispose of during his or her life or at her death. That was why in *Taylor* v. *Williams* [1] a devise by a testatrix in her will of her undivided share in a family property was held to be null and void, as the testatrix could not by will or otherwise dispose of her undivided share in a family property *even where the devise was to her son.* The son will take his mother's share of her family property, not in virtue of her mother's devise of it which is clearly invalid, but because he is entitled to it under the customary law. In such a case it can be said quite definitely that the rules of customary succession cannot be influenced for better or for worse by the will of a family member purporting to devise that member's undivided share in the family property. It is one of the peculiarities of the indigenous institution of family property.

There is, however, nothing to prevent a testator from excluding the devolution of his individually-owned property from the customary rules or from making the vesting of it in some or all of his children conditional upon certain contingencies. For instance, in *Alake* v. *Halid & anor.* [2] a testator devised his property to trustees upon trust that they apply the revenue from the land as to one-half to its repair and as to the other half to Momo Busari, a son, and to Moriamo, a daughter equally. Then followed the provision 'that if Momo Busari in his life-time, or any of his children after his death shall at any time erect at his own expense a solid and brick building and dwelling house on his own portion then that portion of the property shall be conveyed to him or any such of his children in fee simple'. Momo Busari survived the testator but never built on the land in question, and he was also alive at the date of the acquisition of the proprety by the Lagos Executive Development Board. Later, Momo Busari died and his mother claimed to be entitled to his share of the compensation money. It was held that the erection of a brick building was a condition precedent to the vesting of Momo Busari's interest in the land and that the ultimate impossibility of performance of the condition precedent imposed by the testator, though due to the acquisition

[1] (1935), 12 N. L. R. 67.   [2] (1935), 12 N. L. R. 22.

by the Lagos Executive Development Board, did not excuse its performance by Momo Busari who was alive up to the date of acquisition without having fulfilled the condition. If, therefore, Momo Busari did not acquire a vested interest before his death, his mother had no right to which to succeed. It was accordingly ruled that the trustees should hold the whole property in trust for the maintenance of Moriamo and on her death for the benefit of the children and grandchildren of the testator.

Another case on the vesting of a contingent interest in a will is *Bickersteth* v. *Shanu* [1] where a testator devised to the appellants as trustees certain property in Lagos to his son, stating that 'these devises shall take effect upon my said son attaining the age of twenty-five years'. The testator died in 1918 and the son, on attaining twenty-five in 1930, brought an action against the appellants claiming an account as from the date of the testator's death of the rents of the properties. It was held by the Privy Council (1) that the established rule for construing devises of real estate is that they are to be held to be vested unless a condition precedent to vesting is expressed with reasonable clearness; (2) that, considering the will as a whole, the words: 'shall take effect' related to the devise taking effect in possession, and were not intended to impose a condition precedent on the devise which therefore vested in the son at the date of the testator's death, subject to divestment if the son should fail to attain twenty-five, but was not contingent on his attaining that age. The son was accordingly entitled to the rents claimed. We need hardly point out that the whole will was made in English form and intended to be governed entirely by English law, so that no question of customary law arose there.

We may briefly note two more cases involving the construction of ineffectual clauses in the wills of testators made in English form. In the case of *In re Will of Wright* [2] a testator devised (*a*) his town-land to a Church, but if it should prove too small for the purposes of the church, then there should be a gift over to his sister; (*b*) his farm-land to be maintained by the Church, but if that should be impracticable, the land should be sold and the proceeds divided between the Church and his sister. *Held*: that the first devise was valid as an absolute gift to the Church to the exclusion of the sister, but that the second devise was void for uncertainty and that, therefore, the land should be sold and the proceeds shared between the Church and the sister.

[1] (1936), A. C. 290.   [2] (1929), 9 N. L. R. 81.

Tom Jones Memorial Hall. In *Shaw and anor.* v. *Taylor & anor.*[1] the testator, Thomas Jones, devised to his trustees certain real property not including the particular property upon which the testator directed them to build a hall 'which shall be and remain for the absolute use of my countrymen of the Lagos community forever'; the first floor of the building to be used for public meetings and the top floor to be supplied with a library for the educated portion of the community. The building on completion was to 'bear and be known by the name of the Tom Jones Memorial' for ever. Both the Divisional Court and the Supreme Court at Lagos held that, in the absence of a specific devise of the property on which the hall was to be built, the testator must be taken to have died intestate with respect to this property. On appeal to the Privy Council, however, their Lordships held (1) that, notwithstanding that the will contained no express and formal devise of the property to the trustees, the property was by the terms of the will to be affected with a permanent trust; and (2) that, having regard to the expressions therein contained, the will should be construed as effecting a devise of the property to the trustees for the purposes therein indicated to them. Thus were disappointed the two children of the testator who had taken out an Originating Summons claiming a declaration that their father be regarded as having died intestate with respect to the property in question.

Finally, an interesting commentary on the new vogue of making wills so as to displace the customary local rules of inheritance and succession is constituted by *Apatira & anor.* v. *Akanke & ors.*[2] in which a Mohammedan made a will in English form and the question arose as to what law should govern the devolution of the estate comprised in the will. The facts were briefly as follows: the Mohammedan testator made a will in English form but, with respect to signature and attestation, the will did not comply with the requirements of the Wills Act, though it satisfied the requirements of the Mohammedan law. It happened that the two attesting witnesses of the will signed it on two different but consecutive dates after the testator's date of executing and signing his self-made will: the deceased could not, therefore, be said to 'sign or acknowledge his signature in the presence of two witnesses both being present at the same time', as required by the Wills Acts 1837 and 1852. On the other hand, the Maliki School of Mohammedan law which obtains among the Moslems of Nigeria does not require

[1] (1918), 3 N. L. R. 72.
[2] (1944), 17 N. L. R. 149.

a will to be in writing or signed and/or witnessed; but, under it, a testator can dispose by will of only one-third of his property to persons other than his heirs who are entitled to share in his estate, and he cannot effect any alteration of the shares of their heirs in the remaining two-thirds (unless of course they all agree, but they did not in the present case). The Maliki law would appear to be ignored by the testator in this case in that his will disposed of *all* the testator's property. On these facts, Ames, J., held in the Supreme Court that the testator intended his will to be one according to English law and that 'the fact that the deceased was a Nigerian and a Mohammedan cannot make any difference to the necessity of complying with the requirements of the Wills Acts'.[1] The moral of this case is that if a Nigerian testator intends his will to be effective to pass his property, whether by the customary law of succession or by the English law of inheritance, he must comply with the requirements of the formal validity of a will under English law. The conception of making wills is foreign to the indigenous system which knew no writing, and it is only reasonable that any attempt to adopt the will form in order to confirm or vary the customary order of succession should satisfy the requirements of the Wills Acts.

Perhaps we should note very briefly here the famous case of *Sule Noibi & ors.* v. *Imam Noibi & ors.*[2] in which the question of succession to land under a trust *deed* arose. It happened that the Alquranis, a Muslim sect in Lagos, had had land conveyed to them by a trust deed dated 28 July 1879, and had built on it a mosque at Aroloya Street to practise according to their belief a form of the Muslim religion based on the all-sufficiency of the Koran. One Indian, called Nayarr, later arrived in Lagos and purported to convert them in 1921 to Ahmadis in circumstances rendering it dubious whether the alleged converts fully understood their proselytiser or his proselytising. Many years later Nayarr claimed that the property in question had by the alleged conversion of 1921 passed to the new sect founded by him. The Alquranis denied that their mosque had so passed. In delivering the judgment of W. A. C. A., Deane, then C.J. of the Gold Coast, held (1) that the original purpose of the trust must be the guide in determining who had the right to control the mosque; (2) that, according to the celebrated case of *The Free Church of Scotland* v. *Overtoun* (1904), A. C. 515, so long as a remnant of the original beneficiaries of a

[1] F. H. Ruxton's *Maliki Law* (1916), London.
[2] (1934), 2 W. A. C. A. 135.

trust remain they are entitled to the benefit of that trust; and (3) that the Alquranis were therefore the original *cestuis que trust*.

We will now consider very briefly some important Ordinances and Statutes bearing on Succession to property in Nigeria.

E. ORDINANCES AND STATUTES RELATING TO SUCCESSION TO PROPERTY

No attempt will be made here to do more than indicate some of the more important ordinances and other statutes that have an immediate bearing on the law of succession to land in the country. For a detailed statement of the rules the ordinances themselves must be consulted, since it would require a separate treatise to compass the special field of the Law of Succession or, as it is sometimes called, the Law of Executors and Administrators. In so far as succession to any property in Nigeria is expressly made subject to the English rules of succession law, it would be advisable to refer to standard English works on the subject.[1]

Real Estate on Intestacy. The first important ordinance for our present purpose is the *Administration (Real Estate and Small Estates) Ordinance* [2] No. 11 of 1917, which is officially described as relating to the administration of real estate in the case of intestacy and to the administration of small estates. As regards cases of intestacy, ss. 2 and 3 provide as follows:

Real Estate

S. 2. When any person shall die intestate after the commencement of this Ordinance leaving any real property of whatsoever nature of which the intestate might have disposed by will, such real property shall for the purposes of administration be deemed to be part of the personal estate of the said intestate and shall be administered accordingly.

Provided always that the real property the succession to which cannot by native law and custom be affected by testamentary

---

[1] e.g. Parry's *Law of Succession* (2nd edition, 1947); Mustoe's *Law of Executors and Administrators* (4th edition); Williams, *Executors and Administrators*.

[2] Appearing as Chap. XIII, in Vol. I of *The Laws of Nigeria* (1923). This Ordinance repeals the Real Estates (Administration) Ordinance, and the Small Estates Administration Ordinance, both of which formerly appeared as Chaps. X and XI of *The Laws of Southern Nigeria*.

disposition shall descend in accordance with the provisions of such native law or custom anything herein contained to the contrary notwithstanding.

Provided also that the real estate shall not be administered unless the Administrator shows to the satisfaction of the Court that the personal estate is insufficient to pay the intestate's debts and the expenses of his funeral, and of taking out administration.

S. 3. When a person dies intestate possessed of real estate, the Court shall, in granting letters of administration, have, regards to the rights and interests of persons interested in his real estate, and his heir-at-law, if not one of the next of kin, shall be equally entitled to the grant with the next of kin.

There are thus two main provisions: (*a*) whenever a person dies intestate having property of which he could have disposed by will, such real property shall be administered as personalty; (*b*) when granting Letters of Administration the Court is to have regard to the interests of the heir-at-law who is in proper cases equally entitled with the next of kin to receive Letters of Administration.

These provisions came up for consideration in *Fahm* v. *Ogbojulogun & anor*.[1] where the eldest son obtained Letters of Administration of his deceased intestate father's estate which he later found to be insolvent. The administrator son had on 7 April 1924 obtained a Court Order for the deceased's real property to be administered as personal estate. On 25 September 1933, he obtained another order under s. 2 of the Administration (Real Estate and Small Estates) Ordinance empowering him to sell certain properties including the one involved in the present action. He sold it and duly received payment of the price from the purchaser, but, before he executed the necessary conveyance to the purchaser, he discovered that the property was in the occupation of certain relations who claimed that the deceased had in his life-time made a gift of it to them. These relations consequently refused to vacate the property and the administrator was unable to give the purchaser vacant possession. Graham Paul, J., decided (1) that, contrary to the defendants' contention that since the sale of the property by the administrator only the purchaser could sue them for possession, the administrator was in fact the proper person to sue for recovery of possession as, in the absence of a conveyance, the legal estate remained in the administrator; (2) that where the personal estate was insolvent the relations put in possession of the property by the deceased in his life-time could not remain in occupation,

[1] (1935), 12 N. L. R. 47.

without proof of the alleged gift to them, and so prevent the administrator exercising effectively the power to sell given to him under the Administration (Real Estate and Small Estates) Ordinance of 1917.

Similarly, in *Jones* v. *Martins*,[1] the sister of a deceased intestate had afterwards collected rents on part of his estate. The plaintiff sued her as *executrix de son tort* for £105 in respect of professional services rendered to the deceased during his life-time. Held by the West African Court of Appeal (1) that the effect of s. 2 of Administration (Real Estate and Small Estates) Ordinance (1917) was to place real property, left on intestacy, in the same position as personal estate for the purposes of administration, and that such real property thus acquired the character of personal property for administration purposes; (2) that the intermeddling of the defendant in the real estate made her *executrix de son tort*, and that she was liable to the plaintiff for the £105 claimed.

Payment of Wages or Salary of Deceased to his Estate. As regards small estates of which any person may die intestate, the widow or other relatives of the deceased person may be paid wages or salary due to the deceased at his death if the same does not exceed £10 (ten pounds) in the circumstances laid down in s. 4 of the Ordinance as follows:

Small Estates

S. 4. In case any person employed in the service of any Government Department or of a local authority shall die leaving any sum of money not exceeding ten pounds due to him as wages or salary, and probate of his will or Letters of Administration be not produced to the officer responsible for the payment of the said sum; or, if notice in writing of the existence of a will and intention to prove the same or notice of intention to take out Letters of Administration be not given to the said officer within the period of *two* months from the death of such person so employed as aforesaid; or if such notice be given but such will be not proved or Letters of Administration be not taken out and the probate or Letters of Administration (as the case may be) produced to the said officer within the period of *four* months from the death of such person; the officer may after such period of two or four months, as the case may be, pay the sum due as aforesaid, at his discretion to the widow and relatives of the deceased person or any one or more of them.

[1] (1943), 9 W. A. C. A. 100.

Administrator-General's Ordinance, 1938. The most comprehensive enactment relating to all estates in respect of which a grant of probate may be made or Letters of Administration may be granted by the Supreme Court is the *Administrator-General's Ordinance No.* 14 *of* 1938 (with later amendments) which is designed to provide for the powers and duties of the Administrator-General in such matters. This Ordinance is too long to be reproduced or even discussed in any detail here, but we will merely touch on a few interesting aspects of its numerous provisions.

Any testator may appoint in his will the Administrator-General as his sole executor.[1] In any case of unrepresented estate the Administrator-General may apply to the Supreme Court for a grant of probate or Letters of Administration within a period of one month from the death of the deceased.[2] Where there exists any uncertainty as to the succession to the property of a deceased intestate the Supreme Court may at the instance of the Administrator-General or of any interested person order the Administrator-General to hold the estate until further and proper determination of the issue.[3]

Intestate Estates Ordinance of 1928. The main functions of the Curator of Intestate Estates under the *Intestate Estates Ordinance of* 1928 whereby Letters of Administration was formerly grantable to the Curator for the disposal of the intestate estates of persons dying without heirs or next of kin, have now been assigned to the Administrator-General by ss. 41–3 of the Ordinance. After the requisite advertisement for applications or petitions, assets unclaimed for five years shall be transferred to Government.[4]

Estates of Deceased European Officers. The Administrator-General shall administer the estates of deceased European officers upon information received from the Head of the Government Department concerned, if the officer dies in Lagos. Outside Lagos, the Resident or the District Officer, as the case may be, shall be *ex-officio* agent of the Administrator-General in the administration of the estate of such deceased.[5]

Estates of Military Persons. The Administrator-General is also given power to administer the estates of Military Persons in accordance with the provisions of the Regimental Debts Act, 1893, which remains unaffected by the Ordinance.[6]

---

[1] S. 9; Under s. 12 of *The Public Trustee Ordinance No.* 15 *of* 1938, the Supreme Court may grant probate of wills or letters of administration to the Public Trustee whose office was created by that Ordinance.
[2] S. 15.   [3] S. 16.   [4] S. 44.   [5] S. 49.   [6] Ss. 55–7 (Part VIII).

Administration of Small Estates. It is also provided in s. 58 that whenever any person shall die intestate leaving property or assets within Nigeria the gross value of which does not exceed £50, the Administrator-General shall insert notice in the Nigerian Gazette before embarking upon its administration, except that no such notice is necessary where the value of the property is not more than £10.

For fuller detail reference must be made to the text of the Ordinance.

General

In two cases, one relating to the Cameroons (*Martin* v. *Johnson*) [1] and the other to Calabar (*In re Offiong Okon Ata*) [2] the sister and next-of-kin of a deceased intestate in both cases, upon identical facts, was held to be the proper person to whom Letters of Administration should be granted and not the caveators who were claiming a better right in virtue of their being the living heads of their respective families of which the deceased or his predecessor had been an emancipated slave. The abolition of slavery in Nigeria has taken away any such right which the head of a slave-owning family might have had over the property of such slave. [3]

Finally, the decision in *In re Estate of Sholu* [4] should be recorded here on account of its illuminating character. The case concerned an *ex parte* motion made in chambers for an order empowering the administrators of the estate of a deceased James Sholu to control and deal with the estate. The heirs in whom the real estate ordinarily vested had not been notified. If there were no heirs other than the administrators, who in their affidavit alleged that they were the children of the deceased, then unless the Land Transfer Act of 1897 applied to Nigeria, there would seem to be no necessity for the present motion. The control and dealing with the real estate normally vest in the heirs *qua* heirs and not in the administrators of the estate. Except in the cases of the estates of persons married under the Marriage Ordinance and the local estates of persons not domiciled in Nigeria which were formerly administered by the Curator of Intestate Estates (now, under s. 41

---

[1] (1935), 12 N. L. R. 46.   [2] (1930), 10 N. L. R. 65.
[3] In the Gold Coast case of *In re Kweku Damptey* (1930), 1 W. A. C. A. 12, the West African Court of Appeal held that the custom of *Akinkwa* by which a certain class of persons was formerly regarded as dashed to a stool must be regarded as no longer tenable since the abolition of slavery. The stool-holder was therefore not entitled to Letters of Administration in respect of the estate of the emancipated slave.   [4] (1932), 11 N. L. R. 37.

of the Administrator-General's Ordinance 1938, by the Administrator-General), the administrators of an estate deal with the personalty of a deceased's estate and only when the debts of the deceased necessitate the sale of real property can the administrators be empowered to deal with such property if such debts exist and the motion is supported by an affidavit to that effect. Accordingly, Webber, acting C.J., held (1) that neither the Land Transfer Act, 1897, nor the Administration of Estates Act, 1925, applies to Nigeria, and (2) that the estate would therefore vest in the movers of the present motion *qua* heirs, without any necessity for them to obtain permission to deal with it as administrators.

His Honour observed: The succession to intestate property in cases of marriage in accordance with the provisions of the Marriage Ordinance (Cap. 68) is regulated under s. 36 of that Ordinance. In my opinion that section would have been worded differently, had the Land Transfer Act 1897 applied to Nigeria.

Wills under Land and Native Rights Ordinance. It remains to add in conclusion that, under the *Land and Native Rights Ordinance* (1916), the devolution of rights over land in the Northern Provinces of Nigeria, to which English law is applicable, shall not pass to the successor any proprietary right thereover but shall pass only the testator's right of occupancy. The relevant s. 15 is in the following terms:

In the case of the devolution or transfer of rights over land to which English law applies, no deed or will shall operate to create any proprietary right over land except that of a plain transfer of the whole of the rights of occupation over the whole of the land.

Chapter Eleven

LAND REGISTRATION

A. Early Attempts at recording Titles to Land. B. Beginnings of registration of Deeds relating to Land. C. Registration of Instruments relating to Land. D. Registration of Titles to Land. E. Proof of Title to Land

---

UNDER the indigenous land tenure system, as we have seen, certain transactions about land such as gift, loan or pledge invariably require the presence of witnesses on the land to be granted, accompanied by a feasting ceremony of a more or less token nature. The publicity thus secured to the event largely dispenses with the need for any other record, even if such record were possible. In the absence of writing the indigenous system has from the earliest period devised a plan of training certain elders of the community to witness and remember all the dealings in the land belonging to their own community, and the degree of their recollections of such matters years after the events themselves is but remarkable in the circumstances. So long as the system of shifting or expansive agriculture persists in a given community, such rough and ready means of recording transactions appears to be fairly satisfactory. But, as soon as land grows scarce and agriculture becomes intensive, human memory tends to run its gamut and to become incapable of meeting the manifold subtleties of the fraudulent and the clever. Even the fair-minded could sometimes hardly resist the impulse to challenge the authenticity of a record of land transaction which is enshrined in the minds of persons not unsusceptible to later influences of various kinds. The problem becomes even more acute where, as it often has been the case, the witnessing elders have died out and all memory of the original provenance regarding a particular piece of land has faded from the captious minds of the living. Of the difficulties to which the whole system has given rise wherever land has acquired an economic value we have spoken in various parts of Chapter Eight. Land disputes flourish and the spate of litigation in the Local (or Native) Courts, no less than in the Magistrate and higher Courts, is difficult to stem.

When to these incipient trends in the growing inadequacy of the traditional modes of recording land transactions is added the effect of the impact of European economic and social ideas, involving as these do the planting for export of permanent crops like cocoa, palm and kola as well as the necessity of attracting foreign capital in aid of the country's economy, it is easy to see how highly accentuated becomes the scramble for land acquisition and the consequent uncertainties that are bound to follow in its train. At that point, it becomes necessary and even inevitable that the Government of the country should take steps to arrange an adequate system of recording rights and interests in land, if chaos is to be avoided.

The Government of Nigeria has attempted to meet the new situation by a series of piece-meal legislation designed to suit the local conditions and the degree of advancement of the various parts of the country. As a matter of historical interest, if not as an essential preliminary to any fairly adequate study of the problems of registration in the country, we shall briefly trace in retrospect the evolution of the main Nigerian ordinances and proclamations relating to land registration.

There is now in the country a dual system of Registration of Deeds relating to land and Registration of Titles to land, the latter having been introduced only in 1935 while the former has had a long and chequered history dating back to 1863. We shall tell the story of registration of instruments first.

A. EARLY ATTEMPTS AT RECORDING TITLES TO LAND

The earliest enactment affecting the issue of titles to land in the Colony is Ordinance No. 9 of 1863, by which three Commissioners were appointed for the purpose of enquiring into the titles by which or under which all the lands within the Settlement of Lagos were held, and of settling and defining the just rights and titles to such lands. The Commission was to last from 10 April 1863 till 1 April 1864, during which period the Commissioners were to have (a) access to the register of the settlement and all other relative public documents, (b) power to summon all claimants of land titles as well as other independent witnesses and all documents relating to the titles claimed, (c) power to grant certificates of title to those with valid claims, and to inform those with invalid ones that they have no title or right to the land claimed (such fact being by them recorded in a book kept by them for that purpose), (d) the duty to report to the Governor and Council cases of those who neglect or refuse to attend due summons or produce relevant documents, (e) power to take sworn depositions before them, to sit once a week in the Secretary's office and to report proceedings of their Commission to the Governor and Council once every month, and (f) the assistance in due performance of their task of all Magistrates, Constables and other British subjects within the Settlement.

Ordinances No. 10 of 1864 and No. 9 of 1865 extended these provisions to cover respectively the periods 6 July 1864 to 6 July 1865 and 3 August 1865 to 5 August 1866, with these two minor alterations: (i) the Commissioners would by the latter Ordinance thenceforwards sit as a Court in the Chief Magistrate's Court and (ii) by the same Ordinance, the Commissioners could make orders to regulate the costs and fees payable in respect of their duties; such table of fees, having been duly approved by the Governor, to be hung up in the Court.

Ordinance No. 9 of 1869 appointed the Officer administering the Government of Lagos to be Administrator charged with the duty of settling claims to lands, hereditaments and tenements within the Settlement of Lagos and its Territories and to give validity to certain proved possessory titles thereto. Any person in possession by himself or by his tenant of any cultivated land, house, warehouse, factory, brick-works, salt-works, dwelling-houses, place of trade or manufactory or a palm-grove, situate in the Settlement or its Territories, for a period of three years before the passing of the Ordinance without paying rent or acknowledging title to any other person, might apply to the Administrator for a grant of the property of which he was then in possession. After two months' public notice of any application, the Administrator could grant the property in question to the applicant. Those occupying lands who, within six months after being served with notice to produce or obtain grants of their titles thereto, failed to do so, would forfeit their interests in the land, which should thereafter revert to the Crown. All grants were to be dated, numbered and registered in the Secretary's office in Lagos, upon payment of necessary fees: *'unless such grants are so registered they shall not be considered valid'*.

As a result of these four Ordinances, many Crown Grants were issued on the reports of the Commissioners which are preserved in the Lands Registry at Lagos. The Ordinances were repealed by No. 13 of 1877. It has been estimated that in the period between 1863 and 1914 rather more than 4,000 Crown Grants were issued in Lagos to various claimants, many of whom later asserted that the grants conferred upon them absolute and indefeasible titles to the lands subject thereto. That the Crown Grants never have had any such effect in law has been fully demonstrated elsewhere.[1] It is sufficient here to say that the grants were issued to serve only as *prima facie* evidence of the grantees' possessory title and so clarify the uncertainties that prevailed in land matters at the time of their inception.

B. BEGINNINGS OF REGISTRATION OF DEEDS RELATING TO LAND

(*i*) *The Colony.* But the first real attempt at recording instruments affecting land transactions was made in Ordinance No. 8 of 1883 (as amended by No. 12 of 1883) entitled '*The Registration Ordinance, 1883*' which was originally passed for what used to be 'The Gold Coast Colony', but which was, on the separation and establishment of Lagos as an independent Colony, made applicable to Lagos by Ordinance No. 2 of 1894.

The Registration Ordinance 1883 established a Registry Office at Lagos, with power reserved to the Governor to establish others elsewhere, as and when he thought fit. The Registrar was to keep Record Books of all registered instruments and the certificates placed thereon, numbered and indexed alphabetically as regards the names of parties to instruments other than wills and, in the case of wills, the names of the testators thereof. The Registrar should issue certificates of registration in all approved cases and such certificates should be conclusive proof of the particulars of such registration.

All Crown Grants of Land issued after the passing of the Ordinance would be *void* unless registered within thirty days from its date; memorials of Private Ordinances and Inquisitions relating to land should be registered within ten days from the enactment or date thereof; all registered wills of testators dying after the passing of the Ordinance should take effect from the date of their registration, except that such wills would take effect from the testators'

---

[1] See Chapters Two, Four and Six, *passim*.

death if registered within two years next after the testators' death within the Colony and eighteen months elsewhere. Instruments or wills executed prior to the Ordinance were to take effect from the dates of their registration or the dates of testators' death if registered within two years after this Ordinance.

Copies of instruments, the originals of which were preserved in a foreign country, might under certain circumstances be registered. All instruments, relating to land, other than wills, must have in the margin or on the back thereof a plan and a description of such land (s. 15).

All registers were to be deemed to be in legal custody and should be receivable in evidence, as were copies thereof or extracts therefrom, if duly certified by the Registrar. There was, on payment of the proper fee, a right of public inspection of all registers kept at the Land Registry (s. 25).

The provision in s. 19 of the Ordinance for the periodic inspection and attestation, by the Chief Justice or one of the Puisne Judges of the Supreme Court, of all registers kept at the Registry Office was subsequently abolished by s. 35 of 'The General Registry Ordinance No. 9 of 1888' (as amended by No. 9 of 1895) which provided for the establishment for the Colony of a General Registry and a Registrar-General of births, deaths, marriages, alien children and instruments affecting land, until both Ordinances (No. 9 of 1888 and No. 9 of 1895) were repealed and replaced by the more comprehensive provisions of 'The Registration Ordinance No. 5 of 1901' (as amended by No. 12 of 1901).

(ii) *Protectorate of Southern Nigeria.* The first enactment dealing with the registration of all instruments affecting lands in what was formerly the Protectorate of Southern Nigeria was 'The Lands Registry Proclamation No. 16 of 1900' which defined in s. 2 what constituted an 'instrument' within the terms of the Ordinance as follows:

'Instrument' includes (1) a will, (2) office copy of any judgment of the Supreme Court whereby land or the title thereto is or shall be affected, (3) a Judge's Certificate of Title under s. 10, (4) a Judge's Certificate of Purchase of land sold in execution, (5) an affidavit or solemn declaration of ownership in the absence of other documentary evidence of ownership, (6) any other writing whatever affecting land situated in the Protectorate.

Asaba and Old Calabar. 'Land' includes any interest or property in land. The offices of the Registrars of the Supreme Court at Asaba and Old Calabar were constituted Registries of instruments affecting lands in the Protectorate of Southern Nigeria, the Secretary also keeping a register of certified copies of all registered instruments which the Supreme Court Registrar should forward to him. The High Commissioner was empowered to establish subordinate Land Registries in such other districts of the Protectorate as he might deem fit.

All instruments for registration, other than a will or a Court judgment affecting land, must contain a description of the boundaries and abuttals, so far as they could reasonably be described, and the extent and situation of the lands affected by such instruments; there should also be a fairly accurate plan of the land to be registered. The effect of instruments when thus registered was that they became effective, as against other unregistered instruments affecting the same land, from the date of their registration.

An owner of land may apply to the Supreme Court for a Certificate of Title which, if granted, should be registered. Duly certified copies of instruments or even a Certificate of Registration purporting to be signed by a Registrar, were receivable in evidence in any judicial proceeding. A Judge of the Supreme Court was given power of periodic inspection of all the books kept in a Registry. There was a public right to search in any book in the custody of a Registrar.

The next step forward in the history of recording land titles in the Southern Nigeria Protectorate was '*The Lands Registry Proclamation No.* 18 *of* 1901' (as amended by No. 30 of 1903) which was an enactment 'to amend the law relating to the registration of *deeds* in the Protectorate of Southern Nigeria'. It substantially reproduced for the Protectorate the main provisions of 'The Registration Ordinance No. 8 of 1883' which applied only to the Colony, thereby bringing the law applicable to both areas into a measure of harmony. But this 1901 Proclamation defined an 'instrument' within its purview as follows:

'Instrument' includes every instrument in writing affecting land in the Protectorate of Southern Nigeria, including a will and a power of attorney under which any instrument affecting land may be executed.

This may be compared with the definition (already stated above) given in s. 2 of the Proclamation No. 16 of 1900. Also the Asaba Registry Office appears to have since been closed, as s. 3 of the present Proclamation mentioned only Old Calabar.

The detailed rules as to priority of instruments (including wills) registered before and after the making of the Proclamation followed the general lines of the 1883 Ordinance relating to the Colony. But, in cases where land was granted by a Nigerian to non-Nigerians or by the Crown to any person whatsoever, instruments effecting such transactions must, to be valid, be registered within sixty days from the date thereof (s. 14). This was repealed by s. 7 of No. 30 of 1903, but replaced with minor alterations by s. 8 of the same Proclamation. Also, registration shall not cure any defect in any instrument registered, or confer upon it any effect or validity which it would not otherwise have had (s. 30). An instrument endorsed on another instrument would not be registered without the instrument on which it was endorsed, unless the latter instrument had already been registered (s. 31).

An important provision was contained in s. 18 according to which all registers under 'The Land Registry Regulation No. 42 of 1896' of the Royal Niger Company and all registers under 'The Lands Registry Proclamation, 1900' should be delivered to the Registrar-General appointed under the present Ordinance.

(iii) *Colony and Protectorate: Southern Nigerian under Uniform Registration Rules.* With the way so well paved by the Ordinance just above considered it was a short step to establish a uniform set of registration rules of the Colony and the Protectorate of Southern Nigeria as a whole. This task was performed by *'The Land Registration Ordinance, 1907'*, aptly described as an Ordinance to consolidate and amend the law relating to the registration of instruments affecting land in the Colony and Protectorate of Southern Nigeria.

Under it, Registry Offices were established at Lagos, Calabar, Warri and such other place or places as the Governor might appoint. The main provisions followed the lines already considered above for the Land Registration Ordinance 1883 and the Lands Registry Proclamations, all of which it repealed in its s. 25. This Ordinance, which came into operation from 1 October 1907, remained in force until it was superseded by 'The Land Registration Ordinance No. 3 of 1908' which made no material alteration to the law worth noticing here.

(iv) *Protectorate of Northern Nigeria.* Here, because of the strong Government control over land, problems of title gave less trouble in the early days. The first enactment concerning registration of instruments affecting land was *'The Land Registry Proclamation No. 10 of 1901'.* As in the case of the Southern Nigeria Protectorate, a section of the office of the Registrar of the Supreme Court was constituted a Registry for the registration of instruments affecting land situated in the Protectorate of Northern Nigeria. The High Commissioner had power to appoint sub-Registry Offices for such districts and provinces as he might think fit. With regard to certain Land Register books of the Royal Niger Company formerly kept at Asaba (in so far as they covered instruments affecting land within the Northern Protectorate) as well as those instruments relating to land in the Northern Protectorate registered or directed to be registered under the 'Royal Niger Company's Regulations (Embodiment) Proclamation, 1900, Schedule A, Part V', the Registrar of the Supreme Court was by s. 5 of the present Ordinance empowered to embody in the newly established Register books of the Protectorate; all instruments thus re-registered would be deemed to take effect from the date of their original registration with the Niger Company.

Instruments for registration, other than wills, must contain a description as well as a plan of the land concerned; and in the case of the granting of land to persons other than local Northerners, the conditions laid down in 'The Lands Proclamation, 1900' regarding the High Commissioner's consent and written approval as a pre-requisite to the validity of such grants of land rights must be satisfied (s. 8). Court judgments and probates of wills (or copies of either), if relating to land, could be registered without proof upon their production, and Courts were under a duty to transmit to the Registrar judgments relating to land together with relevant plans, if any. Copies of instruments in foreign public custodies might upon certain conditions be registered. For all types of registration proper fees might be charged by the Registrar, who must issue Certificates of Registration in approved cases.

All instruments registered under the Proclamation took effect, as against any other unregistered instruments affecting the same land, from the date of their registration, as did also those executed before the passing of the Proclamation (excluding, of course, the cases under the former Royal Niger Company registers noted above). As in previous enactments, registration alone would not cure any defect in any instrument registered or confer upon it any effect or validity which it would not otherwise have had (except as aforesaid). The public had a right of search in the registers.

The foregoing provisions continued in force until they were superseded by 'the Land and Native Rights Proclamation (No. 9 of 1910, Chapter LXV of Schedule, *Part II*)'. It provided that all instruments affecting land directed by the law of the Protectorate to be registered must be registered within six months of their execution, or in the case of a will, within a year of the testator's death. The Registrar of the Supreme Court should continue to act as Registrar of such instruments until the division of the Protectorate into district Registries. Instruments requiring Governor's consent could not be registered unless such consent was inscribed thereon or otherwise proved. Certificates of Occupancy granted under the hand of the Governor under s. 11 of the Proclamation should also be registered as instruments affecting land. The Proclamation did not affect any existing provincial registration of titles to land other than those conferred by Certificates of Occupancy; but registers under the Proclamation should, in case of conflict with any of these provincial registers, prevail. Otherwise, the provisions of this Proclamation did not differ from those of the one it superseded.

(v) *The Final Phase.* The stage having by now been set for a unification of the principles regarding the registration of deeds affecting land throughout Nigeria, 'the Land Registration Ordinance No. 12 of 1915' (as amended by No. 29 of 1915) was enacted 'to consolidate and amend the law relating to the registration of documents affecting land'. Both the Land Registration Ordinance (Chapter CVI of the *Laws of Southern Nigeria*) of 1908 relating to the Colony and Southern Protectorate and Part II of the Land and Native Rights Proclamation of Northern Nigeria were repealed, without, however, in any way affecting any priority conferred upon any instrument by either such enactment or validate any instrument thereby declared to be void.

This represents the last lap of our journey through the dense maze of early land registration laws in Nigeria. But it also opens to us vistas of 'the brave new world' into which we shall now hurry on our way. Because of the similarity of the provisions of this Ordinance, which came into force on 1 January 1916, to those of the existing Ordinance, we shall not tarry here to describe the details which can be more usefully tackled in the next section.

C. REGISTRATION OF INSTRUMENTS RELATING TO LAND— THE PRESENT POSITION OF

The Land Registration Ordinance No. 12 of 1915, taken together with the amending Ordinances Nos. 29 of 1915, No. 12 of 1918, No. 15 of 1920, thus became the basis of what may be called the modern law of registration of documents relating to land,

and was consolidated and amended into the Land Registration Ordinance (Cap. 87) in Vol. I of the *Laws of Nigeria* of 1923. This Ordinance was itself replaced by *The Land Registration Ordinance* No. 36 of 1924 which remains, with later amendments, the present law on the subject of registration of instruments affecting land throughout Nigeria. We will now proceed to consider in some detail such of its provisions as serve to elucidate our statement here of the principles of registered documents of land transactions:

Establishment of a General Registry. A Land Registry for the whole country was established under 3 (1) of the Ordinance (as amended by No. 15 of 1948), with an office at Lagos and offices at such other places in the Protectorate as the Governor might direct. At the offices of the Land Department at Lagos and of the Secretary, Northern Provinces, at Kaduna, as well as at Ibadan, Calabar and Warri exist the main Land Registries.

It is provided in 3 (2) that all instruments required to be registered under the Ordinance shall be registered in such offices as the Governor may from time to time direct.

Definitions of what constitutes an 'instrument' or a 'Crown Grant' for the purposes of the Ordinance are respectively stated in s. 2 as follows:

(*i*) *Instrument.* '*Instrument*' means a document affecting land in Nigeria, whereby one party (hereinafter called the grantor) confers, transfers, limits, charges or extinguishes in favour of another party (hereinafter called the grantee) any right or title to, or interest in land in Nigeria, and includes a Certificate of Purchase and a power of attorney under which any instrument may be executed, but does not include a will.

(*ii*) *Crown Grant.* '*Crown Grant*' includes a Certificate of Occupancy under the Land and Native Rights Ordinance, and a mining lease, mining right, water right or exclusive prospecting licence granted under the Minerals Ordinance, and a timber licence granted under the Forestry Ordinance, and every other grant, conveyance, lease or mortgage by or on behalf of the Government.

Compulsory Registration. All instruments executed after the commencement of the Ordinance (i.e. 1 January 1925) and all those executed before that date but which were not already registered, must be registered (ss. 6 and 7).

Requisites of Registration. Every instrument executed *in Nigeria* and intended for registration by grantors, one or more of whom is illiterate, must be witnessed and duly attested by a Magistrate.

All instruments executed *outside Nigeria*, but within a British Dominion or Protectorate, must be duly certified or attested by a Judge, a Police Magistrate, a Justice of the Peace, a Notary Public or a resident Administrative Officer. If executed in any *foreign country*, such instruments must be certified or attested by a British Consul or other resident, accredited British Representative.

Apart from a Power of Attorney, all instruments for registration must contain proper and sufficient descriptions and plans of the land affected. Subject to an order of the Supreme Court, the Registrar's decision as to the adequacy or otherwise of such descriptions and plans is final.

A licensed surveyor must have signed and the Surveyor-General must have countersigned all plans or copies of plans of lands covered by Crown Grants executed after 1 June 1918. Also, if any instrument executed after 1 June 1918, has an accompanying plan of the land affected, such plan or copy of plan must be signed by a surveyor as stipulated under s. 10 of the Survey Ordinance No. 13 of 1918 (Cap. 90).

All instruments requiring for their validity the prior consent of the Governor or of any Public Officer must have such consent endorsed thereon, or the Registrar must otherwise be satisfied that such consent has been given. The following instruments shall *not* be registered under this Ordinance:

Non-registrable Instruments. (i) Any instrument declared void by any enactment repealed by this Ordinance; (ii) any instrument which does not comply with this or any other operative enactment at the date of its execution; (iii) any instrument endorsed on another instrument, unless the one on which it is endorsed is itself registered (ss. 11–13).

How Registration is Effected. Any person desiring to register a registrable instrument should deliver it with a copy to the Registrar at one of the established Land Registries in the district. If satisfied with the propriety of both the original and the copy, the Registrar registers the instrument by causing the copy (when duly certified as the true copy) to be pasted or bound in one of the Register books and by endorsing an appropriate Certificate of Registration on the original which will then be returned, upon application, to the person who has submitted it for registration; but if such person fails to apply for its return within twelve months after the date of registration, the Registrar may destroy the instrument. The same fate will befall any properly rejected instrument not claimed within the same period. A rejected instrument may, if all defects have been removed therefrom, be re-submitted for registration afresh (ss. 17 and 18).

Registers and Copies of Entries as Evidence. The registers and other books and files kept at a Registry Office are deemed to be in legal custody and are receivable in evidence, as are any copies of entries therein which are duly certified by the Registrar. Members of the public have a right of search in any register or file of registered documents at the registry (ss. 21–23).

Penalty for False Statement. There is a penalty of £50 or two years' imprisonment against anyone making a false statement respecting any of the particulars required to be known and registered (s. 24).

Legal Consequences of Registration. These are briefly three: Non-registration may (i) render certain documents void, (ii) render them inadmissible as evidence in a judicial proceeding, (iii) make them lose priority as against registered ones affecting the same land.

It must, of course, be remembered that registration does not by itself cure the instrument registered of any defect, nor does it confer upon it any effect or validity which the instrument, apart from the registration, would not otherwise have had. But although s. 19 of the Ordinance thus stipulates, it is nevertheless important to note, at least with respect to that part of the proposition which says that registration cannot validate what would otherwise have been invalid, that s. 14 clearly makes void for non-registration within stated periods certain classes of documents; that is, registration according to the conditions therein prescribed gives such documents the validity which they undoubtedly would lack if not so registered. However, it is still true to say that registration will not of itself cure an instrument of any inherent defect. For example, in *Johnson* v. *Onisiwo* [1] an instrument to which all co-owners of the land in question were not parties was registered. It was held by the West African Court of Appeal that the document was not void but voidable. Registration clearly did not make the document any the less voidable.

On account of the importance of s. 14 and of the two following sections, we will set them out here with a view to analysing their provisions more fully in the light of their judicial interpretation:

Instruments Void for Non-registration. S. 14: Every Crown Grant executed after the commencement of this Ordinance, and every instrument affecting land the subject of a Crown Grant or whereby land is granted by a native to a non-native executed after

[1] (1943), 9 W. A. C. A. 189.

the commencement of this Ordinance shall, so far as it affects any land, be void unless the same is registered within six months from its date (or, in the case of an instrument whereby land is granted by a native to a non-native, from the date on which it receives the Governor's consent) if executed in Nigeria, or twelve months from its date (or, in the case of an instrument whereby land is granted by a native to a non-native, from the date on which it receives the Governor's consent) if executed elsewhere; provided that the Registrar may extend such periods whenever he shall be satisfied that registration has been delayed without default or neglect on the part of the person acquiring the right or interest in the lands in question.

Inadmissibility in Evidence. S. 15: No instrument shall be pleaded or given in evidence in any Court as affecting any land unless the same shall have been registered:

Provided that a memorandum given in respect of an equitable mortgage affecting land in the Colony or the Southern Provinces executed before the 1st day of July 1944, and not registered under this Ordinance may be pleaded and shall not be inadmissible in evidence by reason only of not being so registered. (This proviso was added by No. 13 of 1944).

Loss of Priority. S. 16: Subject to the provisions of this Ordinance every instrument registered under this Ordinance shall so far as it affects any land, take effect, as against other instruments affecting the same land, from the date of its registration as hereinafter defined, and every instrument registered before the commencement of this Ordinance shall be deemed to have taken effect from the date provided by the law in force at the time of its registration.

It may be said here at once that the main alteration effected by s. 16 is that an instrument registered under the present Ordinance enjoys priority from the date of its *registration*, whereas under the Land Registration Ordinance (Cap. 87) an instrument enjoys priority from the date of its *execution*.

Judicial Interpretation. These provisions have been the subject of judicial interpretation in a number of cases.

S. 14 was thus construed, along with s. 15, in *Zard* v. *Diamandis* [1] where the appellant had applied under s. 8 of the Registration of Titles Ordinance (No. 13 of 1935) for a first registration of a fee simple estate in Lagos free from incumbrances. But the conveyance

[1] (1936), 13 N. L. R. 114 (alias, *In Re Property No. 37 Balogun Street, Lagos*).

of the estate to the appellant had not been registered in accordance with s. 15 of the Land Registration Ordinance (No. 36 of 1924). The respondent opposed registration free from incumbrances on the ground that there was a valid, subsisting lease of the property in question. The Registrar of Titles refused registration because of the existing lease, and the issue was taken on appeal to the Divisional Court which confirmed the Registrar's refusal of the appellant's application for registration, though for the very different reasons that (1) the lease regarded as valid by the Registrar was in fact invalid as not having been granted by the proper grantor, and (2) the conveyance to the appellant had not been registered in accordance with s. 15 of the Land Registration Ordinance of 1924. Carey, J., held in the Divisional Court that the alleged lease was invalid only because someone other than the owner of the property had purported to execute it without the owner's authority or knowledge, and was not invalid merely because, as the appellant had contended, the lease had not been registered in compliance with s. 14 of the Ordinance. The learned Judge pointed out that, within the Protectorate, a lease of land by a Nigerian to a non-Nigerian does not become void for non-registration until the expiry of six months from the date of the Governor's approval. There is not in the Colony any restriction upon such alienation of land rights, and it is the existence of restrictions in the Protectorate such as are contemplated in ss. 3 and 4 of the Native Lands Acquisition Ordinance (Cap. 89) that must have influenced or induced the two bracketed alternatives within the wording of s. 14 of the present Ordinance. It is submitted that the draftsman of the section might have phrased it less ambiguously by expressly limiting the requirement of the Governor's approval to those instruments only that come within the four corners of the Native Lands Acquisition Ordinance.

The facts in *Jammal* v. *Saidi & anor.*[1] are of more general interest. The plaintiff claimed recovery of possession of a shop under a Deed of Lease granted him by the owners. The second defendant resisted plaintiff's claim on the ground that he had a prior lease granted him under an Agreement of Lease by the first defendant as representing the head of the owning family. But whereas the plaintiff's Deed of Lease had been duly registered under the Land Registration Ordinance of 1924, the defendant's Agreement of Lease had not. The Divisional Court gave judgment for the defendant simply because the defendant's Agreement of

[1] (1933), 11 N. L. R. 86.

Lease was earlier in date than the plaintiff's Deed. This would have been legal under the previous Ordinance according to which priority of such instruments depended on the date of their *execution* and not on that of their *registration*. But the present case took place after 1 January 1925, and must therefore be governed by the present Land Registration Ordinance of 1924. Now, s. 16 of that Ordinance provides that priority as between two or more instruments shall depend upon the date of their *registration* and *not* upon that of their *execution*. Also, s. 7 of the Ordinance made compulsory the registration of every unregistered instrument executed before 1 January 1925, and the defendant's Agreement being such an instrument as defined by s. 2 thereof should not have been received in evidence without registration. Therefore, the reception in evidence by the Divisional Court of the defendant's unregistered Agreement was contrary to s. 15 of the Land Registration Ordinance, 1924.

On appeal to the Full Court, Kingdon, C.J., set aside the Divisional Court judgment on the ground of its misreception in evidence of an unregistered instrument, and awarded judgment to the plaintiff.

A decision in which the principles of the above case became implicated with those of the Native Lands Acquisition Ordinance was that of the West African Court of Appeal in *Elkali & anor.* v. *Fawaz.*[1] The plaintiffs claimed against the defendant, both of whom being aliens, (*a*) specific performance of the defendant's written agreement to take the lease of a shop at Ibadan from the plaintiffs for three years from 1 November 1937, *or*, (*b*) damages of £192 for breach of the contract. Graham Paul, J., in the High Court at Ibadan, admitted the Agreement in evidence and made a consent order for a formal lease to be submitted by the plaintiff to the defendant who should execute it. Nothing, however, appeared to have been done by either side. So the case came up again for fresh hearing, this time before John, J., on 6 May 1940, when for the first time the defendant objected that the instrument, being one affecting land and not having been registered, was inadmissible in evidence under s. 15 of the Land Registration Ordinance, 1924. This objection was over-ruled by the trial Judge who was of the opinion that the document was not an 'instrument' within the meaning of the Ordinance. The plaintiff admitted that his claim for specific performance was bad in view of the Ordinance provision, but succeeded on his claim for £192 as damages for breach of contract.

[1] (1940), 6 W. A. C. A. 212.

On appeal to the West African Court of Appeal the defendant still relied on his two grounds: (1) that the Agreement was inadmissible in evidence because as an instrument under the Ordinance it had not been duly registered as required by s. 15 thereof; (2) that the claim for damages must fail by virtue of the provisions of s. 3 of the Native Lands Acquisition Ordinance (Cap. 89). *Held*: by the Court: (1) that the instrument was an 'instrument' within the meaning of the Ordinance and was accordingly inadmissible for want of registration, according to s. 15 thereof; (2) that, although the defendant-appellant may have been charged with a duty under the Agreement not to obstruct the obtaining of the Governor's approval which was necessary under s. 3A of the Native Lands Acquisition Ordinance, no breach of that duty is alleged, and the claim for damages must therefore fail also. S. 3A of the Native Lands Acquisition Ordinance reads:

'Where any interest or right in or over any land has been acquired by an alien from a native with the approval in writing of the Governor as provided for in s. 3 such interest or right shall not —(a) be transferred to any other alien without the approval in writing of the Governor.' There was in this case no evidence that such consent had been obtained, nor was there any endorsement to that effect as required by s. 10 of the Land Registration Ordinance. On the main issue in the whole case, namely, whether the document in question was or was not an 'instrument' within the meaning of the Ordinance, the West African Court of Appeal commented as follows:

'If it were an agreement between natives (when of course it would not contain the clause subjecting it to the approval of the Government authorities) there can be no question but that, upon the authority of *Abdullah Jammal* v. *Namih Saidi & Yesufu Fetuga* (11 N. L. R. 86)—with which we see no reason to differ— it would be an instrument within the meaning of the Land Registration Ordinance, 1924.' [1]

The Court was more specifically called upon to determine the principle to be followed in deciding whether or not a particular document is an 'instrument' within the Ordinance in the case of *Coker* v. *Ogunye*.[2] There, two documents, one of which was drawn by a legal practitioner and the other by a letter-writer, were tendered in evidence of certain alleged sales of land. In each document the parties to the sale were described, and the price and the survey-

[1] (1940), 6. W. A. C. A. 212, at p. 214.
[2] (1939), 15 N. L. R. 57.

ing as well as an undertaking by the vendor to execute a conveyance when called upon to do so were stated in four separate,
consecutive clauses. Both documents were duly stamped but not
registered under the Land Registration Ordinance. Against their
admissibility in evidence an objection was lodged on two grounds:
(1) that the documents as 'instrument' under the Ordinance had
not been registered in accordance with s. 6 thereof and so came
under the ban of s. 15 of the same Ordinance; (ii) that the drawing
of one of the two documents by a letter-writer instead of by a
legal practitioner contravened s. 4 of the Legal Practitioners'
Ordinance. At the High Court at Abeokuta, Ames, Asst. J., held:
(1) that the two documents were not such as were required to be
registered under the Land Registration Ordinance, and that the
objection based on their non-registration must be over-ruled;
(2) that the fact of one of the documents having been drawn by a
letter-writer could not bar its admissibility in evidence, even if it
constituted a contravention of the Legal Practitioner's Ordinance
(but whether it did or did not was left undecided). The objection
based on this second ground was similarly over-ruled, the learned
Asst. Judge observing: 'The maker of it would be liable to a
penalty; but the document is not affected. The Ordinance does not
make it void or inadmissible in evidence.'

After remarking that there was no precedent for the case before
him, Ames, Asst. J., postulated these rules of guidance:

'. . . And the principle to be followed in deciding whether any
particular document is an 'instrument' is . . . that only those
which actually are the very means by which a right or title to or
interest in land is conferred, transferred, limited, charged or
extinguished in favour of another party are within the ambit of
the Ordinance and have to be registered. If on the other hand the
right or title to or interest is not conferred, etc., by the document
but was conferred, etc., independently of the document by some
other act of the parties or by some other means and could exist
without the document, so that the document becomes only an
appendage, so to speak, to that other act or those other means, such
a document is not within the ambit of the Ordinance.' [1] As applied
to the documents tendered in evidence before him, the learned
Assistant Judge thought the documents were little more than
'glorified' receipts and records of what was agreed upon between
the parties to them; the so-called purchaser's interest in the
lands concerned was merely equitable and was acquired not

[1] (1939), 15 N. L. R. 57, at p. 59.

by means of these documents but by his payment of the agreed prices.

The principles above suggested would be called in aid only where the character of the document is so doubtful or obscure as to put it outside the recognised categories. Where, on the other hand, a document is fairly clear as to its form and purport, the only further point to decide is whether it has to do with land in the sense of the Land Registration Ordinance; if it satisfies that test then it must be registered; otherwise, not. Thus we see in *Balogun* v. *Balogun* [1] that certain Deeds of Partition relating to family land were duly registered in accordance with the Registration Ordinance of 1883 already considered, and was therefore received in evidence by the West African Court of Appeal in that case.

D. REGISTRATION OF TITLES TO LAND

The above analysis of the principles of registration of instruments affecting land shows that, while it ensures that the date and terms of every document affecting land are recorded in public registers, registration does not cure any defect in any instrument nor does it confer upon it any validity which it would not otherwise have had. Registration does not protect against any fraud or duress that might have been used in the execution of the document later registered, nor does it take account of those questionable transactions in land which are sometimes embodied in instruments never registered and never used in any litigation. In short, it is inadequate as a safe mode of recording land transactions.

On the other hand, a system of registration of titles to land involves (*a*) that the title of every landowner is thoroughly investigated once and for all and placed on the public register, a perusal of which will give an intending purchaser all the necessary information about previous dealings in the land; (*b*) that the registration of a landowner's title is an insurance against any adverse claims by others, and is indispensable to the validity of all transactions relating to the land in question; and (*c*) that instruments are registered, not merely as documents executed between parties, but by reference to the land itself. [2] These advantages first became available in Nigeria by the Registration of Titles Ordinance

---

[1] (1943), 9 W. A. C. A. 78.

[2] See J. E. Hogg, *Registration of Title to Land throughout the Empire* (1920).

No. 13 of 1935. When it is remembered that in England, registration of instruments is now confined to Yorkshire and Kingston-upon-Hull while under the Land Registration Act, 1925, the registration of titles to land is compulsory only in the Counties of London and of Middlesex and the County Boroughs of East-bourne, Hastings and Croydon (though a landowner in any part of England and Wales may ask for his land to be placed on the register),[1] this rather late arrival of the system in Nigeria should not cause any surprise.

Since the Registration of Titles Ordinance No. 13 of 1935 (with later amendments) runs into 101 sections it will be sufficient for our present purpose to give only a brief summary of the salient features which will enable us to understand the principles underlying the new system of registration of titles to land in Nigeria.

Land Registries. The Ordinance provides in s. 4 for the establishment of Land Registries for the registration of titles to land at such places as the Governor may direct. All registration districts will have a common seal which shall be judicially noticed. A Chief Registrar of Titles to have the control and supervision of all Land Registries may be appointed by the Governor; a Registrar of Titles, a Deputy Registrar and a number of Assistant Registrars will be appointed.

The Register. The Register kept at each Registry consists of three parts:

(A) The Property Register,
(B) The Proprietorship Register, and
(C) The Charges Register.

Now, neither s. 69 which lists these three Registers nor any other section of the Ordinance describes their several contents and we are left to glean from Form 16 of the First Schedule attached to the Ordinance the purport of each Register. The Property Register would seem to be designed for the recording of a fairly sufficient description of the land in relation to its locality in the registration district; the Proprietorship Register describes the name, occupation and address of the registered owner, the date of registration, a statement of the price paid for the land, as well as entries relating to Cautions and Restrictions (if any); the Charges Register contains such matters as restrictive covenants, purchaser's covenants and leases in connexion with the registered land, either existing at the date of the registration or created subsequently. These forms

[1] See Cheshire, *Mod. Real Property*, (5th edition) pp. 91-2; Hargreaves, *Introduction to Land Law*, pp. 166-70, 1944 edition.

may be modified by the Registrar to suit the special requirements of any particular case (s. 79 (1)).

Compulsory Cases for Registration. The following species of instruments granting or conveying the legal estate in the freehold or leasehold comprised in them, whether or not the freehold or the leasehold is subject to incumbrances, are declared void unless registered within two months after the date of the creation of a registration district for the area of their location or within a further period of not more than two months authorised by the Registrar or within any other period authorised by the Court:

(*a*) Every conveyance of a fee simple estate in any land for a consideration which consists wholly or in part of money, and

(*b*) every grant of a lease of any land for a term of not less than forty years, and

(*c*) every assignment of a lease of any land having not less than forty years to run from the date thereof for a consideration which consists wholly or in part of money.[1]

Optional Cases. An estate in fee simple or a lease for an unexpired term of not less than five years, whether subject to incumbrances or not, *may* be registered by anyone who has power to sell the fee simple or who is entitled to the fee simple or the lease. There is no time limit within which to make an application to the Registrar.[2]

Registration of Crown Grants and Leases of Crown Lands. The Commissioner of Lands must deliver in duplicate to the Registrar all grants and leases (for more than five years) of Crown lands that are made or granted after the constitution of the registration district in which the land is situated.[3]

Other Registrable Interests. The following categories of interests in and rights or titles to land are by various sections required to be registered:

(i) All estates having priority to that of the registered owner at date of first registration must be registered as incumbrances; as must also Cautions and Restrictions in favour of others having vital interests in the registered land.[4]

(ii) Leases for more than five years and sub-leases as well as charges and sub-charges created on registered lands must be registered as incumbrances thereon.[5]

(iii) Transfers of registered lands and registered charges and of portions thereof must be registered.[6]

---

[1] S. 5 (1).   [2] S. 6.   [3] S. 7.   [4] S. 12.
[5] Ss. 15 (2), 15 (3), 16, 18 (2) and 19.   [6] S. 28 (2) and (3).

(iv) Easements and *Profits a Prendre* as well as the burdens and benefits of restrictive covenants to which any registered freehold land may either on first registration or subsequently be subject, must be registered.[1] But such registration will not prevent the acquisition by prescription of any easement or profit *a prendre* or the extinction by non-user or abandonment of an easement, a profit *a prendre* or a restrictive covenant.[2]

(v) An unregistered estate, interest or claim which, in the opinion of the Registrar, cannot otherwise be adequately protected, may be registered as an incumbrance.[3]

Over-riding Interests. Certain interests in land which are for the time being subsisting in reference to any registered land will not be treated as incumbrances which must be registered under the Ordinance, but all registered land will be deemed to be subject to such interests. They are:

(*a*) Easements;

(*b*) Rights, privileges and appurtenances appertaining or reputed to appertain to any other land, demised, occupied or enjoyed with any other land, or reputed or known as part or parcel of or appurtenant to any other land;

(*c*) Rights of entry, search and user and other rights and reservations incidental to or required for the purpose of giving full effect to the enjoyment of rights to mines, minerals and mineral oils;

(*d*) Leases or agreements for leases for any term less than five years where there is actual occupation under the lease or agreement;

(*e*) Any public highway;

(*f*) Any tax or rate for the time being declared by law to be a charge on land or houses;

(*g*) Rights acquired or in process of being acquired under the Limitation Acts; and

(*h*) The rights of every person in possession or actual occupation of the land to which he may be entitled in right of such possession or occupation, save where equity is made of such person and the rights are not disclosed.[4]

Who may be registered. Having noted the various interests that must or may or may not be registered, we may now consider who may be registered. Naturally, anyone claiming a legal estate in freehold land or in a lease may apply to be registered as such owner; from which it follows that anyone having only an equitable interest in land will not be so registered, although entries regarding

[1] Ss. 39 and 41.   [2] S. 40.   [3] S. 47.   [4] S. 52.

his interests may, as will be indicated, be made along with the registration of the holder of the legal estate. The nominee of an applicant, who is proved to the satisfaction of the Registrar as not thereby intending to evade or defraud his creditors, may be registered instead of the applicant for first registration, such an application being duly stamped as on a conveyance on sale or transfer to such nominee.[1] Also, trustees of settled land or lease under the Settled Land Acts (1882–1889) are entitled to be registered as legal owners of such land or lease, with the consent of the tenant for life in case of first registration.[2] Joint tenants and tenants in common (with their respective shares in the land specified in the Register) may be registered as owners of any registered land or charge. An undivided share in land may, if the Registrar thinks fit, be registered under a separate title.[3] The death of an applicant or an intervening change of his interest in the land does not affect his application for a first registration which may be completed by any person entitled so to apply.[4]

Transmission by Death. If one of two or more joint registered owners of any land or charge dies, his name will be deleted from the Register. If a sole registered owner or the survivor of joint registered owners dies, being beneficially entitled, his personal legal representative may be registered as owner, or a purchaser from such legal personal representative or a person entitled under the deceased's will or on his intestacy may be registered without the previous registration of such legal personal representative. If such a deceased registered owner is not beneficially entitled, his legal personal representative may be registered with necessary restrictions and safeguards. Any change of ownership by operation of law, such as when the registered owner is superseded by a trustee appointed under s. 12 of the (Imperial) Trustee Act, 1893, or someone having an estate superior to that of the registered owner or someone appointed under a Court order or the like, enables any of these persons to apply to be registered as owner of the registered land or charge.[5]

Land subject to Customary Tenure. Any application for first registration of any land which is claimed and proved to be family land under local customary law or, although not family land, is nevertheless subject to some form of customary tenure which confers any rights or interests in the land on others apart from the applicant, may be dismissed by the Registrar; or, the Registrar may register the applicant as owner of the land or the lease accom-

[1] S. 11.   [2] S. 75.   [3] S. 76.   [4] S. 13 (2).   [5] Ss. 37 and 38.

panied by such necessary Cautions, Restrictions, notices, notes or entries as might be agreed by the parties interested in the land or the lease, or as the Registrar might direct. Such registration shall not be open to any later objection on the part of anybody.[1]

Procedure on Application for Registration. Application to be registered as an owner is made to the Registrar who investigates the title to the land or lease in the manner prescribed by the Ordinance. Every application for first registration is advertised by the Registrar at least once in the Gazette and in one or more newspapers circulating in Nigeria. The Registrar also serves notice of such application upon any occupier of the land and upon all adjoining land-owners. Until an objector, who has given due notice of his objection, has been given an opportunity of being heard,[2] no registration will be effected by the Registrar.[3]

Nature of Evidence required. In carrying out his investigation of a title with a view to first registration, the Registrar may accept and act on less than legal evidence or less than the evidence ordinarily required by conveyancers and may even act on evidence of the same facts adduced before him in other proceedings, so long as the Registrar is satisfied of the truth of the facts to be proved. The Regristrar then registers a satisfactory applicant or some other consenting party who appears by the investigation to be entitled to be registered as owner of any land or lease, and he dismisses an unsatisfactory applicant.[4]

Documents intended for registration which are expressed to be made or to operate as a deed will be treated as such without the necessity for sealing.[5] The Registrar may ask for an instrument to be delivered in duplicate or as an original and copy, in which latter case the original will be returned after registration to the person appearing to have the best right to its custody.[6] All unwanted documents are after registration returned to persons who produced them or to their successors in title and, should such persons decline to accept them, the Registrar may order their destruction.[7] The Registrar may retain such documents of title as he considers necessary to show the nature of the applicant's title, except that he cannot retain any documents relating to any other unregistered land or lease or those in the custody of any person having a prior right to that of the applicant, unless these people so agree.[8]

[1] S. 10.
[2] For the Ordinance meaning of 'opportunity of being heard', see ss. 87 and 88. [3] S. 8 (1)–(4). [4] S. 9. [5] S. 80 (1).
[6] S. 81. [7] S. 82 (1). [8] S. 14 (3).

Proof of Documents. Every document for registration must be duly stamped.[1] The Registrar can demand that any instrument for registration under this Ordinance, and the power of attorney by which an instrument is executed, be proved as required in cases of compulsory registration under the Land Registration Ordinance No. 36 of 1924, and may also require the production and a copy of the power of attorney.[2]

Production of Documents and Attendance. Documents relevant to a proposed registration which are in the possession or custody of an applicant, of an objecting party or of any trustee for either party as well as documents in the possession or custody of third parties may be ordered by the Registrar to be produced in evidence before him; the Registrar can also compel the attendance of witnesses and the production by them of any relevant documents.[3]

Statutory Declarations. Before completing a first registration, the Registrar may call upon the applicant and any other person appearing to have knowledge of relevant facts to make a Statutory Declaration that all incumbrances and material facts have been disclosed.[4] Such a declaration is exempt from stamp duty.[5]

The Land must be surveyed. Every freehold land and every lease having more than *twenty* years to run will only be registered if previously surveyed to the satisfaction of the Registrar or of the Surveyor-General. This requirement may be waived in exceptional cases where the land or the lease is otherwise adequately identified and located; but a survey may be demanded at any time later.[6]

Issue of Certificate. After all the formalities of registration have been complied with to the satisfaction of the Registrar, he will issue to the registered owner of any land or charge a Certificate of Title showing all subsisting entries in the Register affecting that land or charge. The Certificate of Title is *prima facie* evidence of the several matters therein contained.[7]

Estates conferred by Registration. The nature and extent of the interest acquired by the registration of the titles of the following four classes of owners may be thus summarised:

(a) *A registered freeholder* has vested in him an estate in fee simple in the land together with all the buildings, erections, fixtures, easements, privileges, etc., appertaining thereto, and free from all estates whatsoever including those of His Majesty; pro-

[1] S. 92. [2] Ss. 83 and 84. [3] Ss. 89 and 90.
[4] Ss. 13 (1) and 91 (1). [5] S. 91 (2). [6] S. 65 (1) and (2).
[7] S. 55 (1) and (4); cf. s. 93 as to proof of abstracts from the Register and proof of acts of the Registrar.

vided that such an estate does not include any right to minerals or mineral oils under either the Minerals Ordinance or the Mineral Oils Ordinance.[1]

(b) *A registered lessee* has vested in him the possession of the land comprised in the lease for the unexpired residue of the term created by the lease, with all implied or expressed rights, privileges and appurtenances attached to the estate of the lessee, and free from all the estates whatsoever, including those of His Majesty.[2]

This plenitude of estate thus acquired by a registered owner of land is, however, subject to:

(a) any registered charges or incumbrances;

(b) any estates declared by this Ordinance not to be incumbrances;

(c) any unregistered estates created by himself or arising by reason of his fiduciary relation to any person or protected by a Caution or Restriction or other notice, note or entry.[3]

It is further provided as follows:

S. 48 (3): The estate of the first registered owner of land is subject to any estate adverse to or in derogation of his title and subsisting or capable of arising at the time of first registration.

(4): The estate of every subsequent registered owner of land, not being a purchaser for value, is subject to any unregistered estate affecting the estate of any previous registered owner through whom he derives title, back to and including the last preceding purchaser for value.

S. 49 (1): The estate of every registered owner of a lease is subject to all implied or expressed covenants, obligations, and liabilities incident to the ownership of the lease, and to any right of re-entry or forfeiture.

Any estate paramount to or in derogation of the title of the lessor to grant a lease is not affected by the registration of the lessee as owner of the lease unless the lessor also inserts, with the Registrar's approval, a declaration in the Register that lessor had a right to grant the lease.[4]

(c) *A registered Crown grantee's* estate is subject to all exceptions, reservations, covenants and conditions contained in or implied by the grant or conferred by any relevant law or Ordinance.[5]

(d) *A registered chargee* has vested in him the rights, powers and remedies conferred by the charge and the right to recover and

---

[1] S. 48 (1) (a).   [2] S. 48 (1) (b).   [3] S. 48 (2).
[4] S. 49 (2).   [5] S. 50.

receive the money secured thereby, free from all estates whatsoever, including those of His Majesty.

But such an estate is subject to:

(i) any registered charges or incumbrances having priority to his charge;

(ii) any estates declared by this Ordinance not to be incumbrances;

(iii) any unregistered estates created by himself or arising by reason of his fiduciary relation to any person or protected by a caution or restriction or other notice, note or entry.[1]

It is further provided that:

The estate of the first registered owner of a charge created otherwise than for value, or of any registered owner of a charge acquired otherwise than for value, whether originally created for value or not, is subject to any unregistered estate affecting the estate of any person through whom he derives title, back to and including the last preceding purchaser for value.[2]

Foreshore not included. On the whole it should be noted that, unless the contrary is expressly stated in the Register, no title granted to a registered owner will include any part of a foreshore, i.e. any land below high-water mark at ordinary spring tides of the sea or a tidal river.[3]

Boundaries not conclusive. The description and plan of registered land, even if duly surveyed, are not conclusive as to the boundaries or extent of such land. The Registrar may at any time summon all interested parties with a view to determining the exact line of any boundary, and thereafter the Register will be suitably rectified and the registered description and plan will then be deemed to be an accurate definition of such boundaries.[4]

Priority of Charges. All registered charges rank, as between themselves, according to the order of their registration and not according to the order of their creation.[5]

Dealings with Registered Land off the Register. Anyone, whether or not a registered owner, may create any interests or rights therein or otherwise dispose of any registered land as if the same were unregistered. But these permitted, though unregistered, dealings with registered land must not fall within the category of cases otherwise expressly required by the Ordinance to be registered, or they would be void for non-compliance.[6] In any case, such dealings can

---

[1] S. 51 (1) and (2).   [2] S. 51 (3).
[3] S. 67.   [4] S. 66.
[5] S. 25.   [6] S. 42.

always be over-ridden by all registered dispositions for valuable consideration.

How Unregistered Estates are protected. We have seen [1] that on an application for first registration anyone, claiming that the land being proposed for registration is family land or is otherwise subject to customary tenure which gives such a one an interest or right in the land, may oppose such an application. On payment of the prescribed fee such an objection, if successful, will be regarded as a Caution within the meaning of s. 43 of the Ordinance, which anyone is authorised by that section to lodge with the Registrar against the first registration of land or lease without notice to the cautioner. The effect of the lodgment of a Caution is to suspend registration of the land until the cautioner has been given an opportunity of being heard. If necessary, both the cautioner's estate as well as the applicant's may be registered, or the latter's estate may be postponed or refused unless he gives satisfactory security for the indemnification of any person likely to be prejudiced thereby. But a Caution will not be entered on a Certificate of Title unless with the consent of the registered owner or an order of the Registrar. [2]

Restrictions. Similarly, anyone claiming an unregistered estate or interest, whether created before or after first registration, may request the Registrar to register a Restriction which has the effect of prohibiting the registration of any disposition or change or ownership affecting the land or charge unless such of the following things as are specified in the Restriction are done or happen:

(*a*) Unless notice of the proposed registration be served on a named person;

(*b*) Unless the consent of a named person be given to the proposed registration;

(*c*) Unless such other thing be done, condition fulfilled, or event happen as may, with the consent of the Registrar, be specified in the Restriction.

But, unlike Cautions, Restrictions may be entered in any Certificate of Title thereby affected. Registration is suspended until the requirements of the Restriction have been fulfilled or until the Registrar otherwise orders. [3]

The Registrar will in every case verify the existence or non-existence of any unregistered estate, interest or claim sought to be protected by a Caution or Restriction or other notice, note or entry; and anyone injured as a result of the lodgement or registra-

[1] At p. 278, earlier.   [2] Ss. 43 and 44.   [3] S. 45.

tion of a groundless Caution or Restriction may recover proper compensation from the person who lodged it or requested it to be registered.[1]

Rectification of the Register. With the consent of all necessary parties, the Registrar may alter the terms of a registered lease, charge or other document as well as the Register itself.[2] Errors or omissions in the Register may also be similarly corrected.[3] Compensation for such correction may be ordered against the party at fault.[4] The Registrar and his staff are indemnified against liability for error or omission.[5] The Register may also be rectified in any of the following events:

(*a*) Where a Court of competent jurisdiction makes an order that a rectification of the Register is required so as to give effect to its judgment that any person is entitled to any estate right or interest in or to any registered land or charge;

(*b*) Where, on an application by an aggrieved party that some entry is made in or omitted from the Register or that some other irregularity exists in the making of any entry in the Register, a Court of competent jurisdiction orders a rectification of the Register;

(*c*) Whenever the Registrar directs a rectification with the consent of all interested parties;

(*d*) Where the Court or the Registrar is satisfied that any entry in the Register has been obtained by fraud;

(*e*) Where two or more persons are, by mistake, registered as owners of the same registered estate or of the same charge;

(*f*) In any other case where, by reason of any error or omission in the Register, or by reason of any entry made under a mistake, it may be deemed just to rectify the Register.

(*g*) Where it is shown to the satisfaction of the Court that the title of the registered owner of any land or charge has been extinguished under the Real Property Limitation Acts (1833, 1837 and 1874) and the Court orders the Register to be rectified accordingly. In such a case the person prejudiced by such rectification will not be entitled to any compensation.

Except for the purpose of giving effect to an over-riding interest, the Register will not be rectified so as to affect the title of the owner in possession, unless such owner is in any way to blame or derives his title from or through a void disposition or for some other sufficient cause.[6]

---

[1] S. 46. [2] S. 59. [3] S. 60.
[4] S. 63. [5] S. 64. [6] Ss. 61 and 62.

Searches. Any registered owner of land or charge or his duly authorised agent, or anyone duly authorised by a Court order or by a general rule of law, *but no-one else*, may inspect and make copies of and extracts from any Register or document in the custody of the Registrar relating to such land or charge.[1]

If we compare this provision of the present Ordinance with that of s. 22 of the Land Registration Ordinance No. 36 of 1924, it would appear that, while the members of the public enjoy a general right of search in the books kept under the 1924 Ordinance, searches under the 1935 Ordinance are limited to a certain class of persons—that is, there is no general public right of search in the Register kept under the Registration of Titles Ordinance (1935).

Purchase of Registered Land. The evidence of title that a purchaser is entitled to demand from a vendor of registered land is by s. 31 limited to the following:

(*a*) The evidence to be obtained from an inspection of the Register or of a certified copy of, or extract from the Register;

(*b*) A statutory declaration as to the existence or otherwise of estates declared by this Ordinance not to be incumbrances;

(*c*) Evidence of the title to or discharge of any registered incumbrances or estates registered as incumbrances.

Purchaser not affected by Unregistered Estates. On the acceptance of such a title by a purchaser for value, his name will on his application be registered as owner, and he will not be affected with notice, actual or constructive, of any *unregistered* estate, interest or claim which may affect the estate of his vendor as the previous registered owner; nor will such a purchaser be concerned to enquire whether the terms of any Caution or Restriction, anterior in time to the date of his own registration as owner, have been complied with.[2]

Forged and Void Dispositions. No one, whose registration as owner of registered land, lease or charge, is based upon or derived from or through a forged disposition or a disposition which without registration would be void, acquires any estate in such land, lease or charge. But if his claim, being *bona fide*, is prejudiced in consequence of any rectification of the Register, he will be entitled to recover compensation from the Government of Nigeria. However, a purchaser for value or anyone deriving title under or through him will acquire a good title if he acquires his estate as a subsequent registered owner.[3]

[1] S. 74 (2).   [2] S. 54.   [3] S. 53.

EXEMPTION OF REGISTERED LAND FROM LAND REGISTRATION ORDINANCE (1924)

In view of the importance of this topic we reproduce as follows the governing provisions of s. 85 of the Registration of Titles Ordinance (No. 13 of 1935):

(1) No document affecting registered land executed after first registration shall require to be registered under the Land Registration Ordinance, 1924, and no registered owner, being a purchaser for value subsequent to first registration, shall be affected by notice of any document registered under such Ordinance.

(2) This section shall not apply to a document affecting a mortgage created before the first registration or to a document affecting an estate registered as an incumbrance in priority to the estate of the first registered owner.

(3) This section shall not affect any obligation to register under the Land Registration Ordinance, 1924, any document affecting other land as well as registered land.

This means (a) that any document relating to registered land which has been executed after a first registration will require to be registered as an instrument within the meaning of the Land Registration Ordinance (1924): (b) that any document registered under the 1924 Ordinance will not constitute notice to a purchaser for value of registered land after a first registration under the 1935 Ordinance; (c) that any document relating to a mortgage created before a first registration under the 1935 Ordinance and any document relating to an estate registered as an incumbrance in priority to a first registered owner's estate under the 1935 Ordinance, may both be registered as instruments under the 1924 Ordinance; (d) that, where a piece of land comprises of registered land within the 1935 Ordinance as well as of other land which is registrable within the 1924 Ordinance, the document affecting such a composite title will be registered in conformity with the Land Registration Ordinance No. 36 of 1924. It is hoped that the whole point will become clearer when we later discuss its judicial consideration in one case.[1]

Appeals from the Registrar. Provisions are made for appeals from decisions or orders of the Registrar, on any issue relating to registration of titles to land, by any person aggrieved by any decision or order, notice of appeal being given to the Registrar within

---

[1] See p. 287, *infra*.

one month of the decision or order appealed from. All parties, including the Registrar, may appear in Court personally or by a legal practitioner.[1] Every person aggrieved by an order of the Court may appeal to the West African Court of Appeal within such time and in such manner as may be regulated by Rules of Court. This right of further appeal to the West African Court of Appeal has been provided for by the amending Ordinance No. 46 of 1943.

Where an appeal to the Court is pending, any dealing for value which has been registered before the Registrar receives notice of the appeal will be valid. A note that an appeal is pending will be registered against the entry in the Register affected by the appeal. The position is the same with dealings occurring between an order of the Court and a further appeal to the West African Court of Appeal.[2]

There is also a provision that the Registrar has power to refer summarily questions of doubt or difficulty, whether of law or of fact, to the Court for determination or guidance, and such reference by the Registrar will be treated as an appeal to the Court.[3]

Illustrative Cases: The principles of the Registration of Titles Ordinance (No. 13 of 1935) with its later amendments have been judically applied or commented upon in many cases, a few of which need be considered here. On account of the importance of appreciating as clearly as possible the relation between the Land Registration Ordinance of 1924 and the present Registration of Titles Ordinance of 1935, we will first briefly note the comment made by Carey, J., on s. 85 of the latter Ordinance in *Zard* v. *Diamandis*,[4] the facts of which have already been given in dealing with the Land Registration Ordinance (1924). The main point in the facts which concerns us here is *whether* the appellant's application under s. 8 of the Registration of Titles Ordinance (1924) for first registration of his freehold title as free from incumbrances was rightly refused by the Registrar of Titles on the ground that the conveyance upon which appellant based his fee simple title had not been registered under the Land Registration Ordinance (1924); *or*, as the appellant contended, his case came within the exemption from registration under the 1924 Ordinance as provided by s. 85 (1) of the Registration of Titles Ordinance 1935. Carey, J., held, on appeal under s. 97 from the Registrar's decision to refuse

[1] S. 97.   [2] S. 98 (as amended by No. 46 of 1943).
[3] S. 99.   [4] (1936), 13 N. L. R. 114.

the appellant's application, that the non-registration under the Land Registration Ordinance of 1924 of the conveyance upon which the appellant founded his title justified the conclusion previously reached by the Registrar, since the exemption provided by s. 85 (1) of the Registration of Titles Ordinance applies only to documents 'affecting registered land executed *after* first registration'. The appellant was just applying for first registration and the conveyance had been executed *before* his application.

(A) In *Dania* v. *Soyenu*,[1] a case twice reported in different connexions, there was an application by the plaintiff for first registration under s. 8 (1) of the Registration of Titles Ordinance. The Registrar then under s. 8 (2) advertised in the Gazette and a newspaper dated 25 and 27 August 1936, respectively, the following notification as provided in the First Schedule to the Ordinance: 'Any person may by notice in writing signed by himself or his agent and delivered at the Registry within two months from the date of the paper containing the advertisement object to the registration.' The defendant's notice of objection, which was lodged out of time on 5 November 1936, was nevertheless accepted by the Registrar as a ground for his refusal of the plaintiff's application. The plaintiff appealed to the Divisional Court under s. 97 of the Ordinance, contending that the objection being out of time should not at all have been considered by the Registrar, though the plaintiff had never raised the point before the Registrar. When the appeal reached the Divisional Court, Butler Lloyd, J., ordered it to be converted into a suit and later held that the Court should not refuse to consider an objection which the Registrar himself thought fit to hear and to which no objection was taken before him. The learned Judge, in thus upholding the Registrar's exercise of his discretion, also drew attention to s. 79 of the Registration of Titles Ordinance which gives the Registrar power to vary the wording or form of a Schedule to the Ordinance.

(B) In the second report [2] of the case under the same name and between the same parties, the plaintiff applied for first registration but the defendant objected under s. 10 of the Ordinance that the plaintiff and his predecessors in title were not absolute owners of the land which they held of the reversionary owners (the defendant and his predecessors in title) under local customary tenure. The plaintiff's application for registration was accordingly refused by the Registrar and the plaintiff's appeal was converted into a suit in the Divisional Court. The big issue in the case was whether the

[1] (1937), 13 N. L. R. 129.   [2] (1937), 13 N. L. R. 143.

proved original reversionary ownership of the defendant's pre-decessors had been extinguished by acquiescence on their part. Adopting a distinction which the West African Court of Appeal had made in *Oshodi* v. *Imoru & ors.* (suit 55/1934), Butler Lloyd, J., held in the Divisional Court (1) that a higher degree of acquiescence was required to extinguish the original owner's reversionary right in favour of the occupier than was required to bar the original owner from ejecting the occupier (as was the position in the leading case of *Akpan Awo* v. *Cookey Gam.* 2 N. L. R. 100); (2) that this higher degree of acquiescence had not been established in the present case; and (3) that the application for registration must therefore be refused. The question of acquisition of ownership by prescription under the local customary law will be briefly examined in a final section on Proof of Title. An ancillary point that arose out of this and the previous cases was whether the conversion of the appeals under s. 97 of Ordinance No. 13 of 1935 into suits had the effect of rendering the point in dispute open to further appeals by the parties, although under the section no further appeal would have lain. That that was the short result of his orders was clear from Butler Lloyd's 'peccavi' delivered at the end of his judgment in the second case.[1] But this remorse would not be necessary since the enactment (in Ordinance No. 46 of 1943) of the enabling amendments to ss. 97 and 98 of the Ordinance, providing for a further right of appeal to the West African Court of Appeal, which we have mentioned already.

We saw in *Zard* v. *Diamandis* [2] that the Registrar was there held within his rights to refuse to register an applicant whose title was based on a conveyance which had not been duly registered under the Land Registration Ordinance, 1924. In very similar circumstances in *George* v. *Pratt*,[3] however, a contrary conclusion was reached by the Registrar who was upheld by the Divisional Court. The plaintiff's application was refused by the Registrar after the defendant had opposed it. The plaintiff appealed to the Divisional Court which converted the appeal into a suit. Certain conveyances founded upon by the plaintiff were not registered and in the Divisional Court objection was taken to the admission of these conveyances in evidence. It was held by Butler Lloyd, acting C.J., that, under s. 9 (1) of the Registration of Titles Ordinance, 1935, the Registrar could accept and act on the unregistered conveyances and that, on appeal, the Appeal Court could also do so: 'By s. 9 (1)

---

[1] (1937), 13 N. L. R. 143, at p. 145.   [2] See p. 287, earlier.
[3] (1937), 13 N. L. R. 133.

of the Ordinance the Registrar may accept and act on less than legal evidence and it would to my mind be an absurdity if this Court in hearing an appeal from him were to be barred by a technicality from taking cognisance of documents which were properly admitted by him.' It looks at first as if the fortunes of an application for registration vary with the state of the Registrar's digestion. But the Court's supervision of the exercise of his discretion is some check against arbitrariness and makes one less cynical about the charter of immunity granted him by s. 9 of the Ordinance.

Another aspect of the 1935 Ordinance was in issue in *Animashawun* v. *Mumuni & ors.*[1] where the plaintiff was, under a conveyance dated 27 February 1940, the purchaser of certain premises in Lagos and succeeded in getting his title registered against an objection by the first defendant and two others who all claimed in the same right. There was no appeal from the Registrar in this case. The plaintiff subsequently brought an action for recovery of possession of a portion which remained in the defendants' occupation and for £3 5s. 0d. for the use and occupation of that portion. Butler Lloyd, J., in the Supreme Court, held that the plaintiff claims succeeded, and said: 'If this litigation has served no other purpose it at least gives me the opportunity of pointing out that the registration of a title under the Registration of Titles Ordinance, 1935, affords no protection whatever to the first registered owner, not even against an unsuccessful objector to the registration, even apparently if that objector has appealed unsuccessfully to the Supreme Court.'

Effect of Registration on Title. Now, this is a very serious judicial reflection on the real effect of registration of land titles under the Registration of Titles Ordinance No. 13 of 1935 and lends colour to the view that no more than a *possessory title* is conferred upon a registered owner under the Ordinance. The overcautious vagueness of certain sections—e.g. 10 (2), 42 (1), 43 (2) and (3), 48 (2) (3) and (4)—as well as the whole mechanism of registration and of protection of unregistered dealings, even in registered land, only leaves one with such an impression. It is probably an inevitable feature of a compromise system of registration of titles in a community still largely dominated by a land tenure in which land rights are collectively held and such individual titles as have emerged are often subject to the vagaries and, no doubt, some virtues of group ownership. If the rights, so frequently

[1] (1941), 16 N. L. R. 59.

undifferentiated, of people other than the usually sophisticated applicants for registration are to be safe-guarded, some such wary steps must be taken during the present period of transition from group to individual ownership of land.

Let us take an important point in the *Mumuni Case* which Butler Lloyd, J., also stressed. He declared that the defendants' claim to the ownership of the land, which was their unsuccessful ground of objection to the plaintiff's application for registration, failed because the plaintiff's vendors had acted as owners of the property for many years: e.g. (1) they had for years collected rents and paid rates on the property; (2) they had had it surveyed in 1912; (3) one of the vendors had in 1923 successfully sued one Sori for possession of a part of the premises—and all these things had been done without a word of protest or any form of intervention on the defendants' part until this case came up. In other words, the defendants' claim of ownership of the land failed on the ground of their laches and acquiescence. This brings us to the larger problem of the nature and extent of acquisition of land by prescription under local law and custom, and the amount and scope of the evidence necessary to ground a title which the Registrar or the Court will recognise as sufficient for registration under the Ordinance.

E. PROOF OF TITLE TO LAND

In seeking to establish title to land in Nigeria, it often happens that the plaintiff has to rely on long occupation and user of the land being claimed. Such right of occupancy may have been granted to the plaintiff or plaintiff's predecessors in title under the customary law of tenure by the defendant or defendant's predecessors in title. The plaintiff later alleges that the land in question was originally acquired by him or by his predecessors from the grantor as a gift or under a sale. Where neither allegation is feasible, he confines him simply to acquisition by prescription on the ground of laches and acquiescence on the part of the grantor or his successors. While it is quite clear that land granted merely for stranger's occupation and user under customary law can never be prescribed by the grantee against the reversionary grantor and that no period of limitation operates under local law and custom to bar the grantor's right to the reversion of the land if any of the conditions of customary occupancy are ever broken. It is not true, however, to say, as is sometimes said in some quarters, that there is no form of time limit in customary law outside which land rights may be lost. Abandonment, or an unreasonably long absence, non-user and ineffectual occupation and user are, as we have seen, some of the ways in which rights to land may be lost. As regards grants of group land to stranger-occupiers, however, it is difficult to imagine a circumstance in which the grantor's reversion is lost to the grantee merely on the ground of the latter's long possession and user.

In the leading case of *Akpan Awo* v. *Cookey Gam* [1] there was uncontradicted evidence that the defendants had been in undisturbed possession of the land they were claiming with the plaintiff's full knowledge and acquiescence for a period of not less than twenty-one years and this, despite the fact that as far back as 1894 the defendants dealt with the land by permitting a European firm to erect thereon a factory. It was the erection of this factory that stirred the plaintiffs into the present action in which they for the first time claimed ownership of the land. On an appeal from a Divisional Court of the Eastern Province to the Supreme Court, Webber, J., held: [2] 'In our opinion it would be wholly inequitable to deprive the defendants of property of which they have held undisturbed possession and in respect of which they have collected rents for so long a term of years with the knowledge and acquiescence of those who now dispute their title, even if it were as clear as it is upon the evidence doubtful that they entered into possession, contrary to the principles of native law. We do not decide this point in accordance with any provision of English law as to the limitation of actions, but simply on the grounds of equity, on the ground that the Court will not allow a party to call in aid principles of native law, and least of all principles, which, as in this case, were developed in and are applicable to a state of society vastly different from that now existing, merely for the purpose of bolstering up a stale claim.' The plaintiffs' appeal for a declaration that they were the owners of the land therefore failed.

But in *Tobias Epelle* v. *Ojo* [3] where the plaintiff sought a declaration of title to land in Aba district, basing his claim on an alleged sale to him of the land in question some twenty years previously, the defendants contended that there had never been any sale of the land but only a grant to plaintiff in perpetuity subject to all the incidents of the local customary tenure. The plaintiff prayed in aid *Akpan Awo* v. *Cookey Gam* which Webber, J., in the Divisional Court at Calabar, distinguished from the present case for the

---

[1] (1913), 2 N. L. R. 97.   [2] Ibid., at p. 98.
[3] (1926), 7 N. L. R. 96.

reason that the plaintiffs in that case had suffered the defendants there to do some overt act in exercise of ownership without objecting until years later, whereas in the case before him, the very first pretension to ownership on the defendant's part brought the plaintiff quickly to his feet and led to the present action. Webber, J., therefore warned that the principle of the *Cookey Gam Case* was not to be indifferently applied and that where there had been no laches or acquiescence, either express or implied, by the grantor in the stranger-occupier's assumption of full ownership, the defendant's long occupation and user did not help him.

The Real Property Statutes of Limitation, being statutes 'of general application', apply to Nigeria so as to engender a right to land by prescription in proper cases. Thus, in *Green* v. *Owo*,[1] a certain piece of land bought by the plaintiff in 1932 was included in a conveyance made in English form and, in the event that happened, the defendants had come to be in occupation for more than the statutory period of limitation. It was held that, in the absence of proof of any local law to the contrary, the situation was governed by the Real Property Statutes of Limitation and that the defendants were entitled to remain in possession.

Rules for Proving Titles. The next question for us to examine is: What must a plaintiff prove in order to obtain from the Court a declaration of title? Kingdon, C.J., in his dissenting opinion in the Supreme Court decision in *Balogun* v. *Oshodi*[2] gave the following answer:

(1) 'They (the plaintiffs) must not only show that the respondent is estopped from contesting their claim but must satisfy the Court that they are entitled to the declaration for which they ask. They must show not only that they are the persons entitled to occupy the land, but also that they hold it upon a fee simple tenure.'

(2) In *Ekpo* v. *Ita*[3] Webber, J's., ruling was: 'In a claim for a decree of declaration of title, the onus is on the plaintiff to prove acts of ownership extending over a sufficient length of time, numerous and positive enough to warrant the inference that the plaintiffs were exclusive owners—if the evidence of tradition is inconclusive the case must rest on question of fact. *It is different in a claim for the recovery of possession of land where the issue between the parties is which of them can prove a better title.*'

---

[1] (1936), 13 N. L. R. 43; also *Morayo* v. *Okiade & ors.* (1940), 15 N. L. R. 131; (1940), 6 W. A. C. A. 67.

[2] (1931), 10 N. L. R. 36, at p. 55.

[3] (1932), 11 N. L. R. 68, at p. 69. (The italics in the passage are by the writer).

(3) To these two judicial pronouncements we may add a third by Berkeley, J., in *Orku Sowa & anor.* v. *Chief Amachree*: [1] 'It is impossible to make a declaration of title without a plan to which such a declaration can be tied.'

(4) Yet a fourth point was made by Webber in the West African Court of Appeal in *Baruwa* v. *Ogunshola* [2] when he said: 'Now it is the first duty of a plaintiff who comes to Court to claim a declaration of title to show the Court clearly the area of land to which his claim relates.'

(5) That the description of the land as to area and extent must agree with the plan submitted in evidence was the fifth and final point which we may deduce from Francis's J., dictum in *Alade* v. *Dina*: [3] 'Now assuming for a moment that the plaintiff has succeeded in proving "acts of ownership extending over a sufficient length of time numerous and positive enough to warrant the inference that he is the exclusive owner" . . . of land at Onikankan to what precise area and which plan could a declaration be tied?' In the case itself the plaintiff sought against the defendant a declaration of title to land at Ijebu Ode Province. The evidence as to the extent of the area did not agree with the plan first submitted. A second plan shows an area more than twice that of the first plan, and the evidence of the plaintiff and of his witnesses could not be reconciled with this second plan. Francis, J., held that the plaintiff's claim for a declaration of title accordingly failed for variance between the plans and the area claimed and for uncertainty as to the boundaries of the land in dispute between plaintiff and defendant.

Disputes about Inter-tribal Boundaries. Disputes as to the boundaries of the lands of two contiguous tribes sometimes arise as in the case of two adjacent individual owners, and the problems for solution are as intriguing in the one case as in the other. But whereas those between two individuals are more readily susceptible of solution by the Courts, those between communities are often better solved on the administrative level. To this end, the *Inter-Tribal Boundaries Settlement Ordinance* No. 49 of 1933 (as amended by No. 38 of 1938), which applies only to the Protectorate

---

[1] (1933), 11 N. L. R. 82, at p. 85.

[2] (1938), 4 W. A. C. A. 159.

[3] (1943), 17 N. L. R. 32; also *Rufai* v. *Ricketts & ors.* (1934), 2 W. A. C. A. 95; *Okoye* v. *Ojiefo* (1934), 2 W. A. C. A. 130; *Kodilinye* v. *Mbanefo Odu* (1935), 2 W. A. C. A. 336; *Ita* v. *Asido* (1935), 2 W. A. C. A. 339; *Udofia & anor.* v. *Afia & ors.* (1940), 6 W. A. C. A. 216.

of Nigeria (including the Cameroons) but not to the Colony, provides that any District Officer may with the approval of the Resident in charge of the Province investigate and decide any dispute as to the boundaries between the lands of two or more tribes. In carrying out his duties, such an Officer has power to summon assessors whose opinion must be recorded. The Resident can review any decision of a District Officer, and the Governor can review the Resident's decisions. S. 8 of the Ordinance expressly requires that any settlement of such boundaries should be duly registered and preserved by the Resident in charge of the Province.

In *Ovat Ebenyam* v. *Chief Ayigo*,[1] the plaintiff representing the people of Osobong and the defendant representing the people of Ikwo held adjoining lands. In 1920, the parties mutually agreed to a boundary which was demarcated and beaconed, except as to a portion called Oboma forest—a stretch of some three miles—which was unexplored forest and swamp and which could not therefore be conveniently beaconed. It was never decided whether the boundary was to pass through this unbeaconed portion, or along the plaintiff's or along the defendant's side. Later, disputes arose between the parties and the plaintiff sued for a declaration of title to what he considered to be his people's. But he could not establish that there ever was any boundary in existence in the portion claimed. Pearson, Asst. J., held in the High Court at Enugu that the plaintiff, having failed to prove an existing boundary to the portion he was claiming and since the Court had no power to demarcate a boundary for the parties, the plaintiff must be non-suited. Pearson, Asst. J., concluded: [2] 'Failing to find an existing boundary, this Court has no power to demarcate; no power to partition land. Such partition is essentially an executive act; e.g. by commissioners under the Inclosure Acts, 1845–1878; or under Inter-Tribal Boundaries Settlement Ordinance No. 49 of 1933. . . . Manifestly this matter can only be settled by demarcation by an Administrative Officer, by consent as in 1920, or under the Inter-Tribal Boundaries Settlement Ordinance.'

[1] (1941), 16 N. L. R. 30; see also: *Nnaji Nwa-Ogaba* v. *Okenwaeji* (1944), 17 N. L. R. 117 (a case of boundary dispute between two Onitsha villages).
[2] Ibid., at p. 31.

Chapter Twelve

CONCLUSION

FAMILY or Group Ownership of Land still Prevalent. It is obvious from our consideration of the problems of land registration in the previous chapter that, in the present state of land rights in Nigeria, there can be no question of a supersession of the system of registration of deeds affecting land by that of registration of titles to land. The whole law and custom of tenure in the country remain subject to the institution of group or family ownership of land which, although slowly breaking up in sophisticated and urban areas due to the various influences already mentioned, impedes the emergence of absolute individual titles in any very large number even in the Colony area. Thus observed Butler Lloyd, J., in the Supreme Court case of *Bajulaiye & anor.* v. *Akapo:* [1] 'Now with all due respect to the opinion expressed by Speed, acting C.J., in the case of *Lewis* v. *Bankole* (1 N. L. R. 83) to the effect that family ownership is a dying institution, I am bound to place on record my view that notwithstanding the lapse of nearly a generation since that judgment was delivered the institution of family ownership is still a very live force in native tenure in Lagos.' There is no doubt that this positive assertion applies with even stronger cogency to the Protectorate, as witness this dictum of Webber, J., in his Divisional Court judgment at Calabar in *Bassey* v. *Cobham & ors.*: [2] 'In view of these expressed opinions and decisions I am not prepared to accept the opinion of the majority in this case: I go further and say that their opinion is wrong and inconsistent with native custom. The institution of communal ownership in Calabar is not dead yet and the native law as to gifts is the same now as it was in 1911.'

That is why the Registration of Titles Ordinance No. 13 of 1935 (with its amendments) cannot yet guarantee an absolutely indefeasible title to the registered owner, but rather gives strong recognition to the rights of those claiming under any valid form

[1] (1938), 14 N. L. R. 10, at p. 10.   [2] (1924), 5 N. L. R. 90, at p. 93.

of customary tenure, firstly, by allowing them to object to any application inconsistent with their interests in the land, and, secondly, by enabling them to deal in certain prescribed cases with registered lands off the Register.

But Changes have set in. But the process of change in the traditional land tenure system is everywhere apparent, and is in the direction of individualisation of land holdings, especially in areas of comparatively great economic activities. The requirements of commerce and the need for capital money, the spread of education and contact with European ideas, these and perhaps other factors are all fostering and engendering the development of individual tenure in urban and some semi-urban areas. In the rural or agricultural areas, however, the ancient system is, to all intents and purposes, still largely immune from these disintegrating influences, and the collective idea, so suited to effective primary agriculture, abides.

Whether or not efforts should be made by the Government to preserve these pristine virtues of land holding and utilisation depends on the administrative aim that informs any particular policy. If the country is to stay agricultural, then administrative control of the exploitation of land in farming areas will have to be ensured against waste and other uneconomic abuses of land usage. If, on the other hand, the country is being planned to become industrial or partly industrial and partly agricultural, less centralised control will be needed, and development may be allowed to take its natural course with, of course, necessary safeguards. In any case, excessive fragmentation of group land, with its concomitants of squalor, unhealthy over-crowding and often uneconomic sub-divisions of holdings, should be discouraged by general legislation designed to give the Court sufficiently wide discretion to order in appropriate cases partition or sale, if partition were either impracticable or undesirable. The criticism of Ordinance No. 73 of 1945, essayed earlier in Chapter Eight, may be re-iterated here in so far as it gives the Local Authorities power to control land usage as well as the limits of holdings consequent upon partition or succession. It is submitted that the Courts would be better guardians of cases of partition or sale than the Local Authorities. Already, in the Colony and other Southern areas of the country, the Courts are usefully and admirably performing that function. There is no reason why the Courts should not be able to carry out most of the objectives outlined at the 1939–40 Conferences of Northern Chiefs.

Government Control not a Claim of Ownership. Nor is the assumption by Government of control of land in Nigeria necessarily an exercise of or claim to absolute Crown ownership thereof. One of the prerogatives of the Government of any State or country the civilised world over is the inherent right to control the use of land and its proper developments for the common weal. This political attribute of government is quite independent of any possible right to certain pieces of land to which the Government might be entitled by public acquisition or the like. In British Constitutional theory, the Crown owns the land in any of His Majesty's Dominions and Colonies; in practice, however, this is interpreted as meaning that while the radical title is in the Crown, the land itself with all its incidents of customary tenure remains in the occupation and enjoyment for all practical purposes of the indigenous inhabitants of the territory. This is the *ratio decidendi* of the great case of *Amodu Tijani* v. *Secretary, Southern Nigeria* [1] which we have analysed in detail in Chapters Two and Three.

But, although the Crown's role is more or less that of a glorified trustee of Nigerian land, the display of authority and control over the land has not been uniform. While the powers assumed by the Government of Nigeria (which is practically *the Crown* in our context here) over land in the Northern Provinces approach those of an over-proprietor—and they have indeed been described as 'expropriation'—in the Southern Provinces, on the other hand, the Government has limited itself to mere protection of the private rights of the inhabitants against their alienation to foreigners (i.e. non-Nigerians). There are two unsatisfactory features of this differential treatment.

The first is the discriminatory provisions of the Northern Provinces legislation which forbid not only non-Nigerians, but also non-resident, non-indigenous Nigerians from acquiring any freehold title to land in any area of the North; even a Northerner not indigenous to a particular locality cannot acquire any such right. All that is vouchsafed to every purchaser of land rights in the North, whether he is an alien or a Nigerian to the backbone, is just a right of occupancy and not of property in the land. Even the transfer of such rights is riddled with many niggling restrictions into which we need not enter here. Enough has been said about the whole matter in Chapter Three.

The second anomalous feature of the uneven Government control over Nigerian land is the complete abdication of control of

[1] (1921), 2 A. C. 399.

land disposal in the Colony area, with the result that many aliens (i.e. non-Nigerians) have acquired and can still acquire freehold titles, some of them of doubtful validity if one considers the unequal circumstances of the parties to the bargain. Government indifference to the whole problem of alienation of absolute land rights by all the inhabitants of the Colony alike seems to go on the over-optimistic assumption that all the people in the Colony have the necessary capacity and knowledge to appreciate all the legal and economic implications of such transactions, just as much as Government ultra-cautious legislation against the acquisition of any proprietary right in land even by a non-resident Northerner has been from the first based on the inaccurate hypothesis that the Government was taking over the ancient feudal hegemony of the Emirs over Northern Nigerian lands.

It is submitted that, since both assumptions have been proved wrong, for which one may turn to Chapters Two and Three, the time is overdue for a general review of the position with a view to setting things right on the lines already suggested in Chapter Eight. It is some comfort to note that quite recently the Governor of Nigeria promised to look into the case of Lagos and the Colony. Would that he could also have his attention drawn to the position in the North, so that the reasonably elastic rules of disposal of land in the Southern Provinces under the Native Lands Acquisition Ordinance (Cap. 89) might be made applicable to all parts of the country as a whole!

Were this wished-for legal millenium to be attained in Nigerian property law, it would serve as a bulwark against unwise and improvident alienation to foreign speculators, while it would introduce a uniform set of rules regarding the transfers of land rights as between one Nigerian and another; that uniformity in the land law is the goal towards which tenure developments in all areas of the country must be directed seems hardly arguable. Moreover, it would promote the natural evolution of the indigenous land law and custom into a system capable of absorbing and embracing the more modern notions of sale, lease, mortgage and the like, and ensure that the destinies of these developments would be, in the last resort, in the hands of the Nigerians themselves. Such an idea would get rid of the kind of problems already mentioned in connexion with the Abeokuta controversy over sales and mortgages when the Alake in Council, on being pressed by his people, recommended (and the then Governor of Nigeria endorsed) the suggestion to the Secretary of State for the Colonies that on no account should sales of land, even on foreclosure under a mortgage, be made to a non-Nigerian. The difficulties inherent in such a proposition, especially *vis-à-vis* the foreign investors of capital in the country, led to its being shelved at the time.

If, therefore, absolute titles to land everywhere in Nigeria could be reserved only to Nigerians while non-Nigerians were allowed long leases of up to ninety-nine years, at least until the country should have achieved a relatively higher stage of all-round development, it would save future regrets for all concerned.

Title by Prescription. Another problem worth mentioning here, if only in retrospect, is that of acquisition of land rights by an occupier of land under a claim to a prescriptive title based on long and uninterrupted possession and user. The principle of *Akpan Awo* v. *Cookey Gam*,[1] as enounced and delimited by *Tobias Epelle* v. *Ojo*,[2] should largely dispose of the normal cases where there might have been culpable laches and acquiescence on the part of inert grantors. But it is important to bear in mind the clear distinction drawn by the West African Court of Appeal in *Oshodi* v. *Imoru & ors.*[3] between (1) an occupier's claim that the original owner is barred from ejecting him on the ground of that owner's laches and acquiescence, and (2) an occupier's claim that the grantor's acquiescence is required in the latter case than in the former. Indeed, *Chief Oloto* v. *Williams & anor.*[4] is authority for the proposition that the grantor's right of reversion cannot be extinguished by lapse of time or by acquiescence in another's dealing in his land, although the exercise of such a right so as to oust the occupier may be restricted owing to such acquiescence.[5]

Analogous to the above issue but different in incidence is the type of prescriptive title that is the cumulative result of pledges or loans of land which have become two or more generations old, and with regard to which rights are later being asserted to absolute ownership by the present occupier thereof. It has been suggested that a way out of such situation would be to fix by legislation a period of some ten to twenty years for the redemption of pledges and loans of land by the pledgors and borrowers or their successors, and that the right to redeem should be barred after the

---

[1] (1937), 13 N. L. R. 143.   [2] (1926), 7 N. L. R. 96.

[3] (1936), 3 W. A. C. A. 93; applied in *Dania* v. *Soyenu* (1937), 13 N. L. R. 129.

[4] (1943), 17 N. L. R. 27, applying *Oloto* v. *John* (1942), 8 W. A. C. A. 127. See also pp. 132–3, *supra*.

[5] See A. W. Alexander's *Memorandum* (1910), op. cit., para. 22.

stipulated period should have elapsed.[1] It is submitted that in such an abstruse corner of the customary law of tenure legislative action would be unwise, and that the principles above laid down in other cases of prescriptive claims to land ownership should, with necessary judicial caution and acumen, cover also the present point.

On the whole, there is no doubt that, taken by and large, these unsure developments in the various types of land-holding in Nigeria will gradually crystallise into absolute individual titles, free from the multiple rights of the family or the group. It may be that in the process many hard cases must arise, but that is a natural incident of any developing system of land law. For, has not Savigny defined ownership as 'adverse possession ripened by prescription'? The statement is as true of the Roman or the German system as it is of the Nigerian or any other system.

With the emergence of such individual ownership of land, therefore, the registration of titles will be put on a more definitive basis than at present exists. But the individualisation of holding will hardly occur in some remote agricultural communities of Nigeria for a long time to come.

The spread of education and the diffusion of culture that will attend the country's rapid advance towards a progressive nation-hood should have an important effect on the future shape of the ownership of land by her people. Her people's future fortunes are bound up with the character and destiny of the ownership and control of land, Nigeria's most treasured possession.

[1] See A. W. Alexander's *Memorandum* (1910), op. cit., para. 22.

Appendix One

TREATY between NORMAN B. BEDINGFIELD, Commander of Her Majesty's Ship 'Prometheus', and Senior Officer of the Bights Division, and WILLIAM McCOSKRY, Esq., Her Britannic Majesty's Acting Consul, on the part of Her Majesty the Queen of Great Britain; and DOCEMO, King of Lagos, on the part of himself and chiefs.

6 *August* 1861

Article 1.—In order that the Queen of England may be the better enabled to assist, defend, and protect the inhabitants of Lagos, and to put an end to the slave trade in this and the neighbouring countries, and to prevent the destructive wars so frequently undertaken by Dahomey and others for the capture of slaves, I, Docemo, do, with the consent and advice of my Council, give, transfer, and by these presents, grant and confirm unto the Queen of Great Britain, her heirs and successors, for ever, the port and island of Lagos, with all the rights, profits, territories, and appurtenances whatsoever thereunto belonging; and as well the profits and revenue as the direct, full, and absolute dominion and sovereignty of the said port, island, and premises, with all the royalties thereof, freely, fully, entirely, and absolutely. I do also covenant and grant that the quiet and peaceable possession thereof shall, with all possible speed, be freely and effectually delivered to the Queen of Great Britain, or such person as Her Majesty shall thereunto appoint for her use in the performance of this grant; the inhabitants of the said island and territories, as the Queen's subjects and under her sovereignty crown, jurisdiction, and government, being still suffered to live there.

Article 2.—Docemo will be allowed the use of the title of 'King' in its usual African signification, and will be permitted to decide disputes between natives of Lagos, with their consent, subject to appeal to British laws.

Article 3.—In the transfer of lands, the stamp of Docemo affixed

303

to the document will be proof that there are no native claims upon it, and for this purpose he will be permitted to use it as hitherto.

In consideration of the cession as before mentioned of the port and island and territories of Lagos, the representatives of the Queen of Great Britain do promise, subject to the approval of Her Majesty, that Docemo shall receive an annual pension from the Queen of Great Britain, equal to the net revenue hitherto annually received by him; such pension to be paid at such periods and in such a mode as may hereafter be determined.

DOCEMO.

(Their marks) X TELAKE.

X ROCAMENA.

X OBALEKOW.

X ACHEBONG.

NORMAN B. BEDINGFIELD, Her Majesty's Ship 'Prometheus', Senior Officer, Bights Division.

Lagos, Aug. 6, 1861.   W. McCOSKRY, Acting Consul.

ADDITIONAL ARTICLE TO THE TREATY OF CESSION OF THE ISLAND OF LAGOS TO THE BRITISH CROWN

18 *February* 1862

King Docemo having understood the foregoing Treaty, perfectly agrees to all the conditions thereof; and with regard to the 3rd Article consents to receive as a pension, to be continued during his lifetime, the sum of 1,200 (twelve hundred) bags of cowries per annum, as equal to his net revenue; and I, the undersigned, representative of Her Majesty, agree on the part of Her Majesty, to guarantee to the said King Docemo an annual pension of 1,200 (twelve hundred) bags of cowries for his lifetime, unless he, Docemo, should break any articles of the above Treaty, in which case his pension will be forfeited. The pension shall commence from July 1 of the present year, 1862, from which day he, the King, resigns all claim upon all former farmers of the revenue.

DOCEMO, his X mark.

HENRY STANHOPE FREEMAN, Governor.

We, the undersigned, witness that the above Treaty and ratification was explained to King Docemo, in our presence was signed

by him, and by Henry Stanhope Freeman, Esq., as representative
of Her Majesty the Queen of England, on this the 18th day of
February, in the year of our Lord, 1862.

JOHN H. GLOVER, Lieut. R.N.
SAMUEL CROWTHER.
J. C. THOMAS, Secretary to the King Docemo.
S. B. WILLIAMS, British Interpreter.

Appendix Two

LAND AND NATIVE RIGHTS

NO 1 OF 1916

AN ORDINANCE to define and regulate the Tenure of Land within the Northern Provinces of the Protectorate.

(25 February 1916.)

Whereas it is expedient that the existing customary rights of the natives of the Northern Provinces to use and enjoy the land of the Protectorate and the natural fruits thereof in sufficient quantity to enable them to provide for the sustenance of themselves and their families should be assured, protected and preserved;

And whereas it is expedient that existing native customs with regard to the use and occupation of land should, as far as possible, be preserved;

And whereas it is expedient that the rights and obligations of the Government in regard to the whole of the lands within the boundaries of the Northern Provinces of the Protectorate and also the rights and obligations of cultivators or other persons claiming to have an interest in such lands should be defined by law;

Be it enacted by the Governor of the Protectorate of Nigeria as follows:

1. This Ordinance may be cited as 'The Land and Native Rights Ordinance, 1916', and shall apply to the Northern Provinces of the Protectorate.

2. The whole of the lands of the Northern Provinces, whether occupied or unoccupied on the date of the commencement of this Ordinance, are hereby declared to be native lands;

Provided that nothing in this Ordinance contained shall affect the rights of the Governor or of the Niger Company in, to or over the lands specified or referred to in the agreements or instruments mentioned in the second and third schedules or either of them to the Niger Lands Transfer Ordinance, 1916.

3. All native lands, and all rights over the same, are hereby declared to be under the control and subject to the disposition of the Governor, and shall be held and administered for the use and common benefit of the natives: and no title to the occupation and use of any such lands shall be valid without the consent of the Governor.

4. The Governor, in the exercise of the powers conferred upon him by this Ordinance with respect to any land, shall have regard to the native laws and customs existing in the district in which such land is situated.

5. A title to the use and occupation of land shall be termed a right of occupancy, and the grantee thereof shall be termed the occupier.

6. It shall be lawful for the Governor

(a) to grant rights of occupancy to natives and to non-natives.

(b) to demand a rental for the use of any native lands granted to any native or non-native; and

(c) to revise the said rental in the case of land granted specifically for building purposes at intervals of not more than twenty years, and in the case of all other land at intervals of not more than seven years.

7. Such rights of occupancy may be for a definite or for an indefinite term, and may be granted subject to the terms of any contract which may be made between the Governor and the occupier not being inconsistent with the provisions of this Ordinance, or any of them;

Provided that, subject to the provisions of section 19, the Governor shall not grant rights of occupancy free of rent or upon any conditions which may preclude him from revising the rent in accordance with the provisions of section 6.

8. Except with the consent of the Secretary of State, no single right of occupancy granted to a non-native shall exceed 1,200 acres if granted for agricultural purposes, or 12,500 acres if granted for grazing purposes. Every native resident on such land shall remain under the control of the native authorities and subject to the same taxation as though he were not so resident.

9. Subject to the provisions of the next succeeding section and of any laws relating to prospecting for minerals or mineral oils or to mining and to the terms and conditions of any contract under section 7, the occupier shall have exclusive rights to the land the subject of the right of occupancy against all persons other than the Governor.

10. (1) Every right of occupancy shall be subject to any easement affecting the land at the date of the grant of the right of occupancy.

(2) The holder of a right of occupancy shall, if required by the Governor, allow a road of access over the land the subject of his right of occupancy to any person occupying land which is so situate that such road of access is, in the opinion of the Governor, reasonably required.

(3) The person requiring a road of access shall pay to the holder of the right of occupancy in respect of the land to be traversed compensation in respect of any growing crops or improvements damaged or destroyed by the construction of the road.

(4) In the event of the holder of a right of occupancy and the person desiring or using a road of access over the land the subject of such right of occupancy being unable to agree as to the direction or width of the road of access or as to any matter in connexion with the construction, repair or use of the road or as to the amount of the compensation to be paid in accordance with the provisions of sub-section (3), any of the parties concerned may appeal to the Governor who may appoint any officer to determine the matters in dispute, and the decision of such officer shall be binding on all persons concerned.

11. Except as may be otherwise provided by the Regulations in relation to native occupiers, it shall not be lawful for any occupier to alienate his right of occupancy or any part thereof by sale, mortgage, transfer of possession, sub-lease or bequest or otherwise howsoever without the consent of the Governor first had and obtained, and any such sale, mortgage, sub-lease, transfer or bequest, effected without the consent of the Governor, shall be null and void.

12. It shall not be lawful for the Governor to revoke a right of occupancy granted as aforesaid save for good cause. 'Good cause' shall include:

(a) non-payment of rent, taxes, or other dues imposed upon the land;

(b) alienation by sale, mortgage, transfer of possession, sub-lease or by testamentary bequest or otherwise of any right of occupancy or part thereof contrary to the provisions of this Ordinance and the regulations thereunder;

(c) requirement of the land by the Government for public purposes;

(d) requirement of the land for mining purposes or for any purpose connected therewith;

(*e*) abandonment or non-use of the land for a period of two years; Provided that when land is allowed to lie fallow for purposes of recuperation of the soil it shall not be held to have been abandoned;

(*f*) breach of the provisions of section 17; and

(*g*) breach of any term contained in the certificate, or in any special contract under section 7.

13. (1) If the rental demanded from an occupier be raised on revision, he may appeal to the Provincial Court of the Province in which the lands are situated, and such Court, whose decision shall be final, may either reduce the revised rental, in which case no costs shall be payable, or it may confirm the revision, in which case the costs of the Provincial Court shall be paid by the occupier. If, however, he so prefer, instead of appealing to the Provincial Court as aforesaid, he may appeal to the Governor who shall appoint as arbitrator such competent officer not responsible for the revision as he may see fit. Such arbitrator, whose decision shall be final, may either reduce the revised rental, in which case no costs shall be payable, or he may confirm the revision, in which case the costs of the arbitration as fixed by the arbitrator shall be paid by the occupier. If the occupier be dissatisfied with the decision of the Court or of the arbitrator, as the case may be, he may surrender his right of occupancy, and the Governor may award him such compensation for his unexhausted improvements as in his discretion he may think fit.

(2) Should a right of occupancy be revoked owing to the requirement of the land by the Government for public purposes, or for mining purposes, or for any purpose connected therewith, the occupier shall be entitled to compensation for the value at the date of revocation of his unexhausted improvements and for the inconvenience caused by his disturbance.

14. The devolution of the rights of an occupier upon death shall be regulated, in the case of a native, by the native custom existing in the locality in which the land is situated, and in the case of a non-native, by the English law governing the devolution of a lease for a term of years: Provided that a right of occupancy shall not be divided into two or more parts on devolution by the death of the occupier, except with the sanction of the Governor.

15. In the case of the devolution or transfer of rights over land to which English law applies, no deed or will shall operate to create any proprietary right over land except that of a plain transfer of the whole of the rights of occupation over the whole of the land.

16. (1) It shall be lawful for the Governor when granting a right of occupancy to issue a certificate thereof under his hand and the seal of the Protectorate; such certificate shall be termed a Certificate of Occupancy and shall be in the form set out in the First Schedule, or to the like effect.

(2) Any person entitled to a right of occupancy may apply for a certificate which may be granted in the same manner and subject to the same conditions as in sub-section (1) hereof.

17. Every such certificate shall be deemed to contain provisions to the following effect:

(*a*) That the occupier binds himself to the Governor to pay compensation for any damage caused to native individuals or communities in the exercise of the rights granted to him, and to accept the ruling of the Governor as to the amount of such compensation;

(*b*) That the occupier binds himself to pay to the Governor the amount found to be payable in respect of any unexhausted improvements existing on the land at the date of his entering into occupation;

(*c*) That the occupier binds himself to pay to the Governor the rent fixed by the Governor and any rent which may be fixed on revision in accordance with the provisions of this Ordinance.

18. In determining the rent to be demanded for any given land, and on any subsequent revision of rent, the Governor shall take into consideration the rent obtained or obtainable in respect of any other like land in the immediate neighbourhood, and shall, subject to the provisions of section 19, fix the rent at the highest amount that can reasonably be expected to be obtained for the land, having regard to all the circumstances of the case; provided that in determining the amount of any rent, whether original or revised, the Governor shall not take into consideration any value due to capital expended upon the land by the same or any previous occupier during his term or terms of occupancy, or any increase in the value of the land the rental of which is under consideration, due to the employment of such capital.

19. The Governor, with the approval of the Executive Council (but not otherwise) and in respect only of an area not exceeding five acres, may grant a right of occupancy free of rent or at a reduced rent in any case in which the Governor shall be satisfied that it would be to the public interest so to do. When the grant to be made under this section is in respect of an area exceeding

five acres, both the approval of the Executive Council and the sanction of the Secretary of State shall be obtained before such grant is made by the Governor;

Provided, however, that unless otherwise expressly provided in the Certificate of Occupancy, there shall be reserved to the Governor, by virtue of this Ordinance, a right to impose a rent in respect of the land the subject of such right of occupancy if and when he may think proper.

20. (1) If the right of the Governor to grant any right of occupancy over any land should be disputed, proceedings may be taken in the Supreme Court, which Court shall have jurisdiction throughout the Protectorate accordingly.

(2) All claims (other than claims against the Government) arising under the provisions of this Ordinance in respect of any rights acquired under a right of occupancy in respect of land situate within the jurisdiction of a Provincial Court, shall be prosecuted before a Provincial Court, and no appeal shall lie from the decision of such Court: Provided that the Governor may transfer any such case to the Supreme Court.

(3) Proceedings for the recovery of any rents payable under this Ordinance may be taken by and in the name of any administrative officer or by and in the name of any other officer appointed by the Governor in that behalf, and when the rent is payable in respect of land situate within the jurisdiction of a Provincial Court, the proceedings may be taken in such Court.

21. Nothing in this Ordinance shall be deemed to affect the validity of any title to land granted to a non-native or any interest therein acquired by such non-native before the date of the commencement thereof, but all such titles shall have the same effect and validity in all respects as though this Ordinance had not been enacted.

22. An occupier under a right of occupancy shall have the sole right to and absolute possession of any improvements effected on his land, but shall be liable to forfeit any claim to compensation for such improvements if the right of occupancy be revoked under section 12 for any cause other than a cause mentioned in paragraphs (c) or (d) thereof.

23. The Governor may make regulations for the purpose of carrying this Ordinance into effect, and particularly with regard to the following matters:

(1) regulating the transfer by sale or otherwise of rights of occupancy;

(2) the terms and conditions upon which special contracts may be made under section 7;

(3) the grant of Certificates of Occupancy under section 16;

(4) the procedure to be observed in revising rents;

(5) the survey and demarcation of areas the subject of rights of occupancy, and the maintenance of boundary marks; and

(6) the fees to be paid for any matter or thing done under this Ordinance.

The regulations contained in the Third Schedule to this Ordinance shall have effect simultaneously with this Ordinance; Provided that the Governor may alter, amend, add to, or revoke, any such regulations from time to time as he may see fit.

24. Definitions:

'Agricultural purposes' includes the planting of rubber, cocoa and other trees and plants of economic value.

'Grazing purposes' includes only such agricultural operations as are required for growing fodder for live-stock on the grazing area.

'Unexhausted improvement' shall mean anything or any quality permanently attached to the land, directly resulting from the expenditure of capital or labour by an occupier or any person acting on his behalf, and increasing the productive capacity, the utility or the amenity thereof, but shall not include the results of ordinary cultivation other than growing produce. 'Native' means a person whose parents were members of any tribe or tribes indigenous to the Northern Provinces and the descendants of such persons, and shall include:

(a) any person one of whose parents was a member of such tribe, and

(b) any person who shall have obtained a certificate from the Governor in the form in the Second Schedule, which certificate the Governor is hereby authorised to grant, at his discretion, to any native of Africa who shall have declared his intention of making the Northern Provinces his permanent domicile and who shall have satisfied the Governor that he has obtained the consent of the Native Communities concerned.

'Non-Native' means any person other than a native as above defined.

'Northern Provinces' means that part of the Protectorate which on the 31st day of December, 1913, was included in the Protectorate of Northern Nigeria, and includes any other part of the Protectorate which has been or may hereafter be included in the

Northern Provinces, and which the Governor, with the consent of the Secretary of State, shall, by notice in the 'Gazette', direct shall be included in the Northern Provinces for the purposes of this Ordinance.

25. The Land and Native Rights Proclamation (Chapter LXV of the *Laws of Northern Nigeria*) is hereby repealed: Provided that such repeal shall not affect any Certificate of Occupancy granted under the said Proclamation, which certificates and the rights thereby conferred and the obligations thereby imposed shall continue to be governed by the said Proclamation as if this Ordinance had not been made.

THE THIRD SCHEDULE

Regulations under Section 23

1. It shall not be lawful for any native holding a Certificate of Occupancy to sell, transfer possession, bequeath or otherwise alienate his title to a non-native, except with the consent of the Governor.

2. Subject to any native law or custom to the contrary, an occupier being a native may sell, transfer possession or bequeath his title to a blood relation being a native: Provided that the transaction shall be null and void unless the change of title is duly registered within a period of six months.

3. Subject to any native law or custom to the contrary, an occupier being a native may sell, transfer possession or bequeath his title to any other native permanently resident in the same district, with the consent of the District Headman and the approval of the recognised Chief, subject to registration.

4. An occupier being a native may sell, transfer possession or bequeath his title to a native not resident in the district only with the consent of the recognised Chief, and the approval of the Resident, subject to registration.

5. If the District Headman under regulation 3 refuses consent, an occupier may appeal to the Native Court, and if the recognised Chief refuses consent under regulation 4 he may appeal to the Provincial Court.

Appendix Three

NATIVE LANDS ACQUISITION ORDINANCE
(CAP. 89) (PROTECTORATE)

AN ORDINANCE to Regulate the Acquisition of Land by Aliens from Natives.

(26th July 1917.)

1. This Ordinance may be cited as the Native Lands Acquisition Ordinance, and shall apply to the Southern Provinces only.

2. Definitions:

'Alien' means any person who is not a native of Nigeria.

'Court' means the Chief Justice or a Judge of the Supreme Court or a Resident in charge of a province or other officer empowered to exercise the full jurisdiction of a Provincial Court.

'Instrument' means any document in writing affecting land, and includes a will.

'Native' means a native of Nigeria, and includes a native community.

3. (*a*) No alien shall acquire any interest or right in or over any lands within the Protectorate from a native except under an instrument which has received the approval in writing of the Governor.

(*b*) Any instrument which has not received the approval of the Governor as required by this section shall be null and void.

4. It shall be unlawful for any alien or for any person claiming under an alien to occupy any land belonging to a native, unless the right of the alien to occupy or authorise the occupation of the land:

(*a*) is evidenced by an instrument which has received the approval of the Governor in writing; or

(*b*) was acquired, if the land is situate in that part of the Southern Provinces which in the year 1900 was included in the Protectorate of Southern Nigeria, before the 1st January, 1900, and in the case of lands situate elsewhere in the Southern Provinces, before the 30th March, 1908; or

314

(*c*) is authorised by or under any Ordinance.

Penalty: on summary conviction a fine of one hundred pounds or imprisonment for 12 months.

5. (1) Where it appears to the Court that any alien, or person claiming to be entitled under an alien, is in unlawful occupation of any land belonging to a native, the Court may, on the application of the Attorney-General, or any person authorised by the Governor, or on its own motion, cause a summons to be issued to such alien or person aforesaid, requiring him to appear before the Court and produce the instrument by virtue whereof the alien, who is occupying the land or under whom the land is occupied, is entitled to occupy or authorise the occupation of the same, or a copy of such instrument certified in accordance with the law relating to the registration of instruments.

(2) If on the hearing of such summons the Court shall find that such alien or person claiming under an alien is occupying land belonging to a native, and such alien or person fails to satisfy the Court that such occupation is lawful, the Court shall order such alien or person aforesaid to give up possession of the land, and shall issue such process as may be necessary for enforcing such order.

6. The Governor in Council may make regulations, with respect to all or any of the following matters:

(*a*) The conditions upon which the approval of the Governor may be had and obtained to instruments by or under which aliens may acquire any interests or rights in or over any lands within the Protectorate from natives;

(*b*) The terms and conditions to be contained in such instruments, and the forms of such instruments; and

(*c*) The fees to be paid by aliens upon the approval by the Governor of such instruments, and upon the execution thereof by the parties thereto.

Bibliography

(a) GENERAL

1. LORD LUGARD, *Dual Mandate in British Tropical Africa* (1929).
2. A. C. BURNS, *A Short History of Nigeria*, 2nd edition (1936).
3. M. PERHAM, *Native Administration in Nigeria* (1937) (Chapters XI and XII on the Yorubas).
4. M. M. GREEN, *Land Tenure in an Ibo Village* (London, 1941).
5. H. L. WARD PRICE, *Land Tenure in the Yoruba Provinces* (1933).
6. S. F. NADEL, *A Black Byzantium* (Bida, 1942).
7. C. K. MEEK, *Land Law & Custom in the Colonies* (1946).
8. SIR WILLIAM GEARY, *Nigeria under British Rule* (London, 1927), pp. 312.
9. SIR WILLIAM GEARY, *The Occupation of Hausaland* (1900–1904), edited by H. F. Blackwell (Lagos, 1927).
10. LADY LUGARD, *A Tropical Dependency*.
11. A. F. CALVERT, *Nigeria and Its Tin Fields* (London, 1912).
12. C. J. GOLLAN, 'Land Tenure in Northern Nigeria' (*Jnl. of Soc. of Comp. Leg.*, Vol. IV, pp. 164–7).
13. C. K. MEEK, *The Northern Tribes of Nigeria* (1925), 2 Vols.
14. C. K. MEEK, *Tribal Studies in Northern Nigeria* (1931).
15. C. K. MEEK, *Law & Authority in a Nigerian Tribe* (1937).
16. C. W. ALEXANDER'S *Memorandum on the Subject of Native Land Tenure in the Colony and Protectorate of Southern Nigeria* (1910). (Colonial Legal Pamphlet, Vol. 1, No. 26 Folio.)
17. J. LEWIN, *Studies in African Native Law* (1947).
18. R. F. IRVING, *Titles to Land in Nigeria* (1916).
19. M. F. LINDLEY, *The Acquisition and Government of Backward Territory in International Law* (1926).
20. G. STONE, *The Mining Laws of the British Empire*, Vol. 1, Nigeria (1920). H.M.S.O.
21. SIR W. GEARY, 'Land Tenure & Legislation in British West Africa' (1913). (*Journal of The Royal African Society*, Vol. XII, No. 47, pp. 236–348).

22. E. P. C. GIROUARD, *Memoranda on Land Tenure and Land Revenue Assessment in Northern Nigeria* (1908). (Colonial Office Legal Pamphlet.)

23. A. K. AJISAFE, *The Laws and Customs of the Yoruba People* (1924).

24. C. K. MEEK, 'A Note on Crown Lands in the Colonies' (*Journal of Comparative Legislation and International Law*, No. 28, Parts III and IV (1946), pp. 87–91).

25. L. P. MAIR, 'Modern Developments in African Land Tenure', *Africa*, July 1948, pp. 184–9.

26. HERTSLET, SIR EDWARD, *Map of Africa by Treaty*, Vol. I (1909).

27. R. L. BUELL, *The Native Problem in Africa*, Vol. I.

28. P. T. MOON, *Imperialism and World Politics*.

29. C. L. TEMPLE, *Native Races and Their Rulers*.

30. LORD LUGARD, Memo. No. 16—*Titles to Land, Northern Nigeria*.

31. SIR JOHN SALMOND, *Jurisprudence* (10th edition).

32. JENNINGS & YOUNG, *Constitutional Laws of the British Empire* (1938 edition).

33. WADE & PHILLIPS, *Constitutional Law* (3rd edition).

34. A. E. SOCKETT, *East Africa as a Protectorate* (1917). (Colonial Office Legal Pamphlet.)

35. A. N. COOK, *British Enterprise in Nigeria* (1943).

36. A. S. DIAMOND, *Primitive Law* (1935).

37. W. A. ROBSON, *Civilization and Growth of Law* (London, 1935).

38. SIR H. MAINE'S *Ancient Law*.

39. SIR H. MAINE'S *Village Communities*.

40. C. W. ROWLING, *Notes on Land Tenure in Benin, etc.* (1948).

41. L. P. MAIR, 'Chieftainship in Modern Africa', *Africa*, Vol. IX, No. 3 of July 1936, pp. 305–16.

42. L. P. MAIR, *Native Policies in Africa* (1936).

43. F. H. RUXTON, *Maliki Law* (London, 1916).

44. G. C. CHESHIRE, *The Modern Law of Real Property*, 5th edition (London, 1944).

45. J. E. HOGG, *Registration of Title to Land Throughout the Empire*, Toronto & London (1920).

46. H. G. LEMMON, *Public Rights in the Seashore* (London, Pitman's, 1934).

47. C. W. ROWLING, *A Study of Land Tenure in the Cameroons Province* (Govt. Printer, Lagos, 1948).

22*

48. L. T. CHUBB, *Ibo Land Tenure*, Gaskiya Corporation, Northern Nigeria, 1948, p. 97.
49. J. S. HARRIS, 'Papers on the Economic Aspect of Life among the Ozuitem Ibo' (*Africa*, Vol. XIV, No. 1 of January 1943).
50. J. O. FIELD, 'Sale of Land in an Ibo Community', *Man*, Vol. LXV, No. 47 of 1945.
51. D. F. H. MACBRIDE, 'Land Survey in the Kano Emirate' (*Journal of the Royal African Society*, April 1938).
52. E. S. C. HANDY, 'The Religious Significance of Land' (*Royal African Society*, Vol. XXXVIII, pp. 114–23 (1939)).
53. C. D. FORDE, 'Land and Labour in a Cross River Village' (*Geographical Journal*, V, 90, July 1937).
54. C. K. MEEK, *A Sudanese Kingdom*.
55. FORDE & SCOTT, *Native Economies of Nigeria* (London, 1946).
56. West African Land Tenure Committee's Report & Minutes of Evidence: Colonial Office Library Folio.
57. G. C. I. JONES, 'Agriculture and Ibo Village Planning' (*Farm & Forest*, Vol. V, pp. 9–15, 1945).
58. T. R. BATTEN, 'Problems of African Development', Part I (*Land & Labour*, (London, 1947)).
59. V. LIVERSAGE, *Land Tenure in the Colonies* (1945), pp. 145, C.U.P.
60. G. T. BASDEN, *Niger Ibos*.
61. F. M. KEESING, *The South Seas in the Modern World*.
62. GOODEVE & POTTER, *Modern Law of Real Property* (1929).
63. A. D. HARGREAVES, *Introduction to Land Law* (2nd edition).
64. M. M. GREEN, *Ibo Village Affairs* (London, 1947).
65. PARRY, *Law of Succession* (2nd edition, 1947).
66. MUSTOE, *Law of Executors & Administrators* (4th edition).
67. WILLIAMS, *Executors and Administrators*.
68. E. C. S. WADE, 'Act of State in English Law: Its relations with International Law'; in *The British Year-Book of International Law* (1934).
69. G. PADMORE, *How Britain Rules Africa*.
70. L. P. MAIR, *An African People in the Twentieth Century* (1936).
71. H. L. WARD PRICE, *With the Prince to West Africa* (1925).
72. T. O. ELIAS, 'The New Development Corporation.' A paper read at the W.A.S.U. Conference in London in July 1948.
73. J. B. MOYLE, *Institutes of Justinian*, Book II, Title I.
74. E. A. SPEED, *Report on Land Tenure in Ibadan* (1916).
75. N. THOMAS, *Anthropological Report on the Ibo-speaking Peoples of Nigeria*, 6 Vols. (1913–14.)

76. R. Firth, 'Social Problems and Research in British West Africa—Part II (A paragraph on 'Studies in Land Tenure', *Africa*, Vol. XVII, No. 3, of July 1947, pp. 173–4).
77. Northern Nigeria Lands Committee's Report: Cmds. 5102 and 5103 of 1910.
78. R. Firth, *Primitive Economics of the New Zealand Maori*.
79. Malinowski, *Coral Gardens and their Magic*, Vol. I.
80. Caseley Hayford, *Native Institutions* (Gold Coast).
81. Vinogradoff, *Historical Jurisprudence*, Vol. II.
82. Lee, *Roman Law*.
83. Hunter, *Introduction to Roman Law*.
84. Lord Lugard, *Political Memoranda* (1918).
85. J. M. Sarbah, *Fanti Customary Law*.
86. Buckland, *A Manual of Roman Private Law* (2nd edition).

(*b*) OFFICIAL PUBLICATIONS OF NIGERIAN GOVERNMENT
(REFERRED TO)

1. *The Laws of Nigeria* (4 volumes).
2. *Nigeria Law Reports* (17 volumes).
3. *Supplement to the Laws of Nigeria* (1933–1948), (16 volumes).
4. *Nigeria Handbook* (1936), 11th edition.
5. *Nigeria: Colonial Annual Report*, 1946.
6. *Nigeria: Colonial Annual Report*, 1947.

Index

Chamba tribe, rules of descent among, 233
Cheshire, G. C., 179 fn.1, 212 fn.3, 227 fn.3, 233 fn.6
Chief's powers over land generally, 101–9
Chief's protest against treaties of cession, 12, 29–32
Chiefs
  as trustee of land, 112–18
  legal position of, 110–12, 133–4
  right of revocation and eviction, 118–127
  right to reversion, 127–33
Chubb, L. T., 174 fn.4
Clifford, Sir H., 187
Colony, history of, 2–3
Communal land
  general principles of, 189, 296 ff.
  in Cameroons, 163–4
  in Eastern Provinces, 189
  inaccuracy of term, 92–3, 98, 142–3, 155–8
Compensation for land acquired, 76–85
Compound, rights of individuals in, 118–19, 137, 145–7, 159–60
Conditions of cesser of land rights, 164–171
Conditional Sale distinguished from Mortgage, 204–5
Conference of Northern Chiefs, 192, 234, 297
Consent, when necessary to alienation, 195–6
Constitution of the country, 5
Contingent interests under a Will, 247–8
Corporate ownership of land (*see also under* Communal land), 98
Courts cannot demarcate land boundaries, 295
Covenants in leases, breach of, 214
Cowries, as *media* of exchange, 180–1
Crown
  control described as 'expropriation', 36–7
  grants not evidence of ownership, 21–5, 129–33
  ownership of land, 7 ff., 18–20, 36–8, 298
  title subject to native rights, 25–6
Crown land
  definition of, 45–53
  lease of, 46–50
  under Registration Ordinance, 276, 281–2
Curator of Intestate Estates, 254–6

Custom varying the rules of succession, 235
Customary land tenure
  prescription under, 291 ff.
  registration of, 278–9, 283
Customary succession made conditional, 247

Daughter's land, mother as trustee of, 241
Death-bed declarations as to inheritance, 223
Declaration of title to land, action for, 293 ff.
Declarations, Statutory, 280, 285
Deed of Partition of family land, 274
Deeds of land, registration of, 260
Definition of "Land", 41
Demarcation of boundaries, 295
Denial of grantor's title by grantee, 169
Description of the country, 1–2
Distribution *per stirpes*, 146, 246
Docemo, King, power of, over Lagos land, 9 ff., 96
Document
  drawn by letter-writer, 272–3,
  proof of, for registration, 280
  purporting to be Mortgage Deed, 204–5
  relating to land by illiterates, 200–1
Donatio mortis causa, 223

Easement
  generally, 210–13
  of passage, 198
  registration of, 277
  reserved by statute, 213
  under English law, 211 ff.
Eastern Nigeria, land rights in, 184, 189, etc.
Ebute Metta, land at, 133, 196, 198
Effect of registration on title, 290
Egba refugees at Ebute Metta, 131 ff.
Egbaland, sale of land in, 186–8
Eldest son as family head, 225
Epetedo lands, 24–5
Equitable mortgage working a severance, 205–6
Estates
  conferred by registration, 280–1
  Royal, 97–100
Eviction, chief's right of, 118–27
Executrix de sont tort, 253

Family compound, mortgage of, 187, 245

For Product Safety Concerns and Information please contact our EU
representative GPSR@taylorandfrancis.com
Taylor & Francis Verlag GmbH, Kaufingerstraße 24, 80331 München, Germany